GULF OF MEXICO

Tropic of Cancer

Bahía de
Campeche

AROUND MEXICO CITY

THE GULF COAST

MEXICO CITY AND SURROUNDINGS

THE GULF COAST AND THE SOUTH

OAXACA

THE YUCATÁN

TABASCO AND CHIAPAS

MEXICO

PLAN & BOOK
YOUR TAILOR-MADE TRIP

BRAZIL   CHILE   ECUADOR

TAILOR-MADE TRIPS & UNIQUE EXPERIENCES CREATED BY LOCAL TRAVEL EXPERTS AT INSIGHTGUIDES.COM/HOLIDAYS

Insight Guides has been inspiring travellers with high-quality travel content for over 45 years. As well as our popular guidebooks, we now offer the opportunity to book tailor-made private trips completely personalised to your needs and interests. By connecting with one of our local experts, you will directly benefit from their expertise and local know-how, helping you create memories that will last a lifetime.

HOW INSIGHTGUIDES.COM/HOLIDAYS WORKS

STEP 1

Pick your dream destination and submit an enquiry, or modify an existing itinerary if you prefer.

STEP 2

Fill in a short form, sharing details of your travel plans and preferences with a local expert.

STEP 3

Your local expert will create your personalised itinerary, which you can amend until you are completely satisfied.

STEP 4

Book securely online. Pack your bags and enjoy your holiday! Your local expert will be available to answer questions during your trip.

BENEFITS OF PLANNING & BOOKING AT
INSIGHTGUIDES.COM/HOLIDAYS

PLANNED BY LOCAL EXPERTS

The Insight Guides local experts are hand-picked, based on their experience in the travel industry and their impeccable standards of customer service.

SAVE TIME & MONEY

When a local expert plans your trip, you save time and money when you book, even during high season. You won't be charged for using a credit card either.

TAILOR-MADE TRIPS

Book with Insight Guides, and you will be in complete control of the planning process, from the initial selections to amending your final itinerary.

BOOK & TRAVEL STRESS-FREE

Enjoy stress-free travel when you use the Insight Guides secure online booking platform. All bookings come with a money-back guarantee.

WHAT OTHER TRAVELLERS THINK ABOUT TRIPS BOOKED AT
INSIGHTGUIDES.COM/HOLIDAYS

Trip to Portugal

Every step of the planning process and the trip itself was effortless and exceptional. Our special interests, preferences and requests were accommodated resulting in a trip that exceeded our expectations.

Corinne, USA   ★★★★★

Trip to Vietnam

The organization was superb, the drivers professional, and accommodation quite comfortable. I was well taken care of! My thanks to your colleagues who helped make my trip to Vietnam such a great experience. My only regret is that I couldn't spend more time in the country.

Heather   ★★★★★

DON'T MISS OUT
BOOK NOW AT
INSIGHTGUIDES.COM/HOLIDAYS

CONTENTS

Travel tips

Maps

LEGEND
🔍 Insight on
📷 Photo story

THE BEST OF MEXICO: TOP ATTRACTIONS

△ **Teotihuacán**. The immense pyramids and majestic, silent geography of this giant city, abandoned since around AD 650, encapsulate the mystery and dramatic grandeur of Mexico's ancient cultures. See page 159.

△ **Baja California's astonishing sea life**. Gray, blue, humpback, and other whales, dolphins, sea lions, turtles, rays, and countless other rare sea creatures gather off the long, often empty beaches of the Sea of Cortez and Baja's Pacific coast, in one of the richest marine environments in the world. See page 188.

▽ **Uxmal and Chichén Itzá**. The two ruined cities that represent the peak of Maya architecture: Uxmal has the most strikingly refined buildings; Chichén Itzá, voted one of the "New Seven Wonders of the World," is the most intensely dramatic in its style and huge scale. See pages 307 and 313.

△ **The Riviera Maya**. Some of the world's finest, softest white-sand beaches, exquisite turquoise seas and dazzling coral reefs provide the essential setting for Mexico's biggest tourist region. Crowds flock to Cancún and Playa del Carmen, but elsewhere you can still find much more space to yourself. See page 319.

△ **Mexico City**. Vast, sprawling, sometimes overwhelming, the capital is almost a continent by itself, within which there are fabulous museums, exquisite restaurants, imposing plazas, placid districts full of old-village charm, and an enormously varied, vibrant, constantly surprising humanity. See page 129.

△ **Colonial Oaxaca**. With its colonnaded main square, extravagant churches, distinctive cuisine, rich craft traditions, and constant calendar of highly colored, intricate fiestas, and its utterly delightful hotels with plant-shaded old patios, Oaxaca epitomizes the rare charm of Mexico's colonial cities. See page 273.

△ **Mexican folk art**. Made with enormous skill and an ever-exuberant love of color, using materials from fine silks to recycled cans, Mexico's endlessly varied ceramics, textiles, woodcarvings, and other folk arts are an irresistible demonstration of the country's imagination and creativity. See page 105.

△ **Palenque**. Rising out of the Chiapas rainforest, Palenque is the most atmospheric of all the Maya cities, and its temples, multi-roomed palace and their refined carvings and inscriptions have yielded up the most complete history of the dynasty of its kings. See page 293.

▽ **Copper Canyon**. Deeper and four times wider than the Grand Canyon, crossed by a spectacular railroad, the Barranca del Cobre is an awesome rift in the world's surface, an intricate maze of gorges, waterfalls and giant rock walls, home to the Tarahumara people, and with unforgettable hiking and biking routes. See page 200.

△ **Pacific beaches**. Mexico's long Pacific coast is lined by fabulous, palm-fringed beaches, many with crashing waves that provide some of the world's best surfing spots. Behind some beaches there are gleaming resorts like Ixtapa-Zihuatanejo, Acapulco and Huatulco, but elsewhere there are laid-back villages, and miles of idyllic bays you can have just to yourself. See pages 254 and 280.

THE BEST OF MEXICO: EDITOR'S CHOICE

Colors of Guanajuato.

BEST CITIES

Mexico City. The city that has everything, from ancient ruins and bustling markets to all-night clubs and ultra-chic hotels. See page 129.

Puebla. A busy modern university city, but still a multi-colored jewel of colonial architecture, with many of its old buildings clad in bright Talavera tiles. See page 163.

Cuernavaca. Famed for its exquisite year-round climate, with magnificent gardens spread around its steep hills, the old town of Cuernavaca has an ideal mix of a lush natural setting and gracious colonial architecture. See page 169.

Guanajuato. The most attractive of the colonial "silver towns," with narrow streets of churches and 18th-century mansions winding up and down the flanks of a dramatic ravine. See page 220.

Oaxaca. One of the cities with the most atmosphere, the most special cuisine, and the most intriguing culture and traditions. See page 273.

San Cristóbal de las Casas. Maya and Spanish traditions are inextricably intertwined in the fascinating capital of the Chiapas highlands, together with a touch of modern style. See page 290.

BEST ANCIENT SITES

Templo Mayor. Mexico City. The core of Aztec Tenochtitlán, discovered only in the 1970s right next to the city's modern heart, the Zócalo. See page 134.

Teotihuacán. From the massive Pyramid of the Sun to the Avenue of the Dead, "the place where men became gods" cannot fail to inspire awe. See page 159.

Monte Albán. A spectacular feat of ancient engineering, built by leveling off an entire mountain top high above Oaxaca. See page 277.

Palenque. A ruined city where it's still easy to imagine King Pakal and his descendants stalking the patios of their palace. See page 293.

Bonampak. Deep in the Chiapas jungle, one small temple in this remote Maya site contains the finest of all surviving pre-Hispanic wall paintings. See page 295.

Uxmal. The most sophisticated architecture of any Maya city is startlingly modern in its rhythmic geometry. See page 307.

Chichén Itzá. The giant temples, ball court, and Castillo Pyramid of Chichén can seem like a set for a science-fiction movie, rising up out of the flat Yucatán. See page 313.

BEST BEACHES

Baja California. Baja is one vast peninsula, replete with idyllic beaches for sun-basking, fabulous surfing, and – now – world-class links golf. See page 183.

Bahía Concepción. South of Mulegé are miles of wild, often empty, beaches with water of ever-changing colors. See page 188.

Puerto Vallarta and the Costa Alegre. The most beautiful of the big Pacific resorts; seekers after solitude can find plenty of empty coves ringed by fabulously lush forest down the Costa Alegre to the south. See page 245.

Playa Troncones. North of Ixtapa-Zihuatanejo, with an idyllic laid-back feel, remote Troncones beach is a surfers' paradise, but also great for kayaking and turtle-watching. See page 250.

Zicatela and Zipolite. Puerto Escondido's Zicatela beach has the country's most spectacular surf; Zipolite, farther east, is perhaps the ultimate tropical hang-out. See page 281.

Cancún. Every kind of entertainment is to hand, along with a giant 23km (14-mile) strip of white, powdery sand. See page 316.

Tulum, Quintana Roo. One of the most beautiful 14km (9 miles) of white sand imaginable has a ruined Maya city above it. See page 320.

Puerto Vallarta.

BEST ADVENTURES

Hiking Copper Canyon. Tarahumara guides can lead you through the forests, gorges, and great vistas of one of the world's most extra-ordinary landscapes. See page 200.

Surfing the Pacific Coast. Baja, Troncones, and Puerto Escondido offer some of the ocean's most challenging breaks. See pages 250 and 280.

Find the monarchs. Michoacán and Mexico State. Hike or ride horseback into the remote high-mountain valleys that are the winter home of millions of monarch butterflies. See page 237.

Rafting the rivers of **Veracruz.** Speed through tree-shrouded canyons on the flashing whitewater Río Filobobos, and hike far away from any road. See page 265.

Cavern and cave diving and Snorkeling. The Yucatán's hundreds of kilometers of underwater caves are a magnet for divers, and even the less-experienced can see a lot just with a snorkel. See pages 82 and 298.

Dive the Great Maya Reefs. Cozumel and the Riviera Maya. Colorful coral and fish, and a huge range of dives from inshore reefs to vast undersea walls, caverns and wrecks. See page 318.

BEST FIESTAS

Carnaval. Late Jan–Feb. Celebrations take many forms, from Rio-style extravagance to intense Catholic-Maya rituals. See page 88.

La Guelaguetza. July. The most brilliantly colorful demonstration of Mexico's music and folklore. See page 277.

Feria de Huamantla. Aug. With flower-carpets created across the town in one night, to be destroyed by crazy bull-running the next day, this is a classic Mexican mix of piety, craftsmanship, color, danger and wild partying. See page 88.

Day of the Dead. Oct 31–Nov 2. Among the best places to experience this most Mexican of fiestas are Lake Pátzcuaro, Michoacán, and Oaxaca. See page 90.

La Vírgen de Guadalupe. Dec 12. The entire country gets involved in this homage to its foremost patron, with intense pilgrimages and religious processions. See page 22.

Divers exploring the Dos Ojos cenote, Tulum.

Playa La Entrega, Huatulco.

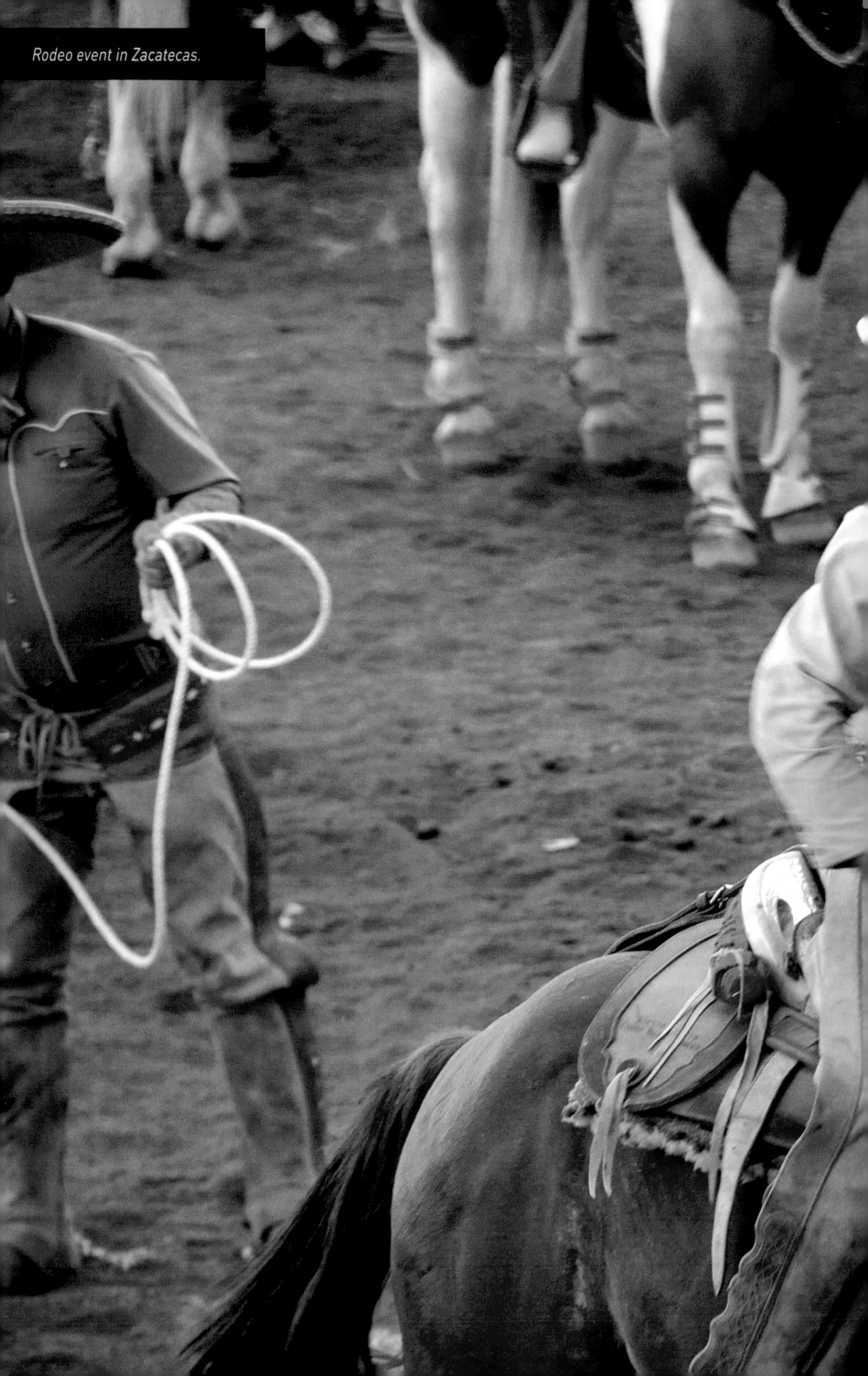
Rodeo event in Zacatecas.

Dancers from Guerrero State celebrate Carnaval in Plaza Tapatía, Guadalajara.

¡QUE VIVA MÉXICO!

Fabulous beaches, spectacular festivals, alluring ancient cultures, dynamic cities brimming with astounding colonial architecture...and all that peppered with one of the world's feistiest cuisines – Mexico is a tropical treasure trove.

A shining example of quaffable Mexican beer.

Mexico, as we know it today, has only existed for a little more than 160 years. Before, its borders stretched north through Texas, New Mexico, Arizona, and California. Now, although it is only one quarter the size of its northern neighbor, it is still a vast country full of surprises and startling contrasts, geographical and social.

In Monterrey, glass-and-steel office towers and factories rise out of the desert; in northern Veracruz and along the Tabasco coast, oil rigs loom like exclamation points, while in the capital, Mexico City, the sheer density of snorting traffic overwhelms any first-time visitor. On Mexico's Pacific and Caribbean beaches some 20 million visitors each year bask under the tropical sun and party through the balmy nights. And yet, not far away, you can find the pyramids left by ancient Mesoamerican civilizations, and forests and lagoons full of rare wildlife. In villages and mountain valleys, indigenous Mexicans continue to perform age-old rituals.

Keel-billed toucan.

Fiery murals blanket many of Mexico City's public walls, but thick smog blankets the sky, all too often obscuring the snow-capped volcanoes – Popocatépetl and Iztaccíhuatl – only 60km (37 miles) to the southeast. With a population of more than 21 million, Mexico City is one of the biggest megalopolises on earth.

Yet beyond the sprawl of the ever-expanding Ciudad de México (the new name of the Distrito Federal, which you may still hear), the air is often still wonderfully clear, and, although Mexico has 332,000km (207,000 miles) of roads, there are still many spectacular parts of the country that are remote and inaccessible. And even apparently plain-looking towns on main highways can surprise you with a raucous fiesta that seems utterly bizarre.

Two-thirds of Mexico's 130 million people are under the age of 30. Most Mexicans are Spanish-speaking, mixed-race mestizos, but some 60 native languages are still spoken, by more than 50 indigenous groups.

So, how do you explain it all – this fantastic, frenetic country? "One does not explain Mexico," says the philosopher Manuel Zamacona in *Where the Air is Clear*. "One believes in Mexico, with fury, with passion..."

THE MEXICAN MOSAIC

The product of many, very disparate, influences, Mexico's people and their cultural tapestry have a constant ability to surprise.

Mexicans are particularly concerned with their identity. To most outsiders, theirs is one of the most recognizable countries in the world, with its own distinctive music, food, and colorful visual style, and a set of unmistakable symbols, from *mariachis* to *charro* cowboys to traditional blouses. Many Mexican writers, on the other hand, have spent a great deal of time considering the nature of *Mexicanidad*, "Mexican-ness," and Mexicans' place in the world.

In good part this is because Mexico is genuinely very difficult to sum up. Mexican men especially can be loud and boisterous at times, lovers of the fiestas that are a national trademark, but oddly reserved at others. Extravagant displays of sentimental patriotism are another feature of Mexican life, from the nightly flag-lowering ceremony in Mexico City's Zócalo and the major national holidays, to the drunken singing of patriotic songs, but Mexicans can also be unremittingly negative about their own country. One could also say that Mexicans are very religious, and reverential toward religious symbols, but amid the piety you can also easily find plenty of raucous, earthy, often off-the-wall humor. It is true to say that most Mexicans, above all in the south, place great value on courtesy; it's also true that some can catch you out by being extremely brusque. A nation often associated with machismo can be surprisingly accepting of homosexuality, and contains communities that are declaredly matriarchal. Lately, through the drug wars, parts of Mexico have been heavily associated with violence, and their crime statistics are frightening; but, arrive in country areas elsewhere, or even small towns, and all you will feel is a pervasive courtesy and gentleness.

Charros (Mexican cowboys) at a rodeo.

The degree of disconnect between these last two images, especially, is something foreigners find baffling. In their folk arts and fiestas, Mexicans also show immense inventiveness and creativity, and yet economically the country has often seemed dogged by inertia. Paradoxes, and the unexpected, are actually part of the essence of Mexico, and even more so now that the country's middle classes are determinedly embracing a modern, consumerist way of life.

This is a country that, more than most, defies generalizations, so that the best one can hope for is to capture just some parts of a changing mosaic. Negotiating, and appreciating, all these contrasts is central to enjoying the country. Mexico is a continent in itself: neither a very old country, nor a very new one. It is both at the same time. It has the most leading-edge modern technology, while nearby people are living according to 2,000-year-old traditions.

> *Under Spanish rule, an attempt was made to keep racial mixing at bay by means of a complex scale of legal castes, arranged according to the amount of a person's European ancestry.*

MESTIZAJE

Many of these paradoxes can be traced back to modern Mexico's very origins in colonial society. When Europeans settled North America or Australia, they generally pushed the native inhabitants aside, or exterminated them. In Mexico and Latin America, the Spaniards dominated the local population, eliminated their rulers, exploited and blatantly mistreated them, but they also lived with them and mixed with them. The Catholic Church, instead of keeping "Indians" at bay Puritan-style, insisted that they be baptized and converted, even if this only produced a syncretic religion, creating the often-bizarre mixes of Catholic and pre-Conquest beliefs that are characteristic of many indigenous communities today.

The great majority of Mexico's 130 million people today are *mestizos*, or "mixed race," of both European and indigenous American descent. This process of *mestizaje* or "racial mixing" that has taken place since the Conquest is the central element in Mexican identity. Rather than the one Spanish Catholic tradition overwhelming the older native American one, the two became subtly entangled, to the extent that no one can quite tell where one begins and the other ends, and indigenous American traditions are still visible in every part of Mexico, not just museum exhibits of national folklore. The complex intertwining of the two is expressed in countless aspects of Mexican life, from the ever-present cult of the Virgin of Guadalupe (see page 22) and the celebrations of the Day of the Dead, to the delicious, rich variety of Mexico's regional cuisines. Other communities have arrived in Mexico since the first Spanish colonists – Africans brought by the Spaniards as

slaves to Veracruz and Guerrero, 20th-century Spanish refugees, Jews, Poles and other eastern Europeans, and Lebanese – but they have found their place alongside the dominant *mestizo* culture.

Today "multiculturalism" is often seen as a positive, and Mexico City's Plaza de las Tres Culturas is one of many monuments around Mexico that celebrate the country's "Three Cultures" – pre-Hispanic, Spanish, and the modern Mexican synthesis. For many Mexicans, however, having mixed origins has often been a source of neurotic

Independence Day celebrations.

insecurity, as if it would be simpler just to be one or the other. The Conquest, after all, was not some peaceful meeting of cultures but a bloody drama, and has often been compared to a mass rape. One of the best-known, most emblematic figures in the Conquest is *La Malinche*, the indigenous princess who became interpreter and mistress to Hernán Cortés, and so mother to one of the first mestizos, before being cast aside when Cortés married a Spanish aristocrat. The powerful, sombre mural by José Clemente Orozco showing *Cortés and Malinche* as a kind of Adam-and-Eve to the new Mexican people, in the Colegio de San Ildefonso in the capital, sums up all the many, frequently contradictory feelings Mexicans can have toward their dual origins.

A NATIONAL CULTURE

At one time Mexicans were pretty much officially encouraged to indulge in self-hatred, and to see the presence of so much indigenous blood in the country as a failing, above all during the dictatorship of Porfirio Díaz at the end of the 19th century. European models were seen as superior in all things, and although General Díaz was himself very much a mestizo from Oaxaca – as is evident in any photograph – he and his followers made it virtually an article of state policy that one of Mexico's major

Aztec dancers in the Zócalo, Mexico City.

problems was its own people, and especially the indigenous communities, who were lazy, apathetic and lacking any initiative. Hence they looked around determinedly for new migrants – Germans, Japanese, Lebanese – to improve the stock and boost the economy.

This produced an intense reaction in the vast upheaval of the 1910 Revolution. The cultural revolution that followed was one of its most lasting consequences, and laid down the basis of the new, inclusive national culture that survives today. In his great murals in the Palacio Nacional in Mexico City, Diego Rivera idealized the pre-Conquest world, while his bohemian partner Frida Kahlo began dressing in the brilliantly colored blouses of the Zapotec women of Tehuantepec. "Aztec" and other pre-Hispanic motifs became a feature – often a cliché – of new Mexican architecture, and the state took its first steps toward taking charge of Mexico's immense archeological heritage, which had previously only been of interest to foreigners. In a complete break with previous centuries, instead of Mexico's pre-Hispanic past and traditions being ignored and treated with contempt, they were comprehensively re-evaluated, celebrated, even venerated, as an essential part of the national identity.

And yet, as usual in Mexico, there is still plenty of room for paradox and ambiguity. The many indigenous communities, especially, may have been enshrined as symbols of the nation, but everyday attitudes toward them can be very variable. Many indigenous communities

⊘ HISTORIC TITLES

One practice that came in flamboyantly with the Mexican Revolution, and which has survived, is the revival of personal names of Mexica or Aztec, and sometimes Maya, origin. The radical artist Gerardo Murillo was a forerunner in the trend, by taking the name "Doctor Atl" (from the Náhuatl for water). Others followed, and for a while it was very fashionable for officials of the new revolutionary political regime to take on names reminiscent of the Aztec warrior aristocracy. Most popular of all was Cuauhtémoc, name of the heroic last Aztec emperor who led the final defense of Tenochtitlán; the most prominent examples are Cuauhtémoc Cárdenas, former mayor of Mexico City and son of the great 1930s president Lázaro

Cárdenas, and Cuauhtémoc Blanco, Mexico's best-loved soccer player-turned politician. Other names that have stayed common are Tenoch, short for Tenochtitlán, for boys, and Xóchitl, from the Náhuatl for flower, for girls.

Before the Revolution no Mexican with any wealth or social position would have given their children an indigenous name. Even today, it can still seem strange to come upon a well-groomed, suited gentleman introduced with the name of a Mexica warrior (plus, foreigners, including other Spanish-speakers, commonly have no idea how to pronounce these names and words ending in –tl). But they remain another sign of Mexico's much-treasured sense of identity.

complain that they are still treated as primitive, and discriminated against, one of the sources of the Zapatista conflict in Chiapas. The integration of the indigenous way of life – based on community, tradition, and a sense of maintaining a balance in the universe rather than change – with a more individualistic Western outlook is a still-continuing process that goes on in people's heads and hearts, rather than any settled matter.

INDIGENOUS PEOPLES

Around 12–13 percent of Mexico's population, or about 16–17 million people, is still made up of indigenous communities (pueblos indígenas), in one of more than 60 different groups who have all maintained their identities and resisted full integration into Hispanic-mestizo culture ever since the Conquest. After centuries of mestizaje, however, the limits of these peoples are often a little vague, and, rather than just genetics, a truer test of belonging is whether someone lives in a community, maintains its traditions and speaks one of the many indigenous languages. As said, the attitudes of other Mexicans to them are very mixed. Cultured middle-class opinion acknowledges them and their traditions and crafts as special national symbols, but in economic life they are commonly at a constant disadvantage. Poor mestizos frequently admire the "Indians'" pugnacious exercise of community solidarity, but, since they themselves are excluded from it, also often find it threatening and an irritation.

With their colorful and intricate crafts, complex, interesting beliefs, and sense of contact with an ancestral past, the indigenous peoples are often the Mexicans that are most fascinating to foreigners, especially those communities, including several in the north, that have maintained their traditions in the purest form. The Tarahumara of the Copper Canyon are one such group, known for their extreme endurance – as seen in their ritual sport of rarajipari, a kind of soccer game played for several days over mountain tops – and their legendary running ability. The Seri are another group, a tiny community of under 1,000 who live by fishing on the shores of the Sea of Cortés in Sonora, and are known for their striking basketware. Northern Jalisco is the home of one of the most

famous communities, the Huicholes, known for their stunningly colorful woven images, their beautiful embroidered shirts and their use of the cactus-drug peyote in shamanic rituals. Each community has its own particular set of beliefs, often incorporating a few Catholic elements beside ancient, entirely pre-Hispanic gods and earth spirits, which have been study material for legions of anthropologists. Equally, each group has a powerful sense of community life, over and above each individual within it, and in most cases there is a similarly ancient system

Carpet weaving, Oaxaca.

of authority based on councils of elders, with, in many, a complex rotation of responsibilities between the men of the community.

These communities in northern and central Mexico, however, have typically maintained their traditions in such pure form because they have retreated to remote places, as far as possible from mainstream Mexican society, and often keep all contact with the mestizo world to an absolute minimum. In major cities in the same regions, however, such as Chihuahua or Guadalajara, there is often scarcely any sign of an indigenous presence at all. It is in contrast to the south of Mexico, in Oaxaca, Chiapas and the Yucatán Peninsula, where the Mixtecs, Zapotecs, Maya and others still make up half or even

GUADALUPE: THE EVER-PRESENT VIRGIN

The Virgin of Guadalupe is found everywhere in Mexico, and ensures that Catholicism here, like so many things, has a very special national tone and color.

A mind-boggling 6 million pilgrims arrive at the vast Basílica de Nuestra Señora de Guadalupe in Mexico City every year to pay tribute to Mexico's patron, making this the single most-visited Catholic site in the world. Some arrive on foot, from the remotest parts of Mexico. Individuals come to ask for help or to make a pledge to the Virgin; business groups often send representatives, and sometimes a whole village will arrive.

Pilgrimage to the Basilica of Guadalupe, Mexico City.

In the week leading up to the Virgin of Guadalupe, December 12, devotees run along roads throughout Mexico carrying flaming torches, on pilgrimages to local churches dedicated to her. The red, white and green image of the Virgin graces nearly every home as one of the world's most pervasive religious icons.

Octavio Paz wrote that the Virgin of Guadalupe is the real core of Mexican Catholicism, ahead of Christ or God the Father, and some writers say Mexicans are not really Catholics but *Guadalupanos*. She is entwined with Mexican life in innumerable ways, a symbol of the racial and cultural mix that is Mexico.

THE LEGEND OF GUADALUPE

The shrine of Guadalupe is on the hill of Tepeyac, which was outside Mexico City in 1531, when, the traditional account goes, the Virgin Mary appeared there to a recently baptized Mexica peasant, Juan Diego, original name Cuauhtlatoatzin. Speaking in Náhuatl, she told him she wanted a temple built there, for all the people in Mexico who loved her. Diego took the message to the Spanish bishop, but was turned away and mistreated; he begged the Virgin to use someone important instead, but she insisted she had chosen him as her messenger. He tried again, until the bishop sneered that, if Diego's apparitions were true, he should show them a sign. The Virgin appeared again, and told Juan to go back to Tepeyac and gather everything he found there.

At the top of the hill, normally an arid, rocky place, he found a field of dazzling, exquisite flowers. Carrying as many as he could in his plain *tilma* (poncho), he returned to the city. The Spaniards abused him again, but when his *tilma* fell open and the flowers spread across the floor, the image of the Virgin appeared through them, leaving the bishop stunned and ashamed. Juan Diego's *tilma* is now the centerpiece of the Basilica of Guadalupe, and he himself was made a saint in 2002.

This was the first manifestation of the Virgin Mary anywhere in the Americas to be recognized by the Catholic Church; it was also a remarkable coming together of the new beliefs and the old. Tepeyac hill had previously been a shrine to an Aztec fertility goddess, Tonantzin. The emphasis on the downtrodden Indian as the Virgin's messenger, and the inclusion of such pre-Hispanic elements as the role of flowers and color as symbols of divine life, also had resonance.

The cult of Guadalupe gave Catholicism here a distinct, Mexican identity, separating it from its Spanish roots, which also made the Virgin a patriotic as well as a religious symbol. When Hidalgo called for revolt against Spain in 1810, he invoked the protection of the Virgin of Guadalupe for an independent Mexico, and military leaders from Porfirio Díaz to the revolutionary Emiliano Zapata have ridden under her banner. And today, no sensible politician would ever dare criticize the Virgin of Guadalupe.

In the work of one of Mexico's greatest living artists, the Oaxaca painter and engraver Francisco Toledo, indigenous imagery has been brought directly into contemporary art.

more of the population, where the multi-faceted indigenous heritage is all pervasive, visible in every market and on every street, an inescapable part of everyday life.

In Oaxaca, it is reflected in the explosive variety of local craft work, or the completely unexpected ways of towns such as Zapotec Juchitán, which is traditionally matriarchal, and where women like to have gay sons since they are deemed more helpful than straight ones. In Chiapas, though the Highland Maya communities have long kept themselves apart like the smaller groups of the north, in recent years they have flooded in to towns like San Cristóbal de Las Casas. In the Yucatán, the influence of the Maya, gentle and reticent, is everywhere, and gives local life its distinctive tone and charm. Another aspect of the south is that the macho brashness often found in northern Mexican cities is far less evident, giving way to a much softer, courteous, tropical grace.

TRADITION AND ITS NOVELTIES

Whether in loud, industrial Monterrey or the placid, heavily indigenous colonial cities of the south, the interaction between pre-Hispanic, Spanish and other influences equally plays itself out in many aspects of the lives of the 87–88 percent of the population who are not part of strictly indigenous communities. This is perhaps most marked in fields where the two main influences actually agree, and so reinforce rather than oppose each other. One of the most striking is the importance given to tradition in itself, a characteristic of the ancient Mexican peoples but also highly regarded in the past by the Spaniards. Compared especially to English-speakers, for whom, some say, "life is what you make it" and can theoretically be reinvented every day, Mexicans historically have a strong sense of tradition as setting down the basic markers of behavior. In food, music, and the pattern of daily life, traditions have often been

seen as a refuge, an important source of stability in a shifting world.

The sense of time is one particular area where pre-Hispanic and Spanish elements coincide. All the pre-Conquest cultures, but above all the Maya, were obsessed with marking the passage of time and the movements of the heavens, as indications of the cycles of the universe. The Spanish Catholic Church, equally, brought with it an intricate calendar of saints' days and other festivals. These two sides of a coin combined together perfectly, and the result was a devo-

Performers with the Ballet Folklórico de México.

tion to *fiestas* even stronger than anything in Spain itself. The great Nobel Prize-winning poet Octavio Paz wrote in his remarkable dissection of his country's psychology, *The Labyrinth of Solitude,* that "we are a ritualistic people," and the fiesta remains one of the foremost Mexican institutions. Not only does each town and village have one to honor its principal patron saint, but there are also special *fiestas* for individual districts, churches, trades, and of course the big national ones like the Virgin of Guadalupe. *Fiestas* are occasions for collective enjoyment with all one's neighbors, when the everyday look of things is transformed by color, music, and fireworks. Many incorporate strange, part pre-Hispanic traditions, and/or are occasions for wonderful demonstrations of popular skills and creativity, so that *fiestas* can themselves be reinvented within a tradition. Utilitarian minds may be horrified when they discover what proportion of its resources a poor village will spend on *fiestas*, but just to treat every day as the same, Protestant-style, would seem to most Mexicans ridiculously dull.

The love of color and decoration is another Mexican characteristic of pre-Conquest origin that seems to run in tandem with the love of *fiestas*, and is seen at its best in curious details

The actor and singer Jorge Negrete, on the right.

like the painted papier-mâché butterflies made in many regions, or the endless range of textile designs. In the 1540s the Spanish Friar Diego de Landa wrote with great admiration of the way the Maya decorated their homes with flowers, and the association of flowers and color with the sacred can be seen in the story of the Virgin of Guadalupe (see page 22). In this case, the modern Mexican enjoyment of color is a tradition that has also been deliberately revived, as it was artists such as Frida Kahlo who made an appreciation of Mexico's brilliant indigenous colors newly fashionable after the Revolution.

The importance of family is another inescapable feature of Mexican life. This could perhaps be not so much a matter of time-honored

tradition as a reflection of people's lack of confidence in any other institution (except perhaps the Virgin of Guadalupe), particularly politics and government. Children are naturally the focus of the family, and are liberally smothered with affection; the American traveler Charles Macomb Flandreau was so impressed by what he saw here in the 1900s that he wrote that *all* children should be born Mexican, to give them a good start in life. Equally, many indigenous people in particular do not really understand how anyone can *not* have several children. Among country people, particularly, this emphasis on caring for family contributes to the atmosphere of warmth and kindliness, the attitude of quiet, live-and-let-live tolerance that is palpable in many small towns and villages.

SOLITUDE AND SENTIMENT

Alongside this color and friendly warmth there are, as always in Mexico, other more complex and contradictory characteristics, such as the much-remarked reserve of Mexican men in particular. Quiet courtesy and apparent affability can sometimes fade into an almost oriental distance and formality. Equally, the counterpoint to this traditional Mexican liking for courtesy is the brash, sharp street-talk of many youth in Mexico City and other big cities, which goes to another extreme with chippy attitude and torrents of obscenities. Octavio Paz wrote that the central condition of the Mexican man was solitude, and that much of his behavior – from elaborate formality to the exaggerated sociability of the *fiesta* – represented only different means of defense, to keep people at bay and protect his isolation. Some say that the reliance on family is itself part of this, in that many Mexicans do not, ultimately, trust anyone outside their immediate family or circle of *compadres* (lifelong friends), an attitude that has naturally contributed to recurrent political corruption. Paz argued too that as a result of his own chronic insecurities the Mexican really saw no point in trusting others, and felt that there were only two attitudes to take when dealing with others: take advantage of them, or have them take advantage of you; "screw or be screwed," in the language of the street.

The views expressed by Paz have often been criticized since they first appeared in the 1990s, and the image of the Mexican male ready to challenge all he meets has become an often-ridiculed cliché, but this all-or-nothing approach is certainly enshrined in popular culture, particularly the classic culture of *mariachis*, *ranchera* songs, and the great Mexican movies of the 1940s that are still favorites on TV. The common thread is that they are melodramatic, romantic, and unreservedly sentimental, but in a peculiarly negative, even vaguely masochistic, way. The great leading men of Mexican cinema – Jorge Negrete, Pedro Infante – perfected a kind of haughty male smoulder; their heroines, like

disappointment than the naïve and drama-free world of happy-ever-after. In the south, the macho bravado of the northern *rancheras* and *corridos* is absent in traditional music such as the *boleros* of the guitar trios of Yucatán, but is replaced by a much more languid, tropical, but still hugely sentimental romanticism.

Most recently, the stereotypical image of the northern Mexican male as in a doomed struggle with the world has also been taken up keenly by those most macho of modern Mexicans, the *narcos* or drug traffickers, many of whom, like

Musicians performing "Danza de los Viejitos" in Plaza Vasco de Quiroga, Pátzcuaro.

the superstar María Félix, smouldered haughtily back. Passion was at the center of the story, but nearly always with the idea that their love was ultimately doomed. The most popular *rancheras* always deal in tragedy, in betrayal, the futility of love. According to Mexican journalist Alma Guill-ermoprieto, a Mexican's idea of a good party is not one where everybody ends up laughing, but one where at least some of the guests, helped by a few tequilas, end up crying their eyes out on each others' shoulders after singing some sentimental old traditional songs, releasing pent-up emotion and so perhaps breaking out of their proverbial solitude. In film and in song, love is always worth embarking upon, but with the implication that it's more likely to lead to

all the Mafia mobsters who modeled themselves on characters from *The Godfather*, exult in their self-cultivated image as lonely heroes ready to take on the Mexican army and anyone else who crosses their path. And there is perhaps no bet-ter evidence for Paz's thesis on the solitude and distrust of a certain kind of Mexican male than the *narcos'* terrifying readiness to turn on, and murder, each other.

THE MODERN WORLD

However, even such a multi-faceted weight of traditions can still not explain Mexico com-pletely, for no country stands still. Mexico has undergone vast changes in the last century, and is still feeling them every day. Massive urbanization began in the 1930s, reaching galloping pace from the 1960s onward. Curiously, one of the first effects of urbanization was perhaps to increase the prominence of tradition, since it was in the 1940s that *mariachi* music – via radio – and other classic images of "Mexicanness" such as the movie heroes with their moustaches and big sombreros, first became popular throughout the country as reassuring, familiar images of rural life for the new city dwellers. In the last few decades, though, urban growth has gone beyond all expectations, above all in the immense, sprawling mass – sometimes just called *el monstruo*, "the monster" – of Mexico City, creating huge challenges to traditional ways of life and generating entirely new ones.

With its size, pollution, traffic chaos, and dire warnings from locals on how not to take a taxi and which areas not to stray into, its catalog of environmental and other problems, Mexico's capital can appear out of control. In its worst problem areas – easily avoided by most visitors – the tension created by crime and insecurity is unavoidable. However, it can also be seen as an example of the resilience of ordinary Mexican people, with very few resources. Even in the most ragged districts, with the greatest deficiencies in housing, water supply, power, and other basics of modern urban life, people establish local organizations, build up local networks, place religious shrines and flowers on street corners, and generally try to take care of their neighborhood. New urban Mexicans enthusiastically keep up district *fiestas* – or observe some they have brought with them from the countryside – and also invent new traditions, such as their crazy love of masked *lucha libre* wrestlers.

Tortilla vendor, Pátzcuaro.

Mexico's biggest problem, as it has long been, is its difficulty in providing a decent standard of life for a great proportion of its population, in the great city and especially across vast areas of the countryside. This has a greater impact than the corrosive chaos of drug violence, to which it also contributes,

⊙ PICK YOUR TELENOVELA

Mexico has a modern institution that easily rivals fiestas in popularity, in part because it's available every day: *telenovelas*, the soap operas that dominate Mexican TV schedules. They differ from most English-speaking TV soaps in that they are not never-ending, but each is a mini-series, with about 100 episodes leading up to a very clear, dramatic end. They are among Mexico's most successful exports, as they gather huge audiences not only throughout the Hispanic world but also in Russia, China, and many Arab countries.

Telenovelas nearly always stick to a few well-tried formulas; melodrama is the key, and family tensions are at least somewhere in each tale. One favorite storyline is the poor girl who falls in love with a rich man and has to overcome the opposition of her family and rivals to reach the happy ending. Historical romances give an opportunity for different costumes and more variety. One traditional constant has been that most of the actors are unusually white-skinned for Mexico, and in modern settings even the "poor" characters seem unusually comfortable, considering that these series are gobbled up by mestizo and indigenous people living in very different conditions throughout the country. Aware of this criticism, some producers have tried to introduce social issues, and give their *telenovelas* a more realistic look. But it's hard to change a formula when the fantasy has been so successful.

since, the fewer the economic opportunities, the fewer the alternatives there are to accepting the pressures and blandishments of the drug lords. The scale of migration and dependency on it has placed immense strain on traditional family life, as whole villages are left made up of old people, sometimes nearly all women, caring for small children after their parents have left for Mexico City or *El Norte*, the US border, and the first question hanging in the air when anyone reaches teenage years is when they might leave. It is another indication of Mexican resilience, and ability to improvise, that so much of social life has survived in such circumstances. Outside Mexico, Mexican migration is often presented as a problem above all for the US, as to whether or not people should be let in. This rhetoric has become especially pronounced under the US administration of President Trump, with his dream of a dividing wall along the Mexican border. After his election victory in 2018, Mexican President Andrés Manuel López Obrador (aka AMLO) and his administration provided an alternative take on the issue. They took steps away from using rhetoric that criminalizes would-be migrants or paints the issue as one of national security, preferring to reflect instead on the need for Mexico itself to offer its poorest people valid alternatives.

Beyond the overriding problem of rural poverty, the modern world has also exerted particular pressures on indigenous communities, despite their apparent protective ring of tradition. In Chiapas, many Maya have joined in a frontal challenge to their place in society through the Zapatista movement, but this has also led to clashes with other, more traditional Maya groups. More challenging to indigenous life across Mexico as a whole has been the arrival of evangelical Protestantism. Most indigenous communities had long got used largely to ignoring the official Catholic Church, but since the 1940s many have been emphatically targeted by a variety of mostly US-based evangelical sects, who have won many converts. Since so much of indigenous life has traditionally revolved around shared rituals, any division in religion is profoundly disruptive of community life. And without the community, indigenous people are all the more vulnerable in the outside world.

MIDDLE MEXICO

Yet again, of course, these tensions represent only parts of the Mexican reality. Another – often passed over by foreigners, but hugely important – is the urban middle class, a substantial section of the population with full access to all aspects of the modern world. Some of the richest, in a tradition of wealthy Mexicans that goes back centuries, go whole-hog to embrace foreign, and especially American, culture. An acrid debate has flowed in Mexico recently over the accusation that many well-heeled teenagers

Staying connected through Wi-fi in a Querétaro park.

are more familiar with Halloween parties copied from movies than they are with the Day of the Dead. Others, however, have a far more creative approach to their own background, as seen in the wonderful, but wholly Mexican, inventiveness of the country's pop music and arts scene.

Mexico has always struggled to combine its great weight of tradition with modernity. Its political system is another example; while extensively democratized since the 1990s, it retains huge elements of long-established cronyism and inertia, and yet now faces its greatest test in the confrontation with the drug cartels. Nevertheless, Mexicans have a long record of imaginatively recreating and adapting their own culture.

DECISIVE DATES

PRE-HISPANIC ERA

c.20,000 BC
First human migrations to the Americas from Asia across the Bering Straits.

c.18–10,000 BC
Settlements of hunter-gatherers established in the Valley of Mexico.

Olmec mask.

c.2000 BC
The beginning of agriculture, with the cultivation of corn, beans and chilies.

1500–400 BC
Preclassic period. The Olmec culture, the "mother culture" of Mesoamerica, develops near the Gulf Coast, with centers at San Lorenzo (Veracruz) and La Venta (Tabasco).

300 BC–AD 250
Late Preclassic period. The Pyramid of the Sun and other major structures are built at Teotihuacán. A distinctive Maya civilization takes shape in the south.

AD 250–800
The Classic era of Mesoamerica: many different cultures flourish, and create large, complex centers.

Teotihuacán dominates a huge area until its still-unexplained collapse around 650. In the south, Maya civilization reaches its peak in more than 60 city states.

AD 800–1000
The Great Collapse: many cultures go into a rapid decline. The Collapse is most acute among the Maya, and most southern Maya cities are abandoned over the next two centuries.

AD 1000–1520
The Postclassic. Warlike Tula emerges as a new center in the Highlands from 900–1100. Mixtec civilization expands in Oaxaca. Around 1200, the Aztecs occupy the Valley of Mexico.

1325
Aztecs found their capital Tenochtitlán on an island in Lake Texcoco, site of present-day Mexico City.

SPANISH CONQUEST AND THE COLONIAL ERA

1517
Francisco Hernández de Córdoba makes first Spanish landing in Mexico.

1519
Hernán Cortés and his conquistadores land at Veracruz and march to Tenochtitlán, where they are initially greeted as honored guests by Moctezuma II.

1520–21
Cortés and his men take Tenochtitlán and overthrow the Aztec empire.

1526–42
Spaniards conquer Maya Yucatán in the face of fierce resistance.

INDEPENDENCE 1810–1910

1810–21
Miguel Hidalgo makes his famous *Grito de Dolores* – Cry for Independence – initiating Mexico's bloody 10-year war of independence.

1821–2
Agustín de Iturbide, Mexican-born commander of the Spanish army, changes sides and so allows Mexico to become independent, declaring himself its first emperor.

1823
Iturbide is overthrown and Mexico becomes a republic.

1836
Texas gains independence.

1846–8
The United States invades Mexico and takes Mexico City. In the concluding Treaty of Guadalupe Hidalgo, Mexico cedes Texas, New Mexico, Arizona, and California – half its territory – to the USA.

1847–50
"Caste War," a massive Maya revolt, in Yucatán.

1855–9
Wars of *La Reforma*, as liberals led by Benito Juárez struggle against conservatives to give Mexico a modern state.

1862–7
French troops occupy Mexico City and attempt to impose the Austrian prince Maximilian as a new emperor of Mexico. Following another bitter war, Juárez is restored as president and Maximilian is executed.

1876–1910
General Porfirio Díaz establishes a 34-year dictatorship, the *Porfiriato*. Foreign investment is encouraged and the economy expands enormously, but chronic poverty worsens in many parts of the country.

MEXICAN REVOLUTION AND ITS AFTERMATH, 1910–80

1911
Armed rebellions finally oust Díaz and install Francisco Madero as president.

1913
Reactionary generals assassinate Madero, but are resisted by revolutionary groups.

1917
New Constitution announced; Venustiano Carranza elected president.

1929
The official state political party, the Partido Nacional Revolucionario – later known as the Partido Revolucionario Institucional (PRI) – is founded to bring together all the different groups that were identified with the Revolution.

1938
President Cárdenas nationalizes Mexico's oil.

1968
Several hundred students and civilians are gunned down by government forces in Mexico City while protesting the spiraling cost of the upcoming Olympic Games.

THE MODERN ERA

1994
Ejército Zapatista de Liberación Nacional (EZLN) seizes San Cristóbal and other towns in Chiapas.

2000
Partido de Acción Nacional (PAN) candidate Vicente Fox is elected the first non-PRI president of Mexico in 71 years.

2005
Hurricane Wilma, the worst hurricane in Mexico's history, rips across the Yucatán's coast, causing thirty billion dollars of damage and killing roughly 11 in Mexico.

2006
Felipe Calderón (PAN) is declared winner of the presidential elections by the narrowest of margins over Andrés Manuel López Obrador of the PRD.

2006–9
President Calderón launches a massive military and police campaign against drug cartels; violence intensifies, especially in cities on the US border.

2012
The election of Enrique Peña Nieto as the 57th President of Mexico is hoped by many to usher in a more peaceful chapter for Mexico, with reduced drug violence. It doesn't.

2013
One of the world's most complex drug-smuggling tunnels is discovered beneath the US–Mexico border – yet another indication that the war on drugs is far from over.

2014
After commandeering three buses to attend a commemoration of the Tlatelolco Massacre, 43 male students are intercepted by police in the State of Guerrero. They are never seen again.

2018
Andrés Manuel López Obrador (AMLO), fronting a left-wing coalition, wins the presidency on his third attempt with over 53 percent of the vote.

2019
Mexico's president demands Spain apologize for colonial abuses of its indigenous populations.

Cross-border tunnel used by drug traffickers.

Statue of a jaguar headdress
from Monte Albán.

PRE-HISPANIC CIVILIZATION

The Maya and Aztecs are the best-known cultures, but ancient Mexico contained a remarkable array of diverse, complex peoples.

According to archeological research, Mexico has been inhabited for around 20,000 years. It all began in Siberia, with ancient hunter-gatherer peoples crossing the Bering Straits in search of food during the Ice Ages. From Alaska they moved south down the coast, and eventually reached Mexico and Central and South America.

Some time around 9000–7000 BC, people in what is now Mexico first began to use a crude stone implement to grind wild corn into maize flour. This was the forerunner of the *metate*, the slab upon which rural Mexicans still grind corn today. By 5000 BC ancient Mexicans had begun to grow maize and beans, and around 2000 BC they began to mix lime powder with corn to create the much more nutritious *nixtamal* flour, the essential ingredient for making corn tortillas. These have been the staple of the Mexican diet ever since.

THE MESOAMERICAN TIMELINE

Mesoamerica is the term commonly used for the cultural region that in pre-Columbian times extended through Mexico, Guatemala, and much of Central America. Within it there were two main "hubs," the Central Highlands and the southern Maya region, from Guatemala up into Yucatán, with many "offshoots" such as the valleys of Oaxaca. Our knowledge of Mesoamerican civilizations is continually changing and expanding, and has been transformed by discoveries in the last 30 or 40 years.

A common Mesoamerican historical division into "eras" has been developed. Very broadly, the first complex cultures emerged in what is known as the "Preclassic" era, from about 1600 to 300 BC; this was followed by a transitional period usually called the "Late Preclassic," from about 300 BC to AD 250, when the growth of major cultures

Colossal Olmec head.

such as Teotihuacán or the southern Maya accelerated. The Classic era of Mesoamerica, from about AD 250 to 800, saw these civilizations reach their greatest wealth and extent, but was followed by a period often called the "Great Collapse," when some cultures, above all the southern Maya, went into rapid decline, for reasons that are still continually debated. In the "Postclassic," from about 1000 to the Spanish Conquest, the Maya revived on a more limited scale in Yucatán, while cultures proliferated in the Central Highlands, culminating in the empire of the Aztecs.

THE MOTHER CULTURE

The first of Mexico's great ancient cultures was that of the Olmecs, who flourished, not in either of Mesoamerica's hubs, but in the apparently unfavorable setting of the low-lying jungles and delta swamps of southern Veracruz and Tabasco, between about 1500 and 400 BC.

Many things about the Olmecs, or "people from the land of rubber," remain an enigma. We know they were the first builders of large, well-organized centers or "cities," and that they channeled water to grow their crops. But unlike the Maya, the Olmec did not have a writing system that can be deciphered, so we must rely entirely on the testimony of their art.

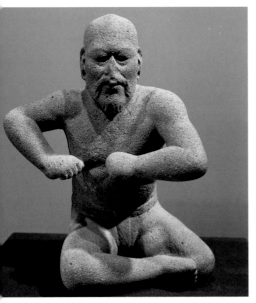

"The Wrestler," an Olmec sculpture.

Their best-known legacies are the astounding, monolithic basalt heads – many of which are now in Parque La Venta in Villahermosa – measuring up to 3 meters (10ft) in height, and weighing between 6 and 50 tons. No one can be certain what they portray, but it is widely believed they are gigantic portraits of Olmec rulers. All 17 discovered have generally similar features – flat wide noses, thickened lips – but all are different from each other. Their slightly "African" appearance has given rise to suggestions the Olmecs had some kind of contact with the other side of the Atlantic, but this idea has been thoroughly discredited, and it is believed the heads were given their apparently non-Native American features to increase their

dramatic effect and evoke the jaguar that was such a theme in Olmec imagery.

One of the great mysteries about the Olmecs is how they ever made these heads and other monuments. They had only simple tools, but the heads are carved out of hard basalt from the Tuxtla mountains, up to 100km (60 miles) from the centers where they were found. It can only be assumed they were hauled down from the hills or on rafts along rivers, but exactly how remains unknown. The enormous workforce required is proof in itself of an organized, hierarchical society.

Not all Olmec art is monumental; there are also exquisite jade miniatures, and delicate jewelry made from pottery and obsidian. The Olmecs created an extensive trading network to obtain materials such as jade, obsidian, and serpentine, and Olmec relics have been found in Puebla, the Valley of Mexico, Oaxaca, and Guatemala.

As in all pre-Hispanic cultures, Olmec art and religion were inseparable. A recurring motif in Olmec art is the jaguar, as the terrifying forest predator played a central role in Olmec religion. The Olmecs were the first people to set out the essential Mesoamerican cosmological vision of existence as divided into three, between the heavens, this world, and a threatening underworld, all equally "alive" and with constant contact between them. This vision allowed space for a complex variety of gods and mythical or semi-mythical creatures.

The first great Olmec center, San Lorenzo in Veracruz, grew up around 1300 BC. It was largely abandoned around 900 BC, but was succeeded by two more Olmec centers, at La Venta in Tabasco and Tres Zapotes to the northwest, which each thrived for another 400–500 years.

Olmec civilization finally came to an end with the disintegration of La Venta around 400 BC, the first of several Mesoamerican "collapses" that give rise to constant discussion of their possible causes. However, as the "mother culture" of Mesoamerica the Olmecs had laid down patterns – in their cosmic vision, social organization, the role of monumental cities with symbolic temple-pyramids as the "core" of each community, and even the ball game – that would influence all subsequent civilizations in the region.

THE SOUTH: THE MAYA

Strongly influenced by the Olmecs, the Maya first emerged as a city-building culture in Chiapas and central Guatemala around the beginning of the Late Preclassic (around 300 BC), and spread across the whole of modern Guatemala, Belize, part of Honduras, Tabasco, and the Yucatán Peninsula. In the Classic era the Maya were the most sophisticated of all the ancient Mesoamerican cultures, in art, astronomy, mathematics – using the concept of zero centuries before it was known in Europe – and many other fields.

The Maya had the only really complete glyph writing system in pre-Hispanic America, used in bark books, on ceramics and in thousands of carved inscriptions. Maya glyphs have only been extensively deciphered since the 1960s, but this has made it possible for the Classic Maya to become the only ancient Mesoamerican people with an extensive history of known names, rulers, and dates.

The Maya were also among the region's finest builders, and their harmoniously proportioned buildings are often beautifully decorated with

Dating from pre-Hispanic times, the Maya backstrap loom is still in use today.

⊘ THE BALL GAME

The ancient Mesoamerican ball game is one of the world's oldest sports, traced back 4,000 years. It seems it was played for sport and to keep warriors fit, but also had huge ritual significance. In societies preoccupied by cosmic forces and cycles of time, it represented a chance to challenge destiny. In the Maya *Popol-Vuh* myths, the "Hero-Twins" Hunahpú and Xbalanqué play against the Lords of Death for days and nights on end, and eventually triumph. It also played a part in sacrifice, with losers – often already captive – put to death. The stakes varied: one Toltec king reportedly played against challengers to his throne, with the winner getting to rule over the others.

It's impossible to know exactly how it was played, but it seems that in the relatively small, earlier courts most common among the Classic Maya and in Veracruz, two or four players took part, scoring just by getting the ball past the opponent and out the far end of the court. In later, larger courts – like the enormous one at Chichén Itzá – there were probably teams of around seven, and scoring involved getting the heavy, rubber ball through stone rings either side of the court. In both styles, players could only touch the ball with their heads, shoulders, and especially hips, protected by leather belts.

A more modern (less brutal) version, called *ulama*, is still played in some indigenous communities.

fine carving or stucco. Like other Mesoamerican cultures they never discovered the true arch, but the Maya did invent what is known as the corbelled vault, or "Maya arch," an upturned V of flat slabs topped by a coping stone.

One of the most important discoveries in the Maya world came in 1952, when a rich burial chamber was found in the Temple of Inscriptions at Palenque, the tomb of the city's greatest ruler, Pakal "the Great" (ruled AD 615–83). Since then many more tombs have been excavated beneath Maya pyramids, notably at Calakmul.

events on earth to repeat themselves too, as the planting season does each year.

The ending of each 20-year *katun* period was marked with special ceremonies, and politi-

> *The memory of the giant city of Teotihuacán always remained in the minds and folklore of the peoples of central Mexico, as the place where civilized life began.*

Maya mural painting in Bonampak, Chiapas.

Another major find was that of the extraordinary battle murals at Bonampak – the only full-size survivors of thousands of Maya wall paintings – which revolutionized our knowledge of Maya art and warfare, with intricate details of dress, musicians, and rituals.

TIME KEEPERS

The passage of time was all-important to the Maya, and no other culture was so obsessed with recording time, plotting the movements of the stars with astonishing precision. The Maya needed such exact calendars because co-ordination of the heavenly bodies affected everything they did. Their vision of the world was cyclical: since the stars and the universe move in regular cycles, they expected

cal events, such as battles and the accessions of kings, were also timed to coincide with the stars. This is also why so many monuments were rigorously inscribed with Long Count dates, making it possible to "date" Maya history with such precision.

GODS OF THE MAYA

The Maya pantheon was as complicated as their calendar. Though commonly translated as "gods," Maya and other Mesoamerican deities would be better described as spiritual or natural forces. For the Maya there were at least 166, each of which could express itself in several different ways. Since the Maya believed themselves to be descended from people of corn, the staff of life, the Maize God, sometimes called Yum Kaax, was of fundamental importance, and in the Yucatán Chac, the Rain God, Itzamná, the Sun God, and his wife Ixchel, Goddess of the Moon, and of weavers, and women, were all prominent. The Maya were also ready to "absorb" gods from other cultures, such as the Teotihuacán war god Tlaloc.

Sacrifice was a central feature of Maya religion, as it was in all Mesoamerican cultures. Humans and spiritual forces were conceived as interdependent: in the same way that humans were "fed" by the gods, with rain and corn, so too the gods needed to be "fed" to survive, above all with human blood. Royal blood was especially powerful, and in elaborate rituals Maya kings and queens let their own blood from ears, tongues or penises. Wars were also fought to secure prisoners to be killed as sacrifices.

COMMON GROUND

The Maya had a common culture, but were never politically united. They were divided, in the Classic era, into around 60 separate city-states, each with a hereditary *ahau* or "sacred king," who was simultaneously the community's ruler and its great shaman, its link to the heavens. They were often at war with each other, and the deciphering of Maya inscriptions has revealed a complex history of battles, rivalries, alliances, and dynastic struggles.

In the early Classic era, many Maya cities had strong links with Teotihuacán. Some Maya centers were linked by stone roads, or *sacbeob*. Maya communities enjoyed a virtual "boom" in size and building from about 600 to 800, when the largest cities, such as Palenque or Calakmul, had populations of 60–70,000.

Then, remarkably quickly, Classic Maya civilization entered a fatal decline. The "Maya Collapse" is one of history's great enigmas, and there are many theories to explain it. It seems most likely the Maya were torn apart by a spiral of environmental and political disasters. The growth in population itself stretched their agricultural techniques to the limit: soils were exhausted, ever more forest was cut down, productivity fell, and malnutrition spread. The main response of the *ahau* lords was more wars, which only made things worse. A crisis point seems to have been reached with a general collapse in faith in *ahau* rule: over a century,

beginning around 800, virtually all the dynasties of the southern Maya cities fell, taking much of refined Maya culture with them, and the cities themselves were mostly abandoned over the next 200 years.

The "Collapse" arrived later, and was never as complete, in northern Yucatán, where cities such as Uxmal and Chichén Itzá were still reaching their peak around 900, but by the year 1000 they too had suffered a decline, often terminal. The southern Maya cities never revived, but from around 1200 Maya culture raised its head again on

Palenque's Temple of Inscriptions.

> For all the Mesoamerican cultures, natural phenomena – caves, waterfalls, mountains, animals – could represent spiritual forces, and act as conduits between the three levels of existence.

a smaller scale in Yucatán, reflected in the fierce resistance given to the Spaniards in the 1530s.

CENTRAL HIGHLANDS AND TEOTIHUACÁN

In contrast to the Maya, the first great civilization on Mexico's highland plateau was highly centralized, around the vast city of

Teotihuacán, just north of modern Mexico City. It first emerged some 200 years before the Christian era, and many of its main structures, including the 75-meter (246ft) -high Pyramid of the Sun, had been built by AD 100. Everything about Teotihuacán was immense: at its peak it probably had more than 150,000 people. It was a ghost town when the Aztecs arrived in the 1300s, but its ruins were so awe-inspiring that they revered it as "The Place of the Gods," and believed the Sun and the Moon had been created there. However, the Teotihuacános did not develop a full writing system like the Maya, so their history has remained far more vague and anonymous.

The exact origins of Teotihuacán are another mystery, though it too was influenced by the Olmecs. It was a warrior city, conquering other peoples around it, but was also a great commercial hub, with trading links throughout Mesoamerica. It controlled large deposits of obsidian, treasured for making tools, weapons, and jewelry, and Teotihuacán craftsmen excelled in jewelry and ceramics. Pyramids and other

Detail of the large puma mural discovered at the ruined Maya city of Teotihuacán.

⊘ MAYA CALCULATIONS

The Maya used a simple bar-and-dot number system, with three symbols: a shell (often more like an eye or a cacao bean) for zero, a dot for one and a bar for five. While our numbers go from right to left by factor 10 (ie 2,345), larger Maya numbers were written in vertical columns from bottom to top, increasing by 20 in each row. An essential use of numbers was to mark time. Dates could be identified with three calendars. Two were used throughout Mesoamerica: the 260-day *tzolkin* cycle and the 365-day *haab* year, which were normally used together, interlocking like cog-wheels in a cycle that repeats every 52 years. More intricate was the "Long Count" perhaps first developed in Oaxaca but only used by the Classic Maya. Again it is mainly based on 20: 20 days make up one uinal month, 18 of which form a 360-day *tun* or year. Twenty *tuns* make a *katun*, and 20 *katuns* a *baktun* (around 400 years) of which 13 make up a Great Cycle (around 5,200 conventional years), the most important division in the movement of time, although even more vast multiples could be used too. The current Great Cycle began in August 3114 BC and ended in December 2012. This was interpreted by the media as a prediction of the end of the world, but merely means the beginning of a new cycle. However, it provided a handy marketing tool for a tourism industry plagued by the continuing drug wars.

structures were adorned with fine carvings and spectacular painted murals.

INFLUENTIAL GODS

So pre-eminent was Teotihuacán that its influence was felt throughout Mesoamerica, in art, architecture, warfare, and religion. One of its foremost deities was the goggle-eyed Tlaloc, god of rain and fertility: in the *Paradise of Tlaloc mural* people are shown frolicking, singing and dancing in a lush, fertile land. However, like most Mesoamerican gods he could have positive and negative aspects, for he was also associated with lightning and war, in which guise he was "adopted" by many Maya cities, along with Teotihuacano fighting techniques. The cult of Quetzalcóatl, the plumed-serpent god of wind and the dawn, also developed in Teotihuacán. He would be one of the gods most revered by the Aztecs, and in late Classic and Postclassic Yucatán, where he was given the Maya name Kukulcán.

Nevertheless, despite – or perhaps because of – its power and wealth, Teotihuacán also suffered a general collapse, around 600–650. As with the Maya 200 years later, there is still no definitive explanation why, but it seems likely it was due to a similar amalgam of overpopulation, agricultural crisis, drought, revolt, and invasion.

THE TOLTECS

The centuries after the fall of Teotihuacán saw smaller-scale cultures rise and fall in the Central Highlands. Some time around 850 a group of Chichimecas, nomadic hunters from the northern deserts, settled down around a new city at Tula, now in Hidalgo state. The Aztecs later called them "Toltecs," but since this could also mean "craftsmen" it has never been clear whether this identified them as a distinct ethnic group or simply meant that they had become "civilized."

Tula society was highly militaristic, and at one time dominated much of central Mexico. While every culture practiced sacrifice, the Toltecs are thought to have been the first to carry out the mass human sacrifices so prominent among the Aztecs.

The Toltecs were also skilled masons, weavers, and featherworkers. Apart from the serpent, predominant motifs in Toltec sculpture – overwhelmingly revolving around power, war, and sacrifice – include the *chacmool* figures,

reclining back to receive sacrificial hearts; the famous *Atlantes*, massive columns of warriors; eagles and jaguars devouring human hearts, and the *tzompantli*, or human skull rack. It was long thought that the presence of similar sculptures at the Maya city of Chichén Itzá indicated that there had been a Toltec invasion of Yucatán, but it is now believed that this was due to a more diffuse spread of central Mexican influences, and that no such "Toltec invasion" ever happened. Nevertheless, Toltec commercial ties were far-reaching, and artifacts from Tula have

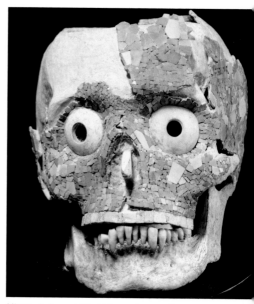

Mixtec skull overlaid with turquoise mosaic.

been found as far north as Paquimé in Chihuahua, and even in northern New Mexico. However, Toltec power was fairly short-lived, and Tula, like Teotihuacán before it, was partly destroyed by fire during the 1170s.

THE AZTECS

Around 1200, another formerly nomadic people arrived in the Valley of Mexico. They called themselves the Mexica – the origin of the name Mexico – and like other migrant peoples in the same area spoke a variant of the Náhuatl language. The Aztecs later elaborated extensive "histories" of their origins, combining fact and myth in a way that makes the two very hard to disentangle. According to legend, the Mexica once lived on an island in a lake called Aztlán, somewhere in the north of Mexico. However, they were oppressed there by other tribes, and so their paramount god Huitzilopochtli instructed them to leave, summoning up a vision of an eagle perched on a cactus and devouring a serpent, and telling them to stop only when they saw a similar vision again.

Guided by Huitzilopochtli, they wandered for over a century, until, on an island in Lake Texcoco in the Valley of Mexico, they finally saw the prophesied eagle. About a year later, in 1325,

Replica of the Codex Mendoza depicting the founding of Tenochtitlan.

the Mexica founded what was to be the great city of Tenochtitlán, named for their leader Tenoch, and which means "Place of the Cactus." Their cosmic symbol – the eagle representing the sky and the sun, the snake symbolizing the earth, and the cactus as sustenance of a wandering desert people – is today the national emblem of Mexico.

THE TRIPLE ALLIANCE

At first they lived off snake meat, fish, and ducks. However, the shallow lake was ideal for the network of *chinampas* or drained-marsh gardens that was created around the central island, and which soon became extraordinarily

productive. The lake also provided an easy, fast means of communication.

The Mexicas were originally only one of many Highland settlements, but in 1428 they formed an alliance with two smaller Náhuatl-speaking cities nearby, Tlacopán and Texcoco. Led by the Mexica king or *Tlatoani*, this "triple alliance" formed the core of what would later be called the Aztec Empire. Under Moctezuma I (1440–69), especially, Tenochtitlán became an imperial capital, as campaigns were launched against Oaxaca and the Gulf Coast. Under later *Tlatoani*, Aztec power extended from coast to coast and even as far south as the Pacific coast of Guatemala, where they went in search of cacao.

The Aztecs demanded obedience from cities they defeated – so that they are one of the few great powers of pre-Hispanic America that can justifiably be called an empire – but were not interested in occupying the lands of the vanquished. They left the conquered peoples with their own leaders, but demanded hefty tributes of luxuries such as shells, quetzal feathers, jaguar skins, precious stones, and cacao.

Huge numbers of prisoners were also taken to Tenochtitlán to be sacrificed. The dedication of the temple-pyramid of Huitzilopochtli in 1487 required the sacrifice of thousands of prisoners who, according to some accounts, were marshalled four abreast, then driven to the sanctuary on top of the pyramid for priests to tear out their hearts.

FIVE SUNS

More than 2,000 spiritual forces were worshipped in the complex Aztec pantheon, but the main temples at Tenochtitlán were dedicated to Huitzilopochtli – "Hummingbird," the Sun God and the city's chief protector – and to Tlaloc. Two other major temples stood nearby: one was dedicated to Tezcatlipoca ("Smoking-mirror"), and the other was the round temple of Quetzalcóatl. The Mexica believed the world had been through five time spans, or suns, each one lasting for several hundred years.

Each of the first four suns was presided over by a different god – the Earth god Tezcatlipoca, Quetzalcóatl the god of the Wind, Tlaloc the god of Rain and Fire, and Chalchiuhtlicue, a female water god – and were ended by titanic struggles between them. The fifth sun, the contemporary era, was said to have begun when Tezcatlipoca and Quetzalcóatl joined together at Teotihuacán to recreate the world.

AZTEC ART

The Aztecs also developed powerful artistic styles. They were skilled sculptors, potters, jewelers, and painters, and though they did not have a full writing system like the Maya, their illustrated books – the codices – are vivid and beautiful. As well as the highly stylized temple sculptures, there was a strong strain of naturalism in Aztec representation of grasshoppers, coyotes, frogs, rabbits, monkeys, and other animals.

Perhaps the greatest masterpiece of Aztec art, however, was the magnificent city of Tenochtitlán itself, set in the middle of the lake, with vibrant markets and surrounding gardens fed by an intricate system of dikes.

OAXACA: ZAPOTEC AND MIXTEC

The ritual center of Monte Albán, in a remarkable location on a mountain top above the city of Oaxaca, was one of the oldest and most enduring settlements in ancient Mexico. Its first structures date from around 500 BC, and it was occupied, built and rebuilt for more than a thousand years, until after AD 750. The greatest achievement of the Zapotec culture, in the early Classic it was the hub of a vigorous "state" that controlled much of modern Oaxaca.

The Zapotecs developed an extensive glyph writing system, and used the same bar and dot numbers as the Maya. Zapotec art was notably sophisticated, and among its greatest works are the extraordinary bas-reliefs at Monte Albán called Los Danzantes (The Dancers). Their ceramic funerary effigy urns, depicting seated deities wearing flamboyant costumes and jewelry, are unique. They were placed in elaborate stone tombs, where they were believed to guard the noble dead.

Around AD 1000 the Mixtecs, originally from the Cholula-Puebla area farther north, moved down into Oaxaca and took over Monte Albán, which was already in decline. They mixed with the Zapotecs, but also built new centers of their own. The most striking of them was Mitla, east of Oaxaca City, where the long, low "palaces" are decorated in finely cut stone mosaic, with

a geometrical style slightly reminiscent of late Maya buildings such as Uxmal in the Yucatán.

The Mixtecs were famed as master craftsmen, goldsmiths, and potters, and their superbly painted polychrome pottery was traded and imitated from central Mexico to Guatemala. They also left especially rich tombs: Tomb 7 at Mitla was found to contain more than 500 pieces of intricate jewelry and other precious artifacts, the greatest single treasure trove found in Mesoamerica. The Mixtec codices, or deer-skin manuscripts, up to 12 meters (39ft) in length,

Palacio de los Danzantes, Monte Albán.

are a vital source of information on pre-Conquest America.

The Aztecs greatly prized Mixtec jewelry and mosaics, which in part was their downfall, for in the 1490s the Tlatoani Ahuitzotl invaded Oaxaca and conquered both Zapotecs and Mixtecs. They never disappeared, however, and there are still large numbers of Zapotec- and Mixtec-speaking

At a time when most Europeans never washed at all, many Aztecs took daily baths, and hundreds of men were employed to clean the streets of Tenochtitlán every night.

people in Oaxaca today. Many have also emigrated to the US.

THE GULF COAST: THE VERACRUZ CULTURE AND HUASTECS

The fertile, tropical Gulf Coast of Mexico was home not only to the Olmecs but also, later, to the Totonacs in central Veracruz and the Huastecs in the north.

Totonac was the name of the people who lived in Veracruz at the time the Spaniards arrived (and are still numerous today), and

Mixtec ceramics.

The Veracruz and Huastec peoples made figurines to push about on wheels, but only as toys, perhaps because there was no point in making wheeled carts with no animals to pull them.

is also often used to refer to the culture that flourished through the Classic era in central Veracruz, although some experts dispute that these were the same people. The most prominent ancient Veracruz centers are at Remojadas, a relatively small site that is closed to visitors, and El Tajín. The Remojadas culture is not known for its monumental architecture,

but was outstanding for its mastery of clay. The dead were buried with clay vessels and figurines, often painted with fine geometric designs, hundreds of which are now in the region's museums.

The *sonrientes* or "smiling face" figurines, often also in the form of whistles or rattles, are this culture's most distinctive creation. Compared with the often fearsome style of Maya or Aztec sculpture, these jolly little figures of men and women, bring an instant change of tone. Their symbolism has been variously interpreted. Some think they portray the ritualistic use of hallucinogenic substances (hence the smile), while others see them simply as an expression of the generally festive character of the coastal people.

The great hub of the Veracruz culture was the huge city of El Tajín, with its famous Pyramid of the Niches. Veracruz culture seems to have been more obsessed than any other in Mesoamerica with the ritual ball game – some 17 courts have been found at El Tajín, and carvings depict many rituals and sacrifices related to the game. The many beautiful carved stone *hachas* (axes), *palmas* (palms), and *yugos* (yokes) at the site were also part of the ball game ceremony. Building continued at El Tajín until about 1200, but it was later attacked by primitive invaders, and by the time of the Conquest it had already been abandoned.

THE HUASTECS

The pre-Conquest Huastecs occupied an area extending from northern Veracruz into the surrounding states, and many of their descendants still live in this region, La Huasteca, today. Curiously, their language is of Maya origin, and there are many theories as to when and why they moved north, probably some time in the Preclassic era, about 1000 BC.

Considered primitive by their neighbors – in part because they usually went naked – the Huastecs only became prominent in the Postclassic era. Their buildings are relatively crude, and they are best known for their extraordinary art work, especially the highly stylized sandstone sculptures that depict almost abstract body shapes of women and men, many with conical headdresses, and bent-over figures of hunchbacks.

The Aztecs conquered the Huastecs some time around 1450. The Mexica were shocked by the Huastecs, who faced their enemy naked, their bodies painted with brilliant colors, their heads flattened and deformed.

WESTERN AND NORTHERN CULTURES

Much less is known about the cultures of western Mexico, although effigy pottery found in caves and tombs has revealed much about the beliefs of the people who inhabited this area 2,000 years ago. The settlements of Colima, Jalisco and Nayarit never merged into unified kingdoms, but remained under chieftains who controlled small areas, often warring with each other.

Life after death was, as usual, a central element in their beliefs, and so men were buried with ceramic replicas of their wives, servants, and slaves to enhance their lives in the afterworld. Lacking the refinement of the Maya or the skill of the Mixtecs, the work of the western potters is distinctive, thanks to its simplicity of design and its joyfulness. They portrayed everyday life as well as spiritual themes: a ball game with spectators, lovers embracing, phallic dances, musicians, warriors, and animals; one of their most common models was the *itzcuintli*, the plump and hairless native Mexican dog.

The peoples of the Central Highlands customarily dismissed those to the north of them as primitive, nomadic Chichimecas. However, in the Postclassic era, around 1200, yet another city developed in the far northwestern desert of Chihuahua at Paquimé, part of a culture that extended into Arizona. The Tarahumara in the Copper Canyon area in northern Mexico are one of the most distinctive groups from this region today. They live either in caves or, increasingly, in small houses within the canyons, produce incredible woven products, often on sale to tourists, and – perhaps most famously – can run for incredibly long distances, sometimes up to 20 hours without rest, across mountainous terrain, with nothing sturdier than sandals on their feet.

THE TARASCANS

We know a good deal more about the Tarascans of Michoacán, an independent kingdom, because by the time the Spaniards arrived, they had been resisting invasions by the Aztecs for more than a hundred years. Shortly after the Conquest a priest, Friar Jerónimo de Acalá, compiled his *Chronicles of Michoacán*, a history of the Purépecha, as the Tarascans called themselves, that gives an insight into their culture.

Michoacán means "Place of the Fishermen," a reference to Lake Pátzcuaro, the centre of Tarascan life. However, the religion of the Purépecha was based not on water but on volcanoes. The chief deity, Curicáueri, the

Totonac figures, El Tajín.

"Great Burner," represented the young Sun. In his honor, the Purépecha kept fires burning constantly on top of huge stone structures called *yácatas*, the largest of them at Tzintzuntzan, their lakeside capital. As an enemy of the Aztecs, the last Tarascan king, Tangáxuan II, thought the Spaniards could perhaps become his allies. Spanish emissaries arrived in 1522, and rather than resist he agreed to accept the overlordship of Cortés while retaining his own autonomy. However, once the conquistadors discovered that he was passing on to them only a small part of the tribute he gathered from his people, retaliation was swift. Tangáxuan was burned alive, and the Tarascans were subjected to Spanish rule.

📷 THE ANCIENT MEXICAN WORLD

Mexico's ruined cities are echoes of a 3,000-year-long history, and a complex, intricately interconnected world that can at times seem familiar, and at others feels very alien.

Perhaps the most astonishing feature of the pre-Conquest civilizations of Mexico is their sheer variety, scale and extent. World-famous ruins such as Teotihuacán or Chichén Itzá are only a few among hundreds of sites, from Paquimé near the New Mexico border to the forest cities of the Yucatán and Chiapas in the south, part of a Maya region that extended still farther into Guatemala and Honduras. A complex series of cultures developed and succeeded each other for nearly 3,000 years, from the emergence of the first Olmec communities in Veracruz and Tabasco around 1300 BC to the time of the Spanish Conquest. They adapted to every part of the region, from the northern deserts and highland valleys to the rainforests of the south. Look beyond the most obvious features, and exploring their differences, individualities and enigmas is endlessly fascinating.

Architecturally the pre-Hispanic cultures were commonly crude in some ways – their reliance on pyramid-mounds rather than load-bearing walls for height – and sophisticated in others, including carving and water management. The central place of ritual was reflected in the theatricality of major buildings. While the great pyramids and plazas grab the eye first, just as interesting are some of the details found in palaces and residential areas at sites such as El Tajín, Palenque or Kohunlich, which give a feel of daily life. Nor is ancient Mexico a closed book, for more sites are being excavated all the time, revealing further historical insights.

The Niches Pyramid at El Tajín, Veracruz, dates from around AD 700.

One of the only surviving complete Maya murals, at Bonampak in Chiapas, portrays courtly ceremonies and rituals.

Carving of a bird on a pillar in the Palacio de Quetzalpapalotl, Teotihuacán.

A stone jaguar head on the steps of the Templo Mayor at Tenochtitlán.

Ancient arts

The artistic creations of the ancient cultures were as inventive as their buildings. Many symbolized the power of their rulers or were associated with rituals and sacrifice, such as the fearful carved altars, or the elaborate Maya ceramic incense-burners representing supernatural beings. Others show a less forbidding side of each culture, such as the disarming "smiling head" sculptures of Veracruz. Among the Mixtecs and the Maya, scenes of everyday life, as well as legends, were painted on ceramic pots. And a Maya specialty was tiny Jaina figurines, charming figures that give an image of a whole society.

All the cultures had a very vivid, imaginative visual sense, which has survived unbroken in Mexican folk arts today. The Maya had the most complete glyph writing system, followed by the Mixtecs, who left many books. Other cultures excelled in jewelry or more abstract designs. Many cultures had sophisticated painting traditions, but only a few examples have survived, such as the murals at Teotihuacán, Mitla, and above all Bonampak, Chiapas.

The ideal first stop to get an idea of the range of pre-Hispanic art is the Museo de Antropología in Mexico City, but there are other fine collections in Xalapa, Palenque, and Mérida.

A hummingbird goblet (AD 800–1521) on display at the Museo Nacional de Antropología in Mexico City.

Geometric mosaics in the Templo de las Columnas, Mitla.

The Tenochtitlán site museum is beautifully designed and contains a fascinating collection of artifacts, such as this ceramic figure.

CONQUEST AND COLONIAL RULE

Spanish adventurers and Mexico's indigenous cultures locked together in an epic struggle, and the fissures in the society this created can still be seen 500 years later.

The Spanish conquest of Mexico centered on the violent clash between two empires, both of which were cultured, cruel and well organized. But it was there the similarities stopped.

From an outsider's point of view, this is one of the world's most exciting adventure stories. Against tens of thousands of Aztec warriors, Hernán Cortés, the leader of the Spanish conquistadors, initially had fewer than 400 soldiers, 16 horses – "fearsome beasts," never before seen in the New World – 10 heavy guns and four lighter pieces of artillery. The success of Cortés' expedition would have been impossible without the help of other indigenous groups who were hostile to the Aztecs and sick of paying tribute to Tenochtitlán, most of all the Tlaxcalans, who provided thousands of men to fight alongside the Spaniards.

NEWS OF GOLD

The first Spanish expedition to set foot in Mexico was led by Francisco Hernández de Córdoba, who in February 1517 sailed west with three ships from Cuba, conquered by the Spaniards six years earlier. They landed first on Isla de Mujeres and sailed west around Yucatán, turning back after a skirmish with the Maya lord of Kin Pech (modern Campeche). Nevertheless, they had already seen buildings and goods of sophistication far beyond anything the Spaniards had found on the Caribbean islands.

The following year another expedition, led by Juan de Grijalva, sailed south around the Yucatán coast and landed in what is now Veracruz state, where they first saw some of the wealth, fine textiles, and above all gold of the Aztec empire. Once news of this reached

Portrait of Hernán Cortés.

Cuba, it could be said that Mexico's fate was sealed.

Hernán Cortés had been just 19 years old when he arrived on Hispaniola in 1504. Later he obtained land in Cuba, but, intelligent and ruthless, he craved more wealth and adventure. In 1519 the governor of Cuba, Diego de Velázquez, proposed that he lead a third, larger expedition of 11 ships, men, and horses to Mexico. However, like most conquistadors both men were intensely ambitious and suspicious of each other, and the rivalry between them would play its part in subsequent events. Distrusting Cortés, Velázquez tried to cancel the expedition, but Cortés ignored the order and set sail regardless.

BURNING THE BOATS

Like Grijalva, Cortés landed first on Cozumel, and then sailed west around the Yucatán. He won a victory against a local chieftain in western Campeche, after which, in Mesoamerican tradition, he was given tribute that included 20 women slaves, among them *La Malinche*, who would become Cortés' invaluable interpreter. On April 22, 1519 they landed again at a point further north, where Cortés decided to found the first Spanish settlement in Mexico, naming it "The Rich Town of the True Cross," or Veracruz.

The next thing he did was order the destruction of all but one of his ships. Cutting himself, and any would-be mutineers, off from any line of retreat, he clearly intended to make his men as desperate to conquer or die as he was.

THE JOURNEY TO TENOCHTITLÁN

The Spaniards were well received by the Totonacs of nearby Cempoala, and Cortés soon became aware of the advantages he could gain by exploiting the resentment of other communities toward Aztec domination. In Tenochtitlán, reports of the Spanish landings were heard by the Aztec emperor or *Tlatoani*, Moctezuma II. The reasons for his strangely passive response have been a great cause of speculation. Traditional accounts from Spaniards and Aztec chroniclers – who blamed him for their defeat – portray Moctezuma as refined but weak, indecisive, and fearful.

It was said that there had been bad omens in the previous year, and that Moctezuma was acutely aware of the legend foretelling the return from the east of the god-king Quetzalcóatl. The description of the Spanish arriving in their "floating towers" coincided with the legend, as they, like Quetzalcóatl, were fair-skinned and bearded. Recent accounts cast doubt on the strength of these legends, but, for whatever reason, Moctezuma did not send warriors to meet Cortés but messengers, who tried to persuade him not to venture farther inland. Cortés, however, ignored them.

Leaving 150 men at Veracruz, Cortés took his time to make the 312km (194-mile) march to Tenochtitlán, stopping at Tlaxcala, where he gained his most vital allies. When the invaders – accompanied by several thousand Tlaxcalans – finally reached the outskirts

of Tenochtitlán, on November 8, 1519, they beheld a marvelous city, then one of the largest in the world, set in a lake, with broad main streets, temples, terraces, gardens, and distant snowcapped mountains.

An essential source on the Conquest is Bernal Díaz, a common soldier who served on all three expeditions to Mexico. In his journal he described the wonder he felt when he first saw the Aztec capital. "[The city] seemed like an enchanted vision from the tale of Amadis," he wrote. "Indeed some of our soldiers asked

Cortés enters Tenochtitlán (detail of a painted screen from the colonial period).

> When Cortés arrived in Mexico he was a mutineer on the run from a Spanish royal governor in Cuba, and could only expect severe punishment if he returned empty-handed.

whether it was not all a dream." The Spaniards saw the people, the canals, the bridges, and the boats gliding on the lake, carrying produce to the great market of Tlatelolco, patronized by some 20,000 people a day.

Moctezuma greeted Cortés with great ceremony, gave him many gifts and arranged for him and his men to be quartered in the former palace of his own father, Axayacatal.

GUESTS OF MOCTEZUMA

There followed weeks of meandering discussions between Moctezuma and Cortés. The *Tlatoani* entertained the Spaniards in luxury, but would promise nothing. Cortés and his men were increasingly bold and restive; Aztec lords, meanwhile, resented their presence and urged Moctezuma to attack them, but he refused to comply. Eventually, in a daring stroke, Cortés's

men seized Moctezuma and insisted he move into their palace with them, effectively taking him hostage. Even then, he still sought to keep his people from rebelling.

Then, news arrived that a much larger Spanish force had landed at Veracruz under Pánfilo de Narváez, sent by Governor Velázquez to arrest Cortés and take over the expedition. In yet another demonstration of his phenomenal willpower, Cortés left Pedro de Alvarado in command in Tenochtitlán with 80 men, and traveled remarkably quickly back to the coast,

Hernán Cortés at the Battle of Otumba, 1520.

⊘ MALINCHE, MYTH AND REALITY

La Malinche, original name probably *Malintzin*, is a powerfully symbolic figure in the conquest of Mexico. Born in the late 15th century (most likely 1496–9), she seems to have been the daughter of a lord from southern Veracruz, but was enslaved at Xicalango in Campeche, where she was given to Cortés after his first victory. She spoke Náhuatl and Maya languages, and began to serve Cortés as an interpreter. He already had with him Jerónimo de Aguilar, a priest who had learnt Yucatec Maya while shipwrecked in Yucatán; between them they gave Cortés a doorway into Mexico. She was soon baptized into the Catholic faith and learnt Spanish, so that she could translate directly, and is said to have given

Cortés vital advice in outwitting the Aztecs.

She also bore Cortés's first son, Martín, one of the first of the mestizos who now make up most of Mexico's population. Malinche can thus be endlessly reinterpreted. The most traditional Mexican view of her is as a traitor, Cortés' whore, selling herself and then cast aside when he married a Spanish noblewoman. *Malinchista* is a word of contempt for any Mexican fascinated with all things foreign. Others see her as an intelligent survivor. And the same contempt is not heaped on men who helped Cortés to succeed, such as the largely forgotten king of Tlaxcala, Xicotencatl. Her image survives in the Monumento al Mestizaje in Chetumal.

where he ambushed and imprisoned Narváez and persuaded his men – more than 1,000 Spanish troops – to join him. With this much larger army, he set off back into the highlands.

In Tenochtitlán, the situation had exploded. Alvarado was brutal but lacked Cortés's cunning. Things came to a head at a festival for the god Huitzilopochtli on May 10, 1520. Exactly what happened is unclear, but the Spaniards, perhaps fearing an attack, set upon the crowd at the Templo Mayor, killing hundreds of priests and nobles. The city rose against them, and the

silence, padding their horses' hooves to escape detection. However, they were seen crossing one of the causeways linking the island city, and attacked by thousands of warriors, many in canoes on the lake. The Spaniards fought back, and then ran for their lives while the Aztecs, no longer fearful of the invaders, harassed them along the bridges and paths.

Bernal Díaz wrote that during this *Noche Triste* (Sad Night), as it became known, the Spanish lost more than half their men, all their artillery and munitions, and many of their horses. Many

Aztec warriors defending the temple of Tenochtitlán against conquistadors, c.1520.

Spaniards were chased back into the palace, taking Moctezuma with them.

Despite this Cortés was still able to rejoin Alvarado with his reinforcements, but they were now besieged. Cortés looked to Moctezuma to cool the situation, but, according to Díaz, when he appealed to his people he was met with a hail of stones, and died soon afterwards. He was succeeded by his brother Cuitlahuac, who began to organize Aztec resistance.

SAD NIGHT AND THE END OF TENOCHTITLÁN

Cortés realized their only hope of survival was to escape from Tenochtitlán. On the night of June 30, the Spaniards attempted to break out in

died from greed, as, weighed down with Aztec gold, they could not fight or swim to safety or even move effectively.

However, the Aztecs failed to follow up their victory. In October 1520 Tenochtitlán was hit by a devastating epidemic of smallpox, brought by the Spaniards, which killed thousands, including Cuitlahuac himself. Aztec society was plunged into deeper disarray, with many of its ruling and warrior elite dead. Cuitlahuac's young nephew and successor, Cuauhtémoc, chose to stay in the city, perhaps believing it was now safe from attack.

Cortés and his few surviving men were thus able to reach Tlaxcala, after living on berries and ears of corn from the fields. Once there, undaunted, he launched into a whirlwind of activity. He set out on a round of diplomacy to win the support not just of the Tlaxcalans but many other Highland states, making all kinds of promises in return for their support, most of which were disowned by later Spanish governors. He also received fresh reinforcements from Cuba, intended for Narváez.

When he moved again on Tenochtitlán, in February 1521, Cortés had 86 horsemen, 818 Spanish foot soldiers and around 80,000 indigenous warriors, and had prepared a careful plan for

and frontal attacks. The Spaniards conquered the causeways first, and then the city, street by street. Their numbers severely reduced by smallpox and famine, the Aztecs were less and less able to fight. Cuauhtémoc was captured, and the Aztecs surrendered on August 13, 1521.

Tenochtitlán had lost perhaps 100,000 people, and the Spaniards and their allies sacked what was left. Cortés had the center completely razed, to be rebuilt as a new, Spanish city, with the remaining indigenous communities confined

Sixteenth-century engraving of Francisco de Montejo and his troops encountering the Maya of the Yucatán in 1526.

Since the Mexican Revolution Cuauhtémoc, the 18-year-old last Tlatoani who defended Tenochtitlán, has been enshrined as a national hero, and Cuauhtémoc is a popular name for a man.

the assault on the city. His master-stroke was to have 13 small ships built on Lake Texcoco, some with cannon, to allow the Spaniards to enforce a complete siege.

They still did not have an easy victory. Cuauhtémoc proved an inventive commander, and the assault on Tenochtitlán lasted for months, between the siege, Aztec breakouts,

to the outskirts. The dismantling of the Aztec empire was near complete.

THE SPREAD OF SPANISH POWER

The overthrow of the greatest state in Mesoamerica gave the Spaniards an aura of immense power, and an essential base from which to extend their tentacles throughout the region. Beginning in 1522 Cortés' men took control of the Tarascan kingdom in Michoacán, and in 1524 Pedro de Alvarado led a bloody march southward through Chiapas to conquer Guatemala and Honduras. The "Chichimeca" deserts north of Zacatecas, however, would be settled by the Spaniards only gradually, over the next 200 years.

Yucatán proved a particularly hard nut for the Spaniards to crack. In 1526 the commission to conquer it was granted by Charles V of Spain to Francisco de Montejo. However, it would take three attempts before Montejo, his son, and his nephew (both also called Francisco de Montejo) were able to inflict a decisive defeat on the Maya lords and found their new capital of Mérida, in 1542. And even then, the last independent Maya kingdom, on Lake Petén-Itzá in Guatemala, continued to survive until 1697.

The conquistadors were driven by lust for gold, but also by a sense of divine mission. They believed God was on their side. Bernal Díaz said their triumph was achieved "not of our volition, but by the guidance of God. For what soldiers in the world, numbering only 400... would have dared to enter a city as strong as Mexico, which is larger than Venice and more than 4,500 miles away from our own Castile?"

IMPERIAL SYSTEM

Spain governed Mexico for three centuries. At the beginning of the 16th century Spain was one of the most dynamic countries in Europe, with a new burst of energy after the final expulsion of the Moors in 1492. Its different Christian kingdoms had recently been unified under one crown, although they still did not form one state, and the new American colonies were actually claimed for Castile. Castile was an absolute monarchy, and below the Crown the two most powerful elements in society were the aristocracy and the Catholic Church. A rigid hierarchy prevailed, and any deviations from Catholic orthodoxy were not permitted.

The same pattern of society would be extended to "New Spain," as Mexico was now called, as the Crown asserted its authority. Charles V and his ministers distrusted the freebooting conquistadors – many of whom were fighting each other for the spoils of conquest – and set out to bring them under control. Cortés was only the most prominent of the many who bitterly resented their treatment: initially confirmed as Governor of New Spain, he was later made subordinate to an *Audiencia* or high court of royal officials, and then passed over for the post of Viceroy in favour of a more aristocratic candidate.

The Spanish Crown aimed to bring order to its colonies with a set of rules. They were all to be governed in line with the *Leyes de Indias*, the "Laws of the Indies," which attempted to cover every possible field: the role of governors, the treatment of indigenous people, taxation, and so on.

ENCOMENDEROS AND FRIARS

Spanish colonists were initially rewarded through the *encomienda* system, with which they were "entrusted" *(encomendado)* an area

Spanish priests destroying Aztec idols.

⊘ THE MANILA GALLEONS

New Spain was not only a source of wealth for Spain by itself, it also became its route to the riches of the Orient. From 1565 until 1815, one or two ships sailed each year from the Philippines to Acapulco, loaded with Asian spices and other treasures, and back again with Mexican silver to pay for them. From Acapulco the cargoes were carried overland to Mexico City and then Veracruz, to be shipped onward to Spain.

The Spaniards used this route to avoid the pirates of the Indian Ocean and, later, hostile colonies around the coasts of Africa. This trans-Pacific trade left many influences in southwest Mexico, such as the lacquerwork of Michoacán, Guerrero, and Chiapas.

of land and all the indigenous people on it, with the right to their labor and the (often theoretical) obligation to teach them Christianity. This effectively gave *encomenderos* the power of life and death, and denunciations were rife of the abuses of the system, with many cases of indigenous people being literally worked to death.

The main challenge to *encomendero* power came from the Church and particularly the various orders of friars – Franciscans, Dominicans – who arrived on the heels of the military conquerors to begin the "Spiritual Conquest"

were given responsibility for entire parts of the country, such as the Dominicans in Oaxaca and Chiapas, the Franciscans in Yucatán.

The missionaries concentrated many of their efforts on teaching the children of the native aristocracy. In 1528, the Colegio de Santa Cruz in Tlatelolco was founded for this purpose. For a wider audience, open-air "Indian chapels" *(capillas de indias)* were built to hold services for as large a number of indigenous people as possible. One of the most important moments in the *conquista espiritual* came in 1531 with the beginning

Nineteenth-century engraving of Bartolomé de Las Casas.

> The Leyes de Indias stipulated the grid layout of all Spanish colonial cities, around a central plaza with a cathedral or church on the east side, a governors' palace on the north and town hall on the west.

of the Americas, the conversion of its people to Catholicism. This required a phenomenal effort by the Spanish Church, but was of fundamental importance to Church and Crown, as a God-given mission that could excuse, even sometimes justify, the cruelty of other aspects of the Conquest. Different missionary orders

of the cult of the Virgin of Guadalupe, a vital step in giving Catholicism a distinctly Mexican – mestizo – tone (see page 22).

DISAPPEARING PEOPLES

Encomenderos complained that friars and Crown officials only denounced mistreatment of indigenous people because they wanted power and local labor for themselves, but there were also priests who were dedicated defenders of indigenous people, such as Bishop Vasco de Quiroga in Michoacán, and the extraordinary Bartolomé de Las Casas in Chiapas, who in his *Brief History of the Destruction of the Indies* questioned the whole moral basis of the Conquest. In 1542 he even persuaded Charles V to revise the *Leyes de Indias*, giving indigenous people more protection from the Crown. The difficulty was in getting laws to apply on the ground, and throughout the colonial era there were complaints that many settlers treated colonized people as slaves.

Las Casas was also perhaps mistaken in thinking that conquistador brutality was the immediate cause of something all the Spaniards could see around them: the catastrophic decline in the indigenous population. In 1520 Mesoa-

were in operation. Indigenous people were forcibly recruited to work in them, and when their numbers fell African slaves were imported. By 1800 Mexico was producing 66 percent of the world's silver.

COLONIAL LIFE

In most of New Spain life settled into a fairly unchanging pattern as the Conquest receded into the past. It was based on the aristocratic Castilian model of society, and the sectors the Spanish Crown relied on to run its empire – the

Apache prisoners were forced to work in the silver mines.

merica had a population of at least 12 million; a century later, almost 90 percent had disappeared. Indigenous people had no defenses against European diseases, above all smallpox; at the same time, the disruption of the traditional economy had a disastrous effect on the food supply. This population collapse was not at all uniform, and some areas – notably Oaxaca, Chiapas, and Yucatán in the south – retained large indigenous populations, but in many areas of the Central Highlands an ever-greater proportion of the survivors was made up of mixed-race mestizos.

It did not take very long for the Spanish to discover silver in Zacatecas, Pachuca, and Guanajuato, and by 1548 more than 50 silver mines

Spanish aristocracy, local landowners and the Church – were not ones to encourage innovation.

The Catholic Church was omnipresent and enormously wealthy, receiving a 10 percent tithe from agriculture, commerce, mining, and the native economy. The missionary orders had begun to build chapels and monasteries as soon as they arrived in Mexico in the 1520s, but the great age of colonial religious building was the 17th century, when magnificent Baroque churches spread across the country.

The great sources of wealth were mining, agriculture, and trade. Cattle and horses the Spaniards had introduced into the country flourished, and huge areas were given over to ranching. Sugar cane was another Spanish introduction. The *encomienda* system largely gave way to one of hacienda estates, so that settlers swapped direct control over indigenous people for ownership of often vast extensions of land. Even so, indigenous families were still commonly bound to the same hacienda for generations, by debt servitude or just the lack of enough land of their own.

The Spanish Crown, interested above all in ensuring that its empire added to its own wealth, banned Mexico and its other American colonies from trading with any European country except

Pima Indians convoying a Silver Train in Mexico by Frederic Remington, 1887.

> *Miguel Hidalgo was a very free-thinking Catholic priest: he did not believe in the virgin birth, the supremacy of the pope, or priestly celibacy, and fathered five children.*

Spain. Inter-colonial trade was also prohibited, since it would compete with imports from the Iberian peninsula.

THE CASTES OF NEW SPAIN

Spanish Mexico had a rigid social hierarchy, based on race, wealth, and place of birth. At the top were Spanish-born aristocrats, for only they could occupy the most important state offices. Below them were the criollos, Mexican-born but of entirely white blood, many very rich and increasingly frustrated at the Spaniards' monopoly on power. Below them was a medley of new peoples: mestizos of Spanish and Native American blood were the most prominent, but there were also many *castas* (castes), with varying quantities of Spanish, indigenous, African, and Oriental genes. By the 18th century, criollos and mestizos formed around half the population. At the bottom were the indigenous peoples, who for most of the colonial era were not even allowed to set foot in the centers of the Spanish cities.

In 1759 an energetic monarch, Carlos III, became king of Spain and tried to shake up his decaying empire. Spanish governors were instructed to introduce economic reforms and even challenge the power of the Church, seen as obstructing that of the state. Among many criollos, however, this burst of activity only spurred the thought that they could do better by themselves.

THE CRY OF INDEPENDENCE

Discontent with Spanish rule was widespread – encouraged by the Enlightenment, the independence of the United States, and the French Revolution – but gave rise to little action until Napoleon occupied Spain in 1808, imprisoned the royal family and put his own brother on the Spanish throne. Suddenly, the center of government had ceased to exist. Criollo grandees demanded to be represented in the regency that took charge of New Spain, but the Spanish officials or *peninsulares* stubbornly resisted. Other criollos looked for more radical change, and secret meetings discussed rebellion. One such group, meeting in Querétaro, included the parish priest of the small town of Dolores, Miguel Hidalgo.

They planned an uprising for the end of 1810, but the government got word of the plot. Rather than be arrested, on September 16, 1810, Father Hidalgo gave an impassioned speech to his congregation in Dolores. From the pulpit he called on them to join in a fight for freedom and to take back the land "stolen" from their forefathers, ending by shouting "Long live the Virgin of Guadalupe" and "Death to bad government. Death to the Spaniards." This was the famous *Grito de Dolores*, the "shout" for independence.

It has never been clear how far Hidalgo intended to go, but a characteristic of Mexican revolutions is that small actions can have huge, unanticipated consequences. His *grito* started a peasant revolution.

BITTER BATTLES AND BIRTH OF MEXICO

Armed with machetes, shovels, and slings, poor mestizos and Indians flocked to join Hidalgo, and within a few weeks he had an army of 50,000 that captured Guanajuato, Zacatecas, and Gua-

and convened a congress at Chilpancingo in 1813 that sketched out the basis of an independent state, with civil rights for all. However, he too was caught and executed, in 1815. He was succeeded by one of his lieutenants, Vicente Guerrero, and the struggle continued as a bitter guerrilla war.

By 1819, the insurgents had largely been contained. Then, things turned upside down. In January 1820 a rising by liberal army officers took over the government in Spain. In Mexico, rumors spread that the mother country's new admin-

Congress of Chilpanchingo, 1813.

dalajara. He issued decrees abolishing slavery and the tributes paid by indigenous people to the Church and criollo landowners. However, his ragged army also massacred whites, Spaniards, and criollos in Guanajuato and Guadalajara. Many criollos, horrified at the prospect of social upheaval, rallied to support the Spanish viceroy. The result was years of bloody war.

At the beginning of 1811 the rebels were driven back, and Hidalgo was captured and executed in July. His role as leader of the fight for independence was taken by José María Morelos, another priest, and a mestizo from Valladolid in Michoacán, now named Morelia in his honor. A brilliant general, Morelos led successful campaigns across Michoacán, Guerrero, and Oaxaca,

istration would bombard them with radical decrees challenging the powers of the Church and landowners, and wealthy criollos saw new attractions in independence.

A criollo general in the Spanish army, Agustín de Iturbide, made contact with Guerrero, and called on him as a patriot to join him in support of the so-called "Three Guarantees:" the independence of Mexico; Catholicism as the sole religion; and the "union" of all Mexicans, with the abolition of the Spanish legal distinctions between ethnic groups and classes. Guerrero agreed, and this left the Spaniards with few options. A newly arrived Viceroy, Juan O'Donojú, signed a treaty that finally converted New Spain into Mexico on August 24, 1821.

NEW SPAIN'S HERITAGE IN STONE

The ornate styles of Imperial Spain blended with Mexican sensibilities and love of decoration to create a unique architectural synthesis.

In Mexico, the legacy of the past is rarely far away. Pre-Hispanic pyramids, monasteries, Baroque churches, and ruined haciendas lie off busy highways. After the Spanish Conquest, the fusion of cultures gave rise to a multiplicity of architectural

The gilded altarpiece of the Church of Santo Domingo, Oaxaca.

styles. The missionary friars were the most prolific builders of the 16th century. Far from Spain, in an alien climate and an alien land, they brought with them elements from Romanesque, Gothic, Renaissance, and other Old World architectures. Even an unusual Spanish style such as Mudéjar – the Moorish-influenced architecture produced by Muslim craftsmen under Christian rule – left its mark in Mexico from 1562, notably in the great *Pila* or well in Chiapa de Corzo, Chiapas.

In villages such as Actopan, Huejotzingo, and Yecapixtla, immense monasteries still dominate the landscape. These fortress-like structures were often built with stones from "pagan" pyramids and

temples. Work was carried out by native craftsmen, who were instructed in carpentry, masonry, metal-working, and other European skills. The glory of the Church Militant found expression in immense altar-pieces, gilded images, mural paintings, and carved decoration of wood and stone. Such creations were not mere copies of European models. With time they increasingly reflected an indigenous sensibility, as local craftsmen reinterpreted European imagery. This intermingling of European and indigenous art – sometimes producing bizarre anomalies – is called *tequitqui* by art historians.

Different missionary orders favored different styles. The austere Franciscans in the Yucatán disliked extravagance and built in a plain, late-medieval style that was already archaic in Europe, as seen in the massive monastery in Izamal or countless Yucatán village churches. The Augustinians in the Central Highlands and the Dominicans in Oaxaca and Chiapas had a much greater taste for artistic refinement and contemporary styles, whether Renaissance or the elegant Spanish style known as "plateresque," because it was said to reproduce the effects of silverware *(plata)* in stone. One of the finest examples of plateresque is the 1560s monastery of San Antonio Acolmán north of Mexico City, and the style can also be seen in non-monastic churches such as the first stages of Mexico City Cathedral, begun in the 1570s, and Mérida Cathedral, completed in 1598.

BAROQUE ZENITH

In the 17th century, Mexican architecture became increasingly ornate. High Baroque, the favourite style of Imperial Spain at its peak, encouraged exuberance and invention, and was enthusiastically taken up in Mexico. By 1750, Baroque had become ultra-Baroque, with the arrival of the Churrigueresque style. Originated by the architect-sculptor José Churriguera in Salamanca in Spain, this involved covering every last part of facades and altars with intricate decoration; in Mexico it matched perfectly with local tastes, and was taken to its limits. This was the greatest period of church-building in colonial Mexico, reflecting 18th-century prosperity, and churches and cathedrals were characterized by lavish complexity and richness of detail.

The Sagrario beside Mexico City Cathedral and Zacatecas Cathedral have two of the most astonishing Churrigueresque facades, but there are many more. Gold-clad altarpieces – replete with twisted columns, angels and medallions – dazzled the faithful of Tepotzotlán, Taxco or Querétaro.

In small towns and villages, local craftsmen drew inspiration from what they saw in cities. Their eclectic creations are described as *barroco popular*. Stucco, carved to imitate stone, embellished facades in the Sierra Gorda of Querétaro. A particular Mexican addition to Churriguesque was color: in Puebla, multi-colored glazed tiles covered church exteriors, and at San Francisco Acatepec, outside the city, they encased cornices, capitals, and columns. Clusters of flowers, fruit, animals, and cherubs cover the walls and ceiling at Santa María Tonantzintla.

Neoclassicism, imported at the end of the 18th century, condemned Baroque as showy and vulgar. It was used in the final stages of Mexico City Cathedral – the dome – and would be copied in many public buildings erected in the first years of independence, as a more "modern" style. Some church interiors were stripped of decoration. Yet many Baroque churches and cathedrals survived intact. Decked out today with flowers, candles, and plaster saints – sometimes even neon crosses – they meet the aesthetic and spiritual needs of Mexican worshippers.

CITIES, PALACES, AND HACIENDAS

In the viceregal capital, the ruling class displayed an appetite for luxury. After the destruction of Tenochtitlán Aztec structures were replaced with grand residences and government buildings. Fray Alonso Ponce, visiting in 1585, praised its "very good houses and handsome streets." Today, little remains of 16th-century civil architecture. Buildings not demolished by later generations have been modified to suit changing tastes.

Aristocratic residences of the Baroque era had two or more stories. Lavish exteriors incorporated corner towers, statues in niches, balconies, and monumental entrances topped by coats of arms. Inside, an imposing stairway led from the main patio to the upper levels. Wealthy families built their city mansions with income from country estates. In the 1730s the Condesa del Valle de Orizaba had her 16th-century Mexico City house rebuilt and decorated with blue-and-white Puebla

tiles. Popularly known as *La Casa de los Azulejos* (House of Tiles), it now contains Sanborn's restaurant. Outside the capital, fine houses were built in cities such as Puebla, where Baroque facades were often encrusted with stucco. One such mansion, resplendent with icing-like ornamentation and now a museum, is aptly known as *La Casa del Alfeñique* (The Sugar-Frosted House).

Landowners with haciendas or country estates made fortunes from farming and mining. Haciendas, many established in the 16th century, were constantly remolded to meet prevailing needs, including after independence. Many surviving hacienda buildings have thus acquired a timeless quality, which makes them hard to date.

Haciendas are among the emblematic buildings of the Mexican countryside. Self-sufficient, haciendas operated along feudal lines. Thick,

The ornate courtyard of the 18th-century Casa de la Marquesa.

powerful walls protected the great house, with its lofty rooms, well-shaded verandas, and plant-filled patios. The walls also enclosed the chapel, laborers' dwellings, the cemetery, the stables, cattle yards, and granaries. Today several haciendas have been transformed into very special luxury hotels with delightful gardens, such as Hacienda Temozón and others in Yucatán, or Hacienda de San Gabriel near Cuernavaca. The Hacienda El Lencero outside Xalapa in Veracruz, once home to the 19th-century dictator Santa Anna, is now a museum. Others are still left to decay, as they have been since the 1910 Revolution.

Lázaro Cárdenas signs peasants'
land deed.

INDEPENDENCE AND REVOLUTION

Dreams of freedom, equality and independence were pursued by Mexicans in the face of cynical dictators, foreign invasions, and social upheaval.

The new state was born with very mixed motives. The Ejército Trigarante, or "Army of the Three Guarantees," that entered Mexico City amid great enthusiasm in 1821 included revolutionaries who had been fighting as guerrillas for 10 years, but its commander General Iturbide had taken up the cause of independence precisely to defend the privileges of colonial society. The immense tensions this situation created would be played out over the next century.

Many conservatives still considered a monarchy to be an essential guardian of social order. In 1822, in a lavish ceremony, Iturbide was crowned Emperor Agustín I. But his rejoicing was short-lived; less than a year later one of his cronies, General Antonio López de Santa Anna, rebelled and forced him to abdicate. When Iturbide tried to return in 1824, he was caught and executed.

SHAKY REPUBLIC

The Constitution of 1824 finally made Mexico a republic, and Guadalupe Victoria, a stalwart of the fight for independence alongside Hidalgo and Morelos, became its first president. But it was Santa Anna who dominated the political scene for the next three decades. Born into a criollo landowning family in Veracruz, like Iturbide he had fought for Spain throughout most of the independence wars.

Independent Mexico found itself to be a vast country with vast problems. Trade and mining had been paralyzed. Communications in the troubled land were almost impossible. The mestizo and indigenous majority lived in dire poverty, apathetic toward, and cut off from, politics.

Mexico's political conflicts coalesced into a divide ostensibly between conservative

General Antonio López de Santa Anna.

> Santa Anna said that Mexicans were "not fit" for liberty and needed "despotism" to keep them in line, and called himself the "Napoleon of the West" and the "Mexican Caesar."

"centralists" in favor of an authoritarian state and a powerful role for the Catholic Church, and more liberal "federalists," but even Santa Anna, generally the standard-bearer of conservatism, changed sides when his intrigues demanded. In many areas the only real power was held by local landowners and bosses called *caciques*.

From 1821 to 1855 Mexico was in constant turmoil. In 30 years there were 50 governments, almost all the result of military coups, and 11 of them presided over by Santa Anna, dubbed the "perpetual dictator." Mexico's weakness tempted foreign powers to intervene, spurred on by myths about its mineral riches.

LOSS OF TERRITORIES

Santa Anna is remembered above all in Mexico as the man who lost half the nation's territory to the United States. In 1835 he tried to tear up Mexico's 1824 Constitution and create a centralized dictatorship. American settlers in Texas reacted by declaring independence. Santa Anna marched north, and famously massacred Texans at the Alamo before being beaten by Sam Houston at the battle of San Jacinto. Humiliated, Santa Anna was forced to accept Texan independence. A new government in Mexico City disowned this agreement, but was powerless to reverse it.

Santa Anna did not only antagonize Anglo settlers in Texas, for other states rebelled against

Depiction of a battle in the Mexican-American War.

⊙ BENITO JUÁREZ

If Santa Anna was an early archetype of tawdry corruption in Mexican politics, 26th President Benito Juárez was its foremost symbol of integrity, with a stature comparable only to Abraham Lincoln as his country's greatest statesman. Born in 1806 in a village north of Oaxaca, he was pure Zapotec, and spoke only Zapotec as a child. His parents died when he was three, and he worked in the fields until, aged 12, he walked to Oaxaca City.

His intelligence was obvious, and a local priest arranged for his education. Rather than enter the priesthood, however, he became a lawyer. His rigid belief that a fair application of law would solve Mexico's inequalities was the source of many of his strengths and weaknesses. His most-repeated quotation is "Among individuals, as among nations, respect for the rights of others is peace."

Above all, he was known as utterly incorruptible, and his lasting legacy in Mexico was one of reform, the like of which has rarely been glimpsed throughout the country's recent history. His unbending determination was vital to the survival of the liberal cause and Mexican independence through the struggles of the 1850s and 1860s. And yet, certain measures in his great reform program, ending traditional restrictions on land sales, would be used by landowners under the Díaz regime to grab even vaster estates. His memorial day is March 21st.

him. Most successful was Yucatán (the entire peninsula, not just modern Yucatán state), which had had its own administration under Spanish rule. Yucatán too declared independence in 1840, and beat off an army sent by Santa Anna to Campeche in 1842.

In 1845 the US Congress voted to annex Texas. This sparked the Mexican–American War, described by future president and general Ulysses Grant as "one of the most unjust [wars] ever waged by a stronger against a weaker nation." US troops captured Monterrey and most of California, while an army under General Winfield Scott disembarked in Veracruz and occupied Mexico City.

In 1848, by the Treaty of Guadalupe Hidalgo, Mexico ceded Texas, California, Nevada, Utah, and most of New Mexico and Arizona to the United States. In 1853, Santa Anna sold off one last portion of New Mexico and Arizona for $10 million, in the Gadsden Purchase.

In the meantime, an entirely separate drama had taken place at the other end of the country. The Maya had risen in rebellion across then-independent Yucatán in 1847, in a savage struggle that became known as the "Caste War." It was the largest indigenous revolt in Mexico since the Conquest, and it very nearly succeeded. In fear of their lives, Yucatán's criollo elite agreed to return to Mexico, in return for aid against the Maya.

JUÁREZ AND THE REFORM

In 1855 a liberal revolt drove Santa Anna from power for the last time, and set out at last to give Mexico the institutions of a modern, democratic state, with a sweeping program known as *La Reforma,* The Reform. The key figure in the new government, as justice minister and later president, was Benito Juárez. Reform laws attacked the privileges of the Catholic Church, which liberals saw as consigning the country to social and economic paralysis. Church and communal properties were broken up. In 1857, a new constitution guaranteed freedom of religion and other fundamental liberties.

Juárez's revolutionary venture met with fierce opposition from conservatives. For three years, from 1858–60, the two parties fought the bitter War of Reform. Juárez emerged triumphant, and

on January 1, 1861, the liberal forces marched into Mexico City.

FRENCH INVASION

The victory was short-lived. The new government was bankrupt, and Juárez had to suspend payment of Mexico's foreign debt. Spain, Britain, and France protested, and sent a joint force to Veracruz to secure their money.

The French Emperor Napoleon III, however, had greater ambitions. Encouraged by Mexican conservatives, who refused to accept defeat,

Emperor Maximilian of Mexico.

he ordered his troops to advance on Mexico City. After a brief though famous Mexican victory under Ignacio Zaragoza at Puebla on May 5, 1862 (the *Cinco de Mayo*, now a holiday), the French took over most of the country. Napoleon invited Maximilian of Habsburg, an Austrian archduke, to become emperor of Mexico under French protection.

Emperor Maximilian and his Belgian Empress María Carlota moved into Chapultepec Castle (see page 143), but their reign was brief. Ironically, Maximilian was too liberal for Mexican conservatives; a romantic idealist, he unsuccessfully invited Juárez to become his prime minister. Then, after the American Civil War ended in 1865, the US government put pressure on Napoleon to withdraw his troops. Without the French to support him, Maximilian was captured in Querétaro. The 35-year-old prince was shot at dawn on June 19, 1867.

The Republic was restored, and Juárez set about putting *La Reforma* into practice. He died in office in 1872, of a heart attack. However, all the struggles of the previous years had not ensured stability, and in 1876 there was yet another military takeover, led by General Porfirio Díaz.

President Porfirio Díaz visits the newly built railroads.

> The great dictator Porfirio Díaz is appreciated for his most famous remark: "Poor Mexico!... So far from God, and so close to the United States."

PORFIRIATO AND ECONOMIC GROWTH

Díaz, also a son of Oaxaca, had been a hero of the fight against the French under Juárez. He was to dominate Mexico's political scene for 34 years, an era known as the *Porfiriato*.

Unlike previous military strongmen, he always claimed to be defending the Constitution. He stressed the need for effective government and the pacification of the country.

Political liberty would come later, he promised; what Mexico needed first was strict administration and very little politicking. He used the army and the *rurales,* his much-feared rural police force, to enforce his program. Díaz acted as the great ringmaster of Mexican politics. He knew exactly how to handle truculent local bosses, doling out favors. Conservative former followers of Maximilian were enticed on board, and a rapprochement shrewdly sought with the Church. Open opposition was ruthlessly snuffed out.

Having established order, General Díaz set about modernizing the country. Business-minded ministers, known as *científicos* (scientists), mapped out plans to bring Mexico into the industrial age. Foreign investment was welcomed and capital poured in. An impressive 19,000km (12,000-mile) railroad network was laid, creating a whole new set of economic possibilities. Steel mills in Monterrey processed iron ore railed in from Durango, and cotton from the north was processed in central Mexico. Railroads also allowed the expansion of mining, not only of gold and silver but also coal, lead, antimony, and copper.

Landowners could send cattle and cash crops such as wheat, sugar, and coffee to the cities and for export. In the Yucatán sisal rope, made from the *henequén* cactus – "green gold" – and in huge demand before the invention of artificial fibers, created vast fortunes, and *henequén* haciendas extended across the countryside.

The Díaz regime won great international praise for the order and progress it had brought to Mexico. Díaz favored European investors for some sectors – notably railroads – in order to reduce Mexican dependence on the United States. Nevertheless, American companies still made huge investments – and huge profits – in Mexico. By 1910, foreigners controlled three-quarters of the nation's mineral and oil rights.

The *Porfiriato* boom transformed many Mexican cities, where grandiose French- or Italian-influenced architecture was favored by the Europeanized elite. In Mexico City, buildings such as the Palacio de Bellas Artes and the Palacio Postal post office all date from this period. Mérida, home of the Yucatán *henequeneros*, acquired a "Parisian-style" boulevard, the Paseo de Montejo.

At the same time, millions were barely managing to survive. As export agriculture boomed, production of food staples actually fell and prices rose. Rural villages were particularly affected by the break up of communal lands – originated by Juárez's reform – which gave ample scope for big landowners to seize village lands. The ignorant mestizo and indigenous poor, it was said, could not be allowed to stand in the way of progress. Most

escaped, and an armed rebellion began on November 20, 1910.

The Mexican Revolution of 1910 – the one always written with a capital R – was no straightforward, united fight for freedom and democracy against the oppressive regime of the *Porfiriato*. It was an explosion of rage that led to a decade of violence and starvation. People went hungry, were tortured and shot, and more than a million died.

Groups across Mexico rose up in support of Madero, and Porfirio Díaz was finally ousted in

Madero enters Cuernavaca in 1911.

productive land thus wound up in the hands of some 6,000 *hacendados*, whose holdings ranged from 1,000 hectares (2,500 acres) to areas the size of a small country.

REVOLUTION

Elections under Porfirio Díaz were carefully managed. Then, in an interview with a US journalist in 1908, Díaz said Mexico was ready for democracy, and that he would welcome real opposition. People took him at his word. For the 1910 elections, opposition coalesced around a wealthy liberal, Francisco Madero. Díaz, aged 80, had him arrested and declared himself the winner for a seventh presidential term. But things did not end there. Madero

May 1911. Madero, however, declared he would only take up the presidency after fresh, clean elections in November. A cultivated, philanthropic hacienda owner from Coahuila, he was a democratic reformer who wanted an end to social injustice, but always insisted on carefully following established legal processes. He lacked any sense of urgency, and so did nothing to challenge the power of Díaz appointees in the army and the states. He even allowed a former Díaz supporter, Francisco León de la Barra, to become interim president while he waited for the November election.

TIERRA Y LIBERTAD

This could not satisfy the passions unleashed by the revolt against Díaz. Many of the movements that had won the first revolution for Madero expected determined, radical change, foremost among them the peasants in Morelos and the south led by Emiliano Zapata. Instead, under De la Barra, troops were sent to Morelos to return land taken by the Zapatistas back to the haciendas.

Zapata lost patience with Madero, and in November 1911 the Zapatistas proclaimed their radical program the *Plan de Ayala* and took up arms against the new government around the slogan *Tierra y Libertad* (Land and Freedom). To this day Zapata is to most Mexicans the Revolution's greatest hero, and has never lost the power to inspire, as seen in the Zapatistas of Chiapas.

Other revolts burst out around the country. Madero relied increasingly on the army to keep order, but its generals regarded him with contempt. Foreign investors called for a restoration of order. At the end of 1912, the old dictator's nephew Félix Díaz and US ambassador Henry Lane Wilson conspired with the army commander Victoriano Huerta for the latter to lead

Pancho Villa sits in the presidential chair with Emiliano Zapata to his right.

⊘ NATIONAL HEROS: ZAPATA AND VILLA

Emiliano Zapata and Francisco (Pancho) Villa are worldwide symbols of the Mexican Revolution. Zapata, a mostly indigenous peasant from Anenecuilco in Morelos, was chosen in 1909 to speak for the village in a dispute with a *hacendado* who was seizing its land to extend his sugar estates. Zapata's creed, to which he stayed forever loyal, was simple: that villages should have their lands restored and guaranteed to them in perpetuity. Peasants throughout southern Mexico could relate to him: he was taciturn, and in meetings with politicians often let others talk for him; he felt uncomfortable outside his own patch. He also had, like Juárez, an image of unflinching, unbreakable integrity.

Pancho Villa was never short of a word, and so could be equally typical of the north. Born in Durango and orphaned when very young, he survived at different times as a miner, a bandit, and a horse thief. In 1910 he joined a revolutionary band in Chihuahua and gained a reputation with a string of exploits that have entered Mexican folklore.

His clashes with more conventional leaders such as Carranza – who despised him as a dangerous idiot – were part political, part very personal. His radicalism was instinctive, not systematic: in Chihuahua, he raised wages, lowered prices, and built schools. Pancho Villa also married more than 70 women, and divorced none of them.

a counter-revolution. In the "10 tragic days" in February 1913, Madero was tricked by Huerta, arrested, and murdered.

SHIFTING ALLIANCES

Huerta assumed he could walk into the presidency, but the sheer brutality of Madero's elimination galvanized resistance. The Zapatistas fought back with renewed determination in the south, while a powerful movement formed in the north around the governor of Coahuila, Venustiano Carranza, in loose alliance with Pancho Villa and his ragged "Division of the North." After savage fighting, Huerta was driven from Mexico City in mid-1914.

The victorious revolutionaries, however, were in no agreement on what should happen next. For all its apparent shapelessness, fought by different groups who often had little contact with each other, the Mexican Revolution is said to have been driven by four common impulses. It was expected to: bring Mexico democracy; establish national independence, and an end to the subservience to foreign interests of the Díaz era; modernize, in a way that benefited the whole country; and instigate agrarian reform, with justice for the rural poor. The importance given to these goals, though, varied a great deal. For the northern "Constitutionalists" around Carranza, an effective, inclusive government was their first priority.

A convention held in Aguascalientes failed to reach any consensus. Fighting soon broke out between supporters of Villa and Zapata, who called for rapid change, and those of Carranza. At the end of 1914 Villa and Zapata occupied Mexico City, and Zapata's peasant soldiers were famously photographed in Sanborn's restaurant. However, they failed to capitalize on their success.

The Constitutionalists gained ground, led by the Revolution's most able general, Alvaro Obregón, another northerner, from Sonora. At Celaya in April 1915 he destroyed Villa's forces by using barbed wire, machine guns, and other techniques of modern warfare. Villa retreated northward. Enraged by US support for Carranza, he raided Columbus, New Mexico, in 1916, which led the US Army to follow

him in futile pursuit for 11 months. Zapata meanwhile retreated to Morelos, as he had always tended to do.

A NEW CONSTITUTION

In 1917 Venustiano Carranza convened an assembly in Querétaro to agree a new Constitution. He wanted only a few amendments to the Constitution of 1857, but it was part of the Mexican Revolution's peculiar, diffuse nature that, since victory was never entirely clear-cut, no one leader could ever impose

The governor of Coahuila, Venustiano Carranza.

a single vision on it, and progress could only be made by giving out concessions to other sectors. To Carranza's disgust, the delegates agreed many radical propositions, guaranteeing the right to strike and form unions, and an eight-hour working day. Even though Zapata was still fighting Carranza, to win the support of the rural poor some of the Zapatistas' central demands were included in the famous Article 27. For a century, agrarian changes in Mexico had focused on creating large estates or dividing land into small, individual farms. Article 27 not only made it mandatory for great haciendas to be broken up, it allowed villages to work their lands individually or collectively, in line with indigenous tradition. How this could be put into practice would be a new source of argument, but the 1917 Constitution had enshrined a whole range of social aspirations in law.

Within this colossal drama every state in Mexico had its own stories. And the Revolution continued to devour its own. In April 1919 one of Carranza's generals tricked Zapata into a meeting, and had him shot. A rift developed between Carranza and Obregón, and in 1920, when Carranza seemed set on extending his power beyond his presidential term, Obregón

General Obregón and his wife.

led a revolt. Carranza was killed while escaping, by an ex-Villista band. Villa himself ostensibly made peace with Obregón and retired to his hacienda, but was ambushed and assassinated in his car one afternoon in 1923.

RECONSTRUCTION

In an exhausted country, Obregón began the "consolidation" of the Revolution. Like his closest associate and fellow Sonoran Plutarco Elías Calles, he believed in "national capitalism," not socialism. However, he was far more aware than Carranza of the need to answer the urgent needs of Mexico's poor. During the Revolution he had already forged contacts with labor unions in the cities, and as

president he introduced pro-labor measures and encouraged the growth of friendly unions as a power base. Land reform was begun in states where it was supported by strong local movements, like Morelos and Yucatán.

The 1920s also saw the flowering of one of the most profound changes brought by the Revolution – its cultural transformation. In sharp reaction against the contempt poured on everything uniquely Mexican under Díaz, artists such as Rivera, Siqueiros and Orozco used pre-Hispanic motifs and images from folk art to create a dynamic style that ignored European models. Their foremost expression was in the world-famous murals on public buildings, many commissioned by Obregón's education minister José Vasconcelos, who had schools built across the country.

The revolutionary government also became mired in a fierce battle with the Catholic Church. It had regained strength during the *Porfiriato,* and many Revolutionary leaders saw it as a permanent threat to Mexico's progress. Conflict intensified after 1924 under Obregón's successor, Plutarco Elías Calles, for whom anti-clericalism was a virtual obsession. Anti-Catholic laws were rigidly enforced, and Catholic guerrillas, known as *Cristeros,* with the war cry ¡*Viva Cristo Rey!* (Long Live Christ the King) clashed with *federales* in Jalisco, Michoacán, Guanajuato, and Colima. Tensions only abated after Calles lost his hold on power.

In 1928 Obregón planned a return to the presidency with Calles, causing deep disquiet among old revolutionaries who feared a repeat of Díaz's multiple terms in office. Obregón won the election, but was shot dead a few weeks later, not by one of his former comrades but by a young Catholic.

THE OFFICIAL PARTY

With Obregón dead, the three presidents who followed were all puppets of Calles. The Revolution's greatest power broker, he had already decided to give it some institutional continuity. So far, the Revolution had been dominated by particular leaders, their clashes and alliances. Most political parties were based on individual states. In 1929 Calles invited all the many parties, groups, and local leaders around the country identified with the Revolution to join together in a single party, the Partido Nacional Revolucionario or PNR. It would also include all the pro-government labor and peasants' unions.

If the PNR was sufficiently inclusive, Calles reasoned, its success would be assured without too much electoral manipulation. The presidential succession could be argued out within the party, rather than with street fights. For still more stability, presidential terms would be extended to a *sexenio*, six years. The "offi-

his presidential term, Cárdenas had distributed land to almost one-third of the population.

Cárdenas equally encouraged labor unions, giving them a permanent place in government.

> Before the Revolution Mexico had shunned its indigenous and folk heritage: in the 1920s and 1930s artists and writers reveled in them to create an entirely new set of national symbols.

President Lázaro Cárdenas at the National Congress of Mexican Workers, 1938.

cial party" thus created would remain in power under different names for 71 years.

CÁRDENAS

The PNR candidate for president in 1934, Lázaro Cárdenas, had also been a Calles protégé, but once in office he broke with his old boss to become the most revered – indeed loved – Mexican president since Juárez. No one else did as much to put the social aspirations of the Revolution into practice.

Above all, Cárdenas took land reform seriously. More than 18 million hectares (45 million acres) of land was redistributed to the communally-owned villages or *ejidos*, against less than one million under Obregón. By the end of

In so doing he also used them to reinforce the all-encompassing bureaucratic structures of the national party, subsequently renamed the PRM (Partido de la Revolución Mexicana) and later Partido de la Revolución Institucional (Party of the Institutional Revolution, or PRI).

Nevertheless, Cárdenas's presidency is often remembered as a golden, hopeful age, and his status as a national hero was cemented forever in March 1938 when he nationalized Mexico's oil, until then controlled by US and British companies. Mexicans cheered; the British were incensed, but in the troubled international climate of the 1930s neither Britain nor the US could afford a major confrontation in Latin America, and both, eventually, had to accept the decision.

Mexican President Andrés Manuel López Obrador (AMLO) at his inauguration in 2018.

MODERN MEXICO

Mexicans have few illusions about politicians, but in 70 years the country has left behind one-party rule to become an imperfect and argumentative democracy.

Between World War II and the early 21st century Mexico's population jumped from 20 million to 110 million. Few countries in the world underwent greater transformations in those years. Mexico has been through several economic booms, and become part of the modern world. But it still faces some of its old problems, as well as entirely new ones.

> As the era of revolutionary jefes (chiefs, or leaders) on horseback faded into memory it was replaced by another era of ribbon-cutting ceremonies, speeches, and official cars.

THE REIGN OF THE PRI

For most of those years Mexico was governed uninterruptedly by the Partido de la Revolución Institucional, or PRI. The party structures created by Calles and Cárdenas grew into a vast, intricate bureaucracy, extending into every part of the country. The tangled web of affiliated labor unions such as the Confederación de Trabajadores Mexicanos (CTM, Confederation of Mexican Workers) or the Confederación Nacional Campesina (CNC, National Confederation of Farm Workers) played an essential role in ensuring support. Millions of Mexicans knew they could only get a job through membership of the union, and in return were expected to show loyalty at election time.

Unions and other PRI organizations were run in a rigidly top-down manner. As a reaction against dictators like Díaz or Santa Anna, it was a principle of the Revolution that elected officials, from town mayors to the president, could only serve one six-year term. This, however,

Violent outbreaks between rival revolutionary and independent party supporters during elections.

only replaced personal rule with the collective domination of the party bureaucracy. Officeholders customarily played a part in nominating their successor, and the result was a pervasive atmosphere of cronyism and corruption.

The party that exercised such power was, however, flexible, its positions as diffuse and hard to define as the Revolution it "expressed." In the tradition of the Revolution, its habit was not to resolve – or override – contradictions but find a compromise, however odd the result. The PRI could display a style close to Soviet Communism in its labor unions, but at the same time gave all kinds of support – including keeping down wages – to "national capitalism," enabling friends of the regime to amass giant fortunes. Nationalist rhetoric provided a cover-all for many policies, and after a brief closeness during World War II, later PRI governments were often pointedly suspicious of the US.

The PRI's main purpose became keeping itself in power. For many years the party held every major elected office in Mexico.

BETTER DAYS

For years the regime also seemed remarkably successful. Of the four "goals" of the Mexican

Weighing produce at a coffee cooperative.

⊘ THE PERFECT DICTATORSHIP

Peruvian novelist Mario Vargas Llosa described the rule of the PRI as "the perfect dictatorship," because no one could ever quite say it was one. The party presented itself as Mexico's only viable option for government, and expected only minor opposition from its right and left. Dissent was not always silenced, and intellectual and cultural life was allowed a good deal of latitude. If open opposition arose, a common response was "co-option," calling in a movement's leaders and offering them a job in party organizations. If resistance continued, most elections could be controlled, and the PRI did not flinch from using outright repression as a final option.

Revolution – democracy, national independence, modernization, and land reform – nationalism and modernity were pre-eminent after 1940. Mexico benefited a great deal economically from World War II, joining the war on the Allied side in 1942 and supplying goods to the United States, and on this basis President Miguel Alemán (in office 1946–52) set out a program for industrialization. Major infrastructure projects were undertaken by giant state-run enterprises like Pemex (the national oil company), in collaboration with home-grown private business. Nationalist tariff policies kept out US and other competition. Politicians and party officials were closely involved, handing out contracts, which gave still more room for corruption.

Implicit in Alemán's policies was the attitude that certain social consequences – uncontroled urbanization, inflation, more inequality – were acceptable so long as growth was achieved. Nevertheless, this did provide a basis for a rapid expansion of Mexican industry, which could sell into a growing market. Moreover, this was one period of expansion in Mexico that benefited large numbers of ordinary people. The middle class in the cities, especially, saw their living standards rise steadily during the 1940s and 1950s.

Agrarian reform never again received the same attention as under Lázaro Cárdenas. A "Banco Ejidal" and other organizations had been created to help *ejido* communal villages farm more effectively, but like so many PRI institutions these developed into a top-heavy, increasingly corrupt bureaucracy. The complaint was often made that *ejidatarios* (members of *ejidos*) had gone from being peons on haciendas to peons of the Banco Ejidal. At the same time, government policy shifted to encouraging more productive private agriculture, in the interests of rapid development. This made it still harder for *ejidos* to compete. Instead of a means for taking them out of poverty, the *ejido* came to be seen by Mexican country people only as a last defense against complete exposure to the market. Attitudes to the rural poor became one of post-Revolutionary Mexico's many paradoxes: despite the prime position of peasant revolt in revolutionary mythology – and the hundreds of villages called "Reforma Agraria" or "Tierra y Libertad" – in practice officials often showed little interest in rural poverty, and treated it as something no one could expect to do much about.

THE SYSTEM IN DECAY

The PRI machine began to falter in the 1960s. The economy stagnated, running into the buffers of population growth and its own inflexibility. The growth of Mexico's cities – formerly seen as a symbol of progress – began to spiral out of control, above all in Mexico City itself, as millions of people flooded into the capital from the countryside, seeking jobs and needing services – light, water, transportation – that the system was scarcely able to provide, and creating a string of huge new environmental problems. Tensions

The oil boom came to an equally sudden end in 1982, with a collapse of the peso. Opposition grew, and the PRI began to lose state gover-

> *The privatization of banks and other major economic sectors since the 1990s has encouraged the entrenchment of a super-rich elite, such as Mexico's pre-eminent billionaire, Carlos Slim, the world's richest man.*

Casting a ballot in the 2000 presidential election.

became more evident in the countryside, and student demonstrations before Mexico City's Olympic Games in 1968 were brutally suppressed by government forces, with the Tlatelolco massacre of October 2 claiming the lives of hundreds.

Respite came thanks to the global oil price hike in the 1970s, which brought another spectacular boom. Tourist income began to flow too, especially into the Yucatán Peninsula after the creation of Cancún. This, however, conformed to a common pattern for Mexican booms: it was possible for Mexico to have the highest growth rates in the world for a few years, for many people to feel better and for some to get extremely rich, while chronic poverty was untouched or even got worse.

norships, especially to the Partido de Acción Nacional (PAN), a conservative, free-market party. The PRI's maneuvers to hold back opposition became more blatant. The PRI candidate for president in 1988, Carlos Salinas de Gortari, was only able to win through crude election-rigging against the leftist Cuauhtémoc Cárdenas, son of the revered 1930s president.

Salinas agreed with international observers who saw Mexico's neo-Soviet system of state enterprises as a block to growth. He set out to open Mexico up to the world – and especially the US – economy, with privatizations of banks, telephones, and other sectors, and a new welcome to foreign investment. Another supercharged boom began. Food prices rose; the flow of the poor into the mushrooming megalopolis of Mexico City and toward the United States accelerated, but this was not given too much attention when other economic indicators seemed so positive.

The culmination of Salinas's program was to be the introduction of the NAFTA agreement on January 1, 1994, which required the amendment of the iconic Article 27 of the Constitution, to make it easier to break up *ejidos*. Then, on the same day, the Zapatista rebels emerged from the forests of Chiapas, making it evident the Salinas boom had only covered over the fissures created by chronic pov-

Displaced children at a refuge in Guerrero State.

erty. Their masked spokesman, Subcomandante Marcos, won huge sympathy throughout Mexico by describing the Salinas regime as a sham. Foreign investors fled again, precipitating a massive downturn. No longer a guarantee of stability, the PRI was falling apart. For six years it stumbled on, as corruption scandals emerged so jaw-dropping that even world-weary Mexicans could be shocked.

A NEW ERA

Faced with a barrage of opposition, the PRI had to allow cleaner elections. In 1997 it lost its majority in the Federal Congress, and the mayoralty of Mexico City was won by the left-wing Partido de la Revolución Democrática (PRD), founded by Cuauhtémoc Cárdenas. Then, in 2000 the presidency was won by Vicente Fox of the PAN. Mexico, it was widely said, could at last be called a true democracy.

After 71 years of one-party rule, Mexicans got used to their new democracy remarkably quickly, but without many romantic illusions. Issues the old system kept hidden are now widely aired. There is vigorous political debate – many Mexicans would say too much – about politicians' catfights or ingratiating foreign powers rather than tackling real issues within Mexico. The system of power is more fluid but still very opaque, and so there exist the usual cracks for corruption to seep in. While some commentators suggested Mexico had exchanged a system of domination by a single elite for one of rotation between three, of the PAN, PRI, and PRD, this triad was broken up further by the rise of one of the country's newest parties, the Movimiento de Regeneración Nacional (MORENA), formed by former PRD leader Andrés Manuel López Obrador (AMLO) in 2014.

Federal, state, and local authorities have taken more steps to deal with Mexico's long-accumulating environmental problems, especially in the capital, but a great deal remains to be done. Hopes of radical change have largely gone unsatisfied.

Mexico is now fully a part of the global economy – the eleventh-largest in the world – and especially interlinked with the US. Pemex was – until 2015 – virtually the only survivor of Mexico's once-vast nationalized industries, its privatization resisted by many Mexicans who saw oil ownership as essential for national sovereignty. However, reform had been mooted for some time, and a new bill was passed under President Peña Nieto in 2015, which finally opened the sector up to foreign investment, at a time when oil prices were slumping. Tourism is now a major source of income. Meanwhile, collusion between vested interests and politicians remains a fact of economic life, contributing to the economy's inflexibility and extremes of wealth.

In 2017, Andrés Manuel López Obrador (AMLO) stepped down from his MORENA party to head up a coalition of MORENA and a number of other left-leaning political movements, including the Labor Party, called Juntos Haremos Historia (Together We Will Make History). He swept to a convincing victory in the 2018 presidential elections in July, with 53 percent of the vote, winning 31 of the country's 32 states. PRI was condemned to its worst ever defeat, with only 16 percent of the vote.

Mexico is now facing two major tests, both linked to its complex relationship with the United States.

Two major tests for Mexico tend to dominate headlines. One has been around forever: the need to provide decent living standards for most Mexicans. The other is the battle with the drug cartels. Both reflect the way Mexico is now intertwined with the US.

For years Mexico sought to keep US domination at bay by building a self-sufficient economy behind tariff walls. Since this model stagnated, politicians took a bet on embracing the bear next door as the easiest means to economic progress. Millions of ordinary Mexicans, of course, have done so by migrating northward. Since the 1994 NAFTA agreement, assembly plants for export goods oriented to the US market have proliferated across Mexico. This has left it acutely vulnerable to fluctuations in the US – as the 2008 recession bit, Mexico's exports fell by 32 percent, instigating further emigration to the US.

On November 30, 2018, on his last day in office, President Peña Nieto consigned NAFTA to the history books, signing its successor, the United States-Mexico-Canada Agreement (USMCA). What this means for ordinary Mexicans remains to be seen.

THE DRUGS WAR

The other key issue is created by the vast US demand for narcotics, pumping more resources into Mexican criminal gangs, the "cartels," than whole state budgets.

Determined to demonstrate his authority after his contested election, President Felipe Calderón attacked the cartels right after his 2006 inauguration, using the army in place of local police forces. He was criticized for doing so without sufficient preparation, and without full awareness of the consequences. The cartels made it clear that if the government wanted a fight, it would have one. The number of drug war-related deaths rose from around 3,000 in 2007 to almost 12,000 in 2009.

Calderón's successor, Enrique Peña Nieto, captured two high-profile drug lords in the summer of 2013, but the overall policy on dealing with the cartels did not change noticeably. Violence levels initially dropped lower than in 2011 – the war's most brutal year under Calerón when 24,000 were killed – but that ignominious record was broken in 2017 with over 25,000 murders in Mexico linked to the drug war alone.

Mass graves are regularly uncovered, law officials and politicians have been assassinated, soldiers and police officers not already bought off are brazenly threatened, and *narcos* (traffickers) have fought savage turf wars. Aside from the demand for drugs, the US is also involved as a weapons supplier. In 2013, there were nearly 7,000 firearms dealers along the US–Mexico border, compared to one in the entirety of Mexico.

While there have been important successes – vast amounts of drugs impounded, weapons seized, drug

The Mexican Army incinerates a drug seizure.

lords locked up – the Mexican government has opened up far too many doors for the institutionalization of corruption. Andrés Manuel López Obrador (AMLO) was unequivocal about his desire to seek a solution to end the drugs war during his campaign trail, pushing the war into a new phase.

Yet however much chaos there is in border towns like Ciudad Juárez, they are a small part of a huge country. It is important to keep in mind that very few tourists are ever caught up in drug-related violence and in most of Mexico the drugs war is a news story, not part of everyday life.

Desert in Baja California.

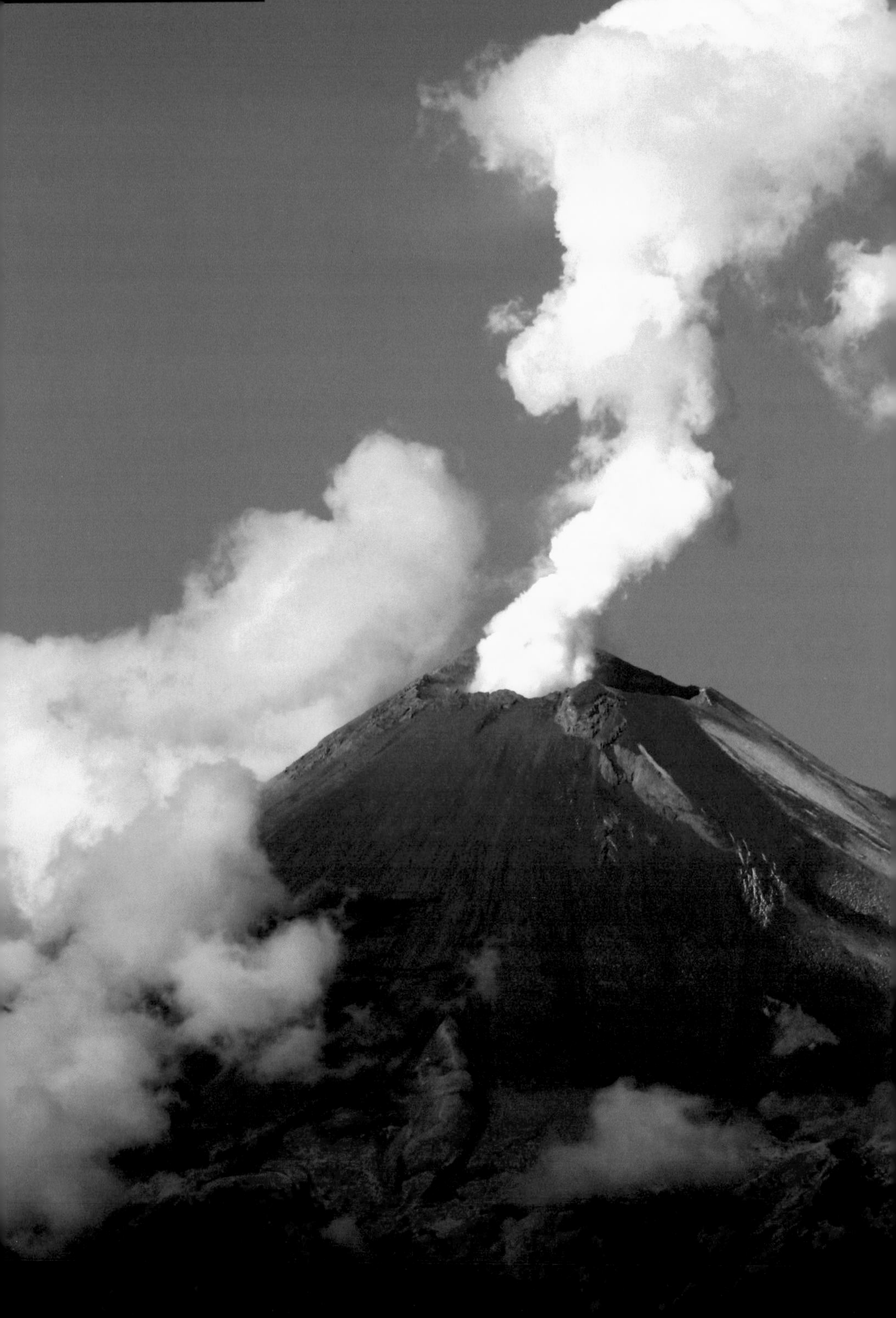

Popocatépetl volcano, the "Smoking Mountain."

SMOKING MOUNTAINS AND FLOWERING DESERTS

A land of extremes, from deserts to rainforests, from soaring volcanoes to vast underwater caverns, Mexico is both barren and lush, rugged and pastoral.

There are many Mexicos, it has often been said. Dramatic physical features make for striking divisions between different parts of the country. Two great mountain ranges, the Sierra Madre Occidental and Sierra Madre Oriental, run down from the US border, flanking the Pacific and Gulf coasts. They meet in the Central Highlands, Mexico's historic heart: covering an area of about 640km (400 miles) from east to west and less than 320km (200 miles) from north to south, this region represents just one-tenth of all Mexico, but contains almost half the country's population. The Central Highlands in turn have a very marked "core," where rivers run not down to the sea but into a giant bowl in the mountains known as the Valle de México, the Valley of Mexico, with Mexico City at its center.

Across the center of the Republic, a 160km (100-mile) belt of mountains stretches between Puerto Vallarta on the Pacific coast and Veracruz on the Gulf. South of this volcanic axis, lesser mountains form the Sierra Madre del Sur, narrowing down at the Isthmus of Tehuantepec – Mexico's so-called waist, with a width of only 160km (100 miles). East of the Isthmus the mountains surge up again into the Sierra Madre de Chiapas, which continue south into Guatemala; to the north, the terrain is very different, even unique, in the Yucatán Peninsula: a vast limestone sheet covered by thin soil, ironed flat by nature.

RAINFALL AND FORESTS

Mountains and highlands characterize much of Mexico, but deserts dominate the north. The Great Arizona Desert continues south of the border through Sonora, Chihuahua, Baja California, and several other states, with vast, arid, empty landscapes where – apart from the desert

There are over 650 varieties of cactus found in Mexico.

flowers that form sudden flashes of color for a few weeks each year – crops can generally be grown only with the help of irrigation.

Nature in Mexico has always tended toward extremes. Many of the northern desert areas get as little as 10cm (4ins) of rain a year. It seems almost perverse that on the Gulf coast, too much rain – as much as 6 meters (240ins) each year – obliges farmers to hack away unwanted growth. Rainfall is also erratic in the central highlands: sometimes a trickle, sometimes a flood.

The denuding of forests by the indiscriminate cutting of timber has long been a major cause of problems, accentuating those stemming from the variability and unpredictability of rainfall. This began in colonial times, when many areas were stripped of trees for planting crops, or for large-scale mining. The silver-mining region of Zacatecas is an example of woodland that was transformed to savannah by tree-cutters.

> *In colonial times, it took more than a year to make the 2,600km (1,600-mile) round trip from Zacatecas to New Mexico and back across the Chihuahua desert.*

Rowing at dusk near El Presa dam, San Miguel de Allende.

In many regions the water table has fallen and climate change has ensued as a result. In the last 50 years, the extension of roads into once-remote rainforest areas of the south has led to large-scale deforestation there, especially in Tabasco and northern Chiapas.

RIVERS AND ROADS

Aside from a few in the south – notably the Grijalva and the Usumacinta, which flow into the Gulf in Tabasco – Mexico's rivers are mostly unnavigable, and communicating between one part of the country and another has always posed special problems. Throughout the colonial period, the road from Mexico City to Veracruz served as the umbilical cord between the New World and Spain; in the

late 16th century land links were also opened to the agriculturally rich Bajío north of Mexico City, and on to the mining district of Zacatecas. However, attempts to extend significant Spanish colonization into New Mexico failed. Neither Spain nor freshly independent Mexico had the resources to integrate effectively into their main territories all the great northern reaches that the conquistadors had claimed, and when the time came the United States was able to seize these lands without much of a struggle.

In the south, too, many regions had only fragile connections with the Valley of Mexico for decades. The Yucatán Peninsula, meanwhile, was virtually an island, with no usable land link with central Mexico through the swamps and forests of Tabasco until the 1940s. Instead, most contacts were carried on by boat, between Veracruz and Campeche or Progreso.

During the dictatorship of Porfirio Díaz (1876–1910), foreign capital poured into Mexico and helped finance the building of roads and railroads, especially between Mexico City and the north. This made it possible to exploit untapped natural resources, such as metals and oil. The governments that followed the 1910 Revolution made improving communications a priority, and in the 1940s the Mexican section of the Pan-American Highway was completed, the first road from one end of the country to the other. While Mexico's railroads have been allowed to fall into decay, road-building has gone on ever since, creating some of the world's most spectacular mountain highways.

VOLCANOES, CASCADES, AND CAVERNS

All the ancient cultures of Mexico saw the land around them as alive with spiritual forces, which could be both friendly and hostile. It's easy to see why, for many features of the Mexican landscape are spectacular, strange, and volatile. Among the most prominent are its many volcanoes, of which the most famous are the two giants that loom up over the Valley of Mexico: Popocatépetl (5,465 meters/17,845ft high), the "Smoking Mountain" or *El Popo*, that as recently as 2016 spewed out high-reaching ash plumes; and its extinct neighbor, Iztaccíhuatl, the "Sleeping Woman" (5,230 meters/17,155ft; see page 163). Mexico's highest mountain, the Pico de Orizaba or Citlaltépetl ("Star Mountain" in Náhuatl), 5,636 meters (18,490ft) high and visible from the road between

Mexico City and Veracruz, is also a volcano, currently dormant but not extinct (its last major eruption was in 1687).

The youngest of Mexico's volcanoes, Parícutin in Michoacán, was born only in February 1943, when local farmer Dionisio Pulido saw a burst of gas and ashes emerging from a cornfield one afternoon. Awestruck, he returned with his *compadres* (friends) the next day to discover a cone already 6 meters (20ft) high. The eruption intensified soon after, hurling molten rock 100 meters (328ft) into the air and putting on a fiery display of orange lava. During its nine active years the fissure covered the village of San Juan Parangaricutiro in ash, and eventually created a cinder-cone mountain 424 meters (1,391ft) high. Since 1952, Parícutin has again been quiet.

In the far south, the massive Tacaná volcano (4,092 meters/13,425ft) that sits astride the border between Chiapas and Guatemala is also potentially still active. Its last significant belch of gas and ash occurred in 1986, but the mountain is constantly monitored.

Mexico's rivers may not be much use as means of communication, but they are often stunning natural sights. The rivers that run down the eastern Sierra Madre to the Gulf descend several thousand meters in only some 100km (62 miles), along spectacular gorges, rapids, and waterfalls, so that rivers like the Filobobos in Veracruz are ideal for rafting and other adventure sports. In the Central Highlands, such mountain rivers as the Amacuzac in Morelos are equally stunning. In the Lacandón forests of Chiapas, many rivers form "ladders" of cascades, torrents, rapids, and exquisite rock pools, often extending over several kilometers.

The Yucatán Peninsula has perhaps the most mysterious landscape of all. There are no rivers of any kind. Instead, rainwater runs straight through the soft limestone, forming a vast labyrinth of caverns and underground watercourses. Investigations by cave divers have shown that most are connected, forming the longest underground river systems in the world. Openings through the rock called *cenotes* – often large, beautiful pools, where a cave roof has fallen in – have been the main (or only) source of water for the Yucatán's people. Nutrients from these mineral-rich caves flow out to the sea, to feed the dazzling coral reefs along the Caribbean coast.

WILDLIFE

Urban areas in Mexico tend to be seriously polluted, and elsewhere deforestation, soil erosion, and the effects of uncontrolled building pose serious ecological threats. Nevertheless, there remain vast thinly inhabited areas of the country that are still isolated and inaccessible, and in which wild animals can roam in relative freedom.

Mexico is a paradise for the nature-lover. It has 2,896 species of vertebrates, including 520 mammals, 1,424 species of birds, 685 kinds of reptiles, and 267 amphibians. Some are

Beautiful cenote Samula in Dzitnup, near Valladolid in the Yucatán.

The Ox Bel Ha cave system, entered near Tulum, is the longest underwater cave system yet discovered anywhere in the world, and has been explored – so far – to a length of 172km (106 miles).

protected in national parks, and others in wildlife refuges. In all, there are more than 50 reserves of different kinds in Mexico.

Tough hikers can sight great horned sheep in San Pedro Mártir National Park in the mountainous interior of Baja California, and in the Cumbres de Monterrey National Park there are black bears.

Off the coast of the Baja Peninsula, the islands of San Benito and Guadalupe (the latter of which is a Biosphere Reserve) are a refuge for fur seals and other species, while the waters around them contain major concentrations of great white sharks. Sea lions bask on many of the small islands around Baja, some of which are also home to the endangered green turtle *(Chelonia mydas)*.

One of the country's newest national parks incorporates the Revillagigedo Islands, which were made a Unesco World Heritage Site in 2016, a unique marine reserve with four volcanic islands.

Millions of monarch butterflies migrate to Mexico in winter.

The most spectacular of the mammals are the gray and other varieties of whales, which migrate yearly from Alaska's Bering Sea to Baja California to mate and calve. For years whales were hunted to near extinction but, thanks to official protection – and despite problems caused by other commercial fisheries in the area – there has been a strong recovery in recent decades. Whales are now easy to spot in their breeding grounds around Laguna San Ignacio on the Pacific coast and in the Sea of Cortés, especially in the December–April breeding season.

From eagles and vultures to hummingbirds and pelicans, birds are never far from view in Mexico; in some parts, wild flocks of parrots are as common a sight (and sound) as the caged macaws in the patios of restaurants or hotels.

As well as having hundreds of native species, Mexico is the winter terminus for many more. Some favor the Pacific coast, and areas such as the San Juan Estuary near San Blas in Nayarit. In Yucatán, thousands of pink flamingos and other water birds flock to the mangrove wetlands around the coast, which can most easily be visited at Celestún, west of Mérida, and Río Lagartos on the north coast.

But perhaps the most spectacular sight of all is found inland, in Central Mexico. Each winter, millions of monarch butterflies transform the Michoacán landscape when they arrive at their breeding grounds high up in mountain valleys after flying thousands of miles, all the way from Canada and the United States (see page 237).

⊘ PROTECTING NATURAL MEXICO

Ecotourism has become ever more popular in Mexico, as it has across the world. Some projects are themselves destructive of the natural attractions they aim to open up – through, for example, careless waste management – but many schemes keep their impact as low as possible. Parallel to this growth has been the expansion of reserve areas, generally with one of three grades of protection: *Reservas de la Biósfera* or Biosphere Reserves, *Parques Nacionales* or National Parks, and protected areas (AFPP). As of 2013 there were 67 such areas across the nation.

In the north, Copper Canyon (Barranca del Cobre) – several times the size in both length and depth of the Grand Canyon – and nearby Cascada de Basaseáchic, with

the highest single-drop waterfall in North America, are both now national parks. In the south, Montes Azules Biosphere Reserve near the Guatemalan border is one of the last wild homes of the red macaw.

One of the most ambitious projects is the vast Sian Ka'an Biosphere Reserve, just south of the Riviera Maya. Its range of habitats includes rainforest, coastal lagoons, mangroves, and coral reefs, containing turtles, howler monkeys, crocodiles, pumas, jaguars, and hundreds of species of birds and fish. The largest of all Mexico's forest reserves, however, is the Calakmul Biosphere in southern Campeche, a giant expanse around the ruined Maya city of Calakmul.

Dazzling coral reef on the Caribbean coast.

📷 ADVENTURE TOURISM

From north to south, in mountains and deserts – even underwater – Mexico offers thrills of a lifetime.

Few countries in the world offer more for the thrill seeker than Mexico. Plop a finger on the map and you'll likely find countless opportunities to plunge, soar, zip, or even scream. Otherwise placid tourist spots such as Los Cabos in Baja will offer parasailing and ATV rides, but adrenalin junkies will find plenty to keep them occupied.

Baja's fame as a surfing hotspot began in the sixties, when those searching for endless waves (if not Endless Summer) started trekking down the 1,600km (1,000-mile) long dirt roads to find beach breaks. This mystique has remained, and Baja offers some of the most spectacular surfing anywhere. Adventure seekers will find more than just waves however: ancient pilgrimage routes, lost treasure, and breathtaking hikes through the astonishing "green desert" all beckon. Mainland destinations such as Sayulita and Puerto Escondido (famous as the "Mexican Pipeline") draw increasing numbers of surfers each year.

Mexico is as varied and spectacular under water as above it. The eerie stillness of freshwater cenotes in Yucatán, the dazzling jewels of the world's second longest barrier reef off Quintana Roo and Cozumél, and the sun-dappled azure of the Sea of Cortés all provide divers with a lifetime's worth of memories.

Jungles offer more than just mosquitoes and humidity: some of the planet's last surviving populations of jaguars still roam in the dense forests in Chiapas, Quintana Roo, and Yucatán, and fascinating birdlife teems in the estuaries in coastal flatlands and Acapulco.

Adventures lie around every corner... go out and explore!

Snorkeling at Cènote Dos Ojos (Two Eyes Cenote), Yucatan

A woman tests her skill and strength on a free climb in the rugged desert terrain near La Paz.

A hot air balloon ride offers a spectacular view of ancient sites such as Chichén Itzá.

Swim with a whale shark in Baja's La Paz Bay.

How green is ecotourism?

Adventure tourism and "eco" tourism are often bandied about and the catchphrase seems to have caught on everywhere – but just because the word has "eco" in it doesn't mean your trip won't be harming the environment. Those going on buggy or horse rides should be sure to ask whether this will be on marked trails or through privately owned lands. Search the internet to check that you're going with a well-known organization that has concern for the environment. National parks are fragile ecosystems and can be easily overwhelmed by large numbers of tourists. Help minimize your effect on the planet by being sure to place your trash in marked receptacles, or consider carrying it back to your hotel. Always make sure to close faucets and preserve water, especially in places like Baja or northern Mexico where rains are infrequent. When hiking, stay on the trails so as not to widen them. Entering the water with sunblock on is increasingly forbidden in areas with delicate marine ecosystems like coral reefs. Divers, snorkelers, and surfers should always take care to avoid direct contact with the fragile coral reefs, which take decades, if not centuries, to grow.

Rent an all-terrain vehicle and cruise across the sand.

Jet skis are available for hire at many Mexican beach resorts.

Coral colonies are beautiful but fragile, growing only a few inches each year.

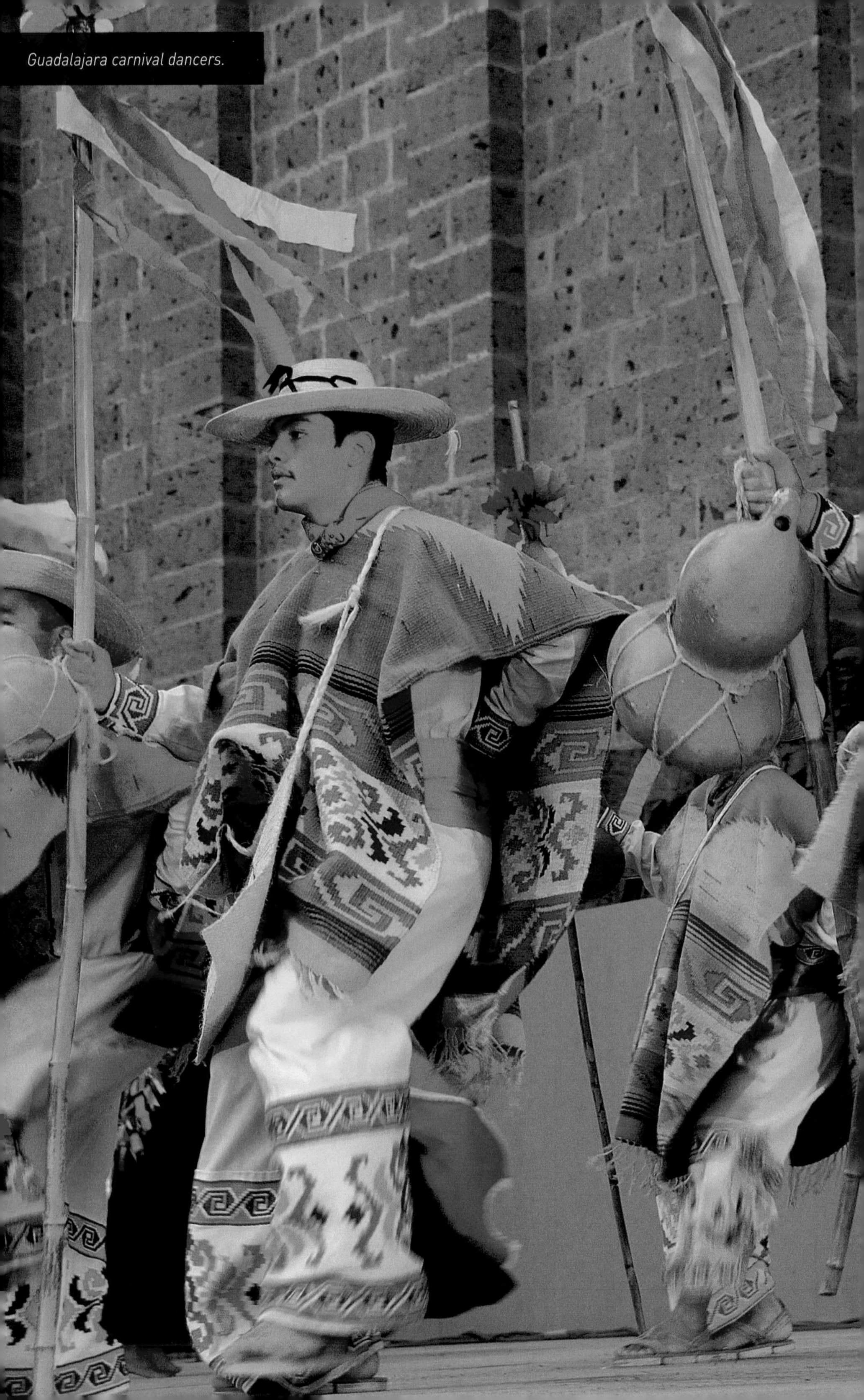

Guadalajara carnival dancers.

FIESTAS

Witness if you can the rituals, costumes, masks, fireworks, song and dance that make Mexico's fiestas an explosion of exuberance.

There is always a fiesta taking place somewhere in Mexico. Aside from the national civic celebrations, every city, town, village, or *barrio* (neighborhood) has its own fiesta, often in honor of the local patron saint. Visitors have a good chance of happening upon one of Mexico's wonderful fiestas, particularly at certain, more traditionally festive times. The calendar lists more than 5,000 every year – that is an average of nearly 14 fiestas a day.

AN EXUBERANT BLEND

Fiestas are a vital part of community life in Mexico. Many can be traced back to pagan pre-Hispanic rituals that relate to ancient customs and aspects of nature such as fertility or the harvest. Others were brought over from Europe with Christianity and have a marked Spanish flavor. But most Mexican fiestas, like the people themselves, are a combination of both.

Fiestas vary greatly from region to region and no two are ever the same, although music, dance, street parades, fireworks, and fire-crackers are almost always present. On religious occasions there are also processions, the reciting of rosaries and the chanting of *novenas* (prayers).

Mexican fireworks are quite breathtaking and unlike any display you are ever likely to witness again. As a general rule, the bigger or richer the town the more impressive the show. Specialized craftsmen are brought in for the occasion to make the *castillos* (castles) and *toritos* (little bulls). The *castillos* are enormous wicker structures, up to 20 meters (66ft) high, to which hundreds of fireworks are wired so as to create a show of spectacular effects. For the *toritos*, especially famous in Cholula, Puebla, the

Danza de los Viejitos (Dance of the Old Men), Michoacán.

wicker framework, shaped like a bull, is worn by a man who twists, turns and charges at the crowds with the fireworks exploding all around.

Fiestas take place in the center of town, around the church and main plaza. A marketplace springs up, with stalls selling crafts, trinkets, mementoes, and the hard-to-resist *antojitos*. A national favorite, *antojitos* include a whole range of Mexican food, from beautifully decorative peeled and cut fruits eaten with lime juice, salt, and chili powder, to the ubiquitous tacos, tamales, and quesadillas.

The *lotería*, a Mexican version of bingo, is usually present too, with its traditional figures of the devil, the moon, the soldier, the señorita, the drunkard, the dandy, and, of course, Death.

Also common to most parts of the country are bullfighting, horse racing (see page 242), and cockfighting. In some towns – like Huamantla in Tlaxcala or Tlacotalpán in Veracruz – they practice Pamplona-style bull-running through the streets. In Huamantla the bulls run through 12km (7 miles) of streets that, on *La Noche que Nadie Duerme* (The Night when Nobody Sleeps), have been beautifully decorated with colored sawdust and flowers for the feast of the Assumption (August 14).

> The Festival Cervantino in Guanajuato began in 1972 when a group of drama students performed works by Cervantes, the author of Don Quixote.

SONG AND DANCE

The variety of traditional music and dance performed at fiestas is enormous. Aside from the obvious Jarabe Tapatío (Mexican Hat Dance), there are dozens more. Some, like the *concheros*, have survived the Conquest; others interpret it. The masked protagonists of the *Danza de la Conquista* (Dance of the Conquest), in Jalisco and Michoacán, are Moctezuma, Cortés, and La Malinche, as well as armed Spanish soldiers and the jaguar and eagle warriors (jaguars and eagles were sacred animals to Pre-Hispanic peoples).

The best known of the many dances formerly dedicated to Huehuetéotl, the "Old God," deity of fire and time, is the extraordinary *Danza de los Viejitos* (Dance of the Old Men) in Michoacán. In Puebla, the Quetzal dancers wear huge, brilliantly colored and feathered headdresses, whilst in Sonora, the Yaqui perform the *Danza del Venado* (Stag Dance), and in Veracruz the Voladores "fly" around a 32-meter (105ft) pole (see page 263) in a hypnotic re-enactment of a Totonac ritual.

Other dances, introduced by the Spanish missionaries, pitch Moors against Christians and include such unlikely characters as Charlemagne and the Knights of the Round Table, as well as the more familiar Angel, Devil, Priest, Maiden, and Death. Newer festivals, such as the Festival Cervantino, celebrate dramatic arts from all over the world.

A Festival Cervantino street theater performance.

⦿ PIÑATAS

The most colorful stall in any Mexican market is the one selling *piñatas*, the terracotta pots decorated with papier-mâché and brightly colored shredded tissue paper. *Piñatas* shaped like a three-dimensional stars are a traditional part of Christmas festivities. They also come in the form of fruit, vegetables, animals, clowns, or even the Disney character of the month. The *piñata* is hung in the patio or street and, one by one, blindfolded children try to hit and break it with a stick. As soon as the pot breaks, candy, fruit, peanuts, and sticks of sugar cane cascade to the ground and the children dive in to grab all they can.

RELIGIOUS FIESTAS

Carnaval is celebrated the week before the beginning of Lent, in February or March. It is, traditionally, the last chance to let your hair down before the 40-day abstinence that precedes Easter. The famous carnivals of Veracruz and Mazatlán (the former claims to be the biggest outside Rio de Janeiro), as well as those of Campeche, Cozumél, Mérida, and other parts of the Republic, are celebrated with colorful parades, extravagant costumes, fireworks, day-and-night dancing, eating, and drinking. The fiesta in Veracruz starts with the ceremonial *Quema del Mal Humor* (Burning of Bad Temper), and reaches its climax several sleepless days later, on Shrove Tuesday (Mardi Gras). The next day, Ash Wednesday, sees the burial of Juan Carnaval and the symbolic beginning of a new era.

Brightly colored papier-mâché devils, or Judases, are sold on street corners the week before Easter and are traditionally burned on the Saturday. Easter in Mexico is a time for candle-lit processions and impressive passion plays

the journey of Mary and Joseph to Bethlehem and are traditionally accompanied by the breaking of the *piñata*. Christmas itself is celebrated on Noche Buena, the night of December 24, with a big dinner and Mass the next morning. Some families still put up the traditional *nacimiento* – or nativity scene – although, influenced by the US, Christmas trees are now more widespread. Customs vary in different regions of the country: in some parts the children receive gifts from the "infant Jesus," while in others it is the Three Kings who bring the gifts on January 6.

Independence Day procession, San Miguel de Allende.

that can last for days. Many people flock to Taxco each year, and millions watch the "crucifixion" at Iztapalapa in Mexico City.

The Feria de San Marcos, around April 25, is a lively affair in Aguascalientes, while Corpus Christi – when children go to church dressed as indigenous people and carrying tiny straw donkeys – is especially interesting in Papantla, Veracruz. The Day of the Dead is Mexico's answer to All Souls' Day, the ultimate combination of pre-Hispanic and Christian ritual (see page 90). Even the celebrations on December 12, when all Mexico commemorates the Virgen de Guadalupe (see page 22), has Aztec as well as Catholic origins. The *posadas*, celebrated on the nine days leading up to Christmas, commemorate

PATRIOTIC FIESTAS

Although religious celebrations are usually the most elaborate, there are lively fiestas in Mexico's political calendar too. National flags are for sale everywhere in September, *El Mes de la Patria* (Fatherland Month), which traditionally begins with the president's state of the nation address (September 1) and builds up to Independence Day celebrations on September 16.

On November 20 schoolchildren parade through the streets dressed as Zapata or Pancho Villa to celebrate the Day of the Revolution, while May 5 marks the Mexican defeat of the French army (albeit short-lived) at the Battle of Puebla.

📷 IN HONOR OF THEIR ANCESTORS

Every year on the first two days of November, the people of Mexico recall their dead relations in a meaningful but festive ceremony.

Of the many religious festivals celebrated throughout the year in Mexico, the *Día de los Muertos* (Day of the Dead) is probably the most fascinating to any outsider and the one that is truest to the country's mestizo spirit.

The original celebration can be traced to pre-Hispanic rituals dedicated to Mictlantecuhtli, the Mexican lord of the underworld, and Huitzilopochtli, the Aztec war deity to whom so many were sacrificed. After the Conquest, in an attempt to turn the fiesta into a Christian celebration, Spanish priests moved the date to coincide with that of All Souls' Day. Far from a macabre, grisly dwelling on darkness and death, Day of the Dead has become a fiesta that celebrates life as much as death, a fun-filled family affair where young and old pay colorful tribute to the spirits that surround them.

Nowadays the fiesta blends both pre-Hispanic and Christian rituals, and celebrations vary from state to state, a warm tradition that brings families together and is anything but somber. The most famous are the Purépecha traditions in Michoacán, where all-night vigils in the cemeteries and candlelit boat processions across the lake to the tiny island of Janitzio attract visitors from all over the world.

Día de los Muertos is a festive occasion for the whole community.

Day of the Dead is a deeply spiritual occasion; a time of personal contemplation, of shared memories, and for reuniting the living with their dead relations.

The bright orange cempasúchil flowers, similar to the marigold, is the "flower of death" and figures prominently during Day of the Dead rituals.

Mexicans dread death but also laugh at it. The ritual is neither morbid nor mocking, but an effort to laugh at the tragically inevitable.

Little angels returning home

It is believed that the souls of the children who have died (called *angelitos* – "little angels") return to their earthly homes on November 1, while those of the adults arrive the following day. A candle is lit for each returning soul and beautiful *ofrendas,* or shrines, are made in homes all over the country.

Photos of the loved ones are placed around the table along with a variety of their favorite foods or *antojitos,* the traditional *pan de muerto* (bread of the dead) and a glass of tequila or mug of *atole* (cornmeal drink). The shrine is decorated with ornately cut tissue paper and orange *cempasúchil* flowers. Little chocolate or sugar skulls, and other decorations are placed around the *ofrenda*, and a type of incense called *copal* is burned. Sometimes a path of orange petals is strewn from the street to the shrine to help the souls find their way home, in this intimate tribute to lost loved ones.

Graves in a cemetery in Guanajuato decorated in honor of the dead.

Lanterns painted with skeleton faces line a street in Oaxaca.

Market stalls fill up with sugar and chocolate skulls – reminiscent of the Aztec tzompantli (skulls racks). There are also lively and humorous skeletons and coffins made of clay and papier-mâché.

MÚSICA MEXICANA

Salsa is the essence, while *cumbia, quebradita, danzón,* and others are not formation showpieces, but everyday dances in bars and *barrios*.

Music is everywhere in Mexico, and just like the people, the music is a rich, varied mix of influences, cultures, and languages. Wherever you happen to be, whether it's in a restaurant, on the beach, on the subway, or a crowded bus in the rush hour, somebody is likely to produce a guitar and strike up a song. Tourists often balk at paying 20 or 30 pesos (or sometimes more) for a song but take a moment to look around and you'll see Mexican families paying the same: in Mexico, music matters.

But you won't hear the same rhythms from Chihuahua to Chiapas. In Mexico the music is as varied as the food, the culture, and the country itself; it is as mestizo as the Mexican people and has absorbed traditional and popular music from all over the world: Spain, Argentina, Colombia, Cuba, and Africa, as well as the more recent influence of rock music from Europe and the US.

Young mandolin player.

MÚSICA POPULAR

In the north of Mexico (and the south of the United States), hugely popular Western-style *norteña* bands pump out Tex-Mex *corridos* on guitars, accordions, contrabass, and drums. The *corrido* always tells a story and its hero is usually on the wrong side of the law; in the old days, the ballads would extol the virtues of the likes of Pancho Villa and Emiliano Zapata; these days, *narcocorridos* focus on the exploits of the drug smugglers, while others tell of illegal immigrants, the fate of the *mojado* (wetback) across the border. Banda, often a group of 10 swaggering men in cowboy hats with accordions, is a frenetic version of this same hallowed theme, but with a polka-like sound, and often with a tuba as the main keeper of the beat.

Canción ranchera is another all-time favorite; it is Mexico's version of country music, which dates back to Spanish romances or chivalric ballads. Mexican *ranchera* music is passionate by definition; the emotions are up-front and the action is melodramatic: heroes and villains, *bandidos* and *pistoleros*, politics, current affairs, and, most of all, tragic and heart-rending love.

Tropical bands play salsa music in the dance halls with a selection of percussion instruments – bongos, *tumbas, güiros*, rattle-gourds, *timbales,* and cowbells – as well as guitars, trumpets, flutes, pianos, and even *marimbas*. Salsa, or *música tropical*, generically includes a whole range of rhythms, from *mambo* and *cumbia* (as popular in Mexico as in its native Colombia) to the frenetic *merengue* and the sedately seductive *danzón*.

The *marimba* itself is most popular in the southern states of Chiapas, Oaxaca, Tabasco, and Veracruz. This large wooden xylophone-type instrument is played by up to four musicians, using rubber-tipped batons. The soloist carries the tune; the other three divide the secondary melody in counterpoint. Traditionally all players came from the same family and could play waltzes, *paso dobles, boleros,* and even excerpts from operas.

considered the most representative of Mexican music. In the region known as the Huasteca, the *son* or *huapango huasteco* is sung in falsetto while in southern Veracruz the *son jarocho* (of which La Bamba is the most famous example) includes harp, *jarana* (small guitar), and sometimes tambourine along with its guitars and violins.

Mexicans, masters of improvisation, come into their own with the *son* and, although the lyrics of many *sones* date from 16th-century Spain, many more verses concerning a particular event or person are ingeniously invented by the *son-*

The marimba is played by up to four musicians.

The nostalgic, romantic *bolero* is probably the most popular type of music in urban Mexico. Its origins go back to Andalusia, but it was enriched by the tropical beat that came over from Cuba. Agustín Lara, the most famous composer of *boleros* in the 20th century, is a household name in Mexico, and in Veracruz there is a museum dedicated to his life.

But probably the most Mexican of all is the ubiquitous *son*, which is interpreted in many regions and with a variety of instruments throughout Mexico. These blends of improvisation using local instruments or melodies rapidly developed into unique local dances that differ greatly from region to region or state to state. In Jalisco, the *son* is the music of the *mariachi* bands and is often

eros on the spur of the moment. Other rhythms may be less well known – the *jarabe* of Jalisco, the *sandunga* of Oaxaca, the *jarana* of the Yucatán, the *pirecua* of Michoacán, and many more – but are still popular in their specific regions and are accompanied, like the *son*, by dances.

NOBLE MUSICAL TRADITIONS

Musical tradition in Mexico has its roots in both pre-Hispanic and Spanish cultures. Before the arrival of the conquistadors, music was an integral part of religious rituals and was unexpectedly energetic and varied. Like the dance, it had to be performed in a plaza, on a platform, or on a pyramid. Priests, nobles, and even kings took part.

Netzahualcóyotl, king of Texcoco, was a poet and a fine singer who encouraged the composers in his court to narrate the glories of his lineage and the history of his kingdom. Many of the songs dedicated to the gods have survived. Manuscripts and codices with rhythmic annotation were set down by the Spanish friar Bernardino de Sahagún in the 16th century and are the first examples of scored music in the Americas.

The songs were generally accompanied by the *huehuetl* and the *teponaztli*, both percussion instruments, as well as by rattles, flutes, conch shells,

Dancing in the Plaza de Armas, Veracruz.

The name mariachi comes from either *mariage*, the French for wedding, or *mariagero*, the Galician for a musician who performs at a wedding. The costume is based on the charro suit, traditional cowboy attire from Jalisco state.

and grooved bones. In some villages of Hidalgo, Veracruz, and Tabasco both the *huehuetl* and the *teponaztli* are considered sacred instruments and are still used to accompany ancient rituals.

Pre-Hispanic wind instruments were sophisticated: reed and clay flutes, multiple flutes, ocarinas, whistle jugs, and conch-shell trumpets. In funerary rites, the sound of conch shells was associated with mourning.

Fray Juan de Torquemada left an excellent description of pre-Hispanic song and dance that were incorporated into religious rites. Musical instruments for ceremonial use in Mexico-Tenochtitlán were kept in a sacred place called Mixcoacalli. A large number of musicians were employed in the service of the temples; men dedicated themselves to the study of song and dance. So important was music to the indigenous peoples that a missionary claimed conversions came about more readily through music than through preaching.

COLONIAL INFLUENCES

After the Spanish Conquest, musicians who had served in Aztec temples were employed in churches. The earliest school to teach music to the indigenous people was founded just three years after the Conquest by Fray Pedro de Gante. It was not long before New Spain started making its own organs and other secular instruments. Some, such as guitars, violins, and harps, became the specialty of certain villages. The Aztecs were a musical people. One early missionary marveled "at the beginning they did not understand anything nor did the old instructor have an interpreter. In a short time they understood so well that they learned not only plain chants but also the songs of the organ and now there are many choirs and singers who are skilful in modulation and harmony, learning everything by heart."

The secular music of the Renaissance arrived aboard the galleons from Spain. Out of the Caribbean came rhythms and musical forms that mixed Latin, Mediterranean, Arab, African, and indigenous music. From all these came the exciting rhythms of the tango, the rumba, the fandango, the *chaconne*, the *saraband*, the *cumbé*, the *habanera*, the *bolero*, and the *danzón*.

During its 300 years as a colony, Mexico was treated to all kinds of music. In 1711, Mexico City played host to the first opera composed and performed in the New World, *La Parténope*, by Manuel de Zumaya. During late colonial times, the *corrido*, accompanied by guitar and harp, became the most popular musical form.

Mariachi music, often thought of as the quintessential "Mexican" music, originated in the 18th century. It is still played all over the country but is most popular in Jalisco and central Mexico. At first the players used only stringed instruments but trumpets were added later for pizazz.

During the 19th century the waltz became popular. The new music spoke of the triumph of the War of Independence. Major composers such as Juventino Rosas gave form to the Mexican version of the waltz combining originality, nostalgia, and melodic imagination.

MÚSICA MODERNA

Stars such as Luis Miguel, with his 2004 hit album "Mexico en la Piel," brought a resur-

easier to state is that no matter where you go, be it in quiet Chihuahua in the north or crazy Cancún in the south, or anywhere in between, venture into any disco and you'll see it packed with young people all enjoying the same thing at the same time: a beat and a place to see and be seen. You won't find a universal music that encompasses all of Mexico. But you will find that music here is inescapable. Don't be afraid to toss a few pesos to a passing troubadour or to kick off your sandals and put on your dancing shoes.

Brass instruments are a key component of traditional Mexican music.

gence in more traditional songs and in Mexican pride, while other Mexican musicians have dominated the pop charts and club scene. Thalía, a stunningly beautiful Mexican singer with a voice to match, has done well not only within Mexico but also in the US, crossing the musical border with English albums, tours, and a fashion clothing line. She became a US citizen in 2006. Another beauty, Belinda, has wooed listeners and viewers with success in both the film and music industry. Modern Mexican music is hard to characterize, in part because it means so many different things to so many different people, and much like the country's people, the music here reflects the unique mix of influences and cultures. What's

⊘ REGIONAL VARIATIONS

As you travel through Mexico you'll find that the differences from state to state are often stark: a mountain range will separate lush tropics from dry plains and desert and the styles of clothing, customs, and food will change. Similarly, the music you'll hear may vary substantially as you journey from place to place. *Banda* is big in Sinaloa and Zacatecas; *norteño* in Baja, Chihuahua, Nuevo Leon; *son* in Oaxaca. In Jalisco, the birthplace of *mariachi* music, being a *mariachi* is a time-honored, respected profession. Just about everything makes its way to Mexico City including Cuban-influenced *danzón* and even Argentine tango.

Preparing fresh fish on the beach, Puerto Escondido.

MEXICAN FOOD

Mexican cuisine goes far beyond chips and salsa. Rich culinary traditions make dining as much about understanding Mexican culture as about flavor or taste.

Like so many other things in Mexico, the cuisine is the result of centuries of encounters and mixings of cultures and peoples. Along with the essential staples of chilies, beans, and corn, the pre-Hispanic peoples enjoyed a varied diet that included turkey, wild pig, *itzcuintli* (a plump, hairless dog), fish, and iguana, as well as avocados, tomatoes, the green *tomatillos*, nopal cactus, tropical fruits like pineapple and papaya, vanilla, pumpkins, herbs, and cacao.

The Spanish conquistadors and settlers, wanting to maintain their own eating habits, brought to the New World their Mediterranean-style foods with chickens, pigs, and cows, cheese and wheat, olive oil and wine, citrus fruits, onions, and garlic. New methods of cooking were adopted to integrate the European and native ingredients, although, for the vast majority of Mexicans, the staples of corn, beans, and chilis have remained unchanged for centuries.

During the colonial period, rice and spices arrived on the galleons from China and the Philippines, and potatoes were brought from South America. Even the brief French occupation is responsible for the addition of several cakes and sweet dishes such as *crème caramel*. Over the centuries, the blending of all these different foods, methods, and styles of cooking has become accepted as Mexico's own cuisine, making it one of the most varied in the world.

THE SPICE OF LIFE

Eating is one of the chief pleasures in Mexico, where the cuisine is as varied as the country itself. Generally speaking, food in the south is much spicier than in the north. Some dishes, although native to certain regions, can be found all over Mexico, while others are found only locally. A trip

Colorful food stalls.

to a market is the perfect way to see or sample the huge variety of unusual fruits, vegetables, chilis, and other strange or exotic ingredients. Mexico City is the culinary melting pot, with many restaurants specializing in regional dishes. As in most big cities, the capital also has plenty of international cuisine as well as good vegetarian restaurants.

NORTH TO SOUTH

Characteristically simple, the non-spicy food of northern Mexico – usually grilled meats – is accompanied by wheat-flour rather than corn tortillas. *Cabrito* (baby goat) is the specialty in Monterrey; grilled and greasy but very tasty, it is washed down with another local favorite, cold Carta Blanca beer. But even the sparse northern cooking offers such delicacies as *caldillo*, which is as close as Mexico gets to chili con carne.

Cooking in the Central Highlands is more adventurous and includes many traditional dishes, such as *pozole*, a hearty soup made of hominy (large maize kernels) with pork or sometimes chicken. Much of the flavor of a good *pozole* lies in the extravagant garnishing of chili sauce, oregano, avocado, lettuce, onion, radish, and lime juice. Other exquisite dishes include the delicate *flor de calabaza* (squash blossom) soup, or the tacos and crêpes filled with *huitlacoche*, a blackish fungus that grows on corn and which has been savored since the days of the Aztecs. These smoky mushrooms are an acquired taste but are well worth sampling for anyone interested in true Mexican cuisine.

Chile relleno is another favorite. The large green *poblano* chili peppers are stuffed with cheese or a mixture of ground meat and spices, dipped in batter, fried, and served with a tomato sauce. Chilis in Puebla are traditionally served *en nogada* – filled with meat, covered with a white walnut sauce, and garnished with red pomegranate seeds, echoing the three colors of the Mexican flag. Though

Cooking tortillas on a hot plate.

⊘ CHILI PEPPERS

Chili peppers, far from being alike in taste or spiciness, are almost endless in variety, depending on the climate in which they are grown, the chemical composition of the soil, and the geographical characteristics of neighboring plantings. The Aztecs and the Incas domesticated chilis about 7,000 years ago, but now these picant fruits are found all over the world, and in many kinds of cuisines. Here is a list of the chilis most commonly used in Mexican cooking.

Serrano is a thin green pepper that's added to sauces, stews, and soups for a touch of piquancy.

Ancho, full-flavored but mild and sweetish, is a dried version of the Poblano, often served with a tomato sauce as *chile relleno*.

Chipotle is the same variety as a jalapeño, but is ripened, smoked, and dried.

Guajillo, the dried version of the Mirasol, adds bite and a yellow color to dishes.

Pasilla is dark brown, and an important chili used in many kinds of moles and other dishes, to which is provides a signature nuanced flavor.

Poblano is a dark green meaty chili, used in the national dish: *mole poblano*.

Pequín, known elsewhere as "cayenne," is very hot, generally exceeded only by Yucatan's Habanero, said to be the world's hottest.

traditionally from Puebla, it is a common offering throughout Mexico and is often served on Independence Day, as a way of showing Mexican pride.

Puebla is the home of the famous *mole poblano*, the curiously rich sauce that's said to have been invented by a nun during colonial times. Mole is, in fact, one of the most obvious Spanish-indigenous combinations on any menu. As many as 40 ingredients go into its preparation, including chilis, spices, tortilla, nuts, and even chocolate. The sauce, served with chicken or the native turkey and accompanied with corn tortillas and rice, is often

food from Veracruz, with its characteristic black beans and giant tropical *macho* banana (plantain), eaten fried. Veracruz also has the most delicious fruit in Mexico – huge pineapples, exquisite mangoes, and juicy oranges and other citrus fruits are sold at the roadside.

Oaxaca is renowned for its *mole negro* and banana-leaf tamales, which are bigger and more elaborate than the others. Oaxaca cheese, not unlike mozzarella, is the best kind to use in quesadillas as it melts beautifully when grilled or fried inside a tortilla.

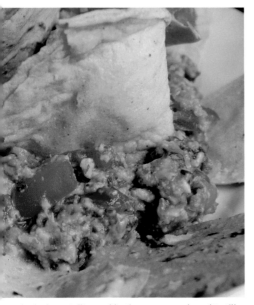

A winning antojito combination – guacamole and tortilla chips.

Shrimp fresh from the Pacific.

eaten at parties or wedding feasts. Every variation of mole can be sampled at the yearly *mole* festival held in San Pedro Atocpán (Mexico City), including the spicier and more robust Oaxaca version of the dish, and the milder and easier to digest *piplán*, as well as *mole verde* (green *mole*), which is made with pumpkin seeds.

Almost 10,000km (6,200 miles) of coastline provides Mexico with an abundance of seafood. Two of the most popular fish dishes are ceviche, (raw fish marinated in lime juice and mixed with onions, chilis, tomatoes, and cilantro) and *huachinango a la veracruzana*, a classic of red snapper with olives, capers, and tomato sauce. As well as the Spanish influence, there is a strong Cuban element in the

The inspiration of cooking in the Yucatán dates back to the pre-Hispanic Maya people. Yucatecan cuisine claims such outstanding dishes as *cochinita pibil*, a sweet and spicy pork dish slow-cooked in banana leaves, and *papadzules* (tortillas filled with egg and pumpkin seeds). Sopa de Lima, similar in many ways to Sopa Azteca of northern Mexico, is delicious – named for its use of the juice from Mexican limes. The salsas are often made with simple lime juice, tomatoes, and habanero peppers. Beer aficionados rate Yucatán's beer as the best in the country – both the light Montejo, and the dark and rich Negro León. *Queso relleno*, another Yucatecan specialty is, surprisingly, Dutch cheese stuffed with spicy minced meat. In relatively recent times Lebanese immigrants have dipped their own spoon into the mix; some of the best restaurants in Mérida offer both local and Lebanese dishes.

ANTOJITOS

Similar to the Spanish tapas, *antojitos* are the Mexican answer to fast food. These snacks or light dishes can be bought – and eaten – almost anywhere, from north to south and from the best city restaurant or most elegant hacienda to the village plaza, the market, and even on the bus or train.

A whole range of Mexican food is classed as *antojitos*, from succulent corn on the cob, to tortilla chips with guacamole, and the delicious tortas, or filled bread rolls. Tamales are also popular; these scrumptious little parcels made from corn husks (or banana leaves in Oaxaca) wrapped around a cornmeal mix are stuffed with highly seasoned meat, cheese or chili sauce, and then steamed. Tamales can also be sweet, the meat replaced with a range of fruits and nuts, including strawberries, pineapple, pecans, or raisins. But whether it is tacos, tostadas, quesadillas, or enchiladas, most *antojitos*, like Mexican food in general, rely on a tortilla base.

Food stall in Guanajuato's Market.

⊘ VERSATILE TORTILLAS

Tortillas, the thin round patties made of cornmeal or wheat flour, are Mexico's culinary soul. They're also in peril: use of corn for ethanol has caused a huge rise in the cost of cornmeal, once the cheapest and most common tortilla base. Now you will often be asked if you'd like corn or flour tortillas, or just be given whichever is less costly. Tortillas are used as a form of bread with just about everything and are the basic ingredient of many of Mexico's wonderful *antojitos* (snacks).

One of the most common manifestations, *tacos* are warm tortillas rolled around any sort of filling; *tacos al pastor* is meat rolled in a tortilla and served with coriander, onion, and pineapple. Another popular tortilla-based snack are *enchiladas*: tortillas folded around meat, cheese, or fish and covered with sauce. *Enchiladas suizas* are served with chicken, a spicy sauce, cream, and cheese. The other cheese-effused tortilla derivatives are *quesadillas* – tortillas folded (generally) around cheese and cooked on a griddle.

Tortillas also come in the guises of *tostados* (crispy fried tortillas spread with refried beans and topped with the likes of chicken, tomato, onion, avocado, chilli, or sour cream), *chilaquiles* (fried tortilla chips in a spicy red/green sauce, sometimes topped with sour cream and cheese), and the much-loved *sopa de tortilla*, a soup of fried tortilla strips.

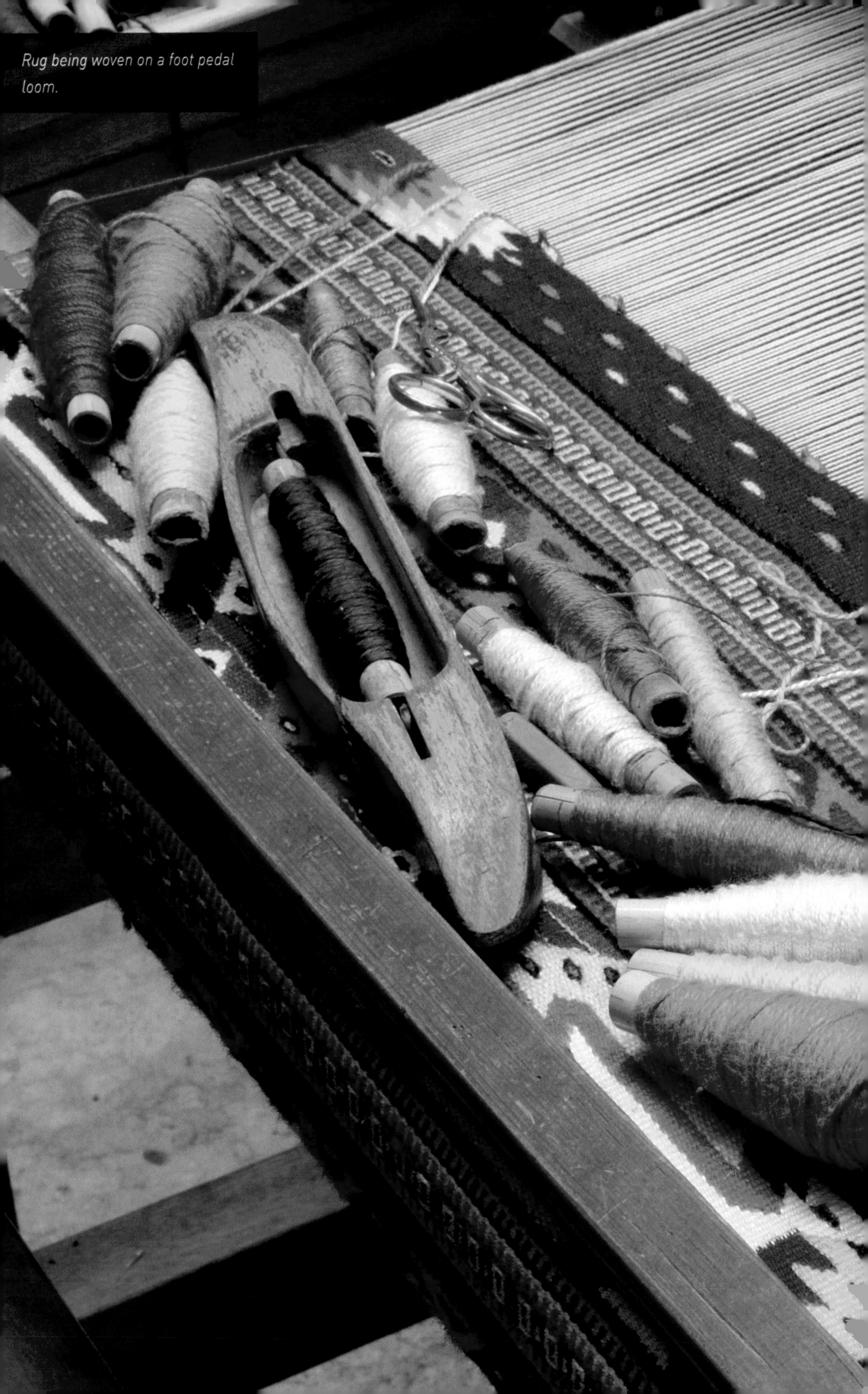

Rug being woven on a foot pedal loom.

ARTESANÍA

After sampling the endless variety of crafts in Mexico, your ideas
of beauty and color may never be the same again.

The craft tradition in Mexico dates back to long before the arrival of the Spanish, and many of the colorful and decorative *artesanías* can be traced to their pre-Hispanic origins. Often the materials and techniques have survived too, although synthetic fibers and colors have taken over much of the market and mass production is threatening some of the more laborious but infinitely more beautiful, authentic creations.

When the Spaniards came to Mexico, they found the native artisans well organized and selling their wares at great markets called tianguis. The Náhuatl word is still in use today, as are the pots, baskets, toys, clothes, sandals, hats, hammocks, and other everyday objects made by the modern craft workers of Mexico.

Among the profound changes wrought by the Spanish newcomers were the introduction of the pottery wheel and the use of metal tools. The Spaniards needed items that were too expensive to import from Spain: saddles and bridles, woolen textiles, furniture, and other household items. So, on the heels of the conquistadors came Spanish craftsmen who taught their specialties to indigenous apprentices. In 1529, a lay brother, Pedro de Gante, established an arts and crafts school in Mexico City for indigenous students, and in Michoacán Bishop Vasco de Quiroga introduced new techniques for working copper and for producing iron and lacquerware.

CHANGING FASHIONS

Initially, native craftsmen were scorned and everything Spanish was considered superior. It was not until the early 20th century, with the new spirit of nationalism that arose from the Revolution, that the pendulum began to swing the other way.

Traditional black pottery.

Artisans often learn their craft from their parents, who have learned from their parents – the skills and techniques are traditions that span generations.

In 1921, President Alvaro Obregón opened a crafts exhibition, the first such official recognition given to the native artisan. Diego Rivera, his wife Frida Kahlo, and other artists of the time praised the artisans and became collectors of their crafts. All of this hype had its effect. Indigenous handicrafts became fashionable and middle-class Mexicans started to buy them; so did visitors from the US. They still do, although the picture is not as rosy as it might seem: so many middlemen get their cut that the artisan seldom fares well.

The majority of artisans in Mexico are peasant farmers or laborers who work at their craft part-time to supplement their income, and generally make objects for everyday domestic use. Those who produce craftwork full time either have their own shops or work for someone who does. They fashion items that are both decorative and useful, but also supply the souvenir trade with

Religious folk art in a Michoacán shop.

cheap stuff that appeals to visitors. Next come those engaged in mass-production, and finally there are the unemployed city workers who live by their wits and, with great ingenuity and skill, fashion toys and trinkets out of factory offcuts and cheap materials such as paper, tin, wire, wood, and cork.

BUYING CRAFTS

Each region and, in some cases, each town or village in Mexico specializes in one or more particular craft (see page 107). Sometimes the same village has made the same item since pre-Hispanic times. In many state capitals there is a *Casa de las Artesanías* where you can admire and buy the particular crafts of the region, although prices may be higher than in the marketplace. Some major cities will have a Fonart shop, too, run by a government agency that promotes the work of artisans and preserves the quality of the crafts. These, or any of the better tourist shops, will provide a good overall view of what is available as well as an idea of the prices.

However, when possible, it is infinitely more interesting to buy the crafts from their region of origin. Markets all over the country are an important source of handicrafts. The daily or weekly *tianguis* usually have a few stalls selling craft items for everyday use such as pots and baskets, while some towns have markets devoted exclusively to the crafts of that region. Often the most exciting buys of all, though, are the crafts stumbled upon on a

Ø STATES OF THE ARTS

Crafts produced in villages around Oaxaca are both beautiful and collectable. Visiting these villages is easy using public transportation.

Arrazola specializes in *alebrijes*, brightly painted wooden animals wrought from the local copal wood.

Cuicatlan is known for embroidered cotton dresses.

San Bartolo Coyotepec produces surprisingly light and highly polished black pottery.

San Martín Tilcajete is a center for carved and brightly painted wooden animals.

Ocotlán de Morelos is home to many renowned potters. Friday is market day and occasionally it is possible to find outstanding baskets.

Santo Tomás Jalieza is the center of backstrap weavings in the form of belts, bags, place mats, and napkins, usually decorated with plant and animal designs.

Santa María Atzompa is famous for intricate pottery renditions of La Virgen de la Soledad, along with other raw clay figures. Much of the pottery is glazed with a green finish, which, owing to its lead content, is unsafe for cooking.

Teotitlán del Valle and Santa Ana del Valle are famous for blankets, rugs, *serapes*, and other woven goods. Motifs range from traditional geometric shapes to portraits of Che Guevara, copies of pre-Hispanic sculpture, or even paintings by Picasso or Miró.

street corner or at the roadside in the middle of nowhere.

REGIONAL SPECIALTIES

Although many of today's handicrafts combine pre-Hispanic, Spanish, and contemporary influences, the majority of wonderful *obras de artesanías* are in the areas with a significant indigenous population like Michoacán, Puebla, Oaxaca, Guerrero, and Chiapas.

Northern Mexico is not known for crafts, but exceptions include the ironwood animal carvings of the Seri; woolen baskets, belts, and dolls of the Tarahumaras and the *serapes* (ponchos) from Coahuila and Zacatecas.

The Cora and Huichol travel to Tepic and Guadalajara to sell their woolen belts and bags, superb beadwork, embroidered clothing, and yarn paintings. Tlaquepaque, a suburb of Guadalajara, is a center for ceramics – including fine copies of pre-Hispanic pieces – blown glass, and furniture. The nearby town of Tonalá specializes in pottery and glass and has a large street market on Thursdays and Sundays.

The best time to buy the delicate *deshilados* (drawn threadwork) and embroidery of Aguascalientes is at the Festival de San Marcos, from April to early May each year. The silk *rebozos* (shawls) of San Luis Potosí are famed for being so fine you can slip them through a wedding ring. In the area known as La Huasteca, the native people weave the traditional white *quechquémetl* (cape for women) with cross-stitch embroidery. They also make rough and inexpensive wool bags and items out of cactus fiber.

Guanajuato has sophisticated Talavera-style pottery, while San Miguel de Allende sells *serapes*, tinware, *piñatas* (a papier-mâché figure filled with sweets and toys for fiestas and children's parties) and masks. Querétaro is famous for its semi-precious stones and silver jewelry, and in Tequisquiapan, you'll find baskets, folding stools, and *serapes*. It can all be bought in the colonial town of San Juan del Río. In the valley of Mezquital (Hidalgo), the Otomí use backstrap looms to weave *rebozos* (scarves or shawls used as baby slings) and belts, while the town of Ixmiquilpan, also in Hidalgo state, is renowned for bird cages in the shape of cathedrals.

Michoacán probably has the greatest variety of crafts in all Mexico. Many of the artisans live near Lake Pátzcuaro and most of the crafts are available in Pátzcuaro town. On November 2, the Plaza Vasco de Quiroga becomes a center for craft workers. Some artisans work year-round in the nearby Casa de los Once Patios (the House of the Eleven Patios), which used to be a convent.

Some Michoacán towns specialize in particular crafts: Santa Clara del Cobre, copperware; Paracho, guitars; Tzintzuntzán, burnished

Hand-crafting a garment in Zacatecas.

⊘ FUNDACIÓN BANAMEX

The Arte Popular program, funded by the Fundación Banamex, aims to preserve and protect unique parts of Mexico's cultural heritage by identifying and supporting certain native traditions, crafts, and artwork. Masters of these arts are contacted and urged to take direct steps, such as teaching others, to ensure that the 250 or so different art forms do not die out completely. Once these masters have begun to instruct others in the particular trade, publicity and exhibitions are phased in so as to promote the craft and explain its value to the world. Tourists can play a role in this process too: that souvenir you bring home may help keep that particular tradition alive.

ceramics; Quiroga, painted wood bowls and household items; Ihuatzio, reed mats and basketry; Patambán, exquisite green-glazed pottery; and Uruapán, masks and lacquerware. In Morelia, capital of Michoacán, some of the state's best handicrafts can be bought at the Casa de las Artesanías, located in the former Convento de San Francisco.

The state of Mexico produces warm wool *serapes*, colorful baskets from Lerma, and the polychrome ceramic "trees of life" in the town of Metepec. In Ixtapán de la Sal, household

Painting ceramics.

utensils and decorative animals are carved out of orange-tree wood. Toluca, the state capital, is known for silverware, and also for chess and domino games made of leather, bone, or wood.

The town and state of Tlaxcala, where wool was first woven in New Spain, is still a center of weaving. *Serapes* are again a specialty of the house, and hand-carved, brightly painted walking sticks are also popular.

Puebla state is one of the richest in the variety and quality of its crafts. Talavera ceramics (see page 165), household crockery and faïence tiles are made in the capital, while onyx is cut in Tehuacán and Tecali. The Baroque ceramic "tree of life" decorations, often seen on travel posters, are made in the town of Acatlán, especially by Herón Martínez, and in Izúcar de Matamoros, by the Flores and Castillo families. Puebla is also famed for its thick, tree-bark *amate* paper and for its textiles and traditional clothing; embroidered *huipiles* (tunics) and the wall hangings and bead-decorated blouses of Cuetzalan and San Pablito Pahuatlán are the best examples. Reed baskets, made in Puebla, are the items most tourists buy.

To the south of Mexico City, the state of Morelos concentrates the sale of its craft production in Cuernavaca. Here, locally made, colonial-style furniture, wooden bowls, *serapes*, palm-leaf strip basketry and jewelry are for sale. The village of Hueyapan, in the municipality of Tetela del Volcán, produces wide, embroidered shawls.

The adjoining state of Guerrero specializes in pottery but also produces, in Olinalá, Mexico's most beautiful lacquerware: gourd bowls,

⊘ RELAXING IN STYLE

If you haven't yet taken the time to lounge in one of those colorful, banana-like hammocks you've seen, you're missing out on some of the most comfortable siestas around. The ones made from cotton are light, airy, and great in dry climates, but they are more expensive and less durable than the brightly colored nylon ones, though these are heavier and harder to dry if they get wet. Seda (literally "silk" but now a mix of silk and nylon fibers) are the lightest and most beautiful hammocks of all, but are unfortunately often fake, so make sure to buy only from trusted sources.

The Mexican, or Mayan, hammock has been

around since before the conquistadors arrived. If you'll be sleeping, lie crossways; if you're napping, lengthwise. A one-person hammock usually costs around US$100–150, a double is US$150–250, and a family-size (which makes for a more comfortable double) would cost in the region of US$200–300. When purchasing a hammock, examine the weaving as a true test of quality. The weave should be dense, even and with at least 10 edge strands (cheap hammocks will have only five to seven). Hammocks made in the Yucatán are particularly well regarded, especially in the region of Tixkokob, as are those produced in Campeche and Michoacán.

trays, boxes, and jaguar masks. Taxco, also in Guerrero, is famous for silverware. In the tropical southern towns Huapanec use bright, even fluorescent colors to paint stories and abstract designs on *amate bark* paper.

Over the border in Oaxaca, the Zapotec villagers make elaborate blouses with tiny flowers and miniature dolls that hold the pleats together. The blouses and wrap-around skirts of Yalalag are dyed with natural colors.

In the town of Oaxaca, artisans create exact copies of the intricately beautiful Mixtec jew-

The indigenous woven woolen clothing worn in the highlands of Chiapas is sold by the Sna Jolobil weavers' cooperative in San Cristóbal de las Casas; alternatively, there are Sunday markets in San Cristóbal and most of the surrounding hill villages. The Tzotzil village of San Juan Chamula produces much of the woolen clothing sold throughout the state, as well as guitars and harps. The town of Chiapa de Corzo is known for its lacquerware, especially the masks used in the festival of San Sebastián, while Amatenango is a center for traditional pottery, which is fired without an oven.

Tin skeleton figures for sale in a shop in Oaxaca.

elry found in the tombs of Monte Albán. The Mixtec coast of Oaxaca is known for its carrying nets, whereas Cuilapan and San Martín Tilcajete produce wooden *animalitos* (little animals) in bright colors and assorted shapes; the village of San Bartolo Coyotepec is famous for its traditional burnished black pottery, and artisans in Santa María Atzompa make ceramic animal figures and green glazed pottery; Teotitlán del Valle produces Mexico's best *serapes*, either in traditional pre-Hispanic designs or as copies of famous modern art paintings. Oaxaca's handicrafts can be found in the many shops and markets (where the prices are cheaper) and especially during the fiestas in December.

The Yucatán Peninsula produces quality mahogany and cedar furniture as well as the county's best hammocks – made either from sisal or cotton – and the best Panama-style hats come from Becal in Campeche.

CAPITAL CRAFTS

Many of Mexico's wonderful crafts can be found in the capital city, which also has plenty of its own gifted jewelers and artisans. The work of the Linares family, for example, who produce fantastical figures they call *alebrijes*, has become increasingly popular. But there are also the skilful and often ignored urban artisans who create art objects and toys from remnants, such as bottle caps and wire.

José Clemente Orozco's ceiling mural of Miguel Hidalgo at the Governor's Palace, Guadalajara.

MURALISTS

Mural painting has been Mexico's greatest contribution to contemporary art, with its origins dating back to pre-Hispanic times.

Dramatic artworks adorn the walls of public buildings all over Mexico. Murals have been painted in Mexico since pre-Hispanic times although many, such as those at Bonampak (see page 295) and Cacaxtla (see page 168), have only recently been discovered by historians and archeologists.

The explosive murals of the post-Revolution were a new departure; the works of Diego Rivera, David Alfaro Siqueiros, and José Clemente Orozco were to become the most powerful visual expression of the emerging modern Mexico, and were to astound the world.

Of the Mexican artists who influenced *Los Tres Grandes* (the three great Mexican muralists), none appears to have been more important than José Guadalupe Posada (1852–1913), whose powerful yet humorous engravings reached the very essence and vitality of Mexico's rich tradition of popular art; indeed, they represent the fullest and most penetrating view of Mexican social life in the years before the Revolution. Posada, whose skeletons were authentically Mexican (a far cry from the foreign models used by artists of his era), laid the groundwork for a whole school of artistry that was vigorous and obsessively nationalistic. The muralist movement remained close to the folk tradition – the so-called *Mexicanidad* – of Posada's wonderful, popular engravings.

THE FIRST MURALS

In 1921, members of President Alvaro Obregón's new cabinet were keen to spread awareness of Mexico's history and culture. None more so than the radical education minister José Vasconcelos, who commissioned murals for the walls of a number of centrally located public buildings.

Diego Rivera in his studio.

And so the Mexican *Muralismo* movement began and Diego Rivera (1886–1957) painted his first mural at the Escuela Nacional Preparatoria in Mexico City.

Rivera was a contradictory painter who aroused deep feelings and controversy. Though an ideologist (he was a Communist, but was expelled from the party), his work is less political than sensual in style, in the tradition of Paul Gauguin, Henri Rousseau, and even Pieter Brueghel the Elder. Rivera's formative artistic influences were by no means exclusively Mexican. In Europe, he had been in touch with avant-garde movements, and the influence of Cubism is apparent in much of his work from that period. However, as a result of the Russian Revolution, and his stated belief in "the need for a popular and socialized art," Rivera distanced himself from the Cubists and sought a more direct and functional artistic style. It is often said that the most important influence on Rivera was not

> The majority of the most famous murals can be seen in Mexico City, although Orozco's finest works were made in Guadalajara, and others in the US.

Mexico, inhabited by brown-skinned girls and dreamy children carrying huge bouquets of exotic flowers.

Rivera himself was a colorful character, a constant source of gossip, who loved to shock. One of his works, entitled *Dream of a Sunday Afternoon in Alameda Park,* originally flaunted the words *Dios no existe* (God does not exist), causing such an uproar among Catholics and Church authorities that they had to be removed from exhibition and were expunged (Museo Mural Diego Rivera –see page 140).

Muralist David Alfaro Siqueiros in front of his March of Humanity mural.

contemporary at all, but came from the frescoes and paintings of the Italian Renaissance. In fact, Uccello's *La Battaglia di San Romano* is said to have been one of the most important influences on Mexican mural painting.

Notwithstanding all these European influences, Rivera acknowledged his debt to José Guadalupe Posada by including the engraver's portrait in some of his most important murals. Rivera was deeply Mexican in his love of color and soft shapes, and in his strong identification with the Mexican native; he was also profoundly influenced by pre-Hispanic architectural form and sculpture. An excellent draftsman and watercolor artist, he created an idealized and sentimental image of a primitive

THE IDEOLOGUE

David Alfaro Siqueiros (1899–1974), like Rivera, continued his training in Europe. Unlike Rivera, he had been a combatant in the Mexican Revolution; he was a strong man of action, a political activist who volunteered for the Spanish Civil War, took part in labor struggles, was involved in a failed attempt to assassinate Leon Trotsky, and was imprisoned several times. His paintings reflect his ideological drive, his taste for bold action, even for violence. Massive and muscular, they become a kind of imprisoned sculpture.

Siqueiros experimented with a combination of painting and sculpture which he called *esculto-pintura.* A great innovator, he was constantly trying new materials and techniques.

Perhaps his best murals are in Mexico City's Chapultepec Castle (see page 143), which offer a powerful interpretation of Mexican history. At the Palacio de Bellas Artes (see page 137) are displayed the best of his easel paintings, but he is best known for the vast, three-dimensional mural in the city's Poliforum Cultural Siqueiros (see page 149).

THE SATIRIST

José Clemente Orozco (1883–1949), a tragic and passionate artist, is often considered the best of

Muralist Rufino Tamayo.

⊘ FRANCISCO TOLEDO

Francisco Toledo – probably Mexico's greatest living painter – has produced numerous important pieces during his lifetime. Born in Oaxaca where he trained as a graphic artist, Toledo was instrumental in regenerating the art scene in his home state after returning to Mexico from Paris, where he spent a formative part of his artistic career. His works are prolific and include oil paintings, charcoal drawings, and assemblages composed of seashells, textiles, crushed eggshells, and household objects. He was awarded the Mexican National Prize in 1998 and the Right Livelihood Award in 2005.

the big three. He was a political skeptic, a biting satirist, but also an idealist who was deeply disturbed by the sordidness of history. Orozco used the mural to convey his troubled feelings; his message transcends the national picture and can be understood by everyone. He has been compared to such German artists as Max Beckmann, Otto Dix, and Käthe Kollwitz. Orozco, always an outspoken man, denounced the tendency to convert the Mexican Revolution into a bloody farce that would result in new servitude for the masses.

The first important Orozco mural was painted in the early 1920s at the Escuela Nacional Preparatoria (see page 136). Stark and simple, it showed some influence from early Italian Renaissance painting. At the Escuela Preparatoria, Orozco does achieve moments of grandeur, especially in *The Trench,* a powerful image of war and human struggle. On the staircase of the same building, he painted *Cortés y la Malinche,* depicting the naked bodies of the Spanish conquistador and Malintzin, his native guide, interpreter, and mistress. The painting makes a clear statement about the relationship between Spain and Mexico, between conqueror and conquered, a theme to which Orozco returned many times.

From 1927 to 1934, Orozco lived in the US and painted murals for Pomona College, California, the New York School for Social Research, and Dartmouth College, New Hampshire. He described the cultural life of the times in his bitter autobiography, and in letters to his friend and fellow artist Jean Charlot.

Back in Mexico, at the Palacio de Bellas Artes, Orozco painted *Catharsis,* whose central figure is a colossal prostitute, the symbol of corruption. Orozco produced many paintings, drawings, and watercolors on the subject of prostitution, viewing the brothel as a place of ultimate horror.

Orozco's greatest works were produced in the late 1930s in Guadalajara – in the Palacio de Gobierno (see page 231), the University (see page 234) and on the walls and ceilings of the Hospicio Cabañas (see page 232). Here he is at the peak of his power, covering straight and curved surfaces with fiery reds and stark blacks, paying homage to Padre Hidalgo, denouncing political manipulation, and searching for deep and universal symbols.

OTHER MURALISTS

Jean Charlot (1898–1979) was born in Paris and is another of the early muralists. His *Massacre in the Main Temple,* a mural completed in 1923 on the stairway of the west court of the Escuela Nacional Preparatoria in Mexico City, is generally regarded as the first fresco painted in Mexico since colonial times. Before his move to Hawaii, Charlot painted in the US, where he helped – with his art, but most of all with his writings – to popularize mural painting during Franklin D. Roosevelt's early years as president.

realism for poetically simplified forms. His decorative murals deal with cosmic and domestic symbology (stars, cats, women) and are indifferent to the direct interpretation of history.

Zacatecas-born artist Pedro Coronel (1922–85) explored much the same ground as Tamayo. His murals are perhaps the best of those painted in recent years. Other mainstream Mexican muralists, whose work is never far removed from realism, include Fernando Leal, Xavier Guerrero, José Chávez Morado, Roberto Montenegro, Raúl Anguiano, Fernando Castro

Juan O'Gorman mural on the Biblioteca Central, Ciudad Universitaria.

Juan O'Gorman (1905–82), a painter and architect of Irish ancestry born in Mexico, transformed the mural into a kind of panorama of miniature scenes. Although they are modern, his paintings are anchored in Mexico's 19th-century popular art. He is famous chiefly for the murals decorating the Biblioteca Central (Central Library) of Mexico City's Ciudad Universitaria (see page 152). Constructed with colored stone, these giant mosaic-murals describe the culture of the world in a Baroque texture that is surprisingly innocent and fresh.

There had grown up a second generation of muralists, one of whom was Rufino Tamayo (1899–1991), a Zapotec from Oaxaca who died at the age of 92. Never political, Tamayo soon abandoned

Pacheco, Manuel Rodríguez Lozano, Alfredo Zalce, and Jorge González Camarena.

CONTEMPORARY MURALS

The Mexican muralist movement sprang out of the Revolution and, in reality, that emotion is gone and done with. In the second half of the 20th century, the new generations of muralists reacted against the movement that they accused of being too obviously didactic and obsessively nationalistic. But disciples of the great muralists continue to cover the walls of public buildings throughout the country. Visitors will be well served by meandering the grounds of Mexico City's UNAM (Universidad Nacional Autónoma de México), where many of the buildings display stunning murals for all to see.

View of Urique, Chihuahua.

Fishing boats, Playa la Entrega.

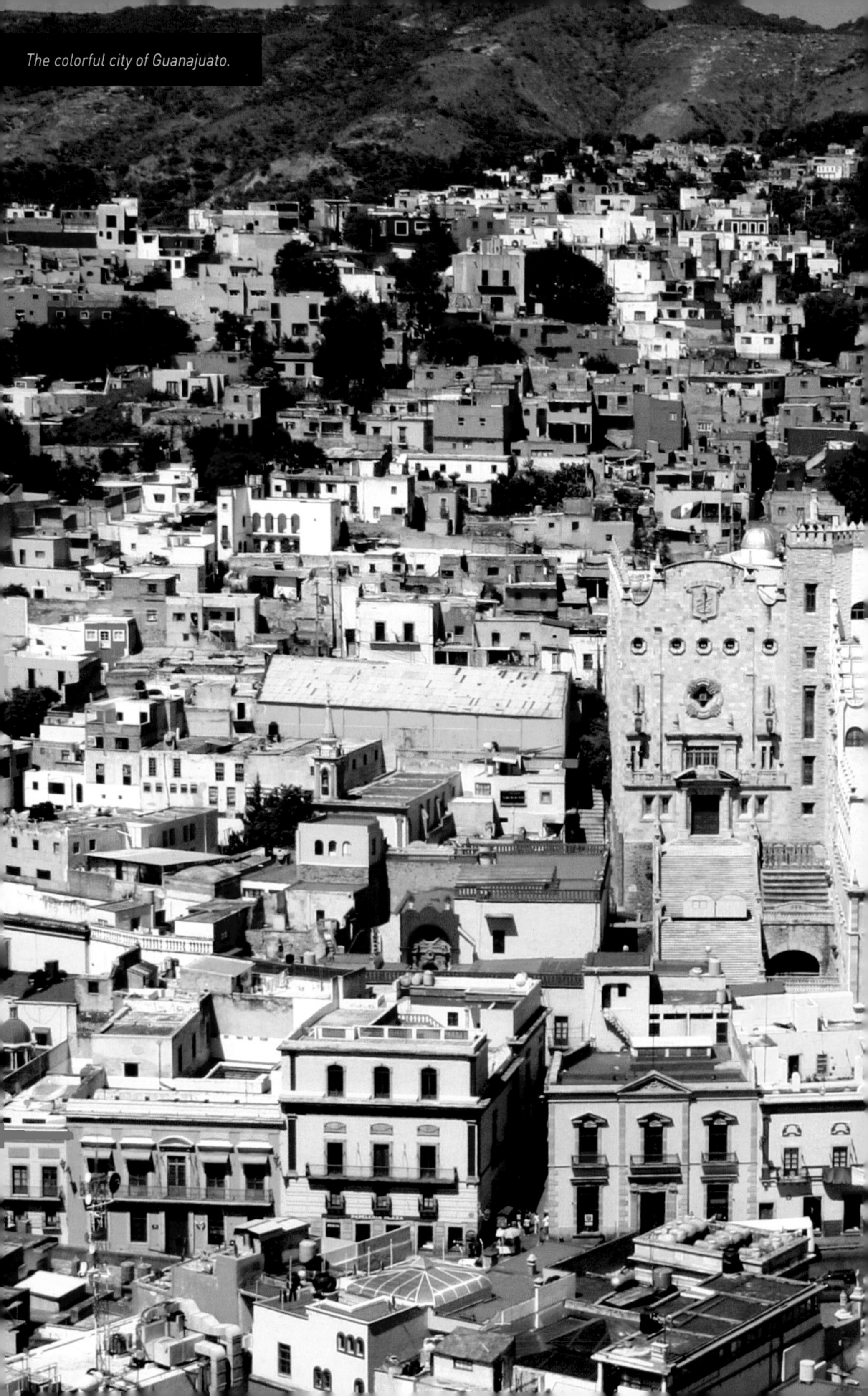
The colorful city of Guanajuato.

The Copper Canyon Railroad, Chihuahua.

INTRODUCTION

A detailed guide to the entire country, with principal sights clearly cross-referenced by number to the maps.

Church of Santa María, Guadalajara.

There's no way to see all Mexico on one vacation. Not only is it far too big, it's also too diverse. Consider just a few highlights: the world's most remarkable train ride through the Copper Canyon from Chihuahua to the Pacific, bigger even than the Grand Canyon; tumultuous Mexico City and the ancient pyramids of Teotihuacán; the Maya ruins of the south, and the coral reefs off the Riviera Maya.

From the arid deserts of Baja California to the mountains of Chiapas, and from the northern border to the mangrove lagoons of the Yucatán and the turquoise waters off Cancún, Mexico has 9,650km (6,000 miles) of coastline. Nearly half the country is more than 1,500 meters (5,000ft) above sea level, and mountain ranges are dotted with still-active volcanoes. Mexico's rugged mountain landscapes are breathtaking; its waters – from the Sea of Cortés in the northwest to the Caribbean – are filled with spectacular marine life.

Agua Azul waterfalls, Chiapas.

The most practical plan is to settle for one region per visit and explore it thoroughly. Or concentrate on one theme – colonial architecture, Maya ruins, wildlife. If you want to be more adventurous, possibilities include mountain trekking and white-water rafting, as well as some of the world's best diving.

And Mexico is a year-round destination. The entire Pacific coast, including the giant Baja Peninsula, is bathed in sunshine for at least three-quarters of the year, and even in the tropical south the summer rains conveniently fall mostly in the afternoons, often leaving the rest of the day clear and sunny. Many of the beautiful colonial cities of the Central Highlands such as San Miguel de Allende, Guanajuato, or Morelia may feel a little chilly at night in mid-winter, but in compensation the air is wonderfully crisp and fresh, and moderate temperatures even on the hottest days of the year provide an ideal setting for exploration. In the sultry Yucatán, winter months are generally the best time to scramble over Maya pyramids, but the powdery soft white beaches of Tulum or Cozumel beckon irresistibly at any time.

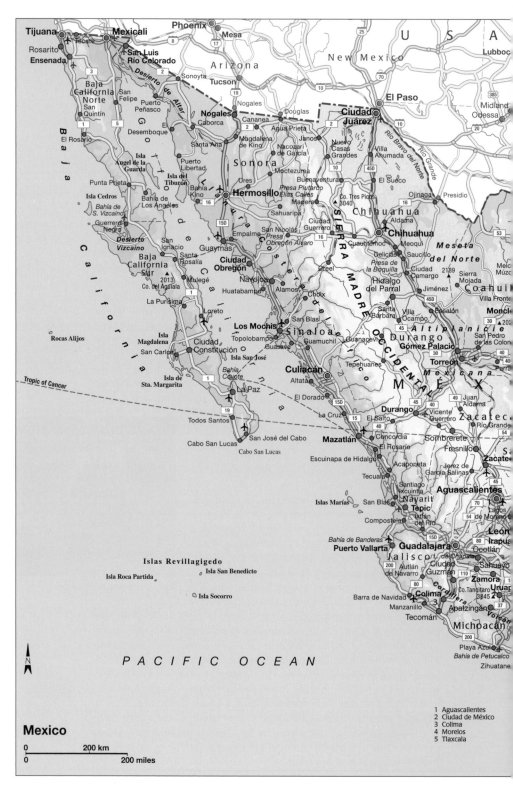

Tijuana
Rosarito
Ensenada
Baja California Norte
San Quintín
El Rosario
Punta Prieta
Isla Cedros
Bahía de S. Vizcaíno
Guerrero Negro
Desierto Vizcaíno
Baja California Sur
Co. del Aguaila 2013
La Purísima
Rocas Alijos
Isla Magdalena
San Carlos
Isla de Sta. Margarita
Ciudad Constitución
Loreto
Mulegé
Santa Rosalía
San Ignacio
Bahía Coyote
La Paz
Todos Santos
Cabo San Lucas
Cabo San Lucas
San José del Cabo

Phoenix
Mesa
Mexicali
Tecate
San Luis Río Colorado
Sonoyta
Arizona
Tucson
Nogales
Douglas
San Felipe
Puerto Peñasco
El Desemboque
Desierto de Altar
Caborca
Santa Ana
Nogales
Cananea
Agua Prieta
Magdalena de Kino
Nacozari de García
Janos
Nuevo Casas Grandes
Isla Angel de la Guarda
Puerto Libertad
Isla del Tiburón
Bahía Kino
Ures
Moctezuma
Buenaventura
Villa Ahumada
Hermosillo
Presa Plutarco Elias Calles
Madera
Sahuaripa
Ciudad Guerrero
El Sueco
Ojinaga
Presidio
Co. Tres Picos 3040
Sonora
Chihuahua
Aldama
Empalme
San Nicolás
Ciudad Obregón Alvaro
Cuauhtémoc
Chihuahua
Meoqui
Saucillo
Delicias
Creel
Presa de la Boquilla
Ciudad Camargo
Sierra Mojada 2189
Meseta del Norte
Guaymas
Santa Maria
Navojoa
Huatabampo
Alamos
Choix
San Blas
Santa Bárbara
Hidalgo del Parral
Jiménez
Villa Ocampo
Coahui
Villa Fronte
Moncl
Los Mochis
Topolobampo
Guasave
Guamuchil
Guanacevi
Durango
Altiplanicie
San Pedro de las Colon
Monclova
Ciudad Constitución
Sinaloa
Gómez Palacio
Torreón
Parra
Culiacán
Altatá
El Dorado
La Cruz
Tepehuanes
Mexicana
Durango
Vicente Guerrero
Juan Aldama
Zacatec
Río Grande
El Salto
Concordia
Sombrerete
Fresnillo
Mazatlán
El Rosario
Acaponeta
Jerez de García Salinas
Zacate
Escuinapa de Hidalgo
Tecuala
Santiago Ixcuintla
Islas Marías
San Blas
Nayarit
Tepic
Ixtlán del Río
Aguascalientes
Lagos de Moreno
León
Irapua
Ocotlán
Compostela
Bahía de Banderas
Puerto Vallarta
Guadalajara
Jalisco
de Chapala
Sahuayo
Islas Revillagigedo
Isla Roca Partida
Isla San Benedicto
Isla Socorro
Autlán de Navarro
Ciudad Guzmán
Zamora
Uruap
Co. Tancítaro 3845
Barra de Navidad
Colima
Abatzingán
Manzanillo
Tecomán
Michoacán
Playa Azul
Bahía de Petucalco
Zihuatane

USA
Lubboc
New Mexico
El Paso
Midland
Odessa
Ciudad Juárez
Río Bravo del Norte
Rio Grande
Tropic of Cancer

PACIFIC OCEAN

N

Mexico

0   200 km
0   200 miles

1 Aguascalientes
2 Ciudad de México
3 Colima
4 Morelos
5 Tlaxcala

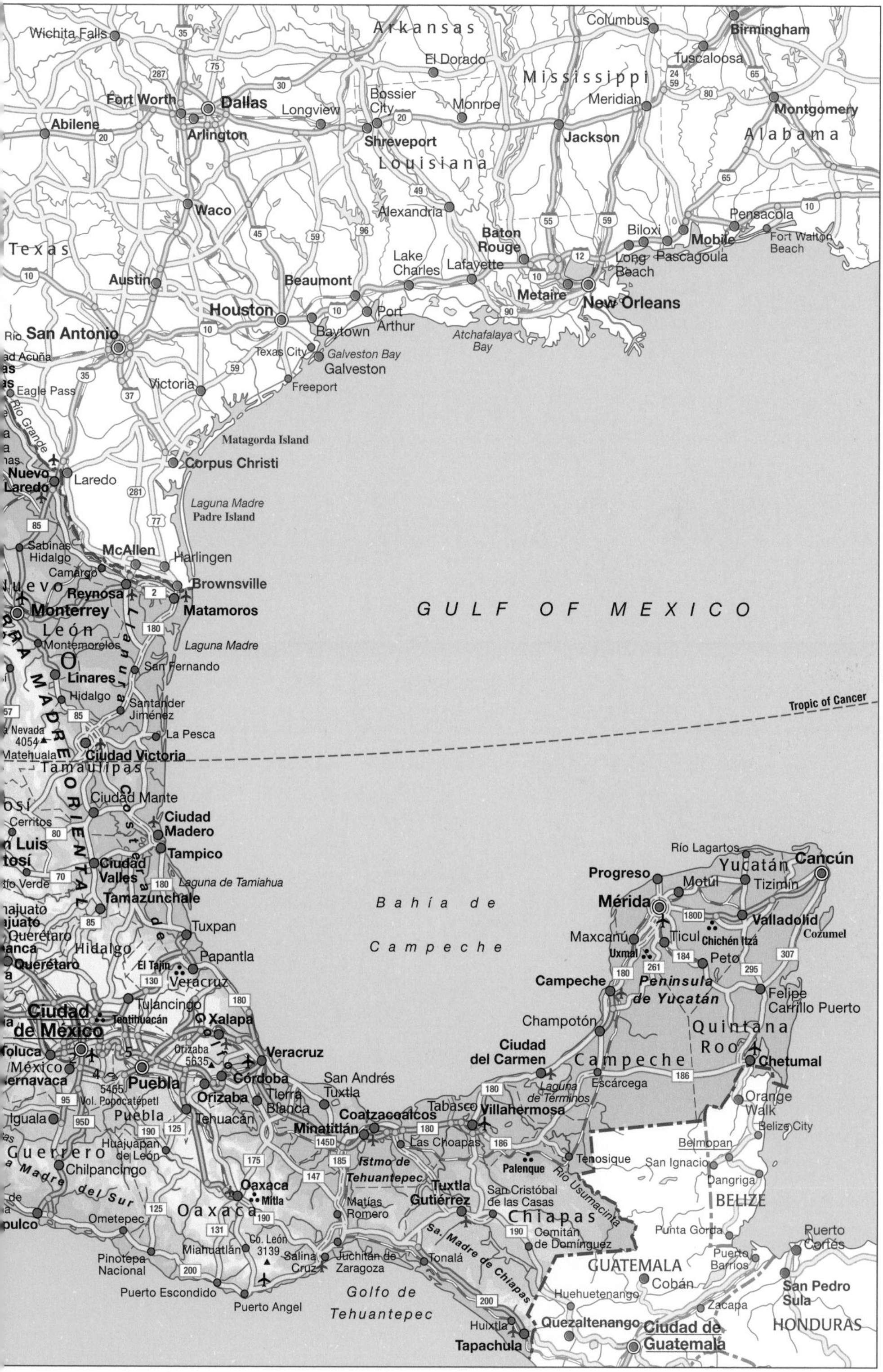

Wichita Falls
Arkansas
Columbus
Birmingham
35
El Dorado
Tuscaloosa
75
287
Fort Worth
Dallas
Longview
30
Bossier City
Monroe
Mississippi
Meridian
24 59
65
80
Montgomery
Abilene
Arlington
20
Shreveport
Jackson
Alabama
Texas
Waco
Alexandria
Louisiana
49
Baton Rouge
Biloxi
Pensacola
10
45
59
96
55
59
Mobile
Fort Walton Beach
10
Lake Charles
Lafayette
Long Beach
Pascagoula
Austin
Beaumont
Metairie
New Orleans
65
Houston
Port Arthur
10
90
10
Baytown
Atchafalaya Bay
Rio San Antonio
10
Texas City
Galveston Bay
ad Acuña
as
35
Eagle Pass
Victoria
59
37
Galveston
Freeport
Rio Grande
Matagorda Island
nas
Nuevo Laredo
Laredo
281
Corpus Christi
85
Laguna Madre
Padre Island
77
Sabinas Hidalgo
McAllen
Harlingen
Camargo
uevo
Reynosa
2
Brownsville
León
Monterrey
Matamoros
O
180
Laguna Madre
Montemorelos
San Fernando
Linares
Hidalgo
Santander Jiménez
GULF OF MEXICO
57
85
Nevada
4054
Matehuala
Ciudad Victoria
La Pesca
Tropic of Cancer
Tamaulipas
osí
Ciudad Mante
Cerritos
Ciudad Madero
80
Luis
tosí
Valles
Tampico
Río Lagartos
Cancún
Ciudad
Progreso
Yucatán
Verde
70
Tamazunchale
180
Laguna de Tamiahua
Mérida
Motul
Tizimín
najuato
juato
85
Tuxpan
Bahía de
Maxcanú
Ticul
Chichén Itzá
Valladolid
Cozumel
Querétaro
anca
Hidalgo
Papantla
Campeche
Uxmal
261
184
Peto
307
Querétaro
El Tajín
Veracruz
130
Campeche
180
Península de Yucatán
295
a
Tulancingo
180
Champotón
Felipe Carrillo Puerto
Ciudad de México
Teotihuacán
Xalapa
Ciudad del Carmen
Quintana Roo
Toluca
/México
ernavaca
Orizaba
5635
Veracruz
San Andrés Tuxtla
Campeche
Chetumal
4
Puebla
Córdoba
180
Laguna de Términos
Escárcega
186
Orange Walk
95
Vol. Popocatépetl
5465
Orizaba
Tierra Blanca
Tabasco
Villahermosa
Belize City
Iguala
950
Puebla
Tehuacán
190
Coatzacoalcos
180
Belmopan
190
125
Minatitlán
1450
186
San Ignacio
BELIZE
Guerrero
Huajuapan de León
175
Las Choapas
Tenosique
Dangriga
Chilpancingo
185
Istmo de Tehuantepec
Palenque
Río Usumacinta
a Madre del Sur
Oaxaca
147
Tuxtla Gutiérrez
San Cristóbal de las Casas
de
a
pulco
125
Mitla
Matías Romero
Chiapas
Punta Gorda
Puerto Cortés
Ometepec
190
Oaxaca
190
Comitán de Domínguez
Puerto Barrios
131
Co. León
3139
GUATEMALA
Cobán
San Pedro Sula
Pinotepa Nacional
200
Miahuatlán
Salina Cruz
Juchitán de Zaragoza
Tonalá
Sal. Madre de Chiapas
Huehuetenango
Zacapa
HONDURAS
Puerto Escondido
Puerto Angel
Golfo de Tehuantepec
200
Huixtla
Quezaltenango
Ciudad de Guatemala
Tapachula

Palacio de Bellas Artes.

MEXICO CITY AND ITS SURROUNDINGS

The core of Mexico's giant capital and its surrounding region is teeming, sometimes overwhelming, but always fascinating.

Casa de los Azulejos.

Commonly referred to by Mexicans simply as México, or DF ('day-efe'), which is short for Ciudad de México's (CDMX) former name of Distrito Federal, Mexico City is one of the most populous places on earth. The city proper has nine million inhabitants, but the whole Zona Metropolitana, or Greater Mexico City area, has some 21 million (as of 2018), or a sixth of Mexico's population. At 2,250 meters (7,380ft) above sea level, it is also one of the world's highest cities – new arrivals may feel a little tired and short of breath – and, despite big steps taken to improve air quality, is still heavily polluted. *Inhabitants* get used to occasional coughs and stinging eyes, but visitors may prefer to avoid the busiest areas at peak times.

Many beach lovers choose to fly directly to Cancún or the Pacific resorts, but Mexico City is the first stop for anyone wishing to explore the center of the country, and an essential transport hub, with connections to every part of Mexico. It is also fascinating in itself, and far less forbidding than its size and reputation can suggest. There are plenty of calm corners among the giant avenues, and superb museums. For anyone with an interest in Mexico's pre-Hispanic cultures and cities, a few hours browsing through the magnificent Museo de Antropología is a must.

Paseo de la Reforma.

Most of Mexico City's major sights are in a central area that stretches west from the Zócalo (main square) to Chapultepec Park, location of the anthropology museum. North and south of the park are the fashionable districts of Polanco, Roma, and Condesa, with many of the best restaurants and most stylish nightlife. Farther south are the charming old *colonias* (neighborhoods) of San Angel and Coyoacán, with their Bohemian feel and memories of Diego Rivera and Frida Kahlo, as well as the floating gardens of Xochimilco.

Mexico City makes a base for all kinds of day and weekend excursions: to pre-Hispanic ruins at Teotihuacán and Tula, colonial towns, and Baroque churches in sleepy villages; or to shop for silver in Taxco, relax at spa resorts in the lush hills of Morelos or sail on a mountain lake at Valle de Bravo.

Casa de los Azulejos.

MEXICO CITY

The statistics of Mexico's capital often beggar the imagination, but there's a wealth of life and spectacular attractions within its sometimes crazy urban fabric.

The vast megalopolis of Mexico City is a love it *and* loathe it kind of place. Much of the nation's wealth and power is concentrated here, along with the finest in music and the arts. If Mexico is the country of surprises and contradictions *par excellence*, then most of them can be found here, all jumbled up together within its vast capital: stylish modernity next to ancient, apparently bizarre traditions, grand monuments beside sprawling markets, hectic highways a few steps from placid squares. It is a huge, exciting, unpredictable city, full of discoveries, where people are often friendly and adventure seems to linger on every street corner. Being one of the largest and most populous cities in the world naturally has its disadvantages too: traffic congestion and pollution can be appalling, and the petty crime of pickpockets and thieves is rife (for some security tips see page 131). Like any giant city, it is a place you need to adapt to, but if you pace yourself, work out how to navigate its multilane traffic junctions, and find the right places to sit and let the crowds pass by, its multicolored verve becomes richly enjoyable.

THE HISTORIC CENTER: ALONG CALLE MADERO

The Centro Histórico, or old town, corresponds roughly to the old colonial capital, centered like all the cities of Spanish America around a main square, the giant Zócalo, which was built on top of the former center of the Aztec capital Tenochtitlán. A great way to begin a tour is with breakfast at the charming **Casa de los Azulejos** or "House of Tiles" between calles Madero and 5 de Mayo. First constructed in the late 16th century, it was extensively rebuilt in the 1730s for the Countess del Valle de Orizaba, with ornate carvings and facades covered with blue and white Puebla tiles, and is one of the best-preserved of Mexico City's colonial mansions. Since 1917 it

⊙ Main attractions

Catedral Metropolitana
Templo Mayor
La Alameda
Palacio de Bellas Artes
Zona Rosa
Bosque de Chapultepec
Museo Nacional de
   Antropología
Museo-Estudio Diego
   Rivera y Frida Kahlo
Museo Frida Kahlo
Xochimilco

**Maps on pages
130, 140, 146**

Tiffany glass window inside the Gran Hotel.

Mexico City
Historic Center

500 m
500 yds
0
0

N

has housed the flagship branch of Sanborns restaurant. Californian brothers Frank and Walter Sanborn created a sensation when they opened their first American-style soda fountain, café, and drugstore in Mexico City in 1903, and Sanborns – long-since Mexican-owned – has become an institution, with branches all over the city and the country. In the days of the Revolution the ragged soldiers of Pancho Villa and Emiliano Zapata were famously photographed sampling unfamiliar luxuries at an earlier Sanborns, just along Calle Madero on the site now taken by the Librería Madero, one of Mexico City's best bookstores.

The glass-roofed patio is the most striking part of the Casa de los Azulejos, with a mural on the staircase by José Clemente Orozco (see page 114), titled *Omnisciencia* (Omniscience). The traditionally dressed waitresses are quietly attentive, and a while spent observing the regulars, many of whom seem to have been coming here for decades, is a fine introduction to Mexico City life by itself.

Opposite Sanborns, the **Torre Latinoamericana** ❷ (http://torrelatinoameri cana.com.mx; daily 9am–10pm) was, in 1956, Mexico's first skyscraper. The panoramic views from the 44th-floor observation platform and its cafés (on the 42nd, 43rd, and 44th floors) are clearest at night. There is a small museum of the building's history on the 37th floor, and even an aquarium on the 38th. Below, busy **Calle Francisco Madero** leads east to the Zócalo. Its landmarks include the sinking church of **San Francisco** ❸, once part of a Franciscan monastery founded by Cortés himself three years after the Conquest, in 1524. Most of the structure, including the stone portal and Churrigueresque facade, is 18th century.

The heavily adorned Baroque **Palacio de Iturbide** ❹, built as an aristocratic residence in the 1780s, is so-named because "Emperor" Agustín de Iturbide briefly made it his palace in 1821. It is now owned by the Citibanamex cultural foundation, and as the **Palacio de Cultura Citibanamex** (daily 10am–7pm;

> **Ⓞ Tip**
>
> The basic security precautions here are the same as in any big city – with perhaps a little extra alertness. Keep cameras and jewelry out of sight, never leave bags on the floor or the back of a chair in restaurants or cafés, and always keep a hold of your possessions, especially on buses and the metro. If you need a taxi, try to use an authorized *sitio* one (based at a taxi rank, which can be phoned). Avoid dimly lit, empty streets at night. Only use ATMs in safer areas, and never after dark.

The cathedral provides a dramatic backdrop for an Aztec dance performance in the Zócalo.

Ⓞ THE SINKING CITY

Walking around the old center of Mexico City it is possible to feel a little dizzy, and not just because of pollution. Some streets don't look quite right, their sidewalks seeming to buckle. You haven't been drinking: many buildings *do* lean at weird angles, especially the massive Spanish stone palaces and churches. They have been quietly sinking for centuries.

Aztec Tenochtitlán was built on a low island in the shallow Lake Texcoco. The Spaniards cut down many trees around the Valley of Mexico, causing most of the lake to silt up. This led to catastrophic flooding at times of heavy rain, a problem solved by building giant drains and aqueducts, from the 1600s to the early 1900s, to take the water away. As the natural water was drained away, however, Mexico City's subsoil got more and more powdery, and softer and softer. Subsidence became especially acute when added to the effects of the 1985 earthquake. The cathedral, especially, was on the verge of collapse. Raising the worst-affected part, the apse, was impossible, so the emergency rescue program actually involved taking away soil from beneath the main facade to lower it, so that the whole building would at least be relatively level. The cathedral was declared out of danger in 2000. It was first built on a platform above the Zócalo; it is now a few meters below it.

Pedi taxis in front of the cathedral.

Military parade at the flag lowering ceremony in the Zócalo.

free) hosts wide-ranging art exhibitions in its sumptuously restored rooms.

Nearing the Zócalo, the somber **Templo de la Profesa** has sunk considerably since it was built in the 1720s. Across the intersection is a brighter attraction, the **Museo del Estanquillo** ❺ (Wed–Mon 10am–6pm; free), with thousands of old postcards, photos, calendars, paper Day of the Dead dioramas, and other Mexican ephemera from the personal collection of author Carlos Monsiváis (an *estanquillo* is the kind of stall where such things were sold). It is in a lovely 19th-century building, and the roof terrace café has a great view.

AROUND THE ZÓCALO

Once the ceremonial center of Aztec Tenochtitlán, with pyramids, palaces and wide-open spaces, the **Zócalo** has been transformed many times. The second-largest city square in the world (beaten only by Red Square in Moscow), over the years it has housed executions, markets, palm trees, and a tram terminal. Today the center is free of trees or permanent structures except for the

pole that supports what is said to be the world's biggest flag. The hub of the city – and at times the whole country – throughout its history, the Zócalo is used for many official ceremonies, but also hosts massive rallies, protests, concerts, and other performances. At any time there is nearly always some kind of political demonstration somewhere on the square, as well as "Aztec" folk dancers and other street performers. The best view of the Zócalo is from the rooftop restaurant of the **Hotel Majestic** (entrance on Madero), and photographs and models of how the square used to be can be seen in Zócalo metro station. The west side of the square is filled by long colonnaded buildings known as the **Portal de Mercaderes**, which have housed jewelers since colonial times.

Filling the block on this side of the Zócalo north of Calle 5 de Mayo, the **Nacional Monte de Piedad** ❻ is an enormous pawnshop and loan bank, founded in 1775. Run as a charity, it has become an important part of local life, especially at holiday time, when people line up to hock their possessions.

The vast, towering **Catedral Metro-politana** ❼ (daily 8am–8pm, bell tower daily 10.30am–6pm), is an encyclopedia of Mexican colonial art. The building took around three centuries to complete, beginning in Spanish Renaissance style and finishing in the neoclassical style of the early 19th century. Most of the lower walls were built between the 1570s and the 1650s; the upper portion of the elegant facade and the unusual bell towers were added in the 1790s by the Mexican-born José Damián Ortiz de Castro, and the dome and the clock were finally finished by the Spanish neoclassical architect Manuel Tolsá in 1813.

Huge and impressive, the cathedral's somber but magnificent interior is illuminated through contemporary stained-glass windows that give a mellow, golden light. The 100-meter (328ft) long and 46-meter (151ft) wide interior is divided into five naves. Close to the main entrance, the **Altar del Perdón** (Altar of Forgiveness), with its huge altarpiece, was the work of the 17th-century architect and sculptor Jerónimo de Balbas. Both the altar and the adjacent choir, with its intricately carved stalls, were severely damaged by fire in 1967 but have been restored.

Dominating the view at the end of the central nave is the magnificent **Altar de los Reyes** (Kings' Altar) – also by Jerónimo de Balbas – one of the masterpieces of the elaborate, ultra-Baroque, Churrigueresque style (see page 56). Completed in 1737, the altar is drenched in gilt carvings, moldings, angels, saints, and cherubim. In the center, two paintings represent the Assumption of the Virgin and the Adoration of the Magi. A massive engineering program has put a halt to the subsidence that long threatened the cathedral with collapse (see page 131), but the strange angles of its walls and giant columns, and the slope of the floor, stand out to any visitor. Monitors around the cathedral check constantly on the state of the building, and a giant pendulum hanging down in the middle allows you to verify just how off-level it is.

The cathedral's neighbour, the **Sagrario Metropolitano** ❽, is in fact

⌖ Eat

One of the most atmospheric places to eat and drink in the center is the Cantina La Opera, at the corner of Calle 5 de Mayo and Calle Filomena Mata, opened in 1876. The gleaming wood and velvet decor is magnificent, and the story goes that Pancho Villa once shot a hole in the ceiling.

The Altar de los Reyes, Catedral Metropolitana.

an entirely separate church, built in 1740–68. It has the most extravagant of all Churrigueresque facades, an explosion of red and white stone. The Sagrario had a special subsidence problem of its own, in that the sinking of the cathedral was pulling it down, and it has only been possible to stabilize the building by separating it from the cathedral wall against which it was built. Just in front of the cathedral and the Sagrario, glass panels in the pavement allow you to see remains of the Temple of the Sun of Tenochtitlán, on the site of which both were built.

RUINS OF TENOCHTITLÁN

The **Templo Mayor** ❾ (www.templomayor. inah.gob.mx; Tue–Sun 9am–5pm) in the northeast corner of the Zócalo stood at the center of the Aztec universe, the exact spot where the eagle was sighted eating a snake on the cactus (see page 40). Today it is the largest surviving relic of Tenochtitlán. Remarkably, its existence was virtually unknown until 1978, when electricity workers laying cables chanced upon the 8-tonne

stone disc of Coyolxauhqui, Goddess of the Moon, showing her dismembered body after her defeat by her brother the Sun God Huitzilopochtli. Excavations began soon after, and revealed the structure of the great pyramid and many other treasures. The pyramid was divided into two, with temples at the top dedicated to Huitzilopochtli and Tlaloc, God of Water. A pathway round the site reveals the multiple levels of construction. The beautifully designed **museum** exhibits artifacts found here, including the original Coyolxauhqui stone, and helpful models of what Tenochtitlán and the Templo Mayor looked like before the Conquest.

Looming up along the Zócalo's east side is the **Palacio Nacional** ❿ (Tue–Sun 10am–5pm; free), built on the site of Moctezuma's palace and the official seat of power in Mexico, although nowadays the president generally only comes here on ceremonial occasions. The Baroque heart of the palace was begun in 1562, but it has been added to and altered countless times. In addition to government offices, preserved

Templo Mayor.

within the giant building are Mexico's first Congress chamber and the office of revered President Benito Juárez, but most visitors come to admire the astonishing murals by Diego Rivera (see page 112) that adorn the main staircase and first-floor gallery. Painted between 1929 and 1935, they dramatically illustrate the history of Mexico, from an idealized pre-Hispanic past through the horrors of the Conquest to Independence and the 1910 Revolution, with Karl Marx and Zapata pointing to the future.

On the night of September 15, the president of Mexico appears on the balcony of the palacio to ring the bell with which Hidalgo summoned the people of Dolores (see page 54), thus starting the War of Independence. *El Grito* (The Shout) is a short but emotional ceremony.

Behind the Palacio along Calle Moneda, the **Museo Nacional de Las Culturas** ⓫ (www.museodelasculturas. mx; Tue–Sun 10am–5pm; free) occupies an impressive edifice first built as the colonial mint (*La Moneda*, or the House of Money), with a flower-filled patio around a fountain. The collection itself is less special, with anthropological artifacts from around the world.

SOUTH OF THE ZÓCALO

One block south of the Zócalo down Calle 20 de Noviembre, the **Palacio de Hierro** department store is worth visiting just to see one of the most gorgeous stained-glass ceilings in existence. Nearby on Calle Pino Suárez, the **Museo de la Ciudad de México** ⓬ (Tue–Sun 10am–6pm; free on Wed), in the magnificent colonial palace of the counts of Santiago de Calimaya, provides an excellent overview of the history of the city from prehistoric origins to contemporary problems.

Across the street is the fort-like **Hospital de Jesús** ⓭, established in 1524 by Hernán Cortés himself. It is the oldest hospital in the New World, and said to be located at the very spot where Cortés first met Moctezuma. The aggressively plain facade on Pino Suárez is part of a modern addition: walk through it to reach the lovely 16th-century patio and the hospital

Replica tzompantli (wall of skulls), Templo Mayor.

Dog training in Parque México.

⊙ LOCAL MARKETS

Every neighborhood in Mexico City has a market of some kind. A Mexican city market is an immense warren of activity, with an overpowering variety of sounds and smells: chickens frying, radios blaring, men with loudspeakers peddling unusual remedies alongside girls heating fresh *tortillas*, and exuberant heaps of pineapples, cactus leaves, and chilies.

One of the largest central markets, and the biggest in the city for traditional foodstuffs, is the **Mercado de la Merced**, near Merced metro station. A couple of blocks south of here is **Mercado Sonora**, famed for its arrays of medicinal herbs and the alleged witch doctors who sell them. One of the most famous markets is **La Lagunilla**, north of Plaza Garibaldi. During the week it is another general market, with a huge, noisy food section and another where you can look over embroidered *charro* hats, children's party dresses, and all sorts of other gaudy or useful things. On Sundays, the Lagunilla becomes a massive **flea market**, with hundreds of stalls selling treasures, trash, and anything in between. Note that this is a place to be on your guard for pickpockets. On Saturdays, in the neighbourhood of San Ángel, the Plaza San Jacinto becomes a handicrafts market known as the Bazar Sábado. Decorative art such as masks and jewelry is sold and cafés sell typical Mexican food. Nearby, other artists sell their wares, ranging from paintings to woven products.

Boy dressed in a Mariachi costume at the Festival of Saint Cecilia in Plaza Garibaldi.

church. The remains of Cortés are in a tomb beside the altar, and the vaulted ceiling is decorated with a mural, *The Apocalypse* by Orozco (see page 114).

NORTH OF THE ZÓCALO

The bustling streets north of the Zócalo, the university area before the vast modern campus was built in the south of the city, house a fascinating mix of museums and other attractions. Right behind the Templo Mayor, the former church of Santa Teresa has been turned into **Ex-Teresa Arte Actual** (daily 10am–6pm; free), a hip contemporary arts center. Two blocks away, **Museo José Luis Cuevas** ⓮ (Tue–Sun 10am–6pm; free on Sun), founded by one of Mexico's best-known living artists, has a wide-ranging collection of mostly Latin American contemporary art, including a *Sala de Erótica*, and presents temporary shows.

Just across Calle Justo Sierra from the Templo Mayor is one of the area's prime sights, the **Antiguo Colegio de San Ildefonso** ⓯ (www.sanildefonso.org.mx; Tue 10am–8pm, Wed–Sun

10am–6pm; free on Tue), also known as the Escuela Nacional Preparatoria (National Preparatory School), where some of the most dramatic revolutionary-era murals cover three floors around the patios of a former Jesuit college. The main work here is by Orozco, but Siqueiros, Rivera and others also feature (see page 112). San Ildefonso also hosts important temporary exhibits. On the next block west is the **Museo de la Caricatura** ⓰ (daily 10am–6pm), in the 18th-century former Colegio de Cristo. The Cartoon Museum engagingly covers the history of Mexican cartoons and related arts since Independence.

Some of the finest of Diego Rivera's work is two blocks north in the twin patios of the **Secretaría de Educación Pública** ⓱ (Education Ministry; Mon–Fri 9am–5pm; free), painted between 1923 and 1928 with more than 120 mural panels on Mexican life, history, and the Revolution. Outside is an immense statue of José Vasconcelos, the revolutionary education minister who commissioned many of Mexico City's murals. The Secretaría can

sometimes, rather unpredictably, be closed to visitors for official reasons.

Delightful **Plaza Santo Domingo** 🔞 is one of the most traditional squares in the capital. Under the colonnade on the west side, the **Portal de los Evangelistas**, public scribes known as *evangelistas,* who used to write letters for the illiterate, today mainly fill out government forms on ancient typewriters. Street printers with old-fashioned hand-presses also vie for trade. At the north end of the plaza is the beautiful Baroque **Iglesia de Santo Domingo**, while across the road is the **Palacio de la Inquisición**, once the local headquarters of the dreaded institution, but now the **Museo de la Medicina Mexicana** (daily 9am–6pm; free). Behind Santo Domingo, the remains of its former monastery have been turned into another striking new contemporary arts center, the **Centro Cultural del México Contemporáneo** (Tue–Sun 10am–6pm; free). By way of contrast, close by is a noisier cultural hub, the **Arena Coliseo**, the number one venue for *Lucha Libre*, the crazy Mexican style of wrestling. Wrestlers, usually masked and with bizarre names, have cult status, and fights attract huge, raucous crowds.

If the Coliseo is Mexico City's wrestling center, a few blocks to the west **Plaza Garibaldi** 🔞 is the traditional home of its *mariachis*, where costumed *musicians* stand around with their instruments until someone pays them for a song, or hires them for a wedding or a party. With *mariachis*, *jarochos* and other musicians playing all day long, this is one of the most characterful parts of the city, but, as Mexico City's foremost tourist trap, it's also a place to visit with care. Many of the restaurants around the plaza have a bad reputation for exaggerated prices and scams such as unannounced *cubiertos* (cover charges), and it has a higher-than-average number of pickpockets. The atmosphere is fine during the day, but it is best not to wander around the main plaza at night.

AROUND THE ALAMEDA

In early colonial times, the stretch of open land west of the old center known as **La Alameda** 🔞 was both a site for the burning of heretics and, according to the Englishman Thomas Gage, who visited in 1625, a place where local "gallants" showed themselves off on horseback to young ladies driving by in their carriages. Around 1700 a reforming viceroy began to make it more orderly, and in the 19th century it was transformed into a romantic park full of trees, fountains, sculptures, and the inevitable bandstand. It is a welcome refuge in the noisy and chaotic capital. Among the park's monuments is the **Hemiciclo a Juárez**, a tribute, in white Italian marble, to the great president; a statue of Beethoven; and two women, also in marble, called, in French, *Malgré Tout* (In Spite of Everything) by Jesús F. Contreras and *Désespoir* (Despair) by Agustín Ocampo.

At the east end of the Alameda is the huge and extravagant **Palacio de**

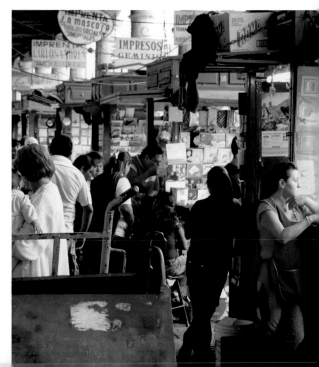

Printers and stationers on Plaza de Santo Domingo.

The ornate interior of the Palacio Postal (Central Post Office).

Chess players on the Alameda.

Bellas Artes N (Palace of Fine Arts; Tue–Sun 10am–6pm; free on Sun), commissioned by Porfirio Díaz in 1905. The original design was by Italian architect Adamo Boari, but building was interrupted by the Revolution and it wasn't until 30 years later that it was finished, by the Mexican architect Federico Mariscal. This time-lapse helps to explain the blend of styles: the Italian marble exterior is a combination of neoclassical with Art Nouveau, full of flying sculpture and florid decoration, while the interior is a sort of Aztec Art Deco. The structure is so massive and heavy that it has sunk noticeably.

Its four auditoria and other rooms are used for concerts, dance performances, and art exhibitions, and the building has yet more fine murals. Most notable is Diego Rivera's replica of a controversial mural commissioned in 1934 for the Rockefeller Center in New York; the subject matter was deemed too left-wing, and the original was destroyed. There are also other works by Rivera, in addition to murals by Orozco, Siqueiros, O'Gorman and Tamayo. The stained-glass mosaic curtain, designed by Gerardo Murillo, "*Dr Atl*," was made by Tiffany of New York. Showing the volcanoes Popocatépetl and Iztaccíhuatl, it is a masterpiece of high-class kitsch, and is lit up for public viewing on Sunday mornings and before evening performances.

Behind Bellas Artes is the almost equally elaborate Venetian-style **Palacio Postal** (Central Post Office), also by Adamo Boari. Nearby, on a small plaza at the western end of Calle Tacuba, is a well-loved monument, **El Caballito** (The Little Horse). This statue, which is not little at all, depicts the Spanish king Carlos IV on horseback. Sculpted by Manuel Tolsá in 1803, El Caballito has galloped all over Mexico City in search of a home; at different times it has adorned the Zócalo, the old university patio, and the busy Reforma–Juárez intersection, where increasing traffic meant it became a nuisance, until in 1979 it was moved to this square, renamed Plaza Manuel Tolsá in honor of its creator. Across the street is the **Palacio de Minería** N (www.palaciomineria.

unam.mx; Wed–Sun 10am–6pm, last Wed of month 10am–10pm), also by Tolsá and one of the best neoclassical buildings in Mexico. Behind the statue on the plaza is the **Museo Nacional de Arte ㉓** or MUNAL (www.munal.mx; Tue–Sun 10am–5.30pm). Occupying a beautifully restored neoclassical edifice built as a government ministry in 1904–11, it displays a comprehensive collection of paintings, sculptures, and graphics tracing the history of Mexican art from pre-Hispanic times to the mid-20th century, with interesting 19th-century landscapes as well as the better-known modern Mexican artists.

TILTING CHURCHES AND MOVING MURALS

Avenida Hidalgo runs along the north side of the Alameda. Two small colonial churches face tiny, peaceful **Plaza de la Santa Veracruz**, which preserves some of the atmosphere of old Mexico City. Next door to the severely tilting Templo de San Juan de Dios, in a beautifully restored 16th-century hospital, is the remarkable **Museo Franz Mayer ㉔**

(Tue–Sun 10am–5pm), showcasing 16th- to 19th-century decorative arts. A German-born financier who moved to Mexico in 1905, Mayer assembled a fantastically rich collection of paintings, furniture, ceramics, rugs, silverware and every other kind of applied art from around the world. The 10,000-piece collection is beautifully exhibited in rooms around a garden courtyard, and the Cafetería del Claustro adds to its charm.

The **Museo Nacional de la Estampa** (Tue–Sun 10am–6pm; free on Sun), on the same plaza, specializes in graphic arts, with a superb collection of the work of José Guadalupe Posada. Another leaning church next door, the 18th-century **Santa Veracruz**, has a fine Churrigueresque facade. Farther west, near the corner of Puente de Alvarado and Paseo de la Reforma, the small church of **San Hipólito** stands on the spot where the Spaniards and Aztecs fought most savagely in July 1520 during the so-called *Noche Triste* (Sad Night – see page 49). This was then the landward end of one of the causeways to

see page 49

> **⊙ Quote**
>
> "Whee!" yelled Dean. "Look out!" He staggered the car through the traffic and played with everybody. He drove like an Indian. He got on a circular glorieta drive on Reforma boulevard and rolled around it... This is traffic I've always dreamed of! Everybody goes!"
>
> Dean Moriarty and Sal Paradise arrive in Mexico City, in Jack Kerouac's *On the Road*

Palacio de Bellas Artes.

Benches in a variety of playful forms line Paseo de la Reforma.

the island-city across Lake Texcoco. Shortly after the battle, the Spanish built the church here, to celebrate their eventual victory, but it has since been greatly altered.

There are two more artistic attractions on the western side of the Alameda. Nearest to Hidalgo is the **Laboratorio Arte Alameda** ㉕ (Tue–Sun 9am–5pm; free on Sun), a dynamic contemporary arts center housed in the former San Diego church, specializing in very of-the-moment, multimedia work. Alongside, the **Museo Mural Diego Rivera** ㉖ (Tue–Sun 10am–6pm, last Wed of the month 10am–9pm; free on Sun) houses Rivera's famous mural *Sueño de una Tarde Dominical en la Alameda* (Dream of a Sunday Afternoon in Alameda Park), which portrays more than 100 historical characters – including himself, Frida Kahlo, and the engraver Posada – under the trees of the Alameda. After the 1985 earthquake, when the Hotel del Prado, its original location, collapsed, a mammoth operation was mounted to transport the wall and mural to its present site.

SEINE IN CEMENT: PASEO DE LA REFORMA

Modern Mexico City owes one of its most emblematic features to poor, sad Emperor Maximilian and his Belgian Empress María Carlota. When they arrived here in the 1860s, they decided their new capital needed a tree-lined avenue to link their favorite residence in Chapultepec Castle with the old city, running across what were then open fields to the Alameda. After his demise in 1867, the leaders of the Republic took to the new boulevard, definitively named **Paseo de la Reforma**, with enthusiasm, and in the Díaz era it developed into a grand promenade, with shade-providing trees and monuments, and lined by the homes of Mexico's elite. The great writer Octavio Paz called the Paseo Mexico City's river, a sort of Seine in cement, majestically crossing the best part of town. But, alas, the horses and carriages were replaced by torrents of automobiles, and many of the French-looking mansions were torn down and replaced by skyscrapers. Nevertheless, the Paseo is still a spectacular avenue;

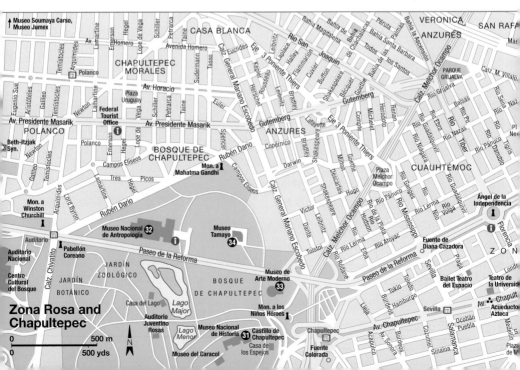

Zona Rosa and Chapultepec

0 — 500 m
0 — 500 yds

extended well beyond Maximilian's original conception, nowadays, like any river, it brings together every aspect of the city at some point along its length.

At the hectic intersection of Reforma, Juárez and Bucareli is the tall tower of the Art Deco **Loteriá Nacional** (National Lottery Building), where public draws take place several times a week. From the crossroads, Reforma marches grandly toward Chapultepec, while Avenida Juárez heads up to the massive **Monumento a la Revolución ㉗**. Some consider this the biggest Art Deco building in the world.

It began as the central dome of a never-completed legislative palace, part of Porfirio Díaz's plan to make Mexico City a Latin American Paris. The Revolution interrupted that grand scheme, and the gigantic structure was left to decay until an enterprising architect transformed it into the imposing, if ugly, monument it is today. The **Museo Nacional de la Revolución** (Tue–Fri 9am–5pm, Sat–Sun 9.30am–6.30pm), in the basement, tells the story of the revolution in detail. The building's 65-meter (213ft) **Observation Deck** (Tue–Thu noon–8pm, Fri–Sat noon–10pm, Sun 10am–8pm) has some wonderful views of the city.

Three blocks northeast on Calle Puente de Alvarado is the **Museo de San Carlos ㉘** (Tue–Sun 10am–6pm; free on Sun), in an 18th-century mansion by Manuel Tolsá. Descended from one of the oldest academies of art in the Americas, it houses Mexico's finest collection of European art up to the 19th century, from medieval altarpieces to works by Goya and Ingres.

Back on Reforma, the flow of the paseo is interrupted by giant traffic circles or *glorietas*, each with a special monument. The **Glorieta Cristóbal Colón** has a statue of Christopher Columbus. Farther south, at the Insurgentes crossing, is the monument to **Cuauhtémoc**, last Aztec emperor and first Mexican hero. Cuauhtémoc, who defended Tenochtitlán against Cortés (see page 50), became the perfect romantic figure, valiant and doomed; he stands erect and proud like a Roman senator, wearing a feather headdress.

Puerta 1808, a sculpture by Manuel Felguerez, in front of the Loteriá Nacional building.

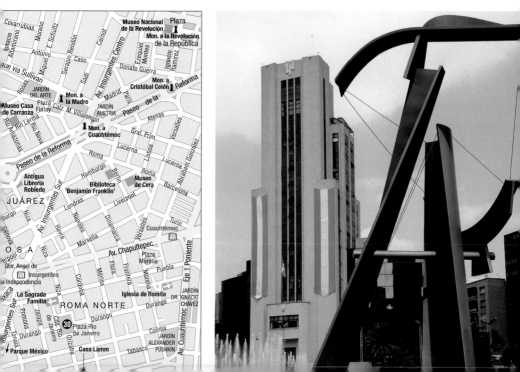

A single central umbrella (paragua) column supports the Museo Nacional de Antropología's vast fountain canopy.

Shopping in the hip Condesa neighborhood.

The **Ángel de la Independencia** is perhaps the most beautiful of all the monuments. Poised gracefully atop a tall and elegant column, the golden angel commemorates Mexico's Independence.

ZONA ROSA, ROMA, AND CONDESA

South of Reforma below the Ángel is the famous **Zona Rosa** ㉙ or "Pink Zone," which in the 1960s became modern Mexico City's most popular area for hotels, restaurants, window-shopping, and nightlife. It still has plenty of hotels and places to eat, which, with a relaxed atmosphere and good communications, makes it a convenient base for many Mexico City visitors. However, it is now less fashionable than other areas farther south, especially for nightlife, and many of its shops have become increasingly shabby as more upscale stores have moved out to neighborhoods such as Polanco and San Ángel.

The areas that have displaced it in fashion are south of Avenida Chapultepec, beginning with the colonias **Roma Norte and Roma Sur**. One key attraction for visitors, aside from the hassle-free atmosphere, is the architecture. Around 1900 the area's streets filled with ornate residences in French Beaux-Arts and other European styles, many of which have been beautifully restored since the 1985 earthquake, especially around **Plaza Rio de Janeiro** ㉚. More specific attractions include the **Casa Lamm** (Mon–Thu 9am–8pm, Fri 9am–5pm, Sat–Sun 10am–4pm), a prestigious private contemporary art center and one of several galleries on or near Avenida Obregón.

The Romas cannot compete in trendiness today, however, with **La Condesa** just to the west (although it is often unclear where one ends and the other begins). If the core of Roma is from the 1900s, most of La Condesa dates from the 1930s and 1940s, and is full of spectacular examples of Art Deco architecture. Buildings of note include Edificio San Martín on Avenida Mexico, restored by the architect Carlos Duclaud, the El Pendulo bookstore, and the turquoise clock in Parque

México, one of the city's most attractive parks. Outside **Parque España**, another pretty park, containing a children's amusement park, is the **Plaza Condesa**, a giant 1950s building that contains movie theaters, restaurants, bars, and music venues. Nearby on Avenida Tamaulipas, at No. 202, an Art Deco 1942 movie theater has been converted into the **Centro Cultural Bella Epoca**, with a gallery and an expansive bookstore. **Avenida Michoacán** is Condesa's main thoroughfare for gallery-browsing, shopping, and people-watching, and on or around it are many of Mexico City's hippest restaurants, bars, and clubs, and some of its sleekest boutique hotels.

CHAPULTEPEC AND POLANCO

At the western end of the main stretch of Reforma, where the paseo bends north, a footbridge leads conveniently over the traffic to six vast columns, the **Monumento a los Niños Héroes**, commemorating the "Boy Heroes," the six young cadets who died defending Chapultepec Castle during the Mexican–American war in 1847. This also marks the entrance to the **Bosque de Chapultepec**, the largest green area in Mexico City, a great verdant lung that is the best place in the downtown area to relax in the open air. It is also a place of great historical importance. It is believed the poet-king Nezahualcóyotl had a palace here, and in pre-Hispanic times the city's drinking water came from the springs of Chapultepec, which means "hill of the grasshopper" in Náhuatl.

The **Castillo de Chapultepec** ㉛, built as a residence for the Spanish viceroy in the 1780s, is said to be inhabited by the ghosts of Maximilian and María Carlota, who lived here during their short reign. Nowadays the castle – a steep 20-minute hike up from Paseo de la Reforma – houses the **Museo Nacional de Historia** (Tue–Sun 9am–5pm; free on Sun), which chronicles Mexican history from the Conquest

to the Revolution. Maximilian and María Carlota's rooms are decorated with period furniture, and artifacts on show include the emperor's carriage. Several rooms contain impressive murals by Siqueiros, O'Gorman, and Orozco, and, smog permitting, there is a fantastic view over the city.

Just down the hill is a lighter alternative, the **Museo del Caracol** (Tue–Sun 9am–4.15pm), the "Snail Museum," so-called because of its spiral shape, which portrays Mexico's modern history through child-friendly dioramas.

THE MUSEO DE ANTROPOLOGÍA

But most of all, Chapultepec Park is home to one of the world's great museums, the **Museo Nacional de Antropología** ㉜ (tel: 55-4040 5300; www.mna.inah.gob.mx; Tue–Sun 9am–7pm). The main entrance is marked by a vast statue, probably representing the Rain God Tlaloc, although it could be Chalchiuhtlicue, another water deity. The 7.5-meter (25ft) monolith was brought here in the 1960s when

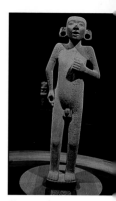

The Museo Nacional de Antropología's fine Huastec figure is believed to be of the young Quetzalcóatl.

Argentinian restaurant mural, Condesa.

Inner courtyard of the Museo Nacional de Antropología.

the museum opened, amid heavy downpours interpreted by some as the god's protest at being moved.

Pedro Ramírez Vásquez, its architect, found his inspiration in Maya architecture, especially Uxmal (see page 307). The museum is a giant quadrangle, with exhibition halls opening separately onto a central patio shaded by an immense rectangular fountain-canopy, held up, amazingly, by a single central pillar.

The different halls cover every one of Mexico's many historical cultures, providing a stunning vision of their sheer variety. It is possible to visit in any order, but they are arranged counter-clockwise around the great patio as follows: first there is an Introduction to Anthropology, and then the *Sala Orígenes*, telling the complex story of the first movement of peoples into the Americas from Asia; the Preclassic hall deals with the region's early cultures, followed by the spectacular halls on central Mexico (*Culturas del Centro*) – Teotihuacán, the Toltecs, the Mexica, or Aztecs; Oaxaca (Mixtecs and Zapotecs)

has a hall to itself, followed by another on the Gulf of Mexico (Olmecs, Totonacs, and Huastecs); a large *Sala Maya*; and, finally, the halls on western (*Culturas de Occidente*) and northern Mexico. While the main archeological exhibits are on the ground level, the floor above has displays on the rich indigenous cultures that survive in the same regions today, emphasizing the continuity between past and present.

Every hall has its treasures. Exhibits in the marvelous **Sala Mexica**, on Aztec art and history, include the famous Sun Stone or Aztec Calendar, and a fascinating model of Teotihuacán. The **Culturas del Golfo** hall has two astonishing Olmec basalt heads from San Lorenzo in Veracruz, and the **Sala Maya** has a model of the tomb of King Pakal from Palenque. Even the less celebrated halls have superb ceramics. For a rest between *salas*, the museum has a relaxing terrace café.

Chapultepec contains many more attractions. The **Museo de Arte Moderno ❸❸** (Tue–Sun 10.15am–5.30pm; free on Sun), in two circular glass buildings,

is Mexico's main depository for the non-mural work of its greatest 20th-century artists: Frida Kahlo, Rufino Tamayo, *Los Tres Grandes* – Orozco, Rivera, and Siqueiros – and more. As well as paintings, there is an impressive sculpture garden. The **Museo Tamayo** 34 (www.museotamayo.org; Tue–Sun 10am–6pm; free on Sun) has a fine collection donated by the great Mexican artist Rufino Tamayo, housed in an ingenious modern building. As well as his own vibrant works, the great highlight is his personal collection of international contemporary art, including works by Léger, Tàpies, and Warhol. Farther west into Chapultepec, the park's facilities include the Auditorio Nacional, the city's foremost concert hall, three lakes beloved by locals for boat rides, botanical gardens, an amusement park, and Mexico City's zoo.

Just outside the park on the south side, by Constituyentes metro station, is the **Casa Luis Barragán** (tel: 55-5515 4908; www.casaluisbarragan.org; tours by appointment Mon–Fri 10.30am–4pm, Sat–Sun 10.30–11am), an extraordinary avant-garde house, making fabulous use of light and color, created by the architect of the same name in 1947. The requirement for visitors to make a reservation is not always adhered to, but it is still best to phone ahead.

North of Chapultepec, **Polanco** is the wealthiest residential district in the city, containing many of its most upscale shops, fine restaurants, and luxury hotels.

The big attraction here is the city's most ostentatious testimony to what money can buy: the **Museo Soumaya** on Plaza Carso (tel: 55-1103 9800; www.soumaya.com.mx; 10.30am–6.30pm; free). Once the world's richest man, Carlos Slim funded the construction of this striking building to house his personal art collection, with works ranging from French impressionist painters to Diego Rivera and other Mexican artists. The building, designed by Slim's son-in-law, Fernando Romero, resembles a clenched fist rising from the earth, and is plated with thousands of glass hexagons. Right next door, **Museo Jumex** (tel: 55-5395

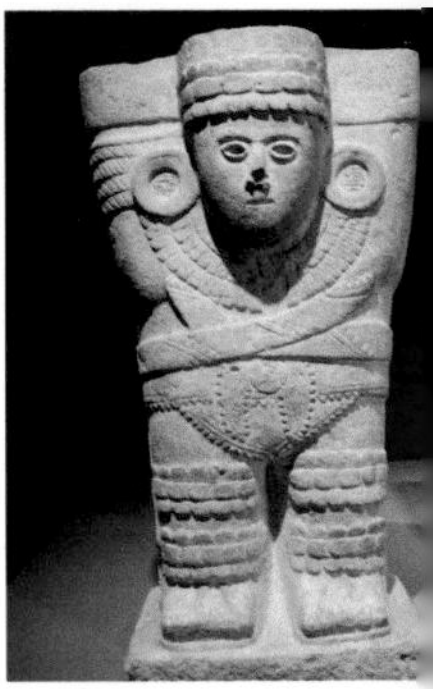

Discovered at Chichén Itzá, the Maya figure Atlantes (c.AD 1000–1250) is on display at the Museo Nacional de Antropología.

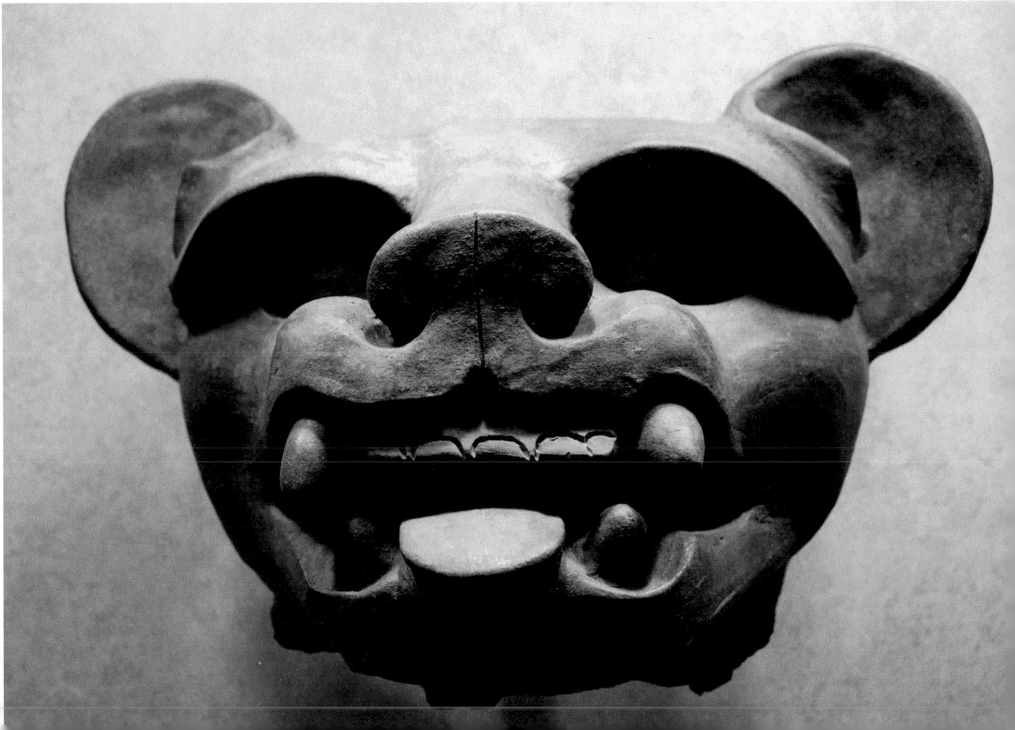

An artifact dating back to 200BC-500AD in the Museo Nacional de Antropología.

Ciudad de México

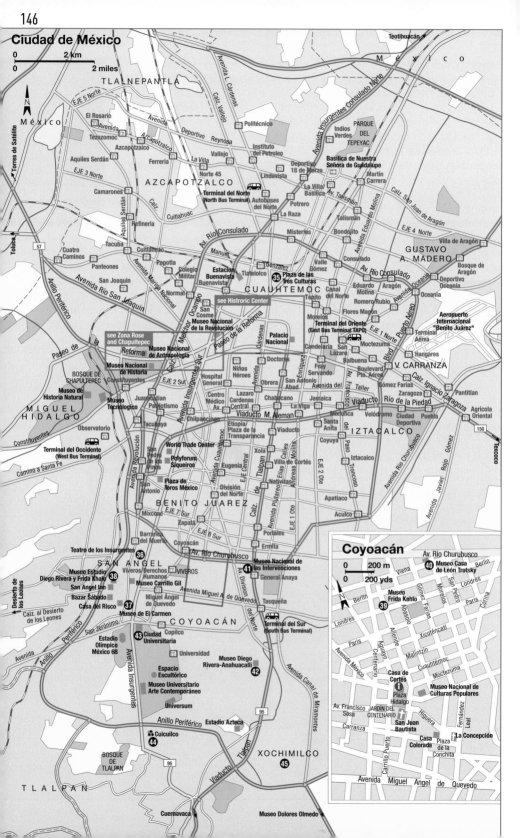

0   2 km
0   2 miles

N
México

Teotihuacán

M É X I C O

TLALNEPANTLA

Torres de Satélite

Toluba

57

ÉJE 5 Norte

El Rosario

Avenida

Deportivo Reynosa

Politécnico

Avenida Insurgentes Consulado Norte

PARQUE DEL TEPEYAC

Indios Verdes

Tezozomoc

Azcapotzalco

Aquiles Serdán

Azcapotzalco

Instituto del Petroleo

Basílica de Nuestra Señora de Guadalupe

Martín Carrera

EJE 3 Norte

Ferreria

La Villa

Vallejo

Deportivo 18 de Marzo

La Villa/ Basílica

Av. Talismán

Camarones

AZCAPOTZALCO

Norte 45

Lindavista

Talismán

Villa de Aragón

Aquiles Serdán

Cuitlahuac

Terminal del Norte (North Bus Terminal)

Autobuses del Norte

Potrero

Bosque de Aragón

GUSTAVO A. MADERO

Refineria

Tacuba

Cuitlahuac

La Raza

Misterios

Bondojito

EJE 4 Norte

Deportivo Oceanía

Cuatro Caminos

Av. Río Consulado

Manuel

González

Valle Gómez

Consulado

Av. Río Consulado

Oceanía

Panteones

Pepotla

Colegio Militar

Estación Buenavista

Tlatelolco

Plaza de las Tres Culturas

35

Eduardo Molina

Aragón

Aeropuerto Internacional "Benito Juárez"

San Joaquin

Avenida Río San Joaquin

Avenida Mérida Nacional

Normal

Buenavista

CUAUHTEMOC

Canal del Norte

Tepito

Romero Rubio

Terminal Aérea

Anillo Periférico

Reforma

San Cosme

see Historic Center

Morelos

Flores Magón

Hangares

BOSQUE DE CHAPULTEPEC

Museo Nacional de la Revolución

Terminal del Oriente (East Bus Terminal TAPO)

San Lázaro

Moctezuma

V. CARRANZA

Museo de Historia Natural

see Zona Rose and Chapultepec

Museo Nacional de Antropología

Palacio Nacional

Candelaria

Boulevard Pto. Aéreo

Paseo de la Reforma

Museo Nacional de Historia

Constituyentes

Doctores

Niños Héroes

Fray Servando

Balbuena

Gómez Farías

Pantitlan

MIGUEL HIDALGO

Museo Tecnológico

Juanacatlán

Patriotismo

Hospital General

Obrera

San Antonio Abad

Avenida del

Taller

Río de la Piedad

Observatorio

Tacubaya

Chilpancingo

Centro Médico Av.

Lazaro Cardenas Central

Chabacano

La Viga

Jamaica

Viaducto

Ciudad Deportiva

Agrícola Oriental

Constituyentes

Camino a Santa Fe

Terminal del Occidente (West Bus Terminal)

Avenida Revolución

San Pedro de los Pinos

Etiopia/ Plaza de la Transparencia

Viaducto M. Alemán

Mixiuhca

Santa Anita

Viaducto

Coyuya

Velódromo

Puebla

150

Texcoco

World Trade Center

Xola

Iztacalco

IZTACALCO

Polyforum Siqueiros

Eugenia

Villa de Cortés

EJE 2 Ote

San Antonio

Plaza de Toros México

División del Norte

Nativitas

Apatlaco

Avenida

BENITO JUAREZ

EJE 7 Sur

Mixcoac

Zapata

EJE 8 Sur

Portales

Aculco

Barranca del Muerto

Coyoacán

Ermita

Teatro de los Insurgentes

36

Av. Río Churubusco

SAN ANGEL

Viveros/ Derechos Humanos

VIVEROS

41

Museo Nacional de las Intervenciones

Museo Estudio Diego Rivera y Frida Kahlo

38

San Angel Inn

Museo Carrillo Gil

General Anaya

Desierto de los Leones

Bazar Sábado

Miguel Angel de Quevedo

Avenida Miguel A. de Quevedo

Tasqueña

Casa del Risco

37

Calz. al Desierto de los Leones

Museo de El Carmen

San Jerónimo

COYOACÁN

Terminal del Sur (South Bus Terminal)

Anillo

Periférico

Estadio Olímpico México 68

43

Ciudad Universitaria

Copilco

Universidad

Avenida Insurgentes

Avenida Canal de Miramontes

Espacio Escultórico

Museo Diego Rivera-Anahuacalli

42

Museo Universitario Arte Contemporáneo

Universum

95

Anillo Periférico

Estadio Azteca

Cuicuilco

44

BOSQUE DE TLALPAN

95

Viaducto

XOCHIMILCO

45

TLALPAN

Cuernavaca

Museo Dolores Olmedo

Coyoacán

0   200 m
0   200 yds

N

Av. Río Churubusco

Museo Casa de León Trotsky

40

Viena

Berlín

Berlín

Av. Río Churubusco

San Pedro

Londres

Paris

Gómez Farías

Morelos

Corina

Museo Frida Kahlo

39

Allende

Aguayo

Aldasolo

Centenario

Avenida México

Xicoténcatl

Malintzin

Cuauhtémoc

Moctezuma

Paris

Londres

Paris

Casa de Cortés

Museo Nacional de Culturas Populares

Av. Francisco Sosa

Plaza Hidalgo

JARDÍN DEL CENTENARIO

Higuera

Fernández Leal

Carranza

San Juan Bautista

Casa Colorada

Plaza de la Conchita

La Concepción

Carrillo Puerto

Avenida   Miguel   Angel   de   Quevedo

2615; http://fundacionjumex.org; Tue–Sun 10am–8pm; free on Sun) is the legacy left by another multi-billionaire, the owner of the Jumex food and drinks company, Eugenio López. It houses his huge private art collection in a giant white cube; the neighborhood is increasingly growing in stature on the international art scene.

Two blocks west of Polanco metro station, **Galería López Quiroga** (tel: 55-5280 1710; www.lopezquiroga.com; Mon–Fri 10am–7pm, Sat 10am–2pm) is one of several good neighborhood galleries, specializing in contemporary Latin American art.

OUTSIDE THE CENTER: GUADALUPE AND TLATELOLCO

The image of the **Virgen de Guadalupe** (see page 22) is everywhere in Mexico: in homes, places of work, even buses and taxi cabs. On December 12, tens of thousands make the pilgrimage to the **Basílica de Nuestra Señora de Guadalupe**, in the north of the city, for the anniversary of her 1531 apparition.

When the beautiful 18th-century **Antigua Basílica** became too small to accommodate the crowds (and began to list noticeably due to subsidence), it was decided to build a new one next door. By the same architect as the Anthropology Museum, Pedro Ramírez Vásquez, the vast concrete **Basílica Nueva** was completed in 1976, and can hold as many as 10,000 worshipers at a time. All around it are shops and stalls selling religious images, incense, food, toys, and lottery tickets.

There is almost always a service in progress in the basilica, while a slow-moving mechanical walkway carries an endless stream of pilgrims past the image of the Virgin. Behind the basilica a path winds uphill to the circular **Capilla del Pocito**, a small but ornate Baroque chapel beside a well.

Back toward the center, the **Plaza de las Tres Culturas** ③⑤ is hailed as a symbol of modern Mexico, with the fusion of two previous cultures (pre-Conquest and Spanish) to create a third, the mestizo Mexican synthesis. In the center of the square are the ruins of **Tlatelolco**, site of Tenochtitlán's biggest marketplace. Today the square is

The upsweeping modern steeple of the Basílica de Nuestra Señora de Guadalupe.

Saturday market, Plaza de San Jacinta.

Bullfighting may not be everybody's idea of fun, but it has been a part of Mexican culture for nearly 500 years.

There's no denying the popularity of bullfighting: in Mexico, there are 225 permanent arenas and around 500 improvised ones, hosting rough-and-ready fights during country fiestas. There are big differences between the kind of bullfights you can see in Mexico, for small-town *corridas* are often pretty chaotic affairs, where the "bullfighters" may be local boys with no experience, and the bull may be too valuable to kill, so that instead it is just chased around for a while.

The traditional Spanish-style bullfight seen in cities is a much more formal, stately ritual. The Plaza México in Mexico City is the biggest bullfighting arena in the world, seating 50,000 spectators. The season runs from late November to March or April.

A bullfight starts promptly at 4.30pm, even if the clock has to be turned back. The opening parade is led by a bailiff, followed by three *toreros*, resplendent in their *trajes de luces* – suits of light – all shiny silk, brilliant colors, and gold embroidery. Behind them come their assistants, the picadors (horsemen armed with lances), and lastly attendants with mules, to haul away the dead bulls. The ring *presidente* waves his

A torero, or matador, in the traditional traje de luces.

handkerchief, and the first bull rushes in. Weighing over 500kg (1,100lbs), he is a raging muscular combatant, itching to fight. The drama unfolds in three acts.

Act 1: The *torero* watches while his assistants handle the bull with their capes. Then he takes a few turns himself to test the animal's behavior. The *picadors* ride in, and push their lances into the muscular hump on the bull's back to expose the "cross" where the bullfighter will thrust his sword in the death stroke. Exit *picadors*, leaving a raging but weakened bull.

Act 2: The *torero's* assistants, or in some cases the bullfighter himself, plant three pairs of *banderillas* (barbed darts) into the bull's hump. The *banderillero* runs to the bull, plants the darts, and dexterously gets out of the way of the charging animal, which by this time is bleeding profusely.

Act 3: *La Hora de la Verdad* (The Moment of Truth). The *torero* asks permission to kill the bull and dedicates the kill. He then has 16 minutes to dispatch it, or be ordered from the ring in disgrace. He first works his magic on the bull with his heavy cape, working ever closer to the horns, before switching to a smaller flannel cape. When the bull has been so weakened that its head droops, the *torero* plunges his sword between the shoulder blades, going over the horns and into the "cross," where the sword can penetrate cleanly and sever an artery or puncture a lung. The bull drops to its knees and usually dies at once, although sometimes a *coup de grâce* has to be delivered.

Depending on his performance, the *torero* can be awarded an ear, two ears, two ears and the tail, and sometimes even a hoof. He does not always win though; many *toreros* are gored, and many are crippled or even die. If a bull puts up a particularly good fight, he can be pardoned and retired to stud, in the hope his sons will inherit his courage.

THE FUTURE OF THE BULLFIGHT

It may well be that the future of the bullfight in Mexico City is extremely limited. There have been numerous protests against the cruelty of the sport by those living in the capital. Mexico City's hallowed Plaza México has rarely been full in recent years, and at the time of writing new legislation to recognize the sentience of animals and the cruelty of blood sports was gaining unequivocal cross-party support.

also remembered for the hundreds massacred here on October 2, 1968, when government forces opened fire on student protesters.

OUTSIDE THE CENTER: SOUTH ALONG INSURGENTES

Avenida Insurgentes runs for 25km (15 miles) from the north of the city across Reforma to the south, where the colonial suburbs of San Ángel and Coyoacán offer a more tranquil side of Mexico City. The first landmark to look out for on Insurgentes Sur is the 50-story **World Trade Center**, which has a revolving restaurant on the top floor.

Attached to it is the unusual and seemingly haphazard **Polyforum Siqueiros** (daily 10am–6pm, sound and light shows Sat–Sun at noon and 2pm), a multi-faceted building designed by David Alfaro Siqueiros (see page 113). Inside the vast main hall is a mural – said to be the world's largest – entitled *The March of Humanity*, which is combined with a light and sound presentation. Another record breaker, just a few blocks farther south, is the **Plaza México**, Mexico City's bullring (see page 148).

The huge mosaic covering the **Teatro de los Insurgentes ㊱**, is by Rivera. Taking the history of theater in Mexico loosely as its subject, it includes many characters from Mexican history books, but pride of place goes to Cantinflas, the national hero of popular comedy, who appears Robin Hood-like, with outstretched arms, taking from the rich and giving to the poor.

SAN ÁNGEL

The fashionable "village" of **San Ángel** lay outside the city until well into the 20th century; it has now been encompassed by the urban sprawl, but has retained much of its charm. The delightful **Iglesia del Carmen**, with its tiled domes, serene cloister, and Churrigueresque altar, was once part of one of the wealthiest monasteries in the area. The convent buildings, now the **Museo de El Carmen ㊲** (Tue–Sun 10am–5pm), retain most of their frescoed walls, furniture, and paintings. However, most people head for

Gorditas, a specialty from La Villa de Guadalupe.

⚽ FÚTBOL!

South of Coyoacán, Santa Ursula Coapa is best known as the location of one of Latin America's soccer magnets, the Estadio Azteca, home to both the national team and one of the city's three big league clubs, Club América. Soccer history has been made in this, the world's ultimate soccer stadium, which can hold a whopping 105,000 spectators – several thousand more than Europe's greatest stadiums, Wembley and Camp Nou. It's also the only stadium to have hosted two World Cup finals, and it was here that Diego Maradona scored the famous "hand of God" goal against England that steered Argentina to the title. Games are spirited affairs, especially when Club América take on bitter rivals Guadalajara. Even neutrals get excited. Tickets are available at www.ticketmaster.com.mx.

the crypt to glimpse the eerie group of naturally mummified bodies of monks in glass-topped cases.

Up the hill, the 18th-century **Casa del Risco** (Tue–Sun 10am–5pm; free) is a lovely example of the district's old mansions, with a fountain composed of hundreds of gaily colored plates, cups, and vases. The house contains an eclectic collection of colonial art and hosts contemporary art shows.

You can still escape the city's bustle along these quiet, bougainvillea-shrouded streets. On Saturdays, crowds descend on San Ángel for the **Bazar Sábado** (see page 135), a handicrafts market with brightly colored stalls on normally sleepy Plaza San Jacinto.

A short walk away on Calle Altavista, the **San Ángel Inn** is one of Mexico's most seductively pretty restaurants, located in the stunning patios and gardens of the 18th-century Goycoechea hacienda, once an aristocrat's ranch. Around the corner is an essential visit – the Modernist, box-like twin buildings, designed in 1931 by Juan O'Gorman (see page 115), that make up the

Frida Kahlo Museum.

Museo Estudio Diego Rivera y Frida Kahlo ❸ (Tue–Sun 10am–5.30pm; free on Sun), where the artist and his equally celebrated partner Frida Kahlo worked in their separate homes, connected by a precarious-looking bridge, and where Rivera died in 1957.

The house will delight any Rivera admirer. On show are some of his later portraits and objects including his characteristic denim jacket, painting materials, newspaper cuttings, and his collection of masks. It is a five-minute walk back to Avenida Revolución and the **Museo Carrillo Gil** (Tue–Sun 10am–6pm; free on Sun), an airy modern building that houses another of Mexico City's fine collections of modern art.

COYOACÁN

After the fall of Tenochtitlán, Cortés set up his headquarters in Coyoacán, east of San Ángel. Still a separate town in the 1940s, it has long been a desirable neighborhood for artists, intellectuals and bohemians. On the corner of Londres and Allende, the **Museo Frida Kahlo** ❸ (www.museofridakahlo.org.mx; Tue

and Thu–Sun 10am–5.30pm, Wed 11am–5.30pm; ticket also valid for Museo Diego Rivera-Anahuacalli) is the bright "Blue House" where Frida was born, where she later lived with Rivera, where she returned whenever their relationship fell apart, and where she died in 1954. Beautifully intimate, it contains some of her work, an inspirational kitchen, and all kinds of memorabilia, including the couple's letters and Frida's dresses.

Three blocks away, the **Museo Casa de León Trotsky** 40 (Tue–Sun 10am–5pm), home of the exiled revolutionary in 1939–40, is surrounded by a high wall and watchtowers. Inside, it is kept almost exactly as when he worked here, with his library containing books in several languages. Bullet holes remain from a failed assassination attempt in 1940 (led by the Communist muralist Siqueiros); three months later, Trotsky was assassinated at his desk with an ice-pick by a Spanish Stalinist agent. His small tomb, by Juan O'Gorman, stands in the gardens, and there is an informative video on Trotsky's life in Mexico.

In the center of Coyoacán, the attractive **Plaza Hidalgo** and adjoining **Jardín del Centenario** have the feel of a real Mexican small-town plaza. They buzz with activity on weekends, and it is worth standing in line at the garden's kiosk, which sells some of the best ice cream in Mexico City. The 16th-century **Casa de Cortés**, now containing the tourist office, lines the north side of the plaza. This is said to be where the Spanish tortured the defeated Aztec emperor Cuauhtémoc – by burning his feet – to persuade him to reveal the whereabouts of his treasure. Opposite is the church of **San Juan Bautista**, begun in the 1560s. One block to the east is the **Museo Nacional de Culturas Populares** (Tue–Thu 10am–6pm, Fri–Sun 10am–8pm; free on Sun), a friendly museum with imaginative, multicolored exhibits covering all aspects of Mexican folk culture.

GARDENS AND WEDDINGS

To the west of Plaza Hidalgo, running away toward San Ángel, **Avenida Francisco Sosa** is one of the best-preserved colonial streets in Mexico City,

Diego Rivera and Frida Kahlo.

ⓞ FRIDA AND DIEGO

Diego Rivera (1886–1957) was already a major artistic figure when he married Frida Kahlo (1907–54) in 1929. In her lifetime he largely overshadowed her, but since the 1980s she has become an international cult figure probably even better known than the great Diego himself.

Rivera's art was very public. After studying in Paris, he returned to Mexico to become the most flamboyant figure in the Muralist movement which, given spectacular spaces to work on by the revolutionary government, deployed distinctively Mexican imagery to create a new sense of cultural identity. Frida's paintings, in contrast, were intensely personal. Aged 18 she nearly died in a bus accident, as a metal rail almost went through her body. She survived, but suffered near-constant pain and needed medical attention for the rest of her life. Her self-portraits often include nightmarish references to her accident, her miscarriages, and operations. A remarkable feature of Frida's work is the way it combines the experience of pain with a vivid energy, expressed in the rich colors that have themselves become part of Mexico's cultural backdrop.

Diego and Frida's tempestuous relationship is inseparable from their mystique. They were both leaders of Mexico's bohemian intelligentsia and met for the first time at a party hosted by the silent movie star Tina Modotti (her interest in him was purportedly initiated when, half-way through the party, he shot the phonograph). Rivera offered her encouragement with her painting and their relationship developed from there. It was also Rivera who suggested she wear traditional Mexican clothes, which, together with her jewelry, hairstyles, and untrimmed thick eyebrows, was even more radical at the time. Their love is immortalised in Mexico City's architecture – Rivera incorporated a likeness of Frida into his famous mural in the Ministry of Public Education – yet he was always unfaithful, and she also had many affairs, with men and women. They tormented each other, but also adored each other. In 1931 they had their "twin houses" built in San Ángel (now the Museo Estudio Diego Rivera y Frida Kahlo), linked by a bridge. In 1939 they divorced, but soon married again, although he stayed in San Ángel and she went back to her family's "Blue House" in Coyoacán. When she died, he was utterly devastated.

The Xochimilco trajineras are very distinctive little boats.

David Alfaro Siqueiros mural, Ciudad Universitaria.

lined with (now much-desired) 17th-century residences. Just to the north is another special feature of Coyoacán, the **Víveros**, a huge area set aside as nursery gardens, where flowers and trees are grown for sale and for use in parks, and where many locals grow their own produce in cooperative gardens. It is also a much-loved park, and a favorite with joggers.

East of Plaza Hidalgo is the picturesque **Plaza de la Conchita**, where the Capilla de la Concepción, with a rare Mudéjar-style facade, is popular for weddings. Overlooking the square is the Casa Colorada, said to have been built for La Malinche, Cortés' interpreter and mistress.

The **Museo Nacional de las Intervenciones** ❹ (Tue–Sun 9am–6pm), in the fortified former Convento de Churubusco, in the northeast of Coyoacán, traces the history of foreign interventions in Mexico's affairs since independence – by Spain, France, and, above all, the United States. Special tribute is paid to the *San Patricios*, Irish soldiers who deserted the US Army in 1847 to fight on the Mexican side, calling themselves St Patrick's Battalion.

About 3km (2 miles) south of central Coyoacán is the unusual **Museo Diego Rivera-Anahuacalli** ❹ (www.museoanahuacalli.org.mx; guided tours only Tue–Sun 11am–5.30pm; ticket also valid for Museo Frida Kahlo), conceived by Rivera himself to house his personal collection of pre-Hispanic art. The somber building of dark volcanic rock is reminiscent of an Aztec temple; aside from the ancient treasures, there are examples of his own work, and a superb view of the city and volcanoes.

CIUDAD UNIVERSITARIA

Farther south again, Insurgentes Sur crosses the vast 1950s campus of Mexico's National University (UNAM), the **Ciudad Universitaria** ❹, with its bold use of color, murals, and sculpture. The **Biblioteca Central** (Central Library) is an extraordinary 10-story block with walls entirely covered by a Juan O'Gorman stone mosaic, and there is another mural by Siqueiros behind the nearby **Rectoría** building.

Across the road, a Rivera mural adorns the **Estadio Olímpico**. Built for the 1968 Olympics and designed to resemble a volcano, the stadium holds up to 80,000 people.

The southern half of Ciudad Universitaria is home to **Universum** (Tue–Fri 9am–6pm, Sat–Sun 10am–6pm), an interactive science and technology center. Nearby is the **Museo Universitario Arte Contemporáneo** (https://muac.unam.mx; Wed, Fri and Sun 10am–6pm, Thu and Sat 10am–8pm) a modern glass and concrete wedge-shaped building filled with subversive modern works by local artists.

South of the university zone, Insurgentes meets the Anillo Periférico, a giant beltway around the city. Near the intersection is the oldest ceremonial center in the Valley of Mexico, the round pyramid of **Cuicuilco** ㊹ (daily 9am–5pm; free), occupied as early as 1000 BC but buried when the Xitle volcano erupted around AD 100. A little farther to the west is the **Estadio Azteca**, one of the world's biggest soccer stadiums (see page 149).

FLOATING GARDENS

The famous floating gardens of **Xochimilco** ㊺ (take the light rail line to Embarcadero from Tasqueña Metro) are the only remnant of the pre-Hispanic lake towns. They are a favorite place for a Sunday outing for local people, who come to eat, drink and be serenaded by *mariachis* on the flowery *trajineras* (boats). Weekdays are not as lively, but the cost can be lower (the hourly rate for a *trajinera*, around US$10 per hour for a whole boat or US$1.50 per person, is posted, but there's room for negotiation).

Just off the district's main plaza is the lovely 16th-century church of **San Bernardino**. At Avenida México 5843 (take the light rail to La Noria) is the **Museo Dolores Olmedo** (www.museodoloresolmedo.org.mx; Tue–Sun 10am–6pm; free on Tue). The late Dolores Olmedo was one of Rivera and Kahlo's foremost patrons, and her magnificent house, a former hacienda, displays an outstanding collection of their work and other 20th-century art.

The floating gardens at Xochimilco.

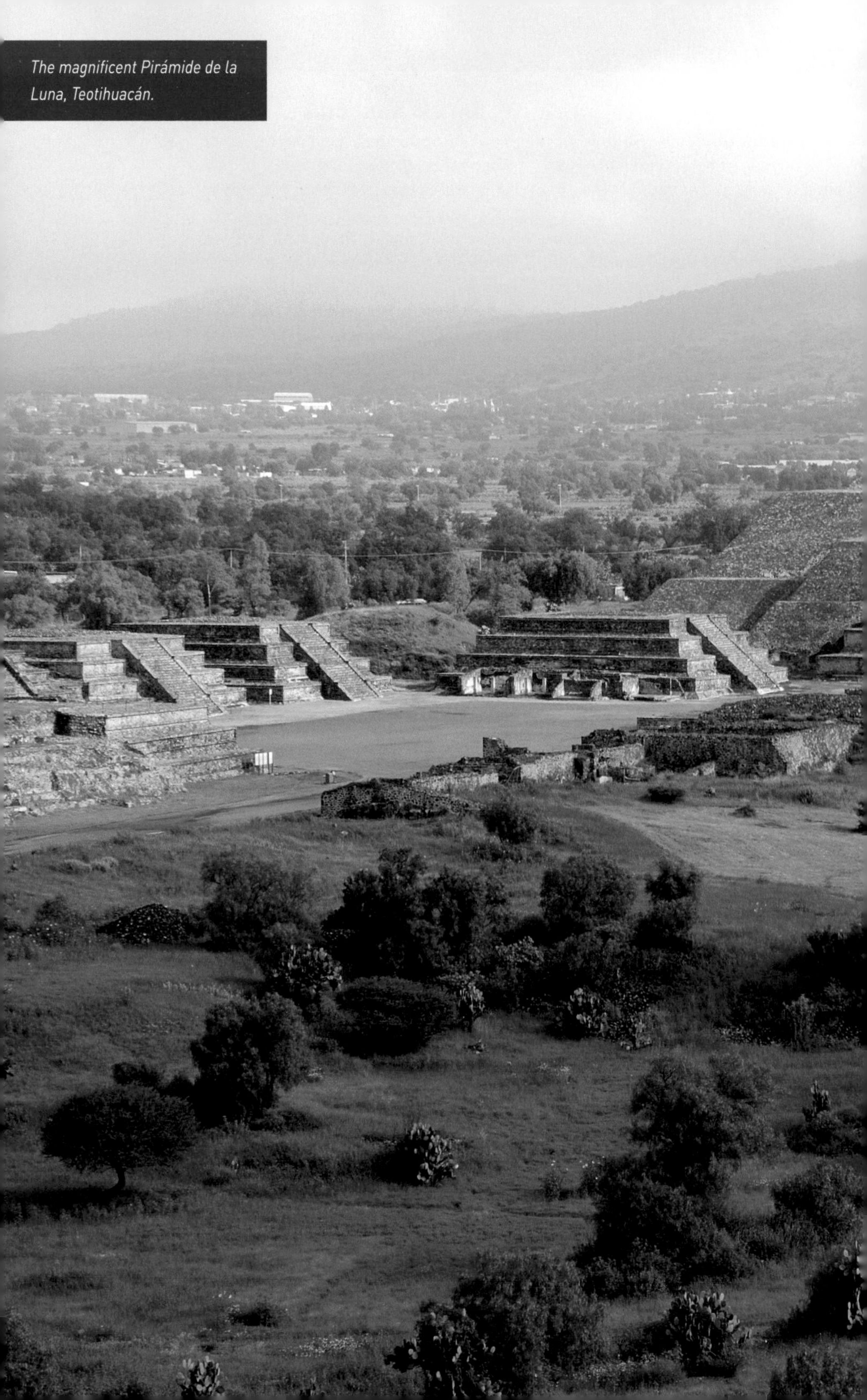

The magnificent Pirámide de la Luna, Teotihuacán.

The Atlantes of Tula once supported the roof of the Temple of the Morning Star.

AROUND MEXICO CITY

Massive pyramids, ornate Baroque buildings, snow-capped volcanoes, subtropical gardens ... whoever chooses Mexico City as a base will find interesting options in every direction.

México City

Although sprawling suburbs have engulfed much of the area around Mexico City, an hour or two's drive in almost any direction will introduce you to the heart of the country – a mosaic of peoples and characterful towns, and geography that ranges from cool, stately pine forests and snow-capped volcanoes to hot, humid valleys bursting with plant life.

NORTH TO TEPOTZOTLÁN AND TULA

Though now on the city fringes, the town of Tepotzotlán is about 35km (22 miles) north of central Mexico City, along the Querétaro road (Mexico Highway 57), which is a continuation of the Anillo Periférico boulevard that runs through the Bosque de Chapultepec. This passes through the **Ciudad Satélite**, a vast area of modern housing initially planned in the 1950s. Its main landmarks are the **Torres de Satélite**, a sculptural group of brightly colored modern towers by German-born artist Mathías Goeritz.

The magnificent Jesuit church and monastery of **Tepotzotlán ❶** are jewels of Mexican colonial art in themselves. The college of San Francisco Javier was founded in the 1580s as a school for indigenous children, but had been left in decay for years when it was made a museum in 1964. As the **Museo Nacional del Virreinato** (Viceroyalty Museum; tel: 55-5876 2270; http://

virreinato.inah.gob.mx; Tue–Sun 9am–4.45pm) it contains Mexico's foremost collection of colonial art.

The church of **San Francisco Javier** is one of the finest examples of Churrigueresque (see page 56) architecture in Mexico. The main nave dates from the 1670s, but the lavishly decorated stone facade and the carving on its single, graceful belfry were added in 1760–2. Inside, golden altarpieces appear to multiply like exotic tropical plants, transforming the walls into a mysterious, glittering curlicued

Main attractions
Tepotzotlán
Tula
Teotihuacán
Parque Nacional
  Iztaccíhuatl-
  Popocatépetl
Puebla
Cholula
Cuernavaca
Xochicalco
Taxco
Malinalco

Maps on pages
158, 160, 164

Tepotzotlán Sunday market.

Step by step to the top of Pirámide del Sol.

mass. It provides an inspiring frame for sculpture and paintings such as Miguel Cabrera's retablo of Our Lady of Guadalupe.

Baroque ornamentation reaches its dazzling extreme in the **Camarín de la Virgen**, a small octagonal side room that was used for dressing an image of the Virgin of Loreto, where every inch is covered with a riot of archangels, cherubim, fruit, flowers, and shells. It is reached through the Casa de Loreto, a little chapel said to be a "replica" of the house where the Virgin Mary lived in Nazareth. It has been said that Baroque style – especially in its most extravagant forms – goes hand in hand with the Mexican psyche: the lavish use of color and movement, and the excesses and unbounded imagination are seen as the soul of Mexican art.

The rest of the monastery, with graceful cloisters and delightfully shady gardens, houses ornaments, jewelry, furniture, clothing, and other objets d'art from the colonial period, as well as displays about life in Mexico under Spanish rule.

TULA AND THE TOLTECS

The ruins of ancient **Tula ❷** (daily 9am–5pm), capital of the Toltecs, are about 50km (30 miles) north of Tepotzotlán. Founded around AD 800–850, the city played a major role in Mesoamerican history. According to local chronicles, Topiltzin, Tula's semi-legendary founder, was expelled by followers of the warrior god Texcatlipoca, who dominated the city until it was destroyed 300 years later. In addition to being skilled artisans, the Toltec seem to have been a particularly warlike culture – even for ancient Mexico – and Tula was the most powerful city in the Central Highlands for around 250 years, with trading links over a huge area. However, many of its main buildings were destroyed by fire – due to an invasion, perhaps, or internal conflicts – and its power dwindled rapidly after about 1170.

The main pyramid is the **Tlahuizcalpantecuhtli** (Temple of the Morning Star), on top of which stand the **Atlantes** – massive basalt figures, 4.6 meters (15ft) tall, that once supported a wooden temple roof. They are Tula's

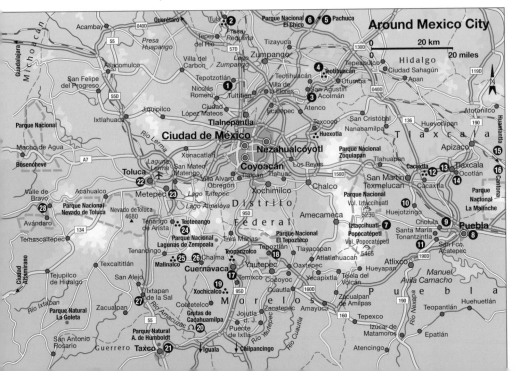

most distinctive contribution to Mexican art, giant images of Toltec warriors, armed with javelins and wearing pectoral adornments in the form of butterflies; on their backs are round shields representing the setting sun, with a human face at the center. The box-like headdresses are decorated with vertical feathers.

Of the other surviving structures, perhaps the most interesting is the **Coatepantli** or "Wall of Serpents," along the north side of the pyramid; 40 meters (130ft) long and more than 2 meters (6.5ft) high, its reliefs show snakes devouring human bodies. Nearby is the **Palacio Quemado** (Burnt Palace), once an exceptionally large palace complex, in front of which is the *chacmool*, the characteristic reclining figure holding a receptacle on which the hearts of sacrificial victims were placed.

TEOTIHUACÁN

Leaving Mexico City in another direction, northeast along Insurgentes Norte and then Highway 132, you will come to one of Mexico's unmissable sights, the immense ancient city of Teotihuacán, "the place where men become gods," 50km (31 miles) from the capital. For once, the over-used description "awe-inspiring" is really unavoidable.

On the way, look for the fortress-like **San Agustín Acolman** ❸ (Tue–Sun 9am–5pm), an imposing church with a fine plateresque facade from 1562. The monastery it served was one of the oldest in Mexico, founded in 1536, and like many missionary monasteries is fronted by a huge open atrium or square, built to hold open-air services for hundreds of recently converted indigenous people.

The setting of **Teotihuacán** ❹ (tel: 594-956 0276; daily 9am–5pm), in a bare, dusty valley, seems perhaps less exotic than those of Maya cities farther south, shrouded in tropical greenery. It impresses most by its majestic geometry and sheer scale, with vast pyramids

and structures lined up along the nearly 2km (1.5 miles) of the "Avenue of the Dead." Teotihuacán began life several hundred years before the Christian era, and the building of its first large structures began around 200 BC. At its zenith, from around AD 150 to 600, Teotihuacán was one of the biggest cities in the world, with a population of around 150,000 – some estimates go up to 250,000 – and an area of 20 sq km (8 sq miles), more extensive even than its contemporary, Imperial Rome. Its influence in politics, culture, and trade extended over a huge area, and, in the same way that ancient Rome contained communities from every part of the Mediterranean, Teotihuacán appears to have had areas inhabited by Maya, Zapotecs, and other peoples from many parts of Mesoamerica. Even so, Teotihuacán was also a virtually illiterate culture, so a great deal about it remains mysterious.

One of the principal "mysteries" of Teotihuacán is just how and why this city declined so rapidly, around 650. The most likely explanation, as in the case of the Maya, is a combination of agricultural

Pre-Hispanic anthropomorphic ceramic figure displayed in the museum at Teotihuacán.

View of Pirámide de la Luna across fields of cacti and wild flowers.

collapse due to overpopulation, drought, invasions by newer, competing cities, and internal revolt – several of Teotihuacán's major buildings seem to have been sacked and burnt around the same time. The shock waves of its collapse were felt throughout ancient Mexico. Teotihuacán's population dwindled away over the next centuries, but it was regarded with awe by all the later cultures of the Central Highlands, especially the Mexica and the Aztecs, who considered it almost the birthplace of civilization.

AROUND THE SITE

Buses from Mexico City drop you at **Gate 1**, in the southwest corner; drivers can continue north around the perimeter to several more gates and parking areas. At Gate 1, you walk up past stands selling clothing and souvenirs, and a small restaurant (there is also a delightful restaurant outside the site to the south, in the Villas Teotihuacán hotel). The site is so huge it rarely ever feels crowded.

Beyond the Gate 1 entrance you emerge at the south end of the **Calzada**

Architectural crenelation representing a bird, on view at the Teotihuacán Museum.

de los Muertos (Avenue of the Dead), the main axis, which stretches 3km (2 miles) north, past the Pyramid of the Sun to the Pyramid of the Moon. In front of you is a broad, sunken square that the Spaniards called the **Ciudadela** (Citadel), because it looked to them like a fortress, and which probably was indeed the primary residential area of the rulers of Teotihuacán. Within it is the **Templo de Quetzalcóatl**, a tiered temple decorated with alternating motifs of the feather-collared Serpent God, and the goggle eyes of the Rain God Tlaloc. The temple was discovered in the 1920s, hidden beneath a cruder later pyramid, probably added by the Toltecs in the 9th century.

To the north, the Avenue of the Dead is lined by smaller pyramids and temples, nearly all in a similar squat, square-sided style. Unmissable about halfway up on the east side is the gigantic **Pirámide del Sol** (Pyramid of the Sun), Teotihuacán's foremost landmark. Most of it had been built by around AD 100. The entire structure, with a base measuring almost 225

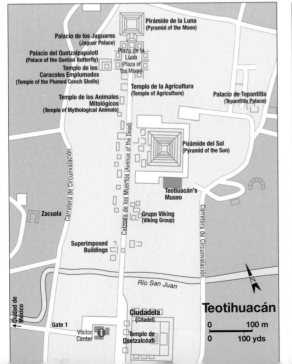

meters (738ft) square, was at one time covered in stucco and brightly painted. For an impressive overview of the city, a steep 248-step climb will take you up the 75 meters (246ft) to the top, where a temple once stood.

Below the pyramid on its south side is Teotihuacán's **museum**, which contains a fascinating scale model of the site, plenty of explanatory displays, and artifacts found here, although many others have been taken to the Anthropology Museum in Mexico City. There is also a restaurant and a shady botanical garden, ideal for a break in the tour.

On the northeast side of the site, the **Palacio de Tepantitla** contains Teotihuacán's finest surviving fresco, the *Paradise of Tlaloc* mural. A reproduction can also be seen in the Mexico City museum.

The **Pirámide de la Luna** (Pyramid of the Moon), though smaller than the Sun Pyramid, is built on higher ground and so their tops stand at the same level. It is also easier to climb. Overlooking a plaza at the northern end of the avenue, the Moon Pyramid is surrounded by a dozen small temples. Nearby, in the **Palacio del Quetzalpapalotl** (Palace of the Quetzal Butterfly), one of the largest residential complexes, there are well-preserved murals and stylized reliefs of creatures that are part bird and part butterfly. Also part of this complex are the **Palacio de los Jaguares** (Palace of the Jaguars), named for its feline mural painting, and the **Templo de los Caracoles Emplumados** (Temple of the Plumed Conch Shells) which still bears traces of the red, green, yellow and white symbols representing birds, maize, and water.

It's easy to spend a whole day at Teotihuacán, and any decent visit requires at least two hours (more than some bus tours allow). The pyramids are at their most impressive first thing in the morning or just before sunset. Like most great Mesoamerican cities, Teotihuacán was aligned with the heavens, and the Avenue of the Dead points precisely 15.5° east of north – just why, is another source of argument. Thousands flock here to greet the dawn on the Spring Equinox, March 21, when the site opens especially early.

⊘ Tip

The same tips that should be followed at all Mexico's ancient sites are even more applicable at Teotihuacán, given its huge size: be prepared for a lot of walking, and some stiff pyramid climbs. Take a snack, a hat, sunblock, and plenty of bottled water; the sun can be fierce and there's not much shade. Afternoon thunderstorms can occur in the summer months.

Mural on display at the Museo Manual Gamio, Teotihuacán.

Distinctive Talavera tiles are used in houses and buildings throughout Mexico.

One of the many ceramic masks found in the vast ancient city of Teotihuacán, and now on display in the site museum.

The surrounding countryside is of interest too. Just to the west is **Otumba**, where the Aztecs were defeated by Cortés in one of the major battles of the Conquest. The region is typical of central Mexico: desert plains and hills, and fields of maguey plants, from which *pulque*, one of Mesoamerica's oldest alcoholic beverages, is extracted. Strong, frothy, beer-like, and loaded with vitamins, *pulque* is said to be very nourishing (the best excuse in the world for a favorite drink). In the 19th century *pulque* plantations were developed, but it is now far less common than beer, which is much easier to produce and to transport.

HIDALGO

Tucked-away Hidalgo is one of Mexico's least visited yet most beautiful states. The capital **Pachuca ⑤**, 94km (58 miles) northeast of Mexico City, makes a good base. Its history is closely linked to its silver mines, worked at different times by Spanish, British, Mexican, and US mine owners. All have left their mark on Pachuca and the quaint town of

Mineral del Monte, especially the miners who came here from Cornwall in the 19th century. South of the Plaza de la Independencia, with its attractive clock tower, in a the 16th-century former Convento de San Francisco is the **Centro de las Artes de Hidalgo** (tel: 771-714 2853; Mon–Fri 10am–8pm, Sat 9am–2pm), which contains various exhibitions, and Mexico's **Fototeca Nacional** (National Photography Museum; Tue–Sun 10am–6pm), the core of which is the extraordinary archive of pioneer photographer Agustín Víctor Casasola, who took many famous images of the Mexican Revolution. There is also a collection of work by Tina Modotti, the Italian photographer who was inspired by Mexico in the 1920s.

Some 20km (12 miles) north of Pachuca, pine forests, lakes, and spectacular rock formations in the **Parque Nacional El Chico ⑥** provide great hiking and climbing terrain. Within the park is **Mineral del Chico**, a picturesque old mining town now one of the most recent of Mexico's *pueblos magicos* (magic towns), defined as such by tourism

⊙ POPO AND IZTA

Mexico City's valley is a volatile place, surrounded by volcanoes – most famously the majestic Popocatépetl (5,465 meters/17,926ft) and Iztaccíhuatl (5,230 meters/17,155ft), affectionately known as *El Popo* and *Izta*. In the past these enormous snow-capped peaks formed a backdrop to the city, 60km (40 miles) away; nowadays, it's a talking point if they are not obscured by smog, but they still make an impressive sight when traveling east toward Puebla or the Gulf – or coming in to land at Mexico City airport. According to legend, Popocatépetl (Náhuatl for "Smoking Mountain") was a warrior in love with Iztaccíhuatl ("White Lady" or "Sleeping Woman," with the four summits representing the head, breast, knees, and feet of the reclining Aztec princess). Fearing her lover had been killed in battle, Iztaccíhuatl died of grief, and when Popo returned alive, he laid her body on the hill where he stands sentinel beside her.

El Popo has been quite active in the past few decades, with regular eruptions in 2016, meaning that access is frequently barred. Izta is much quieter, and can still be explored. The road from Amecameca is open as far as the Paso de Cortés, the saddle over which the conquistadores entered the Valley of Mexico in 1519, from where footpaths lead around the lower levels. Only experienced climbers with a guide should attempt to go higher: several Mexico City agencies offer treks.

authorities because they offer a particularly special experience for visitors.

Monday is market day in **Ixmiquilpan**, 75km (47 miles) northwest of Pachuca along the Highway 85 Querétaro road, and the chief town of the Otomí people, Hidalgo state's original inhabitants. This is the best day to see the beautiful Otomí textiles and fine inlaid woodwork; on the way, stop off at **Actopan** to see the 16th-century San Nicolás Tolentino monastery. Farther on beyond Ixmiquilpan are the waterfalls, hot springs, and caves of the **Grutas de Tolantongo**, a spectacular box canyon.

EAST OF MEXICO CITY

The road to Puebla and the east coast is a continuation of the great avenue called **Calzada Ignacio Zaragoza**, the backbone of proletarian Mexico City. It runs eastward through the sprawling suburb of **Ciudad Nezahualcóyotl** (also known just as Neza), with a population of nearly 3 million, and sometimes called Mexico's third-largest city.

Once the road leaves the urban area behind, it enters the beautiful pine-forested mountains near the **Parque Nacional Iztaccíhuatl-Popocaté-petl** ➐. The volcanoes loom very close, and the climate becomes cooler. The road to these magnificent snow-capped wonders is reached via a turn-off through the pleasant hill town of **Amecameca**, in a green, pastoral landscape.

PUEBLA: CITY OF THE ANGELS

After crossing the mountains, the road descends into the ample valley of **Puebla** ➑, culturally one of the richest of Mexico's colonial cities, known both for the uniquely colorful style of its historic buildings, many clad in Talavera tiles, and the special qualities of its cuisine. In spite of being a growing industrial center, with an enormous Volkswagen auto plant, Puebla has preserved a good deal of its old character, and possesses some of the most impressive colonial art and architecture in Mexico.

One such gem is the elegant **cathedral** ➊, the second largest in the country. Overlooking, naturally, the main square, it was consecrated in 1649, and combines the refined architecture of the

Spanish colonial coat of arms on the facade of a Puebla house.

Basaltic prisms, near Hidalgo.

○ Eat

Puebla's traditional cuisine, *cocina poblana*, is celebrated throughout Mexico: among its most popular specialties are *chile en nogada*, green chili stuffed with meat, white walnut sauce and red pomegranate seeds – the colors of the Mexican flag – and *mole poblano*, a rich savory chocolate and chili sauce. The Fonda Santa Clara, almost opposite the Museo Bello, has long been renowned for its typical Puebla dishes.

Spanish Renaissance with more ornate Baroque styles. The exterior is severe and somber, while inside the main altar, another work by Manuel Tolsá, is like a miniature Roman temple. The angel statues around the atrium are symbols of the town, the original name of which was "Puebla de los Angeles."

The tourist office is beside the cathedral, almost next door to the **Casa de la Cultura** (tel: 222-246 3186; Mon–Fri 10am–5pm, Sat–Sun 9am–4pm, later for concerts; free). Occupying the former Bishop's Palace from 1646, with a lovely Puebla facade in brick and tile, the center has a sculpture garden and an open-air theater. Up the stone stairs is the splendid **Biblioteca Palafoxiana** Ⓑ (Mon–Fri 10am–5pm, Sat and Sun 10am–4pm), the oldest library in America, with 50,000 volumes on ornately carved wooden shelves.

Two blocks west, the **Museo José Luis Bello y González** Ⓒ (tel: 222-232 9475; Tue–Sun 10am–6pm; free on Tue) contains a fascinating collection of decorative art amassed by a local industrialist in the 19th century, displayed in ornate

rooms in his former home. Back to the south of the cathedral, the untypically high-tech **Museo Amparo** Ⓓ (tel: 222-229 3850; www.museoamparo.com; Mon, Wed–Fri, Sun 10am–6pm, Sat until 9pm; free on Mon and Sun), in an 18th-century former hospital, has interactive, multilingual displays to complement its beautifully presented collections of pre-Hispanic artifacts and colonial art and furniture. On the corner of calles 2 Sur and 3 Oriente – behind the cathedral – is the **Casa del que Mató al Animal** (House of the Man who Killed the Animal), a 16th-century house, now a newspaper office, which retains a spectacular Renaissance carved portico with images of a hunter and his dogs.

The 18th-century **Casa de los Muñecos** Ⓔ (House of Puppets), now the University Museum (tel: 222-246 2899; daily 10am–6pm; free on Wed) has the most amusing of Puebla's tiled facades, with panels portraying 16 apparently dancing figures, allegedly caricatures of the first owner's enemies. On the first floor there is also an elegant restaurant.

Puebla

0 ___ 400 m
0 ___ 400 yds

One block east along Avenida Juan de Palafox y Mendoza, the **Templo de la Compañía de Jesús ⒻF**, with its elaborate facade, is said to be the last resting place of the celebrated **China Poblana**, a 17th-century Asian princess who was adopted by a local merchant, and whose statue surmounts a fountain at the east side of town. Her costume of frilly blouses atop embroidered, sequinned skirts have become part of local tradition. Adjoining the church, bordering a cobblestone alley, is the 16th-century Puebla University building, first built as a Jesuit college. A short walk up Calle 4 Norte leads to the **Museo Poblano de Arte Virreinal ⒼG** (tel: 222-246 6618; Tue–Sun 10am–5pm; free on Sun), another fine collection of colonial art in the former Hospital de San Diego, dating from 1647, with a beautifully restored cloister.

The vendors at Puebla's main tourist market, **El Parián ⒽH** (daily), sell everything Mexican, from *serapes* to *piñatas*, but are especially strong on Puebla ceramics. If it's pictures you're after, cross the road and wander through the open studios of the **Barrio del Artista ⒤I**.

Puebla's traditional architecture is a very Mexican adaptation of Spanish Baroque, with the characteristic addition of color, and expressed in a profusion of tiles and plaster decoration. Perhaps the finest example is the sugar-icing stucco, set off against red walls, of the **Casa del Alfeñique ⒥J** (an *alfeñique* is a kind of sugar-and-almond meringue). The interior houses the **Museo Regional**, **containing** fine Puebla ceramics, and memorabilia from the 1862 Battle of Puebla against the French. The museum was forced to close when the building was badly damaged in a September 2017 earthquake, but reopened in late 2018. Just beyond the "artists' quarter," the **Teatro Principal ⓀK** was almost 150 years old – one of the oldest in the Americas – when it suffered a disastrous fire in 1902, after which it had to be rebuilt.

Calle 6 Oriente is a fascinating street, renowned for its *dulcerías*, candy stores with beautiful displays of exquisite handmade confections. There

The splendid ornamentation on the dome of Santo Domingo church.

⊘ THE TALAVERA OF PUEBLA

Talavera pottery is everywhere in Puebla: there are tiles, bowls, vases, flowerpots, jugs, and sculptures. The technique, combining earthenware with a tin-based enamel glaze, takes its name from Talavera de la Reina in Spain, and was introduced into Mexico around 1550, probably by craftsmen from Talavera brought here by Dominican friars to teach new skills to the indigenous people. The original pottery was cobalt blue and white, with strong Moorish motifs, but the Mexican potters added their own touches and also received influences from China and Renaissance Italy. This led to the introduction of new designs and colors, particularly greens, yellows and oranges. Using the original technique, it takes six months to produce one piece of authentic Talavera pottery, and it is fairly easy to distinguish the earthy mineral colours of these items from the bolder hues of mass-produced copies (there is also a difference in price).

There are naturally plenty of shops around Puebla selling local ceramics. The historic Uriarte factory, on Calle 4 Poniente, has a beautiful shop and also offers tours (www.uriartetalavera.com.mx; Mon–Sat 11am, noon, 1pm) that explain the process from beginning to end: first the clay is left to stand for three months, and then wedged underfoot until it is well kneaded; after another month, the piece of pottery is made and left to dry before it is fired, painted, glazed, and fired again.

⊙ Tip

Archeologists have excavated as much as 8km (5 miles) of tunnels inside the Great Pyramid of Cholula, revealing some of the many stages of its construction. Before entering this well-lit warren, have a look at the large cut-away model of the pyramid in the museum opposite the tunnel entrance.

are *camotes* (sweet potatoes with pineapple and sugar), fudge-like *dulce de leche*, limes filled with sweet coconut, and *rompope*, a sort of eggnog, often a child's introduction to alcohol.

The church of **San Cristóbal ⓛ** has sumptuous stucco carvings. One of the first battles of the 1910 revolution took place next door; this was then the house of Aquiles Serdán, a leading liberal conspirator, and in November 1910 he and his family were besieged here by the troops of Porfirio Díaz, firing back from the balconies (the bullet-holes have been preserved). It now houses the **Museo de la Revolución Mexicana ⓜ** (tel: 222-242 1076; Tue–Sun 10am–6pm; free on Tue). Looking west up Calle 6 Oriente you can see the cast-iron structure of the **Mercado de la Victoria**, transformed into a modern shopping mall.

Two ex-convents north of the center are worth discovering. The austere **Ex-Convento de Santa Mónica ⓝ** (tel: 222-232 0170; Tue–Sun 10am–5pm), founded in 1606, was officially closed by the Reform Laws of 1857, but a community of nuns lived on here in secret until 1934.

Today, as the **Museo de Arte Religioso**, it is particularly focused on the life of women in religious houses. Nearby, the **Ex-Convento de Santa Rosa ⓞ** (tel: 222-232 7792; Tue–Sun 10am–5pm; free), also 17th-century, is now a **Museo de Arte Popular**, with a wonderful display of the many crafts of Puebla state. A highlight is the beautiful vaulted kitchen of the convent itself, covered with traditional Puebla tiles. Mexico's famous *mole* sauce (made from, among other ingredients, chocolate, almonds, and chili) is said to have been invented by nuns in this very room. Ongoing refurbishment means some portions of the museum may be closed.

About half a kilometre north of here is the rather fascinating **Museo Nacional de los Ferrocarriles Mexicanos** (Museum of Mexican Railroads; Tue–Sun 9am–5pm), housed in the former train station.

The pride of Puebla's religious architecture, however, is on the way back to the center, tucked away inside the 16th-century **Santo Domingo ⓟ** church: the breathtaking **Capilla del**

Plazuela de los Sapos, Puebla.

Rosario, to the left of the main altar, is a dazzling mass of Baroque gilt decoration, with a host of angels and a heavenly chorus.

CHOLULA AND THE VILLAGES OF PUEBLA

Cholula ❾ is now almost a suburb of Puebla, but it was a major center from around AD 600 up until the Conquest, when it was one of the largest cities in the Central Highlands after Tenochtit-lán. In 1519, Cortés, claiming to fear an ambush, made an example of Cholula by massacring some 3,000 of the city's elite. Then, after being depleted by plague, Cholula rapidly dwindled in size.

Modern Cholula is famous for its many churches; according to tradition, the conquistadors vowed to build one for every pagan temple they found or, alternatively, one for each day of the year. The fortified **Convento de San Gabriel** is the most impressive, its massive walls lining the east side of the attractive **Zócalo** (main square). On one side of the convent atrium is the **Capilla Real**. Originally an open chapel for holding Mass, its roof, with 49 little domes, was added in the 18th century. Sadly, the September 2017 earthquake badly damaged this site, although parts remain open while repairs are underway.

Most people come to Cholula to see what looks like an ordinary hill with a church on top. In fact, this is the **Gran Pirámide** (tel: 222-247 9081; daily 9am–6pm), the largest pyramid and largest man-made structure anywhere in the world, with the Náhuatl name *Tlachi-hualtépetl*, or "handmade mountain." Like all pre-Hispanic pyramids it was built up over centuries; in the final phase, the entire pyramid was covered with a thick layer of adobe, which over time became covered in vegetation. Only part of the pyramid has been excavated, but you can enter tunnels within it, and there are remains of fine murals. From the top, beside the earthquake-battered church of **Nuestra Señora de los Remedios**, there's naturally a superb view.

The villages around Puebla state are rich in folk traditions. **Huejotzingo** ❿, about 14km (9 miles) northwest of Cholula, is a small town known mainly

The queen of one of Puebla's many fiestas poses in full regalia.

View from Nuestra Señora de los Remedios, Cholula.

Church of the Virgin of Ocotlan, Tlaxcala.

for its cider, woolen *serapes* and its **Carnaval**, usually in February, highlights of which are masked dances that re-enact a battle against the French. Just off the main square is the impressive 16th-century **Convento Franciscano** (Tue–Sun 10am–5pm), with original frescoes and artifacts that illustrate life in the early Spanish missions.

Santa María Tonantzintla ⓫, just south of Cholula on the old road to Oaxaca, has a remarkable folk-Baroque church with an interior entirely covered with colorful, vibrant carvings. The decor took 200 years to complete, and is a wonderful example of the way indigenous artisans adopted Spanish iconography. The dazzling tiled facade of the church of **San Francisco Acatepec**, a couple of miles farther south, is one of the region's unmissable sights. Damaged by fire in the 1930s, it was restored in every detail.

INTO TLAXCALA

In the neighboring state of Tlaxcala, 18km (11 miles) west of the state capital is **Cacaxtla** ⓬ (tel: 246-416 0000; daily 9am–5.30pm), "the place where the rain dies in the earth." Once the chief center for a people called the Olmeca-Xicalanca, it flourished between AD 400 and 1000. It was virtually unnoticed until 1975, but excavations of the huge, 200-meter (660ft) platform known as the *Gran Basamento* have revealed some of the best-preserved ancient murals in Mexico, notably the 22-meter (72ft) *Mural de la Batalla*, which vigorously depicts a battle between jaguar and eagle warriors. Only 2km (1.5 miles) away is **Xochitécatl**, a smaller but older site that may have been a subordinate community to Cacaxtla.

The town of **Tlaxcala** ⓭, capital of Mexico's smallest state, is one of its hidden colonial treasures. The center has been beautifully restored, and thanks to a traffic control scheme its plazas are unusually tranquil. Although they lived only 115km (70 miles) from the Aztec capital, the Tlaxcalans always managed to maintain their independence. When Hernán Cortés arrived in 1519, they became crucial allies in the conquest of Tenochtitlán. A mural by local artist Desiderio

Hernández Xochitiotzin, in the **Palacio de Gobierno** on the Zócalo, tells the story.

South of the Zócalo, a steep walk uphill leads to the **Convento de San Francisco**, with a beautiful view over the city and its bullring. The church – which is now the city's cathedral – has a Moorish-style wooden ceiling and the font used to baptize the four Tlaxcalan chiefs; the monastery buildings now house the **Museo Regional** (tel: 246-462 0262; Tue–Sun 10am–5pm), with a fascinating collection of local pre-Hispanic pieces.

Also worth discovering is the **Museo Vivo de Artes y Tradiciones Populares** (tel: 246-462 0262; Tue–Sun 10am–6pm), a "living museum" where local craftspeople demonstrate the intricate work involved in producing Tlaxcala's wonderful handicrafts, which are on sale in the museum shop.

Perched on a hill above Tlaxcala, in the village of **Ocotlán** ⓮, is a twin-towered church that seems as lightly spun as sugar candy. This is the 18th-century **Basílica de Ocotlán**, another of Mexico's most ornate Churrigueresque churches, which was built in honor of an apparition of the Virgin said to have occurred here in 1541. The explosion of Baroque giltwork inside is dazzling.

To the east, **Huamantla** ⓯ is famed for its celebration of the Feast of the Assumption (August 15), when the town is covered in flower carpets, which are destroyed in the following days by the *huamantlada*, when bulls run through the streets Pamplona-style. The **Museo Nacional del Títere** (National Puppet Museum; tel: 247-472 1033; Tue–Sun 10am–6pm) on the main square houses an interesting collection of puppets. Beyond Huamantla a lonely road leads back into Puebla state to a dirt-track for **Cantona** ⓰ (site daily 9am–6pm, museum Wed–Sun 9am–6pm), an archeological site that may have been one of the largest Mesoamerican cities, extending over 12 sq km (5 sq miles). It was at its peak in the late Classic era, about AD 700–1000.

SOUTH: CUERNAVACA AND MORELOS

Mexico City's Insurgentes Sur joins the road to **Cuernavaca** ⓱. After an initial climb, the road descends in 75km (47 miles) to an altitude substantially lower than that of the capital. Cuernavaca, capital of Morelos state, is also a week-end resort where *capitalinos* go for clean air, a pleasant climate and relaxation. It has always attracted the capital's elite: Aztec emperors built temples here, and Cortés a palace; artists, retired North Americans, and even the fugitive Shah of Iran have also chosen to settle in this flower-filled "city of eternal spring." In the 1930s, writer Malcolm Lowry (using its Náhuatl name, *Quauhnahuac*) made it one of Mexico's mythical cities in his novel *Under the Volcano*, as the place where his British Consul drinks himself to death. More recently – in contrast – exhilarating landscapes, the fine climate, and fast-flowing rivers have made Cuernavaca and Morelos one of Mexico's most popular areas for adventure and health tourism. The city itself has grown rapidly, but a weekend here

Fragment of an ancient mural, Cacaxtla Anthropology Museum.

still comes as a welcome escape from the cacophony of the metropolis.

In the center of town, the **Plaza de Armas** is flanked by the **Palacio de Cortés** (tel: 777-312 6996; Tue–Sun 9am–6pm), which the conqueror had built on the ruins of a pre-Hispanic temple. It now houses the **Museo Cuauhnáhuac**, a substantial collection of pre-Hispanic and colonial artifacts from the surrounding area. There is also a series of murals by Diego Rivera (see page 112) depicting 400 years of Mexican history, from the Conquest to the Revolution. For decades, teachers have been challenging Mexican children to identify the heroes and villains of their national saga.

Jardín Juárez, off the square's northwest corner, has a bandstand designed by Gustav Eiffel, who designed the famous Paris tower, where you can buy fresh fruit juice or *licuados* to sip in the shade of the flame trees.

Two blocks west up Calle Hidalgo, the imposing **cathedral** stands in a high-walled, fortified garden. Like the palacio it was begun in the first years after the Conquest, in a massive, plain

style. Inside, some curiously Oriental frescoes were discovered during renovation work in 1959. They seem to depict the mass crucifixion of missionaries in Japan, and are believed to have been painted in the 17th century by a Japanese Christian convert. The Sunday Mass (11am) with *mariachi* musicians is famous all over Mexico.

Also part of the *recinto* or cathedral compound is the **Museo Casa Robert Brady** (tel: 777-318 8554; Tue–Sun 10am–6pm). Brady, a wealthy US artist and collector, lived and worked in Cuernavaca until his death in 1986, and the museum exhibits his extraordinary collection of art, antiques, and crafts from Mexico and other parts of the world. Nearby, in the **Palacio Municipal** (daily 9am–6pm; free), paintings around the courtyard give a romantic vision of local history.

A great deal of Cuernavaca's beauty lies behind high walls in private gardens. However, the prettiest of them, the **Jardín Borda** (tel: 777-318 6200; Tue–Sun 10am–5.30pm; free on Sun), created in the 1780s around the home of Taxco's

Dominican Monastery cloisters, Tepoztlán.

richest silver magnate, is public. Inside its walls, there are fountains, terraces, an artificial lake with row boats for rent, and an outdoor theater. The museum, in part of the old house, has exhibits from the time when this was the summer residence of Maximilian and María Carlota, and their favorite place in all Mexico.

Aside from the large **market** (northeast of the center) and the underwhelming **Teopanzolco Pyramid** (daily 9am–5pm), in a park farther east (a bus or taxi ride), these are the specific attractions of Cuernavaca. It is also known, though, for its excellent luxury hotels. The **Hacienda de Cortés** and **Las Mañanitas** are two of the most opulent. If you've ever dreamed of staying in a place with a beautiful, flower-filled garden where fountains tinkle and peacocks strut; of sleeping in a room filled with period furniture and eating first-rate food, now is the time to indulge. The restaurants are open to non-guests too.

MORELOS STATE

Morelos is the sugar bowl of Mexico. The conquistadors brought sugar cane here,

and during the dictatorship of Porfirio Díaz local *hacendados* seized huge areas of land to plant sugar for export. This laid the seed for agrarian revolution, and Morelos was also home to the Mexican Revolution's most legendary leader, Emiliano Zapata, born in Anenecuilco, a village near Cuautla. Villages around the state still display his portrait: the huge bristling moustache, the *charro* jacket, the sombrero, and the deep, sad look that is ever present in his eyes.

Tepoztlán ⑱ is an attractive town nestling at the foot of the Tepozteco mountain, 26km (16 miles) northeast of Cuernavaca. Its center is dominated by a massive **Dominican Monastery** (Tue–Sun 10am–5pm; free) and its church, built in a near-medieval style in the 1560s. Behind the church, the small **Museo Arqueológico Carlos Pellicer** (Tue–Sun 10am–6pm) has a remarkably good collection of pre-Hispanic pieces. It is a strenuous one-hour hike up to the **Tepozteco Pyramid** (daily 9am–5.30pm), a temple dedicated to Tepoztécatl, Aztec god of fertility and *pulque*. The climb is rewarded with an awe-inspiring view

One of the steep, cobbled streets in the pretty town of Taxco.

Plaza flanked by colorful buildings, Cuernavaca.

Modern architecture in Toluca.

Main ball court, Xochicalco.

of the Tepoztlán valley. With a special atmosphere and balmy climate, Tepoztlán has become an ecotourism and New Age travel hub. A craft market draws the crowds on Sundays, as do the Carnaval celebrations in February and a *pulque* festival in September.

Heading south from Cuernavaca on the old road to Taxco, a short detour leads to the spectacular archeological site of **Xochicalco** ⑲ (daily 9am–5pm), "place of the house of flowers" in Náhuatl. It is one of the most significant sites in the Highlands, covering 25 hectares (62 acres), and flourished between the 7th and 10th centuries, bridging the gap between the decline of Teotihuacán and the rise of later cultures. Sometimes called the crossroads of Ancient Mexico, Xochicalco was declared a Unesco World Heritage site in 1999. The most striking monument is the **Pirámide de Quetzalcóatl** (Temple of the Plumed Serpent), with superb bas-reliefs, at the summit of the terraced platforms. The **Grutas de Cacahuamilpa** ⑳ (guided tours every hour, daily 9am–5pm) caves are unmissable: enormous, intriguing, but forbidding for the claustrophobic. The main tour takes you through just 2km (1 mile) of well-lit paths, past vast chambers with extraordinary rock formations.

SILVER TOWN: TAXCO

Taxco ㉑, Mexico's most famous silver-working town, is 72km (45 miles) south of Cuernavaca and about a third of the way between Mexico City and Acapulco. It is truly picturesque: red-roofed white-washed houses, pretty plazas, cascading bougainvillea, and narrow, cobbled streets twist up and down the steep hills. All tend to lead to the **Zócalo** or main square, overlooked by the pink stone Baroque church of **Santa Prisca**. Completed in 1758, with twin, 40-meter (130ft) towers, its elaborate Churrigueresque facade and tiled dome are more than matched by the dazzling gilded interior. Take special notice of the fine German organ and delicately carved woodwork. The church was entirely paid for by José de la Borda, a Spaniard who redeveloped Taxco's silver

mines in the 18th century and became one of the richest men in Mexico.

To the right as you leave the church is the **Casa Borda** (tel: 762-622 6634; daily 10am–7pm; free), a humble house built in 1759 by the town's wealthy patron for the church priest. It is now a cultural center, with exhibits on local themes. There are a number of jewelry stores nearby selling a rich selection of fine local work. It was William (Guillermo) Spratling, an architect from New Orleans, who sparked off Taxco's modern jewelry boom when he opened the first silver workshop here in the early 1930s, after silver-working had been neglected in the town for centuries. Spratling's apprentices went solo, and today there are more than 300 shops in Taxco, selling an enormous variety of silver work, including some of the finest in the world.

Behind Santa Prisca church, the **Museo de Taxco Guillermo Spratling** (tel: 762-622 1660; Tue–Sat 9am–5pm, Sun to 3pm), Spratling's home until his death in a car accident in 1967, houses his private collection of pre-Hispanic art and antiquities. There is also a small section on local history.

The **Casa Humboldt**, on Calle Juan Ruiz de Alarcón, is one of Taxco's oldest colonial houses, and so-named because the German explorer-scientist and traveler Baron Alexander von Humboldt (1769–1859) stayed a night there in 1803. With an exquisitely ornate facade, this beautiful Moorish-style house now contains the **Museo de Arte Virreinal** (tel: 762-622 5501; Tue–Sun 9am–5pm), a miscellaneous collection of religious artifacts and other items. Easter is a major festival in Taxco, when hotels are often fully booked well in advance.

WEST TO TOLUCA

Many roads connect Mexico City with **Toluca ㉒**, capital of Mexico state and only an hour's bus journey west of the capital, climbing through surprising countryside with pine forests reminiscent of Germany, before typical Mexican landscapes reassert themselves in dry, golden fields, cacti, and adobe houses. Toluca's proximity to the capital has aided its industrial growth,

Picturesque Taxco.

◎ Tip

The lakeside promenade is the center of life on warm weekend nights in Valle de Bravo, lined with restaurants, shops, bars, and clubs, some on rafts floating on the lake. The busiest times are during the Festival Vallesano in March and the Festival de las Almas at the end of October, when the town hosts a whole range of arts and sport events.

and its airport is now promoted as an alternative entry point for Mexico City, 60km (38 miles) away. Toluca's Friday **open-air market** (in the outskirts, near the bus station), reputedly the largest in Mexico, draws huge crowds.

The center of Toluca is typically provincial with colonial churches, a large square (Plaza de los Mártires) and 120 *portales* (arcades). Look for the local specialties – fruit jam, spicy *chorizo* sausages, and *moscos,* orange-based liqueurs served from bottles with long spouts that are known for being *muy traidores* (very treacherous).

One block north of the square, in a magnificent old Art Nouveau former market on Plaza Garibay, is the **Cosmovitral** (Tue–Sat 10am–6pm, Sun to 3pm), a beautiful indoor botanical garden, lit by brilliantly colored stained-glass panels. The best of the area's traditional arts and crafts can be found in the **Museo de Culturas Populares**, one of three museums in the **Centro Cultural Mexiquense** (tel: 722-274 1222; Tue–Sat 10am–6pm, Sun to 3pm; free), 8km (5 miles) west of the city. This ambitious center also

The Cosmovitral stained-glass mural.

contains museums of anthropology and modern art.

MEXICO STATE

Metepec ㉓, now almost a suburb of Toluca, is famed for its craftworkers and especially its colorful ceramic trees of life, offering a very Mexican interpretation of the story of Adam and Eve. Farther south, above Tenango del Valle, are the hilltop ruins of **Teotenango** ㉔ (Tue–Sat 10am–6pm, Sun to 3pm), a fortified center first built up around 750, and later taken over by a people called the Matlatzincas, who were conquered in turn by the Aztecs. Across to the west is the majestic extinct volcano, the **Nevado de Toluca**, 4,680 meters (15,354ft) high.

Not far from Teotenango is the site of **Malinalco** ㉕ (Tue–Sun 9am–5pm), in a spectacular location high up on a rocky crag. First built by the Matlatzinca culture, it was soon taken over by the Aztecs, and the Emperor Ahuitzotl began large-scale building here in 1501 that was still unfinished when the Spaniards arrived. The main

temple, the **Cuauhcalli** (House of the Eagle Warriors), was carved into the face of the mountain itself, and used for initiation ceremonies of young Aztec nobles into the warrior elite. The entrance has the form of the tongue and giant mouth of a fanged serpent, and images of sacred eagles, serpents, and jaguars abound throughout the site. The nearby town of Malinalco has become a fashionable weekend getaway, with a golf club and plenty of shops and restaurants.

Several times a year pilgrims swarm to the village of **Chalma** ㉖, 12km (7 miles) farther east, to worship the Santo Señor de Chalma, an image of Christ said to have appeared miraculously in 1533. It is one of Mexico's most revered shrines, after Guadalupe.

Farther south on the main Taxco road (Mexico 55) is the spa resort of **Ixtapan de la Sal** ㉗, semitropical and flowery, whose mineral waters are said to have rejuvenating properties. On the outskirts of town is the **Parque Acuático Ixtapán** (tel: 800-493 2726; daily, water park 9am–6pm, spa

8am–7pm, hours liable to change during the year; charges depend on activities). Here you can head for the slides and wave machines, swim in the Olympic-sized pool, or relax in Roman-style baths with massage, mud, and beauty treatments. There are also several hotel spas.

One of the state's most popular destinations is away to the west at **Valle de Bravo** ㉘, a picturesque colonial town 80km (50 miles) from Toluca, which acquired a beautiful lake due to a 1940s hydroelectric scheme. Weekend visitors, including many foreigners, enjoy the idyllic mountain scenery and the attractive hotels and cottages overlooking the lake. Watersport enthusiasts are well catered for, while other popular activities include paragliding, horseback riding, golf, and hiking.

To the west and northwest, the remote mountains of Piedra Herrada and **Cerro Pelón** contain valleys that are wintering-grounds for monarch butterflies, and are less exploited than similar locations in Michoacán (see page 237).

Parque Alameda, Toluca.

Unwinding at a bathhouse at Ixtapan de la Sal.

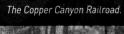

A charro astride his horse.

THE NORTH

South of the border is not just a buffer zone; this often bypassed region has natural and cultural gems all of its own.

Alamos doorway.

The fact that most of northern Mexico is not tourist country is one of its main attractions. This rugged land is starkly beautiful, a region of desert landscapes with huge and varied cacti, lofty mountains, and high plateaus. Renowned for its vast cattle ranches, it is Mexico's Wild West. It also contains some of the country's most fertile agricultural land.

Sadly, recent drug-related crime has overshadowed the many reasons tourists should take the time to come here: ancient ruins, peaceful towns, and beautiful architecture make it well worth visiting, and crime is rarely directed at tourists. In fact, you're far more likely to make friends here.

Baja California is becoming a destination in its own right, and for good reason. One of the world's longest peninsulas, Baja stretches more than 1,600km (1,000 miles) with two of the world's prettiest ocean bodies on either side: to the west, the Pacific, which surfers have long known as paradise; to the east, the Sea of Cortés, with placid lagoons and stunning vistas; in the middle, some of the most curious plant and animal life on the planet; visit parts of Baja and you'll feel like you're visiting the moon. Some of the towns, such as Todos Santos and Loreto, once quiet one-horse villages, are developing fast with big hotels and resort-style development on the horizon; others

Bay of Loreto National Park.

feel more like American suburbs, albeit with much better food. Much of Baja's fame rests now on the beaches and the massive Californian gray whales cavorting in their breeding waters at Scammon's Lagoon.

The far north of mainland Mexico – the vast and monotonous Sonora Desert, the imposing Sierra Madre, and the sprawling industrialized cities – is usually visited en route to somewhere else. But the interminable, barren landscape also conceals some outstanding surprises: the pre-Hispanic Paquimé ruins at Casas Grandes or – the highlight of any trip to northern Mexico – the world's most spectacular train journey, from Chihuahua to Los Mochis, through the breathtaking scenery of the Copper Canyon, one of the world's deepest canyons. And Chihuahua, with its cathedral, broad plazas, and locals clad in cowboy garb, seems like a stopover in yesteryear.

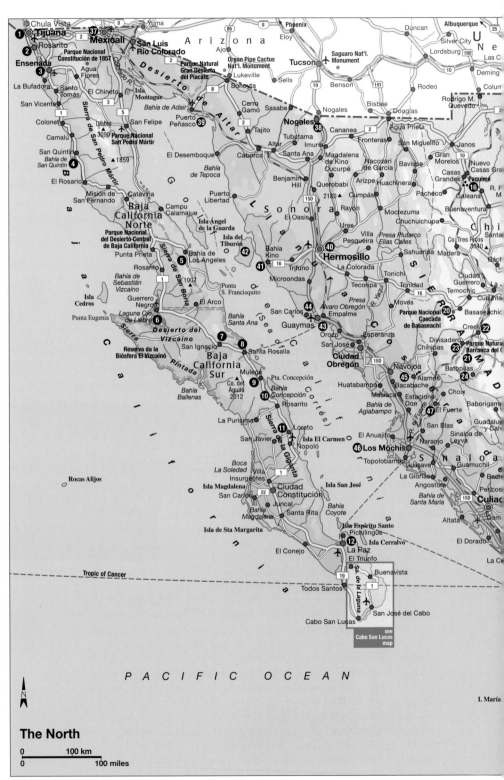

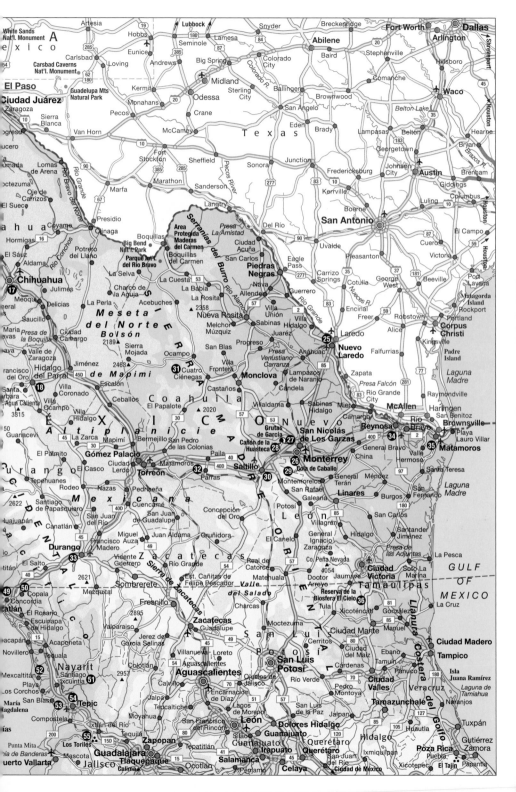

Beach near Loreto.

BAJA CALIFORNIA

Mountains, deserts, and thousands of kilometers of coastline are here for exploring, snorkeling, whale-watching, diving, and some of the best deep-sea fishing in the world.

Highway 1, the 1,690km (1,050-mile) road that spans the peninsula from Tijuana to Los Cabos, didn't even exist until 1973 and although there are half a dozen shorter subsidiary routes, hundreds of kilometers of Baja's coastline and almost all the interior can be comfortably reached only by four-wheel-drive vehicles. While some people deplore this inaccessibility, the majority of Baja fans rejoice in their knowledge of a land that – though a very close neighbor to California and its teeming millions – remains largely unexplored.

The peninsula was opened, Christianized, and depopulated by the Spanish missionaries; in just a few decades, the missions – intended to spread salvation – spread plagues and diseases that depleted the native populations, and with it, their culture. Most missions were subsequently abandoned; their ruins, remote and slowly eroding, make for wonderful photos and interesting side treks, but only a few, such as the one in Loreto, still function today. Pre-European Baja culture is found in intricate, ethereal paintings on cave walls, on pottery, and in legends and lore.

Baja's population and its economy are both concentrated in the north. Bumper crops are produced in the irrigated lands around Mexicali: cotton, alfalfa, wheat, tomatoes, and grapes. Recently

Gulf grouper, Cabo Pulmo National Park.

Baja's wineries have received international recognition, and there's even a Wine Country route north of Ensenada that tourists can follow, tippling as they go. Workers in northern Baja get the highest minimum wage in the country.

ON THE BORDER

There are three major crossings into Baja at the California border – **Tijuana**, **Tecate,** and **Mexicali** – all connected by Highway 2. These places are fun but be aware that staying out after midnight, purchasing drugs or other illegal

Main attractions

Tijuana
Ensenada Wine Country
San Pedro Mártir National
  Park
Bahía de Los Ángeles
Laguna Ojo de Liebre
Santa Rosalia
Mulegé
La Paz
Espiritu Santo
San José del Cabo

Maps on pages
180, 191

⊘ Tip

Don't forget to get your passport stamped at the border if you plan to travel south beyond the "free zone" (Ensenada/San Felipe) either by bus or by car. Currently, anyone crossing the border – including US citizens – will need a passport to enter Mexico and re-enter the US by land.

items, or being rowdy or obnoxious can lead to problems with the police. Drug-related crime is unfortunately high; the best way to avoid trouble is to pass on offers of illicit goods. Needless to say, Mexico already has enough problems created by the demand for drugs.

TIJUANA

Once a rip-roaring, shoot 'em up, anything-goes border town and still living up to its reputation in some ways, **Tijuana ❶** is now one of Mexico's busiest and most prosperous cities. It also claims to be the most-visited border city in the world, with more than 2 million people crossing each year.

Because Tijuana is a duty-free zone, imported goods can be surprisingly inexpensive and there are bargains to be found in Russian caviar, Spanish leather, French perfume, and even Cuban cigars (shoppers should not plan on buying anything illegal here that they plan to bring into the United States: you may be arrested and illegal goods will be confiscated, including non over-the-counter medications for which you do not have

a doctor's prescription). The city's main drag, Avenida Revolución, is lined with popular bars, nightclubs, craft stores, and clothing and jewelry stores mixed among those selling *serapes* and sandals, but shoppers will find even more variety in the Plaza Río Tijuana (www.plazariotijuana.com.mx; daily 10am–8pm) near the river, the largest shopping center in northwestern Mexico. For a massive selection of footwear, head for the Plaza del Zapato (Mon–Sat 10am–8.30pm, Sun until 6pm) within the Plaza Fiesta. While TJ has seen a lot of bad press due to a resurgence of drug-related crime, it's unlikely you'll have problems if you're moderately careful. Caution is advised after 9 or 10pm.

The distinctive red **Tijuana Trolley** runs between the city's main sight-seeing attractions (there is also a San Diego trolley link), but it's a pleasant stroll back northward on Via Poniente along the river. It will bring you to an older, funkier shopping center, **Pueblo Amigo,** which comes alive at night.

TIJUANA ATTRACTIONS

Behind the Plaza Revolución is the **Museo de Cera** (Wax Museum; tel: 664-688 2478; Mon–Fri 10am–5pm, Sat–Sun 10am–6pm), whose motley inhabitants range from Madonna, Mahatma Gandhi, and the Pope to Mexican revolutionary heroes and a gray-haired lady known as **Tía Juana** (Aunt Jane), the legendary *cantina* owner after whom the city was named. The ultra-modern **Centro Cultural** (Cultural Center; tel: 664-687 9600; www.cecut.gob.mx; daily 9am–9pm), with its comprehensive survey of Mexican history, adjoins a building that resembles a giant golf ball. This is the concert hall and 26-meter (85ft) high **Omnimax Theater** where movies about Mexico's history and culture are shown regularly, some in English.

Tijuana is in Mexico's wine-growing region, and the **L.A. Cetto Winery** (Avenida Cañon Johnson 2108; tel:

Mariachi band, Tijuana.

664-636 9200; call for an appointment) offers tours of the vast cellars and wine tasting. **Mundo Divertido** (Fun World; tel: 664-701 7133; www.mundodivertido. com.mx; Mon–Fri noon–9pm, Sat–Sun noon–10pm; free park entry, ride prices vary), at Paseo de los Héroes and José María Velasco, in Zona Río, is a family-oriented amusement park with miniature golf, a roller coaster, miniature train rides, batting cages, video games, go-karts, and more.

The highway west of Tijuana leads to the **Plaza Monumental** bullring, 10km (6 miles) away, beside the sea. Bullfights take place (either here or at the older bullring downtown) on Sundays at 4.30pm during the season, which runs from May to September. There are inexpensive motels along the seashore road and stands selling coconut drinks and seafood.

ROSARITO

The expensive *cuota* toll road to Ensenada includes stretches of fine scenery as it passes along a series of cliffs overlooking the Pacific Ocean (the *libre*, or free road, runs parallel most of the way). About 27km (17 miles) south of the border is **Rosarito ➋**, an over-commercialized town with a good swimming beach, which gained celebrity status after 1927, when the newly opened Rosarito Beach Hotel began to attract the Hollywood crowd and other famous faces. Pacific lobster is a favorite in the town's numerous restaurants and there is even a so-called "Lobster Village" – **Puerto Nuevo** – 10km (6 miles) to the south, where this dish is widely available and uniformly overpriced.

ENSENADA

As you enter the big city of **Ensenada ➌** (population 370,000), 113km (70 miles) south of the border, turn right off Highway 1 and drive up Avenida Alemán into the Chapultepec Hills, a high-rent district that offers a magnificent view of the city set around Todos Santos Bay.

A busy port, Ensenada is a regular stop for cruise ships and the farthest south that the vast majority of tourists penetrate. A favorite haunt of fishermen, it tags itself "the yellowtail capital of the world," with surf fishing along the rocky shoreline and organized trips from the sport-fishing piers off Boulevard Lázaro Cárdenas. In winter, whale-watching trips are also popular. The city stages various regattas and, in November, a noted off-road race.

Ensenada is the center of the area's wine industry, and there are winery tours every day except Sunday at the **Bodegas de Santo Tomás** (Miramar 666; tel: 646-178 3333; www.santo-tomas.com). The main tourist shopping zone is along **Avenida López Mateos**, a few blocks from the bay, but prices are lower around Avenida Ruíz and Calle 11, where every other store or bar seems to bear the name Hussong. The original Hussong's *cantina* (Avenida Ruíz 113; tel: 646-178 3210; www. cantinahussongs.com), with its dusty floor

Mexican flag, Ensenada.

Sea lions resting off Ensenada.

and time-polished wood, is a popular drinking place, and visitors from all over the world have been pinning samples of their currency to the walls for a century. Visit the fish market, at the end of Avenida Macheros, to sample the fish *tacos*.

South of town take the turn-off to **La Bufadora**, where incoming waves are forced into a narrow "V"-shaped wedge, causing great jets of sea water to spout over 18 meters (60ft) into the air, spraying amused spectators. Incoming tides are best, and it is a good idea to consult the *Baja Sun* for the tide timetable.

SAN PEDRO MÁRTIR

Back on Highway 1, at **San Telmo de Abajo**, just south of Colonet, a reasonably good road (in the dry season) heads east to the sprawling Meling Ranch (tel: 646-240 5115; http://ranchomeling.com). You can stay here in comfortable quarters, swim in the pool, and ride horses into the mountainous **Parque Nacional San Pedro Mártir**, with its beautiful oak and pine forests.

La Bufadora.

The National Observatory is located near the highest peak, the **Picacho del Diablo** (3,090 meters/10,135ft).

Productive agricultural land surrounds **San Quintín**, a small town strung out along the highway. To reach the best place for an overnight stop, turn right off the highway just south of the military camp at Lázaro Cárdenas and drive 5km (3 miles) along the unpaved road to the **Old Mill**, a reminder that this area was once colonized by an English land company that went bankrupt; the names of the almost forgotten pioneers are recorded on a group of lonely graves by the shore. The wild peninsula along **Bahía de San Quintín** ❹ is a well-loved camping area for the cognoscenti, whose favorite pastimes include fishing and digging for "chocolate-tipped" clams.

CATAVIÑA

South of San Quintín the road veers inland and you will begin to see the spidery *cirio* trees (*Idria columnaris*) that bear tiny yellow flowers and are sometimes referred to as **boojum** after the mythical species described by Lewis Carroll in *The Hunting of the Snark*. Gigantic boulders carpet the landscape here. Heading southeast, past **Cataviña** (an unexpected oasis with a Pemex station) the road climbs over the summit of the sierra, then drops into the arid bed of **Laguna Chapala**. Near the south end of the boojum area, a paved side road branches east to **Bahía de Los Ángeles** ❺, on the calm waters of the Gulf of California. Protected by the aptly named **Isla Ángel de la Guarda** (Guardian Angel Island), the fishing and shelling here are great; dolphins can often be seen in the bay, and the waters teem with fish; the tiny island of **Isla de la Raza** is a wildlife refuge. The town itself still has few facilities – a minuscule museum, a store, and a couple of hotels and trailer parks

– but the views are splendid and the setting idyllic.

GUERRERO NEGRO

Back on the main road, going south, you reach the 28th parallel, where a looming metal sculpture marks the boundary between Baja California Norte and Baja California Sur. Acres of shallow saltwater ponds lie just beyond this border, at **Guerrero Negro**, the largest salt plant of its kind, producing one-third of the world's supply, where guided ecological tours are available. The town has hotels, restaurants, stores, and gas, although only from January through March is it of much interest to tourists, many of whom come to watch the whales in the **Laguna Ojo de Liebre** ⑥. Scammon's Lagoon, as it is also known, is at the end of a dirt road several kilometers south of town, past the salt-evaporating ponds.

From Guerrero Negro, the highway cuts across the peninsula to the Sea of Cortés. A mandatory stop should be made at tiny **San Ignacio** ⑦, whose plaza, lined with shady laurel trees, is dominated by the San Ignacio mission. Built by the Dominicans in 1786, with 1.2-meter (4ft) thick walls and a vaulted ceiling, it replaced an earlier (1728) Jesuit mission. The church, with its perfect symmetry and Baroque facade, is a delightful example of what is left of colonial architecture in Baja California. An oasis of almost 100,000 date palms, sustained by an underground spring which surfaces here, has become the basis of the town's economy. Remember to set your watches one hour earlier as you cross south into Baja California Sur.

THE SEA OF CORTÉS

After many dramatic curves, Highway 1 reaches the coast, 73km (45 miles) beyond San Ignacio, at **Santa Rosalía** ⑧. In 1887, a French company opened the El Boleo copper mine here. The company left in 1954, but the small wooden houses from the French era still give the town a curiously anomalous look; indeed,

Gray whales near Guerrero Negro.

Road to Cataviña.

⊙ Fact

Baja California is twice as long as Florida, but much skinnier. A great crack in the San Andreas fault created the Gulf of California millions of years ago; the water is 3,290 meters (1,800 fathoms) deep off La Paz.

author John Steinbeck called it the "least Mexican-style city" he had seen. Unexpectedly, Santa Barbara Church, one block from the plaza, was designed by Gustav Eiffel, the French engineer responsible for the famous Parisian tower. This prefabricated metal structure won second prize at the 1889 Universal Exposition in Paris; it was later acquired by the El Boleo company, shipped over from France and assembled here.

From Santa Rosalía, an overnight ferry crosses the Gulf to **Guaymas** on the Sonora coast. Otherwise you can follow the Transpeninsular Highway down the dry Gulf Coast to **Mulegé ❾**. Threatening US warships were frightened away from here by a locally orchestrated subterfuge during the Mexican-American war in 1847. In July and August the town is stiflingly hot, but usually the palm trees and plantings along the Río Santa Rosalía make Mulegé a pleasant oasis. There's a wonderfully situated 1766 mission church on the outskirts of town, and a fortress-like museum – a

jail until 1975 – up the hill. Snorkeling, diving, and fishing are all popular activities, and there are ancient **cave paintings**, now a Unesco World Heritage site, in the San Francisco mountain range.

South of Mulegé the highway skirts the shore, offering tantalizing glimpses of delightful coves and bays that are only accessible with a four-wheel-drive vehicle. Framed to the east by a northward-pointing peninsula, the 40km (25-mile) long **Bahía Concepción ❿** is particularly renowned for its enticing camping beaches, all with at least a few facilities such as restrooms, trash cans, and sheltering *palapas* (beach shacks). Most of the rocks between the beaches are occupied by morose pelicans, gazing silently at the sea.

LORETO

Loreto ⓫, about 136km (85 miles) farther south, was the site of the first permanent mission and for 130 years the capital of Baja. After it was leveled by a storm in 1828, the capital was moved

⊙ WHALE-WATCHING

For centuries, gray whales have traveled from Alaska's icy Bering Sea to mate and spawn in the warm, shallow waters off the coast of Baja California. It takes these gentle giants two or three months to complete the 9,500km (5,900-mile) journey, the longest migration of any mammal. They arrive between December and January and stay until March, or sometimes as late as June.

In 1857 the breeding ground was discovered by a rapacious whaling captain from Maine, Charles M. Scammon – hence Scammon's Lagoon (aka Laguna Ojo de Liebre). For the next 100 years the whales were hunted almost to extinction until, in 1972, the area became the world's first whale sanctuary, the Parque Natural de Ballena Gris. Nearby Guerrero Negro (Black Warrior) is named after a British whaling boat that was wrecked off the coast soon after.

Today's hunters come armed only with binoculars and cameras and the gray whale population has almost fully recovered. Early morning or late in the day are the best times for whale-watching, either from the shore (or observation tower by Scammon's Lagoon), or else from locally chartered

boats, which provide an even closer view of these magnificent, 15-meter (49ft) long, 35 ton plus leviathans.

You don't have to have a skiff to view these gentle creatures either. In peak season, simply pull over to the curb and scan the water for a while – chances are you'll see a whale, sometimes a whole pod, surfacing out there to breathe. Other behavior you may catch (if you're lucky) is full or partial breaching (where the animal leaps out of the water), fluke slaps (where it slaps the water with its tail), or flipper waves.

There are several key places to "gray whale watch," including Laguna Oja de Liebre (Scammon's Lagoon) near Guerrero Negro half-way down the peninsula, the Bahia San Ignacio a little farther south, and, increasingly, Bahia Magdalena just south again. During the main viewing months of January through April, multiple boat trips run up and down the Baja coastline.

It is a little-touted fact, but other whale species are also prevalent in the Baja area – finbacks and blue whales – and plenty of opportunities for catching a glimpse of them and the other marine wildlife around the peninsula's coast.

to the pearling center at La Paz. The twin towers on the restored mission were replaced using money won by the local priest in the national lottery. The town's main street is named after the Jesuit priest Juan María Salvatierra, who established and ran the mission here for 20 years. The tourist complex at **Nopoló**, 25km (15 miles) south of Loreto, has amenities for sports such as golf and tennis, and a pleasant marina.

EN ROUTE TO LA PAZ

The scenery south of Loreto is spectacular; lovely beaches and the reddish-brown slopes of the Sierra de la Giganta sometimes distract attention from the dangerous curves and steep switchbacks on the highway. In the fertile Santo Domingo valley, **Ciudad Constitución** is a fast-growing, busy agricultural center with some of the ambiance of the old American West. Highway 22 heads west from here 57km (36 miles) to the Pacific port of **San Carlos**, a small fishing town overlooking Bahía Magdalena, the largest bay on Baja's Pacific coast, which shelters a commercial fishing fleet and, during the spawning season, Californian gray whales.

Early in the 20th century there were steamboat connections from **La Paz** ⑫ to other Baja ports; now there are daily ferries to Topolobampo on the Sonora coast. La Paz, the capital of Baja California Sur, is a delightful city with a population of almost 200,000. Its streets, with their old colonial buildings, are shaded by coconut palms and laurel trees and, in the spring, blossoming jacaranda, acacia, and flame trees add to the splendor.

Aside from its celebrated sport fishing, La Paz is famous for its spectacular sunsets – best viewed from the terrace café of the popular Hotel Perla, on Paseo Alvaro Obregón (the local **tourist office** has a branch office two blocks from the seafront, on Av. 16 de Septiembre). If you have the time, it is worth visiting the **Biblioteca de las Californias** (Library of California's History; Mon–Fri 9am–4pm) inside the Casa

Mulegé church.

de Gobierno opposite the cathedral on the town square, and the **Museo de Antropología** (daily 8am–6pm), on Altamirano, for information and exhibitions on Baja's history. There is also an aquarium, a serpentarium, and a cactus sanctuary to entertain and educate visitors. Good boat trips to remote beaches and islands where you can snorkel with sealions can be found along the **Malecon**. La Paz is a favorite vacation town for Mexicans, so prices are lower here and those seeking a more authentic Mexico may prefer this peaceful city to the resort-filled Cabos.

Northward out of La Paz, the road goes up the **Pichilingue** peninsula, past the ferry terminal to lovely bays and beaches at **Balandra** and **Tecolote**; there is a bus every hour from La Paz. Another popular destination is the island of **Espíritu Santo** (8km/5 miles offshore), uninhabited today, but once known as the "isla de perlas" after Cortés harvested black pearls here in the 16th century. After centuries of exploitation, the pearl

trade finally came to an end in the 1940s when a mysterious disease wiped out the oyster beds of La Paz.

Though off the beaten path just south of La Paz, the towns of Barriles and Buenavista are excellent for anyone wishing to windsurf – at certain times of year the prevailing winds across the Sea of Cortés are so perfect that you can see hundreds of colorful sails zipping around in the water. Sport fishing and other water sports are also prime attractions. Those wanting fewer people but similar trade winds can head to La Ventana, less than an hour east of La Paz.

LOS CABOS

Of the two famous *cabos* (capes) at Baja's southern tip, **San José del Cabo ⑬** is by far the less glitzy and more typically picturesque. The 32km (20-mile) strip of highway between the two is filling up with resorts, golf courses, and all the trappings of a developing tourist region, but San José itself, at the eastern end of the "corridor," remains relatively

Bahía Concepción.

unspoiled. Rent a bicycle or car, or walk to the beach at **La Playita**, where you can dine on freshly caught seafood, go fishing in a *panga*, or just admire the estuary, home to thousands of birds.

This area has more to offer than its coastal charms: just inland, south of the intersection of Carretera Transpeninsula and Highway 19, is the wild, Unesco-protected **Reserva de la Biosfera Sierra de la Laguna** ⓮: rocky hills and pine and oak forest containing a huge variety of wildlife ranging from coyotes and grey foxes to cougars. Hiking here is remote and due care should be taken.

The highway continues on down to the tip of Baja at **Cabo San Lucas** ⓯, a former supply station for the Spanish treasure galleons from Manila and now a major tourist center bulging with bars, cafés, nightspots, and dozens of luxury hotels; some have private beaches and their own landing strips for small aircraft. On a Saturday night, with two or three cruise ships moored in the bay, you'll find

little difference between Cabo and a college fraternity party, and for many, that's all part of the attraction. Come here and plan on feeling like you've stepped into a Jimmy Buffet song.

The tides in the Gulf are powerful and tricky, and the wind is strong. This means small boats are difficult to handle and it can be very dangerous. You can charter a boat with an experienced local crew at the marina; this is also the place to take glass-bottomed boat trips **to El Arco**, the natural stone arch at the southernmost point of the peninsula.

From the town of Cabo San Lucas you can make your way back to La Paz along the Pacific coast on a good but partially unpaved road past some lovely lonely beaches, though the ocean is rough. The road leaves the coast near **Todos Santos**, a quaint, quiet, surfing and art community, which stands exactly on the Tropic of Cancer. Rumor has it that the "original" Hotel California is here. From Todos Santos, the road loops back across the peninsula to La Paz.

Playa del Amor, Cabo San Lucas.

Adobe house fronts in Cabo San Lucas.

The Paquimé ruins.

THROUGH THE SIERRAS

The mountainous north is different from the rest of the country; this is Mexico's Wild West, where men wear Stetsons not sombreros.

México City

Heading south from the US (Texas) border, you will be confronted by two great mountain ranges, the Sierra Madre Occidental in the west and the Sierra Madre Oriental in the east. The former is by far the more rugged of the two. Between Ciudad Juárez, on the US border, and Guadalajara, 1,600km (1,000 miles) farther south, there are only a few major ways to cross the mountains to the Pacific coast: the railroad from Chihuahua City to Los Mochis, the highway between Chihuahua and Hermosillo (and from there to Guaymas) or, much farther south, the road from Durango to Mazatlán.

STATE OF CHIHUAHUA

About 300km (186 miles) south of Ciudad Juárez, **Paquimé** ⑯ (tel: 636-692 4140; Tue–Sun 8am–5pm), also known as Casas Grande (the name of the surrounding township), is the most important archeological site in northern Mexico. A Unesco World Heritage site, the ruin is a series of beautifully eroded adobe walls and structures, many still preserved in clear detail. Key-shaped entryways and cages for scarlet macaws, which the culture revered, are some of the intriguing legacy of the Paquimé, who lived here from around AD 900. Additionally, they knew how to irrigate the land and build three-story adobe houses. Once an important trading center, Paquimé

combines elements of the Pueblo civilization from the southwestern United States along with Mesoamerican influences. The town was abandoned around 1300, possibly after attacks by Apaches. Paquimé-style pottery is made, using ancient techniques, in Mata Ortiz, a small town located 55km (34 miles) south of Nuevo Casas Grandes – about an hour's drive away. This small town has recently been rediscovered, and the pottery, created using a technique called burnishing which produces a highly polished surface without the use of traditional glaze, is a

Main attractions
Paquimé
Chihuahua City
Hidalgo del Parral
Cuauhtémoc
Cascada de Basaseachic
Barranca del Cobre
Creel
Cuatro Ciénagas
Parras

Map on page 180

Traditional weaving technique.

hot collector's item. Visits to Mata Ortiz can be done either through pre-arranged tours – one company is Agave Lindo Tours (tel: 636-103 6004) – or by taxi from Nuevo Casas Grandes. You will tour the humble homes where the artisans work, and perhaps dine at one of the town's tiny restaurants. Despite the simple way of life and the apparent poverty, the pottery is quite expensive and collectors should plan on bringing plenty of pesos if they wish to take something home.

Founded in 1709, **Chihuahua City** ⑰, with a population of 800,000 and some fine colonial buildings, is worth more than a casual look. Quinta Luz, the 30-room mansion belonging to Pancho Villa, is now the **Museo Histórico de la Revolución** (tel: 614-416 2958; Tue–Sat 9am–1pm, 3–7pm, Sun 9am–5pm). Among the assorted memorabilia is the bullet-riddled Dodge car in which the bandit-turned-hero of the Revolution was gunned down in 1923. Señora Luz Corral de Villa, one of his many female companions, lived here until her death in 1981.

On the main plaza, the twin-towered Baroque **Catedral Metropolitana,** built

Palacio de Gobierno.

in the 18th and early 19th centuries, is one of the few outstanding gems of colonial architecture to be found in the north of Mexico. It was financed by voluntary contributions from miners working in the nearby silver mines.

An aqueduct and the church of **San Francisco** (daily 7.30am–1pm, 4.30–8pm; free) also date from colonial times. Stunning murals inside the **Palacio de Gobierno** (tel: 614-429 3596; daily 8am–6pm; free) tell the history of Chihuahua, while in the inner courtyard stands a monument to Father Miguel Hidalgo, hero of the War of Independence, who was executed here. You can visit the grim dungeon in **Casa Chihuahua** (Wed–Mon 10am–6pm; free on Sun), the former Palacio Federal on the other side of the central Plaza Mayor, where he was imprisoned while awaiting his fate. Another mansion, **Quinta Gameros**, dates from the turn of the century and now houses the **Museo Regional** (tel: 614-410 5474; www.uach.mx; Tue–Sun 11am–2pm, 4–7pm), with elaborate Art Nouveau exhibits and a display of Paquimé artifacts. The house was built as a gift from the owner to his fiancée, but during the construction she fell in love with the architect instead. Chihuahua is well known for rearing great artists, and one of the most famous is Sebastián, internationally recognised for his elaborate metal sculptures. Models of his work are represented in Casa **Siglo XIX** (tel: 614-200 4800; daily 9am–6pm).

HIDALGO DEL PARRAL AND PANCHO VILLA

Driving south from Chihuahua City you will see the state's richest agricultural regions. It is here that they grow many of Mexico's famous chili peppers. Silver was once the main support of the economy in the prosperous old mining town of **Hidalgo del Parral** ⑱. Nearby mines are still active; indeed the star attraction of the city is **Mina La Prieta** (Tue–Sun 10am–5pm), going strong since 1629. Malachite and other ores are currently extracted, but visitors can descend nearly 90 metres in an old elevator to the second of what was originally 25 levels.

The fine 18th-century church of **Nuestra Señora del Rayo** (Our Lady of the Light) is said to have been paid for in ingots by a local man who had struck gold but refused to reveal the location of the mine, even when beaten and tortured to death. Another fine church, **Nuestra Señora de Fátima**, is built entirely out of ore-bearing rock – gold, silver, copper, lead, zinc – right down to the pews inside.

Parral, as it is often called, is notorious as the town where General Francisco "Pancho" Villa was assassinated in 1923. Museo Francisco Villa (tel: 627-525 3292; Tue–Sun 10am–5pm) is a small museum near the center, which contains old photos and a number of mementoes. Some years ago the government decided to rank Villa in with the country's other revolutionary heroes, and his grave was dug up, then the body reburied in the Monument to the Revolution in Mexico City.

The villages around **Ciudad Cuauhtémoc ⓳**, 95km (60 miles) southwest of Chihuahua City, are home to more than 15,000 members of the Mennonite sect, whose families moved here in the 1920s. Cuauhtémoc is the Mennonite center for commercial activity, though the people do not live here. Just north of the city, the **Museo Menonita** (Mon–Sat 9am–5pm) offers an overview on the culture and history of the Mennonites in this region. Guided tours are available in English, Spanish and German.

From Cuauhtémoc a paved road leads to the **Parque Nacional Cascada de Basaseachi ⓴**, containing Mexico's highest waterfall. Be sure to enquire about road conditions before driving this route as access to the waterfall is difficult, especially during the rainy season. The falls plunge more than 300 meters (1,000ft), but it's an easy walk up the road to the top. If you are in good shape, walk about halfway down for a spectacular view. It is best to hire a local guide as the path is not clearly marked.

THE SIERRA TARAHUMARA

The **Barranca del Cobre ⓴** (Copper Canyon; see page 200), one of many

Pancho Villa's Dodge car, Museo de la Revolución Mexicana.

⊘ THE MENNONITES

Speaking their own dialect of old German, the Mennonites are farmers, best known for the mild cheese (queso menonita) they produce. They do not tend to integrate much and few speak Spanish, but their presence has long been accepted, in part due to their exemplary agricultural practices. It is customary from Mennonites to shun luxury and modernization, and most still drive around in horse-drawn carts (although nowadays you may see a pick-up truck or two). Television is still taboo in most of the homes, and 10-children families are not uncommon. Some tours from Creel include sharing a simple lunch in a Mennonite household. During the day you may see them in town: overall-clad men, married women dressed in dark colors, and girls in bright floral dresses.

Valley of the Mushrooms in Copper Canyon, near Creel.

canyons in the Sierra Tarahumara, southwest of Chihuahua City, is even deeper than the famous Grand Canyon of Colorado in the US. This is Tarahumara country. Some 50,000 Tarahumara live in this region, typically in caves or wooden huts in the mountains. Although they are one of the largest indigenous groups left in Mexico, the Tarahumara are also one of the most reclusive, a condition that has exacerbated their dire poverty while at the same time enabling them to maintain many of their traditions.

The Chihuahua–Pacífico train ride has been called "the world's most scenic railroad" with just cause. It winds up, over, around, under, and through the Sierra Madre mountains, passing spectacular scenery the entire way. You can stop off at places like **Creel ㉒**, where there are plenty of good tours to see the surrounding country and Tarahumara communities, or **Divisadero ㉓**, with its remarkable canyon views. The remote hiking centre of **Batopilas ㉔** in the

Basaseachi Falls, Barranca del Cobre.

canyon bottom is best reached from Creel. Here you can explore some of the canyon on foot (there are special trails to follow). Those not stopping should at least disembark the train at the canyon when prompted for a 15-minute viewing.

NORTHEAST MEXICO

Most foreign tourists cross the border into the northeast of Mexico at **Nuevo Laredo ㉕**. From here, it is less than a two-hour drive south to **Monterrey ㉖**, the third-largest city in the country and a center for industry and commerce. Recent spates of drug-related violence have made this city far more dangerous than it once was. Old guidebooks refer to Monterrey as the "Pittsburgh of Mexico," but that description is outdated, for its huge steel industry was shut down years ago. *Regiomontanos* (natives of Monterrey) have an uneasy relationship with the government in Mexico City, and local businessmen often seem to have closer cultural ties with the US than with the rest of Mexico.

The capital of the state of Nuevo León, Monterrey produces about 25 percent of Mexico's manufactured goods, including half the manufactured exports. In the center of town, at the south end of the vast Macroplaza, is the busy **Plaza Zaragoza**, with a Baroque-facaded **cathedral** on its east side and the modern Palacio Municipal to the south. Between the two is the **Museo de Arte Contemporáneo de Monterrey** (MARCO; tel: 81-8262 4500; www.marco.org.mx; Tue, Thu–Sun 10am–6pm, Wed until 8pm; free on Wed), with its Latin American collection. Nearby stands a large free-form sculpture by Rufino Tamayo, one of Mexico's best-known 20th-century artists (see page 115).

Dominating the plaza is the Faro del Comercio, a concrete "beacon of commerce" designed by architect Luis Barragán, with a laser beam that sweeps the city every evening. Just northeast of the Macroplaza, on Plaza Santa Lucía, the **Museo de Historia Mexicana** is one of the best history museums in the country and has free guided tours. It is part of a trio of museums, the other two being the **Museo del Palacio**, showcasing the state's history, and **Museo del Noreste**, a guide to regional history in an impressive modern structure (www.3museos.com; Tue and Sun 10am–8pm, Wed–Sat 10am–6pm; free entry to Museo del Palacio).

Another must-see art gallery in the city center is **Pinacoteca de Nuevo León** (Wed–Mon 10am-8pm; free), a few blocks northwest of the northern end of the Macroplaza. Here the riveting contemporary art on display includes works by members of Andy Warhol's art circle, including Julio Galán.

Horno3 (tel: 81-8126 1100; www.horno3.org; Tue–Thu 10am–6pm, Fri–Sun 11am–7pm), in the former industrial steel-producing area of Monterrey that lies 2.5km (1.5 miles) east of the center, is the shining star of Parque Fundidora, an excellent cultural hub.

Here you can gain an insight into Monterrey's steel industry through exciting interactive exhibits.

Strategically located on a hill 2.5km (1.5 miles) west of the center (take a cab to get there), the 18th-century **Obispado** (Bishop's Palace), now the **Nuevo León Regional Museum** (tel: 81-8346 0404; Tue–Sun 9am–6pm; free on Sun), affords an excellent overview of the city and an impressive mountain backdrop called **Cerro de la Silla** (Saddle Peak). The bullet holes and shellfire scars in the building's walls are souvenirs of the US invasion of September 1846; it was also attacked by the French in the 1860s and witnessed clashes between Villa's troops and Constitutionalists during the Revolution half a century later. A cheerful way to start or finish a tour of Monterrey, especially if you are thirsty, is with a visit to the **Cervecería Cuauhtémoc** (Mon–Fri 9am–4.30pm; free), Mexico's oldest official brewery, which produces Carta Blanca and Bohemia brands – fine Pilsner-type beers.

⊘ **Fact**

Popular local foods include *cabrito al pastor* (charcoal grilled kid), *pan de pulque* (a delicious sweet bread made with the fermented sap of the maguey plant) and *huevos con machaca* (scrambled egg with Mexican-style dried beef).

Church of Our Lady of Perpetual Help, Monterrey.

Fact

Saltillo is famous for its colorful handwoven *serapes*, which can be bought at the market on Plaza Acuña.

OUT OF TOWN

It's worth spending some time exploring the area around Monterrey, although a surge in drug violence has made this area more dangerous. A short drive up the pine-covered slope to the southwest of the city leads to **Chipinique Mesa**, Monterrey's most exclusive suburb, which also has a restaurant, hotel, picnic places, and stunning views over the city and surrounding area. The **Grutas de García** ㉗ (Tue–Sun 9am–5pm), about 35km (21 miles) northwest of town, near Villa de García, are a spectacular series of caverns set high inside a mountain with astounding rock formations, stalactites, and stalagmites. The drive from Monterrey is beautiful, although winding and narrow. You can take a little cable car up to the cave entrance.

Only a 15-minute drive from downtown Monterrey, outside suburban Santa Catarina, the **Cañón de la Huasteca** ㉘ is a dramatic 300-meter (1,000ft) deep canyon (the road is good only as far as the Gruta de la Virgen). The **Cola de Caballo** ㉙ (Horse's Tail)

Sombreros for sale in Reynosa.

waterfall is a 35km (22-mile) drive south of Monterrey. The area around the triple cascade called the **Tres Gracias** is an ideal picnic spot. En-route you pass **La Boca** dam, where there is good fishing and water sports.

MILE-HIGH CITY

The state of Coahuila is almost as big as neighboring Chihuahua. **Saltillo** ㉚ at 1,598 meters (5,245ft) above sea level, is the state capital, with a population of 600,000. This mile-high altitude, with its sunny, dry climate, has made Saltillo a favorite summer vacation spot, especially for visitors from the United States, for many years. There is also a fine university that runs Spanish courses for foreign students in summer.

Founded in 1575 by Captain Francisco Urdiñola, Saltillo became the Spanish headquarters for exploring and colonizing land to its north, and in the early 19th century it was the capital of a large area that included Texas. In 1847 one of the bloodiest and most decisive battles of the Mexican–American War took place at **Buena Vista** (half an hour south on Highway 54). A small monument marks the site. Soon after this battle the war ended and Mexico lost half of its territory to the US. Nowadays, Saltillo is an interesting blend of colonial and modern; the city manages to maintain its charm despite being an important industrial center. The elaborate facade of the late 18th-century **Catedral de Santiago** (daily 9am–1pm, 4–7.30pm; free) on the main plaza is one of the finest examples of Churrigueresque architecture in Mexico.

The elegant **Palacio de Gobierno** on the opposite side of the square is also worth visiting. Among the museums of Saltillo are the fantastic Museo del Desierto (www.museodeldesierto.org; Tue–Sun 10am–5pm), and the **Museo de las Aves de México** (Tue–Sat 10am–6pm, Sun and hols 11am–6pm), an impressive museum devoted to the many birds of Mexico. The 2,000 specimens were collected by Aldegundo Garza de León over a period of 40 years.

For a more hands-on experience of the desert, the dreamy town of **Cuatro Ciénagas** ㉛, five hours' drive north of Saltillo, is the jumping-off point for the **Area de Proteccion de Flora y Fauna Cuatro Ciénagas**, The area's remarkable biodiversity is due to the combination of arid desert landscapes and underground water systems, and many species here (including numerous endemic ones) are key to naturalists unravelling the history of evolution – the *estromatolitos* found here, for example, have much in common with the planet's very first oxygen-producing organisms. Many places in town offer tours.

Parras ㉜, a small town about 160km (100 miles) west of Saltillo, is an oasis in the Coahuilan desert and is also the birthplace of revolutionary leader Francisco Madero. An excellent local wine is bottled at nearby **Casa Madero** (tel: 842-422 0111; www.madero. com.mx; tastings Mon–Sat 10am–6pm, Sun 10am–2pm) in San Lorenzo; this is Mexico's oldest winery, founded in 1626. Another specialty of the famous Saltillo vineyards is Brandy Madero.

South of Chihuahua and Coahuila, but still considered the north, the state of Durango is a cattle and lumber center that was once a popular location for Hollywood Westerns. Excursions to the movie sets at **Chupaderos** and **Villa del Oeste** can be arranged by the local tourist office in the industrial city of **Durango** ㉝, which has an attractive plaza, a Baroque cathedral, and other fine colonial buildings. It is located at a crossroads: to the southeast is Zacatecas and the colonial heartland (see page 215); to the southwest is Sinaloa and the Pacific coast at Mazatlán.

THE GULF COAST
People who cross the US border at Brownsville or McAllen, in the east of Texas, enter Mexico through the towns of **Reynosa** ㉞ or **Matamoros** ㉟, in the state of Tamaulipas. The Gulf Coast of Mexico between the border and Tampico, 619km (384 miles) farther south, has little to offer tourists except a scattering of hunting lodges and fishing camps. The roads are often poor and the coast is littered with oil refineries and tankers. This has also become almost out of bounds since the surge in drug violence. If you do enter Mexico this way, the best diversion is the **Reserva de la Biosfera El Cielo** ㊱ in the south of the state near Ciudad Victoria. Encompassing 1,500 sq km (580 sq miles), the reserve contains some of Mexico's greatest diversity, with a mix of desert and semi-tropical ecosystems. The best starting point for exploration is at **Cumbres Inn & Suites** (tel: 832-236 2218; www.hotelcumbres. com.mx) in Gomez Farias, which can help arrange excursions.

That said, most visitors choose to drive south through Monterrey and down to the colonial heartland of the central states.

Carved wooden doors, Saltillo.

THE WORLD'S MOST SCENIC RAILROAD

Riding on bridges over yawning chasms, viewing awesome scenery and age-old settlements – welcome aboard the Copper Canyon Railroad.

Some of Mexico's most spectacular scenery is found in Chihuahua – the massive canyons and gorges in the Sierra Madre known as the Barranca del Cobre. It has taken millions of years for rivers and wind to mold what is actually a series of five interconneted canyons, covering 64,000 sq km (25,000 sq miles) of rugged land that ranges from below sea level to more than 3,046 meters (10,000ft) at its peak. Mexico's tallest waterfall, the 300-meter (1,000ft) Cascada de Basaseachi is found here, as well as a variety of plant life and one of the world's most interesting indigenous tribes. It is a living museum of natural history – except for animals. Although you may see buzzards and bald eagles flying overhead, the majority of animal life has disappeared.

The Ferrocarril Chihuahua al Pacífico, called "the world's most scenic railroad," hauls lumber and tourists through this spectacular setting. This extraordinary feat of engineering – 661km (410 miles) in all – was begun in 1881 and not completed until 1961, at a total cost of more than US$100 million. It passes through 87 tunnels (one almost a mile long) and crosses 35 bridges. The train ride from Chihuahua to Los Mochis takes anywhere from 12 to 15 hours with short stops along the way to enjoy the splendid views – from alpine forests and rushing rivers to dusty gorges studded with Tarahumara settlements, and the remains of old missions and mining towns.

Key stops along the railroad include **Creel**, a delightful alpine-style town and the main hiking center, and **Divisadero**, which provides the most dramatic overview of the canyon, and now also offers the Parque de Aventuras Barrancas del Cobre, an adventure park with ziplines over the canyons.

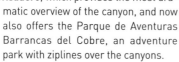

A Copper Canyon passenger train hoves into view.

The railroad project was conceived by US idealist Albert Owen, who came to Mexico to form a utopian colony on the Pacific coast.

The curious rock formations found in the Valley of the Mushrooms in Copper Canyon, near Creel.

A variety of handicrafts are on sale along the route, many of them made with techniques that have been passed down from generation to generation for centuries.

The Tarahumaras

Long before the advent of the railroad, the highlands and deep gorges of the Copper Canyon were inhabited by the Tarahumara indians. Exploited for centuries by the Spanish colonists and the mestizos, these unique people give Copper Canyon part of its character. While some visitors may balk at the obvious poverty (begging at train stops is common), these people have carved a living out of these rough mountains for centuries, despite modern progress, the advent of the train, and missionary zeal. In church, their ancient gods *Raiénari* (Sun) and *Mechá* (Moon) exist side by side with images of Christ and the Catholic saints.

Little writing exists, and few studies have been done on these people, who have lived in small huts and caves within these canyons. They are a shy people, best known around the world for their fabled sporting abilities – they can run for very long distances across demanding mountain terrain, often for almost a whole day, with only sandals for footwear. The Hotel Paraiso de Oso in Cerocahui, in the canyon, is a great source of information about the Tarahumara.

Tarahumara women and children sell tortillas and other snacks at stops along the route.

The Ferrocarril Chihuahua al Pacífico is also known as El Chepe on account of its reporting mark CHP, which is used to identify its rolling stock.

A Tarahumara girl sells necklaces at a train stop.

THE NORTHWEST COAST

From the great desert of Sonora to the tropics of Nayarit, the northwest of Mexico offers fantastic beaches, good fishing, delicious seafood, and spectacular birdlife.

◉ Main attractions

Hermosillo
Bahía Kino
Isla del Tiburón
Alamos
El Fuerte
Mazatlán
Mexcaltitán
San Blas

Map on page 180

Northwest Mexico's vast stretches of barren yet beautiful desert, plateaus, and unique plants, animals, and birds was neglected by European invaders until the missionaries started to work among the tribes in the 17th century. The Jesuit priests introduced domestic animals, showed the indigenous peoples new crops and taught them farming and building techniques, as well as introducing less desirable things, like European diseases. Problems arose when Spanish colonists arrived and tried to take the most fertile lands and force local people into hard labor. The locals resisted and, as they were split into many tribes and spread out over great distances, they could not be conquered in one blow. Rebellion flared, on and off, for many years, particularly with the Yaqui (see page 208).

LA FAMILIA REVOLUCIONARIA

This area was already fiercely independent and cut off, both culturally and geographically, from the rest of Mexico. Thus, by the time the Revolution broke out in 1910, the northwest had developed muscle and conscience and was ready to take part wholeheartedly in ushering in change, providing both troops and the general (Alvaro Obregón) who emerged after the inevitable internal power struggle. For a decade, Mexico was ruled directly or indirectly by one of Sonora's *Familia Revolucionaria*, first Obregón, then Generál Plutarco Elías Calles.

THE YAQUI DEAL

The Yaquis, who had joined Generál Obregón's forces, wanted their tribal lands back, and when Cárdenas became president in the 1930s, he ordered a dam to be built on the upper Yaqui River for irrigation, setting aside some 4.5 million hectares (11 million acres) for the Yaqui tribes. It included the whole north bank of the river and part of the south. Setting up a reservation, the Yaquis took over

US–Mexico border fence, Nogales.

their own tribal lands, which they control to this day. Other northwest natives did not fare so well. The Seris, for example, were either killed or died of European diseases and their population dropped from 5,000 to less than 200. The Opatas, on the other hand, disappeared due to assimilation: they learned Spanish, intermarried, and cooperated in the battles against the Apaches.

The Yaqui have a complex belief system that is in part influenced by ancient tenets and in part by Jesuit priests who established a series of missions in this area of far northwestern Mexico in the 16th century. Few other indigenous tribes have beliefs that so combine colonial (Catholic) and native ideas of faith. Perhaps the most evocative example of Yaqui culture in Sonora is in their ritual deer dance, in which the deer, traditionally essential for sustenance, is personified and a deer hunt re-enacted.

The best source of Yaqui information is www.pascuayaqui-nsn.gov. While this focuses more on the Yaqui who live on the American side of the border (the tribe actually inhabits lands stretching north up to Tucson, Arizona), most of the same information applies.

The northwest is a highly productive region: Sonora leads the nation in cotton, wheat, and soybean production; Sinaloa tops the other states in tomatoes – most of which go to the US – and also raises a hefty crop of wheat, cotton, sugar cane, and chickpeas, which are exported chiefly to Spain and Cuba. Although the silver mines of the northwest are practically exhausted, the mines of Cananea make Sonora the country's leading producer of copper. (The 1906 miners' strike at Cananea was critical in the lead up to the Revolution.)

MEXICALI TO MAZATLÁN

The Pacific beaches are the main attraction of the route from the Arizona border to Mazatlán, but there are also interesting mountain towns and historical sights along the way. An excellent, though expensive, toll super-highway stretches down most of the coast. The alternative *libre* (free) route is longer and the traffic is predictably heavier.

Colorful homes on a hillside adjacent to Mazatlán.

Many people who come south from the US, either through **Mexicali** ㊲ or **Nogales** ㊳, begin with a jaunt to **Puerto Peñasco** ㊴ in the far northwest corner of Sonora. This former fishing village – now more mega-resort – is a popular weekend retreat for Arizonans. Fishing and enjoying the beach are the main reasons for going there. If you are thinking of taking a boat out, be extremely careful as tides are hazardous and winds are strong in the shallow waters at the head of the Gulf of California. Like most of the resorts in the north, Puerto Peñasco offers good trailer facilities, with water and power hook-ups.

Waiting for a wave? Not all waves are surfable. To be "good surf" the waves have to be created by storms far out at sea, called swell, and have long intervals between them. Waves, the higher the better, are improved by a stiff offshore wind, which holds them up and shapes them nicely.

Rocky Point, Puerto Peñasco.

EL GRAN DESIERTO

There is precious little to break the beautiful monotony between the border and Hermosillo. In the small town of **Magdalena**, 20km (12 miles) northeast of the junction at Santa Ana, a glass shrine contains the mortal remains of Padre Eusebio Kino, the Jesuit priest who helped establish missions along the coast, and later in Arizona and California. Often crippled with arthritis,

Kino, a mathematician, astrologer, architect, and economist, died in 1711 but his grave was only discovered in 1966. Just south, Sonora's capital **Hermosillo** ㊵ is a thriving city with a Ford automobile plant, and, despite the fierce summer heat, several of this region's best museums. The **Museo de Arte de Sonora** (MUSAS; tel: 662-254 6397; Tue–Sun 10am–6pm) on Avenida Cultura is a surprisingly wonderful contemporary art museum, while up on Cerro de la Campana, a hill near the city center, is **Museo Regional de Sonora** (Tue–Sat 10am–6pm, Sun 9am–4pm), housed in the old city jail.

SERI IRONWOOD CARVINGS

The next worthwhile stop is **Bahía Kino** ㊶, which just about clings on to its unsophisticated fishing-village atmosphere, despite the many *norteamericanos* who choose to spend the winter months there. The local Seri sell wonderful handicrafts such as baskets and ironwood carvings, so-called because they are made out of an exceptionally hard local wood. The Seri, a nomadic people, were moved to

this part of Sonora from nearby **Isla del Tiburón** ⓐ (Shark Island), which is now a wildlife sanctuary.

COOL WINTER NIGHTS

You can rent a boat for fishing in most of the resort towns along the coast. It is easy to acquire a permit, and most come complete with tackle, crew, and cold beer, though prices do vary, so you would be wise to shop around. Winter nights can get chilly along the coast of Sonora, and although it is sunny during the day, the water is cold for swimming. The ocean can get rough and swimmers should be careful of the big waves and powerful undertow, except in protected bays. There are ocean breezes even when it does warm up, and the Pacific beaches seldom get as muggy as the Gulf Coast.

A GRINGO OASIS

Though many people call **Guaymas** ⓐ a beach resort, it is not. It is a fishing town and Sonora's main port, with ferries to Santa Rosalía in Baja California. The beaches are pretty and you can easily spend an afternoon just watching the

sun sink to the sea as the pelicans glide by in formation. While drivers headed toward Baja won't save any money by taking the ferry, they will save time, and those without cars will find that the cost per passenger is still very reasonable. But don't plan your trip too closely as the ferry times and days change frequently.

Nearby **San Carlos** ⓐ is the beach resort (albeit a very tranquil one); it is a gringo oasis inhabited by many retired Americans and Canadians. There are dozens of hotels and restaurants, and it has one of Mexico's largest marinas, with sailing vessels from all around the world. The 1970 movie *Catch 22* was shot nearby.

Navojoa, south of **Ciudad Obregón**, is the center of a major cotton-producing area and the home of the Mayo people. A detour from Navojoa takes you 53km (33 miles) inland to the beautiful old town of **Alamos** ⓐ in the foothills of the sierras. This was a rich mining center in the 18th century, with dozens of fabulous residences lining its cobblestone streets. After the Revolution, the mines were closed down and the

View from San Carlos.

town was practically abandoned. In the late 1940s Alamos was rediscovered by wealthy Americans, who bought up and restored many of the colonial mansions. The beautiful central plaza is dominated by the Baroque-facaded church of **Nuestra Señora de la Concepción beside the Plaza de Armas.** The town, which has some of the best examples of colonial architecture on the West Coast, is a national monument, and visiting it is like stepping back in time.

LOS MOCHIS

From Navojoa, the main highway continues through some of the richest farmland in Mexico to **Los Mochis** ㊻, a pleasant and friendly town. Most people spend a day or two here while waiting to ride the **Copper Canyon Railroad** (see page 200), which traverses the rugged mountains of the Sierra Madre to Chihuahua, offering one of the most spectacular train rides in the world. It leaves early in the morning and arrives in Chihuahua around nine at night. Los Mochis has become a boomtown, with rice, cotton, winter vegetables, sugar

cane, and marigolds all produced nearby. Tourists will find it quiet, laid back, without a lot to offer aside from a pretty plaza. Hunting and heading for the beach are other options.

The ferry from La Paz in Baja California docks south of Los Mochis in **Topolobampo.** Just off the coast, the rocky island of **Farallón** (sometimes called Isla las Animas) is a breeding ground for sea lions and attracts flocks of sea birds. The marine life around the island is colorful.

El Fuerte ㊼, an important Spanish settlement during colonial times, and once capital of the state of Sinaloa, is a picturesque town 78km (48 miles) northeast of Los Mochis. In addition to the **Museo El Fuerte** (tel: 698-893 1501; daily 9am–7pm), and the church, it is worth visiting the **Posada del Hidalgo** (tel: 668-815 7668; www.hotelposadadelhidalgo.com), a 19th-century mansion that has been converted into a beautiful hotel. Fishing for catfish and carp is possible in the nearby Presa Miguel Hidalgo, one of the best bass-fishing lakes in the country. El Fuerte is far more picturesque than Los Mochis, and many tourists taking the Copper Canyon railroad may want to overnight here. The train stops briefly to pick up passengers, but there is only one train daily in each direction (the train's arrival is quite an event).

From Los Mochis to Mazatlán, the highway cuts through **Culiacán,** capital of Sinaloa, known for its bumper crops of tomatoes and opium, both destined for the US (some opium is legally exported for medicinal purposes). Marijuana is another crop grown in the complex landscape of the Sierra Madre Occidental. Culiacán, along with Sinaloa, are current centers of the Mexican drug trade, and visitors are strongly warned against using or dealing; Mexican anti-drug laws are very strict, and looking for drugs is one of the quickest ways to get mixed up in the usually non-tourist crimes connected with warring gangs.

Mazatlán, the closest Mexican resort to the US.

The toll road from Culiacán to Mazatlán, the most expensive stretch, saves about 1.5 hours, while traffic on the old free route is congested, although the road surface is usually quite good. About halfway between the two, you can make a detour to **Cosalá,** an old mining town with hot springs nearby.

THE PEARL OF THE PACIFIC

Mazatlán ⑱ (meaning "Place of the Deer" in Náhuatl) is a booming resort town about 15km (9 miles) south of the Tropic of Cancer. It is also one of the most important ports on Mexico's west coast and home to the country's largest shrimp fleet. Unlike most Mexican towns, Mazatlán's first plaza, Plaza Zaragoza, was not built around a church and government offices because the city's richest and most influential people were merchants. Only later was the Plaza de la República built. Both plazas are worth visiting. Much of the action occurs along the long Malecón, a pedestrian avenue that follows the white sand beaches. Pulmonias, golf cart-like

vehicles originally designed by a local, are as common as taxis.

The old part of the city, located on a peninsula, centers around the Plaza Principal and the 19th-century twin-towered **cathedral**, whose unusual facade is decorated with intricately carved volcanic rock. Towering over this old part of town, the **Cerro de la Nevería** (Icebox Hill) has panoramic sea views. The trendy spot in the old town focuses around **Plazuela Machado**, a leafy, buzzing area full of fashionable restaurants and some of the most interesting architecture, most notably **Teatro Ángela Peralta**, a superbly renovated theater with regular performances and events. Most tourists spend their time in the so-called **Zona Dorada** (Golden Zone), a long stretch of hotels, restaurants, and shops about 3km (2 miles) north of the old town.

A little farther south, near Playa del Norte, the **Acuario Mazatlán** (tel: 669-981-7815; http://acuariomazatlan.com; daily 9.30am–5pm), with nearly 200 species of fish, is worth a visit. Local travel agencies organize city

Welcome sign in Alamos.

Fresh fish for sale.

and jungle tours. There are also boat trips around the harbor and to the nearby islands.

Winter is the most popular season here, though any time of the year is pleasant. Summer is the "rainy" season, but unless there is a hurricane nearby it will not greatly inconvenience you. *Carnaval* in Mazatlán (the week before Ash Wednesday) is one of Mexico's liveliest fiestas; hotel reservations are essential then, as they are between Christmas and New Year, and for the week before Easter, when all beach resorts are jam-packed. There is plenty in the local area to explore, including the countryside and nearby swamp areas.

On a cloudy day you may want to take a short detour east up Highway 40 into the foothills of the Sierra Madre for a pleasant day trip from Mazatlán. The colonial town of **Concordia** ⓐ, set in lush, tropical vegetation with hot springs nearby, is known for its pottery and hand-carved furniture. Picture-postcard **Copala** ⓑ, 25km (16 miles) farther on, with its cobblestone streets,

House on stilts, San Blas.

red-tiled roofs and wrought-iron balconies, is an old silver-mining town. Keep your eyes (and ears) peeled for wild parrots; sightings are not unusual.

THE HUICHOL

Craftwork from all over the Republic can be found in Mazatlán, but particularly beautiful is the beaded artwork and weavings of the Huichol people. However, if you are on your way south, it is more helpful to them – and more interesting for you – if you wait until you reach **Santiago Ixcuintla** ⓒ. Here you'll find Huichol families making their crafts; any money you spend here goes directly to the tribe, and much of it to the nearby hospital (tuberculosis, malnutrition, and other ailments mean Huichol children suffer a 50 percent infant mortality rate).

THE VENICE OF MEXICO

The small island village of **Mexcaltitán** ⓓ has been nicknamed the "Venice of Mexico" because, during heavy rains, the streets are frequently flooded and you have to pole your way

⊘ THE YAQUI INDIANS

When the Jesuits were expelled from Mexico in 1767, the missions disintegrated and the colonists brazenly encroached on tribal lands. The Yaquis, a fighting race, reacted angrily and the Spanish dealt with them harshly. For centuries the tribes of the northwest were isolated in a remote corner of Mexico. They took little part in the life of the nation and were marginal to the Independence movement of the 1810s. The region was weak and unprotected. The French, led by Gaston Raousset de Bourbon, captured Hermosillo in 1852, and in 1857 Henry Crabb, an American from California, tried to capture northern Sonora. In both instances, the Mexicans reacted vigorously, defeating the invaders and executing the leaders.

The largest campaign against the Yaqui was in the 1880s–90s, under Mexican general Porfírio Díaz, when large numbers of Yaqui were taken to the Yucatán. But several decades later the Yaquis, in exchange for their help during the Revolution, requested their lands back. When Cárdenas became president in the 1930s, he set aside 485,000 hectares (more than 1 million acres) for the Yaqui tribes. It included the whole north bank of the Yaqui River and part of the south.

around town in a canoe (every family has at least one "vessel"). But in recent years more and more of the streets have been filled in, so Mexcaltitán's waterlogged days are probably limited. The seafood here is excellent, but don't look for luxury hotels; the town is a bit run down, although tourists find it fascinating. Some historians believe that Mexcaltitán is the legendary island of Aztlán, the original home of the Aztec people and the place where they first had the vision of the eagle perched on a cactus with a serpent in its claws; this symbol of their promised land was eventually found in Tenochtitlán, now Mexico City.

SURF CITY

San Blas ⑤ is a quiet fishing town noted for the ferocity of its gnats, known as *jejenes*. The insects are at their worst early in the morning, in the evenings, and during a full moon, so be sure to stock up on insect repellent. Surfers flock to San Blas to ride its famous long waves, and ornithologists come to watch the many species of migrating and native birds that take refuge here. Birdwatching trips to the **Santuario de Aves** (Bird Sanctuary) can be arranged. Another popular pastime is to take the jungle boat-ride up the San Cristóbal estuary, through a green tunnel of vegetation to **La Tovara** springs, where you can swim in crystal-clear water, picnic, or eat at one of the *palapa* (shack) restaurants.

Although it is hard to believe now, San Blas was once a shipbuilding center and the point of departure for Spanish exploration of the Pacific Northwest. Vestiges of this period include the old **Aduana** (customs house) by the port and the **Fuerte de Basilio,** a counting house built in 1768. It was the church here that inspired 19th-century US poet Henry Wadsworth Longfellow to write the poem entitled *The Bells of San Blas.*

THE JOURNEY TO IXTLÁN

About 70km (44 miles) inland, **Tepic** ㊹, the capital of the state of Nayarit, has a pleasant square, flanked by a cathedral with impressive neo-Gothic towers, though overall the city does not cater much to foreign tourists and is better as a lunch stop on the way to Tequila or Guadalajara rather than as a destination all its own. The **Museo Regional de Nayarit** (tel: 311-212 1900; Mon–Fri 9am–6pm, Sat and hols 9am–3pm) houses a collection of pre-Hispanic ceramics and the **Cinco Pueblos Casa de Artesanias** (tel: 311-039 4200; daily 9am–8pm; free) exhibits handicrafts by Huichol, Cora, Náhuatl, and Tepehuano people, which can be bought far more inexpensively here than in the resort boutiques.

Just outside the town of **Ixtlán del Río** – made famous by Carlos Castaneda's *Journey to Ixtlán* – is an extensive and largely restored archeological site, **Los Toriles** ㊺ (daily 9am–6pm), which flourished in the 2nd century AD. The main structure is an unusual circular stone temple with cruciform windows, dedicated to Quetzalcóatl.

Carved coconut heads make an unusual souvenir.

Huichol handicrafts.

La Anunciacion (1706) by Cristobel de Villalpondo, Convento de Guadalupe.

Statue of Papila, overlooking Guanajuato.

CENTRAL MEXICO

Famous for its Pacific beaches, tequila, and
Unesco World Heritage sites, above all this
is the heartland of colonial Mexico.

A charro entering the rodeo ring.

The Central Highlands were a source of wealth
for the Spanish colonists, as the silver route from
Zacatecas to Mexico City passed through the magnificent towns of the so-called colonial heartland.
The cathedrals, monasteries, chapels, and mansions that can be visited today are the exquisite
legacy of Spanish prosperity on the one hand, and
of the extreme exploitation of indigenous labor on
the other. In the 19th century the Independence
movement was ignited in El Bajío – the triangle formed by the towns of
Querétaro, San Luis Potosí, and Aguascalientes. El Bajío's San Miguel
de Allende has become one of the most important
tourist towns in all of Mexico.

To the south are the rolling hills of Michoacán, one
of the most beautiful states in the Republic. Visitors
can ride up to the crater of a smoldering volcano or
else witness the spectacular sight of the monarch
butterflies that arrive from Canada in their millions each year. For anyone traveling in November,
nowhere is Mexico's unique Day of the Dead celebrated more fervently than in the delightful town of
Pátzcuaro and on the nearby island of Janitzio.

Monarch butterflies.

Fields of blue-green agave surround the world-
famous town of Tequila. Among other things, Jalisco
is home to the Cora and Huichol people, who live in
the sierra and make yearly pilgrimages to San Luis Potosí – a 1,600km
(1,000-mile) round trip – to collect the hallucinogenic peyote cactus that
is central to their ancient rituals. Guadalajara, the "City of Roses," is a
rose itself, a magnet for language students, artists, musicians, and cooks.

Jalisco is also the gateway to the Pacific coast, where mega-resorts
of Puerto Vallarta, Ixtapa, and Acapulco attract sun-worshippers by
the tens of thousands. Break-bound surfers will find the azure coast-
lines hold a wealth of waves at almost every corner, and anyone who
wants to get away from the crowds will find there are still hundreds of
kilometers of deserted coast fringed with vast plantations of bananas,
mangoes, and coconuts.

A Zacatecas neighborhood at night.

EL BAJÍO AND THE COLONIAL HEARTLAND

For centuries, the mines of central Mexico produced much of the world's silver; their legacy today is reflected in some of the country's finest colonial architecture.

México City

Less visited than the coastal resorts and some parts of southern Mexico, the five states of the central highlands, to the north of Mexico City, have much to offer any traveler who has the time, patience and curiosity to explore. Zacatecas, Aguascalientes, San Luis Potosí, Guanajuato, and Querétaro are the colonial heartland of Mexico. Some of the most impressive colonial architecture can be seen in the cities of this region, which grew and flourished under Spanish rule as a result of the huge quantities of silver and other metal extracted from the local mines. Several of these areas have earned Unesco World Heritage status.

ZACATECAS, THE PINK CITY

The state of **Zacatecas** is the gateway between the huge, barren and empty north and the richer, more fertile and more densely populated highland region of central Mexico. The fortified archeological site at **Chalchihuites ❶**, in the northwest of the state, which flourished from AD 900 to 1200, has yielded ceramic treasures that suggest contact between the Mesoamerican style of the Central Highlands and the simpler geometric art style of the American West.

The city of **Zacatecas ❷**, spectacularly sited between arid hills at an altitude of 2,500 meters (8,200ft), was declared the property of the Spanish

Crown in 1546. Soon after, enormous quantities of silver were being mined and shipped off to Spain. Fortunes were rapidly amassed and Zacatecas, as a result of this prosperity, has some of the finest colonial architecture in Mexico. Declared a Unesco World Heritage site in 1993, the city is one of the cleanest and friendliest in Mexico, and combines the vigor and roughness of the north with the architectural refinement of the Central Highlands. The elegant stone mansions have fancy wrought-iron balconies and window

Main attractions

Zacatecas
La Quemada
San Luis Potosí
Real de Catorce
Guanajuato
Festival Cervantino
Dolores Hidalgo
San Miguel de Allende
Querétaro

Maps on pages 216, 222

Indigenous dance group.

Central Mexico

0   100 km

0   100 miles

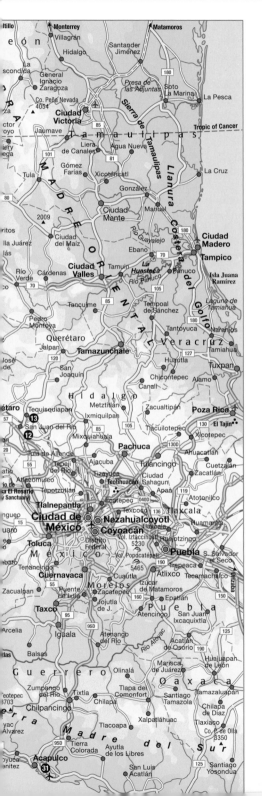

grilles. Meandering the streets, camera or sketchbook in hand, is an agreeable way to discover the city's charm. The main sights are mostly concentrated in a small area of 12 blocks, easily explored on foot. To the north of this area, on the Plaza de Armas, the **cathedral**, with its delicately carved pink stone facade, is considered one of the masterpieces of Mexican Baroque. Also on the plaza are two colonial mansions: the **Palacio de la Mala Noche** and the **Palacio de Gobierno.**

AROUND THE CATHEDRAL

Just south of the cathedral are the 19th-century **Teatro Calderón** and the **Mercado González Ortega**, a turn-of-the-20th century cast-iron structure that has been converted into a shopping center. Uphill from the Plaza de Armas, behind a sober facade, the 18th-century **Santo Domingo** church holds some fine gilded altarpieces. The 17th-century monastery next door, now the **Museo Pedro Coronel** (Fri–Wed 10am–4pm), exhibits an enviable collection of both ancient and modern art and artifacts from all over the world (including works by Picasso, Braque, Chagall, and Miró), which this noted Zacatecan artist bequeathed to his home town. The artist's brother also donated a collection, this one of masks, 19th-century marionettes, and pre-Hispanic pottery. These are displayed in the magnificently restored Convento de San Francisco, now the **Museo Rafael Coronel** (tel: 492-922 8116; Thu–Tue 10am–5pm).

Perhaps the most fascinating local attraction is a trip into the heart of the **Mina El Edén** (tel: 492-922 3002; www.minaeleden.com.mx; daily 10am–6pm), one of Mexico's richest mines, which was worked from 1586 until the 1960s. As the tour passes dramatically lit shafts, subterranean pools, and chasms, the guides describe the deplorable working conditions that existed for the miners in the colonial era. For a thrilling view of the city, a cable car will take you from the entrance to the mine up to the top of the **Cerro de la Bufa**. On weekends there's dancing in a nightclub that has been installed near the entrance of the mine.

The early 18th-century **Convento de Guadalupe** (tel: 492-923 2386; daily 9am–6pm), 10km (6 miles) southeast of Zacatecas, is a remarkable museum and monastery with one of the most elaborately decorated chapels and an impressive collection of colonial paintings. Viewed on a bright day, the majestic exterior, with its pink stone walls and cupola, is postcard perfect. Inside, it seems almost fantastical with its scooped out ceilings, high arches, and pastel blues and golds.

About 45km (28 miles) to the west of Zacatecas, through the best cattle-raising country in Mexico, in the attractive colonial town of **Jerez**, is the horseshoe-shaped **Teatro Hinojosa**, a replica of Ford's Theatre in Washington, DC.

Just off the road to Guadalajara, about 50km (30 miles) south of Zacatecas, the ruins of **La Quemada** ❸ (daily 9am–5pm) spread over the hillside. It is thought to have been part of a trade network, and was inhabited between AD 300 and 1300, when it was destroyed by fire. It is one of the largest sites of that era ever discovered, and is well worth a detour to see it. Like many Mexican archeological sites, La Quemada remains shrouded in mystery – some theorize that this was a temporary settlement used en route to elsewhere, others point to the establishment of defensive walls and additional indicators and claim it was a settlement in its own right. Either way, it's an interesting spot to explore, and some of the ruins are sensitively preserved.

AGUASCALIENTES

The city of **Aguascalientes** ❹ regards itself as Mexico's grape capital. Until recently the small state of Aguascalientes, south of Zacatecas, was an important wine-producing region but the local vintners could not compete with imported wines, either on price or quality. Today most of the grapes wind up in Mexican brandy, which bears only a slight resemblance to Spanish brandy or French cognac. The **San Marcos Winery** north of the city conducts tours. Also north of town are the hot springs from which the town takes its name.

Aguascalientes' **Jardín San Marcos**, west of the town center, hosts one of Mexico's biggest annual festivals. During the end of April and early May, thousands of visitors flock to the **Feria de San Marcos** for the parades, exhibitions, bullfights, singing, dancing, and brandy drinking.

On the main Plaza de la Patria is the impressive 18th-century **Palacio de Gobierno**; brightly colored murals by Chilean artist Oswaldo Barra Cunningham decorate the patio walls inside. The 18th-century Baroque **cathedral** and the religious picture gallery next door both contain paintings by colonial artist Miguel Cabrera. There are several museums in Aguascalientes, but the highlight is the **Museo José Guadalupe Posada** (tel: 449-915 4556; Tue–Sun 11am–6pm; free on Wed), next door to the Templo del Encino. Posada, most famous for his satirical (skeleton) prints (see page 112) and a great social and political critic during the *Porfiriato*, inspired many later artists, including Diego Rivera and José Clemente Orozco (see page 112). The museum houses over 200 works by this local artist. The **Museo de los Muertos** (tel:

The Museo Rafael Coronel in Zacatecas is housed in the restored Convento de San Francisco.

449-910 7400; Tue–Sun 10am–6pm; free on Wed) offers a close, intimate, fun look at the fate that awaits us.

SAN LUIS POTOSÍ

The state of San Luis Potosí is large and diverse: the east is hot and tropical; dry plains stretch across the center; while the west, like neighboring Zacatecas, is mountainous and rugged. The industrial city of **San Luis Potosí** ❺ is the state capital and was the seat of Juárez's government before the defeat of Maximilian. The attractive downtown area has many beautiful plazas, elegant mansions, and pedestrian walkways. The city's pre-eminent jewel is the **Templo del Carmen**, a Churrigueresque church completed in 1764 and adorned with shells on the facade, multicolored tiles on the dome, and a wonderfully intricate retablo inside. The adjacent **Teatro de la Paz** was built in the 19th century, during the dictatorship of Don Porfirio Díaz. Across the street the **Museo Nacional de la Máscara** (tel: 444-812 3032; Mon and Sun 10am–3pm, Tue–Fri 10am–6pm, Sat 10am–5pm; free on Tue) displays more than 2,000 ceremonial masks, both pre-Hispanic and modern, from all over Mexico. The **Museo Regional Potosino** (tel: 444-812 0358; Tue–Sun 9am–6pm) is a regional handicrafts museum housed in a former Franciscan monastery; the richly decorated 18th-century Capilla de Aranzazú is on the second floor. **Museo Federico Silva** (tel: 444-812 3848; www. museofedericosilva.org; Mon, Wed–Sat 10am–6pm, Sun 10am–2pm) is an impressive contemporary art museum in a lovingly restored 17th-century former hospital.

Shopping is a popular pastime here in San Luis Potosí, and you'll find an abundance of handiwork and crafts, especially textiles and fabrics, often handwoven by artisans whose families have been doing similar work for decades or even centuries.

REAL DE CATORCE

Once a thriving silver-mining center housing a royal mint and 40,000

> **⊙ Fact**
>
> The lyrics for the Mexican national anthem were composed by San Luis Potosí poet, Francisco González Bocanegra.

Cathedral of Our Lady of the Assumption, Zacatecas.

The opening to the 2.5km (1.5-mile) tunnel in Real de Catorce.

A swimming hole near San Luis Potosí.

inhabitants, **Real de Catorce** ⑥ is practically a ghost town today. It is located in the mountains west of Matehuala. You have to go through a 2.5km (1.5-mile) tunnel – a former mine shaft – to reach this extraordinary town where street after street of once sumptuous mansions stand eerily in ruins. However, the 1,000-strong population provides rooms to rent, as well as stores, restaurants, silversmiths, and (why not?) mystics.

GUANAJUATO

The city of **Guanajuato** ⑦, which in the local tongue translates to "Hill of Frogs," is the capital of the state and one of Mexico's most famous tourist spots. In colonial days it was the center of a rich mining area and one of the greatest producers of silver in the world. The mines were flooded during the wars for Independence, but reopened again under Porfirio Díaz. Abandoned again in the Revolution, they reopened recently as the price of silver escalated.

A Unesco World Heritage site, Guanajuato is charming, romantic, and sometimes eerie. This well-preserved city is built in a ravine and on the banks of a river; no street runs in a straight line; all go their crooked ways, up and down steep hills, some falling into an abyss; in some houses the entrance is through the roof. Tunnels and streets wind their way along the basements of the town's old buildings, with steps intermittently leading to a square or winding alley. Buildings new and old are brightly colored and give the vistas a fiesta-like feel even when nothing in particular is going on.

CENTRAL GUANAJUATO

At the heart of Guanajuato is the **Jardín de la Unión** Ⓐ, a cool, shady wedge-shaped plaza surrounded by cafés. Across the road is the churrigueresque church of **San Diego** Ⓑ, next door to the magnificent **Teatro Juárez** Ⓒ (Tue–Sun), inaugurated in 1903 by the dictator Porfirio Díaz himself, and with a "French-Moorish" interior. There are often good musical performances here.

Almost all of Guanajuato's sights are to the west of the Jardín de la Unión, with the exception of the **Museo Iconográfico del Quijote** Ⓓ (tel: 473-732 3376; Tue–Sat 9.30am–6.45pm, Sun noon–6.45pm; free on Sun), a few blocks to the east. Dedicated to Cervantes's *Don Quixote de la Mancha*, the collection – ranging from dime-store junk to works by Picasso and Dalí – was donated by a rich advertising executive and avid Quixote-phile.

Two blocks west of Jardín de la Unión, near **Plaza de la Paz** Ⓔ, are some of Guanajuato's richest colonial buildings. The **Supreme Court**, which was designed by the 18th-century architect Eduardo de Tresguerras, was the home of the Condes de Rul y Valenciana, owners of Mexico's

richest silver mine. On the east side of the plaza is the **Basílica de Nuestra Señora de Guanajuato F**, which houses the image of the city's patroness, a gift in 1557 from King Philip II of Spain and said to date from the 7th century.

The **University G**, a huge white building, is an outstanding example of Moorish-inspired architecture only half a century old, relatively new in comparison to its ancient surroundings. It is the pride of Guanajuato and the centerpiece of the **Festival Cervantino** (see page 221), an important international arts festival that's celebrated in Guanajuato every October. The pink stone Baroque **Templo de la Compañía de Jesús H** is the grandest church in town with a fine 19th-century dome and paintings by Miguel Cabrera inside. One block west of the university, the **Museo Casa Diego Rivera I** (tel: 473-732 1197; Tue–Sat 10am–6.30pm, Sun 10am–2.30pm) exhibits a collection of works by the famous muralist, who was born in this house in 1886.

Plaza de San Roque J is renowned for its presentations of *Entremeses Cervantinos*. These light-hearted theatrical sketches by 16th-century Spanish writer Miguel de Cervantes have become a tradition in Guanajuato and are central to the Festival Cervantino. Nearby, in a French wrought-iron structure, **Guanajuato's Market K** is large, noisy, and full of good and bad smells.

OTHER ATTRACTIONS

Originally a granary, the impressive **Alhóndiga de Granaditas L** (tel: 473-732 1112; Tue–Sat 10am–5.30pm, Sun 10am–2.30pm; free on Sun) was used as a fortress for the Spanish and Royalists during the War of Independence before being captured by the rebels after the famous Pípila incident. Carrying a slab of stone on his back for protection, a local miner known as the Pípila rushed the door of the Alhóndiga, set it on fire, and the rebels poured in. Today the building houses a museum with murals by Chávez Morado and a collection of

Statue of Miguel Cervantes, Guanajuato.

GUANAJUATO'S FESTIVAL CERVANTINO

Originally a casual university production of Cervantes' farces (from whence the name), the Festival Cervantino, held each October, has grown in size and scope to become one of Mexico's largest and grandest performance art festivals. As a result of its popularity, the festival has attracted big-name sponsors including Microsoft. Tourists from all over the world flood the city (and the streets) to watch the various events, which include all kinds of dramatic and performing arts, such as plays, music, opera, concerts, recitals, stage events, and so on. Each year the focus is on a particular Mexican state, and a different foreign country is honored, making this truly a uniquely multicultural experience.

Recently there has been a bit of controversy surrounding the problematic and excessive use of drugs and alcohol. In response, city officials have taken steps to regulate drinking, as well as beef up the police presence during the festivities, which has helped keep things from getting out of hand. This is still considered "one big party" by many twenty-somethings, so despite prohibitions on drinking alcohol openly in the streets, visitors should keep in mind that there's plenty of craziness and cavorting mixed in with the more cultured events.

⊙ Fact

The Cerro de Cubilete, a mountain between Guanajuato and León, marks the geographical center of Mexico. On the summit stands a 20-meter (65ft) statue of Christ with open arms, blessing the valley below.

paintings by the 19th-century Guanajuato artist, Hermenegildo Bustos. A grandiose monument to **Pípila** Ⓜ stands on a ridge overlooking the city; it's a steep climb or an easy cable-car trip; the view from the top of the colourful city below is superb.

The best panoramic view of Guanajuato is from **La Valenciana** (daily 10am–7pm), the mine that under its Spanish colonial masters produced a large quantity of the world's silver. The elaborate church of **San Cayetano**, next to the mine, is a masterpiece of churrigueresque style and the interior is quite dazzling. On the way you may want to stop at Guanajuato's most famous attraction, the **Museo de las Momias** (tel: 473-732 0639; www.momiasdeguanajuato.gob.mx; Mon–Thu 9am–6pm, Fri–Sun to 6.30pm). The museum exhibits more than 100 grotesque mummified corpses, mostly found when the public cemetery was extended in 1865 (the combination of mineral-rich soil and exceptionally dry air can mummify bodies in as little as five years).

About 1km (0.5 miles) southeast of here in the suburb of Pastita is **Casa de Arte Olga Costa-José Chávez Morado** (Thu–Sat 9.30am–5pm, Sun until 4pm), containing works by these two well-regarded artists, characterful antiques, and ancient ceramics.

The beautiful 17th-century **Hacienda San Gabriel Barrera** (daily 9am–6pm), about 2km (1 mile) out of town on the road to Marfil, may not be completely authentic, but it does give visitors an idea of the opulence of the wealthy during the colonial era.

DOLORES HIDALGO

Dolores Hidalgo Ⓑ, 45km (28 miles) northeast of Guanajuato, is known as the cradle of Mexican Independence. The beautiful 18th-century **Parroquia** on the main square, where Hidalgo uttered his famous *Grito*, is lovingly preserved. The **Museo Casa de Hidalgo** (tel: 428-685 0309; Tue–Sat 9am–6pm, Sun 8am–5pm; free on Sun), at the corner of Hidalgo and Morelos, is where Hidalgo lived and plotted the uprising with Ignacio

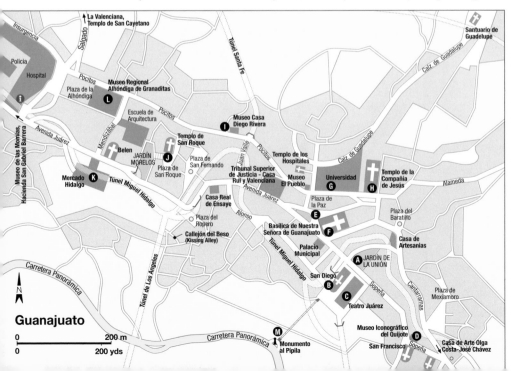

Guanajuato

0   200 m
0   200 yds

Allende and Juan de Aldama. The museum displays personal items and documents related to the life of the priest. Dolores is a typical Mexican town: the houses are solid and secretive, and there are many simple churches. Several workshops in town produce Talavera-type pottery and the ice-cream stands round the square are famous for the unusual flavors they offer.

SAN MIGUEL DE ALLENDE

The pretty colonial streets and buildings of **San Miguel de Allende** ❾ have been protected since 1926, when the whole town was declared a National Monument. Initially a native settlement, owing to the natural spring, the town grew exponentially after mining began in Zacatecas and other places to the north. In 1938, US artist Stirling Dickinson founded an art school here, and soon the town began to attract foreign artists, writers and, eventually, tourists. Even now it is easy to see the attraction. The **Instituto Allende** is still a popular arts and language center and one of the town's chief attractions, housed in what was the 18th-century home of the Conde de Canal. It offers a wide range of courses, including photography, sculpture, painting, and weaving. San Miguel de Allende now has a large community of US expatriates, including many artists and writers.

On the main plaza and dominating the entire town, the neo-Gothic **Parroquia** (parish church) was designed in the late 19th century by self-taught stonemason, Zeferino Gutiérrez, who gained inspiration from postcards of French churches, which is why the rest of the building is so different in construction from the wild facade.

Across the road from the parroquia, the **Museo Histórico de San Miguel de Allende** (tel: 415-152 2499; Tue–Sun 9am–5pm) occupies the elegant house where Independence hero Ignacio Allende was born. Exhibits relate to local history, particularly that of the Independence movement and its heroes. Also on

A bride-to-be arrives at church.

Relaxing at a viewpoint overlooking the Unesco World Heritage site of Guanajuato.

El Charco del Ingenio.

the plaza is the **Casa de los Condes de Canal**, one of the palatial mansions of the aristocratic Canal family, the devout "Medici" of San Miguel. It now houses the offices of Citibanamex, one of Mexico's largest banking institutions. It was Canal money in the 1730s that paid for the **Santa Casa de Loreto**, part of the multi-towered, 18th-century **Oratorio de San Felipe Neri**, a few blocks northeast. Dedicated to the Virgin Mary, the chapel is a replica of one in Loreto, Italy, and contains a lavish *camerino*, or dressing chapel. The main church contains more than 30 oil paintings depicting the life of San Felipe, some by Miguel Cabrera.

Two blocks west of the Jardín on Calle Canal is the church and monastery of **La Concepción**, with a huge dome (added in the late 19th century, again by Zeferino Gutiérrez) that was inspired by the one on Les Invalides in Paris. The former monastery now houses **Bellas Artes** (tel: 415-152 0289; Mon–Fri 10am–5.30pm, Sat 10am–2pm; free), a state-run fine arts education and cultural center. Like the Instituto Allende, Bellas Artes runs arts and crafts courses, although usually only in Spanish. One room contains an unfinished mural by David Alfaro Siqueiros (see page 113) who taught at the institute in the 1940s.

One of San Miguel's major attractions is the excellent shopping. In fact, it's hard to walk for more than 60 seconds without passing a gallery or store. Many of the businesses around the main square sell beautiful handmade items, including the finely woven tablecloths and the tin and brass ware produced in the region. You can also hop in a horse-drawn carriage for a scenic bump over the cobblestones.

El Charco del Ingenio (www. elcharco.org.mx; daily 9am–5pm) is a 65-hectare (160-acre) botanical garden mainly devoted to the cultivation of cacti, but also containing other plants and wildlife native to this semi-arid region. Located on a hill just 2km (1 mile) northeast of

Dome of the Parroquia, San Miguel de Allende.

San Miguel, the view of the town in the valley below is spectacular.

There are several resorts with hot springs and mineral waters in the area surrounding San Miguel. **Taboada**, 10km (6 miles) northwest, is probably the most popular. A little farther, in the village of **Atotonilco ⑩**, is a Baroque pilgrimage church filled with a huge variety of artwork including frescoes by the colonial artist Miguel Antonio Martínez de Pocasangre.

CITIES OF EL BAJÍO

The colonial cities of **León**, **Irapuato**, **Salamanca**, and **Celaya**, also in the state of Guanajuato, are growing rapidly and not much favored by tourists. Lively **León** is an important industrial and commercial center; it is Mexico's shoemaking capital and a good place to buy leather goods of any kind.

Salamanca, once a sleepy agricultural town, has become prosperous and chaotic since it became the site of a huge oil refinery. A redeeming feature is the church of **San Agustín**, which possesses some of the most beautiful retablos in Mexico. South of Salamanca, the farming village of **Yuriria** is the site of a 16th-century Augustinian monastery with an ornate plateresque facade.

Celaya has some late-colonial architecture and the neoclassical **Templo del Carmen**, designed by Francisco Eduardo Tresguerras.

QUERÉTARO

Alongside Guanajuato is the state of Querétaro whose capital, also called **Querétaro ⑪**, is known for its colonial art. It also has a good bullring and its festival attracts famous *toreros* and enthusiastic fans from afar. Querétaro has staged some of the greatest episodes in Mexican history, including the events that accelerated the proclamation of Independence. The Treaty of Guadalupe Hidalgo, which ended the Mexican–American war and handed over half of Mexico's national territory, was signed in Querétaro in 1848. It was here that Maximilian was executed in 1867 and

Hand of Fatima door knocker, San Miguel de Allende.

Independence Day decorations adorn the colonial streets of San Miguel de Allende.

☉ THE CRY OF INDEPENDENCE

On the morning of September 16, 1810, in the town of Dolores, the parish priest Padre Miguel Hidalgo rang the church bells. He addressed the congregation with an impassioned speech and ended with his famous *Grito de Dolores*: "Death to the Spaniards" *(Que mueran los gachupines)* – the "shout" for independence from Spanish rule, and the most famous outcry in Mexican history.

Hidalgo, a creole, soon became the moral and political leader of the Independence movement. He had no military training but with the help of men like Ignacio Allende, his forces – creoles, mestizos, and Amerindians – took control of a large part of western central Mexico and came close to taking the capital itself. Ten months later Hidalgo was imprisoned and executed by firing squad in Chihuahua. After Independence was finally won 11 years later the town was renamed Dolores Hidalgo.

Every year, on the night of September 15, enormous crowds gather to hear the president and politicians in the squares of every town across the whole country repeat *El Grito*: "¡Viva México!" marking the beginning of Independence Day celebrations; and that is the one night of the year when the church bell still rings out in the colonial town of Dolores Hidalgo.

that the Constitution was signed in 1917.

The outskirts of Querétaro are sprawling and industrial, but the preserved historic center has been declared a World Heritage site. The main plaza, Jardín Zenea, is dominated by the church of **San Francisco**, one of the city's earliest. The dome's colored tiles were imported from Spain in 1540. The cloister of the adjoining monastery now houses the **Museo Regional** (Tue–Sun 9am–6pm; free on Sun) displaying local archeological finds as well as some fine colonial paintings.

One block north of the square is the 19th-century **Teatro de la República** (daily 9am–5pm; free). This building has been a venue for two significant moments in Mexican history: where Emperor Maximilian faced the tribunal in 1867 and where the Mexican Constitution was signed in 1917.

Facing the attractive Plaza de Armas, the **Casa de la Corregidora** (now the Palacio de Gobierno) was once the residence of Doña Josefa Ortiz de Domínguez, wife of the local governor. In 1810 Doña Josefa, *La Corregidora*, sent a message alerting the Independence conspirators to the fact that her husband had discovered their plot; her action triggered Father Hidalgo's *Grito de la Independencia* (see page 225).

Curiously enough, the monument in the square is not dedicated to Father Hidalgo or Ignacio Allende, but rather to a colonial aristocrat, Don Juan Antonio Urrutia y Aranda, who built the magnificent 1,170-meter (3,840ft) **aqueduct** with its 74 towering arches, which was completed in 1738. The aqueduct, which can be seen from the *mirador* (viewpoint) in the east of Querétaro, still carries water into the city.

The **Museo de Arte de Querétaro** (tel: 442-212 2357; Tue–Sun 10am–6pm) is housed in a late-Baroque Augustinian monastery with fantastically carved columns and arches. The leering gargoyles are said to be uttering the Ave Maria in sign language. The museum also exhibits a

Horse awaiting its rider outside a San Miguel cantina.

fine collection of paintings from the 16th to the 20th centuries.

SANTA CLARA

Behind a deceptively austere facade, the church of **Santa Clara**, one block north on the corner of Madero and Allende, is wildly Baroque: the interior walls are covered with overflowing gilt retablos, and the grille separating the choir from the congregation is a masterpiece. Outside, the fountain dedicated to Neptune was designed in 1797 by one of Mexico's greatest architects, Francisco Eduardo Tresguerras. **Templo de Santa Rosa de Viterbo** (daily 9am–6pm), southwest of the center at Arteaga and Montes, contains grand altarpieces and a splendid organ. It has a more flamboyant exterior with buttresses that seem more Chinese than European in style.

East of the center, the **Convento de la Santa Cruz** (daily 9am–6pm; donation requested) is built on the site of the Otomí defeat in 1531, and is said to be inhabited by the ghost of Emperor Maximilian, who was imprisoned here before his execution.

To the west of Querétaro, the **Cerro de las Campanas** is a low, barren hill where Maximilian went before the firing squad. Nearby is a humble chapel dedicated to the emperor and a huge statue of Benito Juárez.

PROVINCIAL QUERÉTARO

About 60km (38 miles) south of Querétaro, **San Juan del Río** ⑫ is a popular place for a weekend outing from the capital. A market town with narrow streets and solid provincial houses, it is not as aristocratic as Querétaro, but offers the atmosphere of rural Mexico. Some of the country's best fighting bulls are raised near here, and the town is known for basket-weavers and lapidaries (dealers in opals and amethysts).

Nearby, on Highway 120, is the picturesque village of **Tequisquiapan** ⑬, another weekend resort with thermal springs, fine climate, water sports, and a popular wine and cheese festival in the summer.

The 18th-century Querétaro aqueduct.

Querétaro street performers.

A farmer gathers blue agave for tequila production.

JALISCO AND MICHOACÁN

Guadalajara and Morelia are very Spanish cities, but indigenous traditions and culture are still alive in many of the Purépecha and Huichol villages of Michoacán and Jalisco.

Jalisco, northwest of Mexico City and the Central Highlands, is one of the most important states in the country. It has agriculture, a booming industry, and popular coastal resorts. Its capital, **Guadalajara** , is the second-largest city in Mexico, with a population of more than 4 million. Jalisco is also the home of tequila, the hat dance, and *mariachi* music.

Perched on a "mile-high" plain (actually 1,524 meters/5,000ft high), Guadalajara has been called "the biggest small town in Mexico;" it is a busy metropolis that manages to retain a provincial atmosphere. The city has a pleasant climate, with temperatures averaging 20–25°C (68–77°F) all year round, although the days can be hot in summer (July–August).

PEARL OF THE WEST

Mexico's second-largest city is in many ways one of its most pleasant. The numerous universities, the cooking schools, the language institutes mean a constant influx of foreigners and Mexican youth, and the expansive parks and plazas with fountains and monuments make it an attractive and communal city perfect for strolling and watching the world go by. It has a big-city bustle with all the benefits of great restaurants, delightful B&Bs, and fancy hotels, while the

calm markets, local vendors, and quiet back streets keep it from feeling overwhelming. It is also large enough to attract vibrant cultural events, yet small enough to avoid soaring crime rates of larger urban centers. Guadalajara has the kind of easy ambience that encourages visitors to linger.

Founded in 1532 by Nuño de Guzmán, Guadalajara was not recognized by the Spanish Crown until 10 years later. A cruel and ambitious conquistador, Guzmán, who intended

Main attractions
Guadalajara
Guadalajara Cathedral
Tlaquepaque
Tequila
Morelia
Monarch Butterfly Sanctuary
Pátzcuaro
Tzintzuntzán
Volcan Paricutín

Maps on pages216 230, 237

Cobbled street in Pátzcuaro.

Guadalajara to be the capital of the kingdom of New Galicia, was sent back to Spain in disgrace. Guadalajara managed to remain independent of Mexico City, and its archbishopric was as rich and powerful as that of the capital itself.

Guadalajarans are uniquely proud of their city and their role in shaping Mexico's historical past. The city played a key role in the Mexican War of Independence: it was here that Hidalgo spoke about the importance of ending slavery, and numerous Mexican leaders of the 19th and 20th centuries have visited or lived here. Guadalajara was also one of the largest cities to avoid invasion by American forces during the Mexican–American War.

The city has long been an important commercial center and it always retained some political and judicial autonomy; it is strategically located near one of the few passages leading through the mountains to the fertile Pacific coast. Its university was founded very early on, and students were drawn from as far away as southern Texas,

then part of New Spain; the university remains one of Mexico's best and most popular to this day.

THE CATHEDRAL

Most of the interesting sights in Guadalajara are downtown. Its landmark, the huge **cathedral Ⓐ**, with its yellow-tiled spire, exhibits a mixture of styles, from neo-Gothic to Baroque and neoclassical. Surrounded by four plazas, it provides a welcome oasis amid the bustle of the big city.

Don't miss the tombs beneath the altar, where several religious figures are buried. The cathedral's many exhibits are worth visiting as well – religious artifacts dating back hundreds of years are on public display on the walls and in side rooms. Tipping a local person 20 or so pesos for a short tour is worth it, as he or she can point out many details of the place that you would otherwise miss, and currently there is little to no literature about the cathedral aimed at tourists.

Two blocks west of the cathedral is an interesting market, the **Mercado**

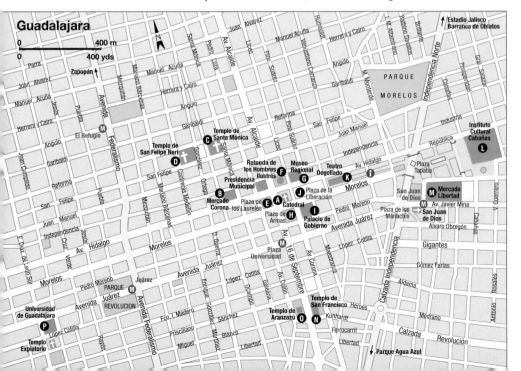

Corona **B**, with stands selling every kind of herbal tea and natural remedy imaginable. These narrow side streets, with their brightly painted walls, street vendors, and little stores are great for exploring. You'll find orange trees, and houses with pretty wrought-iron grilles leading into patios overflowing with bougainvillea, jasmine, and songbirds. Be sure to take some photos.

Two often-overlooked churches in this area are the **Templo de Santa Mónica C** and **Templo de San Felipe Neri D**; the former, a convent church, has a prodigiously carved, late-Baroque facade. Inside, women still pray to St Christopher to help them find a husband (or to get rid of the one they've got). Nearby, 18th-century San Felipe is a very grand church with an exotic belfry and well-proportioned dome.

A fountain in the **Plaza de los Laureles E**, in front of the cathedral, commemorates the founding of the city and serves as a good base for people-watching or as a landmark for a meeting point; along its north side is the porticoed Presidencia Municipal (City Hall). Some of Jalisco's most distinguished men are buried beneath the Greek-style **Rotonda de los Hombres Ilustres F**, which stands, surrounded by Doric columns, in the center of another plaza to the north of the cathedral. Statues of famous *jalicienses* are dotted along the plaza's shady paths. The **Museo Regional G** (tel: 33-3614 2227; Tue–Sun 9am–5pm) occupies an attractive 18th-century building, a former seminary, on the east side of the square. The museum has galleries dedicated to archeology, colonial history, painting, and ethnography.

To the south of the cathedral is the pretty **Plaza de Armas H**, originally Guadalajara's main market square and ancient execution site. The French bandstand in the center hosts concerts every Thursday and Sunday evening. Facing the plaza, the late-Baroque **Palacio de Gobierno I** (Mon–Fri 9am–7pm; free) houses a magnificent mural by **José Clemente Orozco** (see page

Belle Epoque figure detail on the bandstand in Plaza de Armas, Guadalajara.

The dome and twin spires of Guadalajara's cathedral.

114). The mural is a striking homage to Padre Miguel Hidalgo, the "father of Mexican Independence."

The **Plaza de la Liberación ❶**, to the east of the cathedral, is the largest of the four squares. Designed by contemporary Guadalajara architect Ignacio Díaz Morales, the plaza blends with the buildings framing the rear of the cathedral and the facade of the 19th-century **Teatro Degollado ❷** (Tue–Sun 10am–2pm and during performances). The recently restored theater has a sumptuous red velvet and gilt interior and a ceiling painted with a scene from Dante's *Divine Comedy*.

HOSPICIO CABAÑAS

Behind the theater, the **Plaza Tapatía** is a long pedestrian precinct that leads down to the elegant **Instituto Cultural Cabañas ❸** (https://hospiciocabanas.jalisco.gob.mx; Tue–Sun 10am–6pm; free on Tue) in the **Hospicio Cabañas**, which was founded and financed by one of Guadalajara's great benefactors, Bishop Juan Ruiz de Cabañas. More than 20 patios interconnect the different sections of this neoclasssical building, which was designed by Manuel Tolsá in 1805. At the center is the Capilla Tolsá, whose walls and ceiling were decorated in the late 1930s with what are considered to be Orozco's finest murals. These dramatic, symbolic works depict, among other things, the destruction and suffering caused by the Spanish Conquest. As the city's most important cultural center, the institute also organizes many other artistic activities such as plays, concerts, and movies. The odd bronze statue rising up near the fountain is actually a headless snake. The head, which fell off in the 1980s, lies on the ground nearby, a testament to creative – if unsuccessful – engineering.

MARKET STANDS AND MARIACHIS

Guadalajara has a host of great shopping opportunities for just about anyone with a few pesos to

Plaza Tapatía, Guadalajara.

burn, so many, in fact, that shoppers will find themselves overwhelmed by the possibilities. Bargaining is commonplace, and in crowded areas it isn't a bad idea to keep some change in a separate place, away from your wallet, just in case a pickpocket comes along. While this kind of crime is rare, a little caution can make a big difference in the long run. Just south of the Hospicio Cabañas, at the core of Guadalajara's traditional center, the **Mercado Libertad** is a vast, colorful, covered market. Better known as San Juan de Dios after the nearby church, the market sells everything from herbal remedies, fresh food, and handicrafts, to imported jeans and stereos. Beside the church, the **Plaza de los Mariachis** comes alive in the evening when the musicians gather in the square to play traditional songs and *corridos* (ballads) outside the cafés and restaurants. If you stop for an *helada* (ice-cream cone) and sit on a park bench as the musicians play, you'll find yourself fitting right in with the easy pace of life here.

In the southern part of the downtown area, **San Francisco** and **Aranzazú** are two remarkable colonial churches built by the Franciscans in their ambitious attempts to extend their missions all the way to the Californias. Now located in a busy financial district, these churches, with their attractive gardens, were once at the heart of one of the city's best neighborhoods. The Templo de Aranzazú has a highly elaborate interior with three golden Churrigueresque altarpieces. The retablos in the older San Francisco church were destroyed by arson in the 1930s.

Farther south, toward the train station, the large, well-kept **Parque Agua Azul** (Tue–Sun 10am–6.30pm) offers relief from the city noise with an aviary, butterfly dome, and orchid house. In the southeastern corner of the park, the **Museo de Paleontología** (Mon–Fri 9.30am–5pm, Sat 10am–5pm, Sun 10am–3.30pm) houses a collection of prehistoric fossils. The **Casa de la Cultura Jalisciense** (Mon–Fri 10am–6pm), on the

Rotonda de los Hombres Illustres, Guadalajara.

Getting a shoeshine in downtown Guadalajara.

north side of the park, showcases arts and cultural exhibitions from around the state.

THE UNIVERSITY AND BEYOND

Farther west, on Avenida Juárez, is the **Universidad de Guadalajara** ⓟ, whose central building dates from the 1920s. More impressive Orozco murals decorate the dome and back wall of the *Paraninfo* (main hall). The building also houses the **Museo de las Artes** (tel: 333-134 1664; Tue–Sun 10am–6pm; free), which exhibits a permanent collection of mainly local modern art, and temporary shows from farther afield. Behind the university, the neo-Gothic church, modeled on the cathedral of Orvieto in Italy, is known as the **Expiatorio**. The area just beyond the university, along Vallarta and Chapultepec, offers relief from the downtown noise and traffic with its broad, tree-lined streets and inviting sidewalk cafés.

Vegetable market stalls in Guadalajara's Mercado Libertad.

Calzada Independencia is the backbone of popular Guadalajara. It is not a beautiful street, but it is busy and full of life. Due north along the street is a huge soccer stadium, the **Estadio Jalisco**, a shrine to Mexico's most popular – some might say fanatical – sport. A few kilometers farther north is the **Barranca de Oblatos**, a superb 600-meter (1,970ft) canyon with dramatic stone walls softened by lush vegetation and an impressive waterfall, the **Cola de Caballo**. At the bottom of the canyon the Santiago River slides into the tropics and toward the distant Pacific. There's a great view of the Barranca from the nearby **zoo** (tel: 363-674 4488; www.zooguadalajara.com.mx; Wed–Sun 10am–5pm, open daily during school vacations) at **Huentitán Park**, which has more than 1,500 animals and also features an amusement park and planetarium.

In the northwestern suburbs of Guadalajara, **Zapopán** is visited for its basilica, a Baroque church that houses the miraculous image of the Virgen de Zapopán. Every summer, the Virgin is paraded from church to church through the streets to Guadalajara; then, on October 12, in what must be among the best-attended pilgrimages in the world, the image is brought back to Zapopán. Next door to the church is the small but interesting **Museo de Arte Huichol Wixárica** (tel: 333-636 4430; Mon–Sat 10am–6pm, Sun 9am–2pm), with displays that relate to the art, crafts, and traditions of the Huichol people. There's also a shop selling some of these crafts on site.

TLAQUEPAQUE AND TONALÁ

San Pedro Tlaquepaque, in the southeastern suburbs, is famous for pottery and craftwork, though it pays to shop carefully, as the quality varies and many pieces are now mass-produced. However, there are still many beautiful, handmade crafts to be found and the **Museo Regional de la Cerámica** (tel: 333-635 5404;

Mon–Sat 10am–6pm, Sun 9am–4pm; free on Sun) is worth visiting for its display of local pottery and to get a sense of the range of quality that's out there. Then wander along Tlaquepaque's cobbled streets and browse around the 19th-century houses that have been turned into shops and restaurants, looking for deals (or meals) that suit your fancy. **El Parián**, the covered market on the central Jardín Hidalgo, is especially favored by *tapatíos* – the nickname given to people from Guadalajara – who flock here on weekends to drink beer, eat *birria* (a local dish of barbecued kid/young goat), and listen to the *mariachis*.

Much of the pottery and glassware sold in Tlaquepaque and Guadalajara is produced in the *fábricas* (factories) of nearby **Tonalá**. On Thursdays and Sundays practically the whole town becomes a street market, although many of the stands sell factory seconds, and sometimes it is better to go directly to the shops.

TEQUILA

What the town of Cognac is to France, so **Tequila ⑮** is to Mexico – and then some. Mexico's best-known spirit is of course distilled in other places in the state of Jalisco but this is the spirited center of tequila tourism, and one of the Mexican government's *pueblos magicos* (magic towns) to boot. *True* tequila must be made with the variety of blue agave growing only in the area around the town here, but in addition to giving the drink Geographical Protection Status the Mexican government has invested significant money in promoting (largely drinks-based) tourism locally.

At **La Perseverencia Distillery** (tel: 374-742 7100; www.casasauza.com) in Tequila's Colonia Centro, visitors can see the tequila nurseries where the blue agave plants are reared and learn how agave harvesting works, then head on to the distillery itself for a run-down of the production process and tastings.

CHAPALA, TAPALPA, AND BEYOND

Southeast of Guadalajara is **Lago de Chapala**, Mexico's biggest (although fast shrinking) lake, renowned for its glorious sunsets. The comfortable weekend homes of wealthy *tapatíos* and retired *norteamericanos* line its north shore. The town of **Chapala ⑯**, only 40 minutes from Guadalajara, can get crowded on weekends; you can rent a boat to take you to one of the tiny islands for lunch. Farther west along the shore is the attractive, sleepy village of **Ajijic ⑰**, largely populated by US expatriates, and the thermal spa at **San Juan Cosalá**.

The town of **Tapalpa ⑱**, with its delightful old wooden-balconied houses in the cool pine-forested hills southwest of Lake Chapala, offers a complete change of scenery, and makes a delightful weekend escape from the city.

Mosaic wall in a Tlaquepaque side street.

Sculptures along Plaza Tapatía, Guadalajara.

TEQUILA

Straight, with salt and lime, or in a *margarita*: chances are you won't leave Mexico without a taste of this venerable spirit.

Like Jerez in Spain, famous for sherry, or Cognac in France, the town of Tequila has achieved a reputation far out of proportion to its size. Millions who would otherwise never dream of going to this small town will rhapsodize about its name, referring, of course, to the eponymous liquor.

Less than an hour's drive northwest of Guadalajara, Tequila is surrounded by thousands of acres of bluish-green, spear-like, cultivated maguey (agave) plants. Although there are hundreds of different species, under Mexican law at least 51 percent of any tequila must be from the *Tequilana weber* agave, which grows only in this region. The best tequilas use pure maguey juice; cheaper brands are usually supplemented with cane juice.

After eight to 10 years' growth, the maguey is trimmed down to its 50kg (110lb) heart, the *piña*, which is steamed, then shredded and squeezed. Sugar is added and it is fermented for four days before undergoing two distillations. Most of this colorless liquid is then bottled; the rest is aged in oak casks for up to

A lorry-load of blue agave.

seven years, during which time it assumes the golden color and mellow flavor of *tequila añejo*.

Mezcal and *pulque* are also derived from the maguey cactus. *Pulque* is fermented rather than distilled (the distillation process was unknown before the Conquest) but it is becoming hard to find these days. Mezcal, primarily produced in Oaxaca but made here in Jalisco as well, is a fiery, flavorful, high-proof alcoholic drink, which, like tequila, is distilled, although the methods used are less complex. The small *gusano* worm in the *mezcal* bottle is considered a delicacy, but there is no unified theory as to how it came to be placed there. The most plausible is that a genuine *mezcal* should have a high enough alcohol content to effectively pickle the grub, thus proving the legitimacy of the drink. Many excellent brands opt to forgo the hapless larvae, preferring to sustain their sales on brand name alone.

Tequila is the only one of the three liquors to have taken its place on the top shelf, especially in the US, which annually imports several hundred thousand dollars' worth from its southern neighbor. There are three common varieties – *blanco*, *reposado*, and *añejo* – primarily distinctions of color, flavor, and age. *Blanco* – as the name suggests – is white, young, and strong. *Reposado* has been aged and has a golden color and a medium taste. *Añejo*, meanwhile, has been aged for at least four years and will have lost a lot of the punch that most people attribute to tequila. For someone who prefers cognac to tequila, *añejo* will be the best choice, while hardened tequila afficionados may prefer a shot of *blanco*.

THE TEQUILA EXPERIENCE

The ritual of correct tequila drinking begins with placing salt on the fleshy area between the thumb and forefinger. After licking the salt, take a shot of tequila, then suck on a slice of lime. This establishes a precise and satisfying balance of strong flavors in which the tequila's pure, sweet fire is complemented by the acidity of lime, and the relief given by those grains of salt. However, a good quality añejo tequila, in particular, needs no accompaniment, and it is just as acceptable to sip tequila straight, as one would a fine cognac. Others prefer their tequila mixed with Sangrita, a spicy concoction with tomato and orange juice, or in the ever-popular, ubiquitous *margarita*.

But for anyone seeking a few lei-surely days at the beach, **Puerto Vallarta** – Jalisco's sophisticated Pacific coast resort – is just minutes away by plane and three hours by car (see page 245). For those who prefer less activity and more privacy, there are long stretches of creamy-colored sand beaches such as Sayulita north of Puerto Vallarta, and romantic rocky coves to the south.

MICHOACÁN

With its lakes, rivers, indigenous villages, volcanoes, and colonial cities, Michoacán is like a miniature model of Mexico. In the northeastern part of the state, the capital, **Morelia** ⑲, formerly known as Valladolid, was renamed in 1828 for José María Morelos, one of the heroes of the Independence movement. The roads (toll and free) from Mexico City are marvelously scenic. The slow but beautiful free road passes **Mil Cumbres** (Thousand Peaks), through shady pine forests, mountain vistas, cool waterfalls, and rural villages. Those taking the

coastal route from Puerto Vallarta to Acapulco along Mexico 200 will find a beautiful shoreline, remote beaches, banana and coconut plantations, and laid-back locals.

The climate is mild and life moves at a slow tempo in Morelia, a pretty colonial town built of rose-colored stone. The **cathedral** ⓐ, which took more than a century to build (1640–1744) is a grand combination of Herrerian, Baroque, and neoclassical styles. Sadly, much of the Baroque relief work inside was replaced in the 19th century. However, there is a magnificent German organ, and a corn-paste statue of Christ wearing a 16th-century crown, a gift from Felipe II of Spain. In the **Palacio de Gobierno** ⓑ, a former seminary on the other side of Avenida Madero, local artist Alfredo Zalce has painted colorful murals that reflect the beauty of Michoacán and its rich history.

The **Casa Natal de Morelos** (tel: 443-312 2793; Mon–Fri 9am–8pm, Sat–Sun 9am–7.30pm; free) on the corner of Corregidora and Obeso,

Santuario de Mariposas El Rosario.

⊙ BUTTERFLY PARK

One of nature's most spectacular sights is the annual monarch butterfly migration, which begins in the United States and Canada and ends here in the mountains near the village of Angangueo. Though threatened by severe frosts, logging, and climate change, there are still between 30 and 100 million monarch butterflies that breed in the eastern part of Michoacán. Not far from the Mexico City–Morelia highway is the **Santuario de Mariposas El Rosario** ⑳ (Nov–Mar daily). It is best to visit the sanctuary in the morning when the butterflies flutter from the trees to the humid ground as the day becomes warmer. The butterflies blanket the entire landscape: covering trees, bushes, the ground, everything. Blur your eyes slightly and they look like flakes of fluttering orange snow.

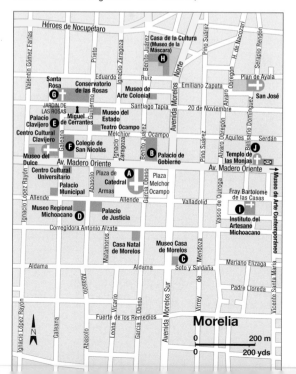

Morelia

Eat

It's worth stopping for a creamy *nieve* (ice cream), as this state is supposed to have the best. In fact, all over Mexico you'll see ice cream shops that have adopted the name Michoacán as a mark of their quality.

was the birthplace (in 1765) of José María Morelos y Pavón, who studied under Padre Hidalgo and also became a priest. One block east, the **Museo Casa de Morelos** C (tel: 443-313 2651; daily 9am–7pm; free on Sun), where Morelos lived from 1801, has exhibits on his life along with memorabilia, such as the blindfold he wore when he was executed in 1815.

Just off the square, the **Museo Regional Michoacano** D (tel: 443-312 0407; Tue–Sun 9am–5pm) has exhibits on archeology, history, ethnology, and, most interestingly, a complete pharmacy dating from 1868.

The elegant **Palacio Clavijero** E, a former Jesuit seminary founded in 1660, now houses the **Centro Cultural Clavijero** (**Tue**–Sun 9am–6pm). The building, a multi-use space with concerts and exhibitions, was named in honor of Francisco Xavier Clavijero, a Jesuit who taught here and who wrote what many believe to be the best historical account of

Lago de Chapala.

Mexico. The nearby **Colegio de San Nicolás** F, where Morelos studied as a young man, is one of the oldest universities in the Americas. One block north, facing a peaceful plaza with a statue of Miguel de Cervantes, is the pretty Baroque church of **Santa Rosa** G and the adjoining 18th-century **Conservatorio de las Rosas**, which still functions as a major music academy and arranges classical music concerts from time to time.

MARVELOUS MASKS

A small but fascinating collection of ceremonial masks associated with dances from different regions of Mexico is on display at the **Museo de la Máscara** H (tel: 443-312 8898; Mon–Fri 10am–2pm, 4–8pm, Sat–Sun 10am–2pm, 4–6pm; free). The museum is part of the Casa de la Cultura, a lively cultural center in the converted **Convento del Carmen**, which hosts arts workshops, performances, and temporary exhibitions.

Three blocks east of the square, in the converted Convento de San Francisco, the **Instituto del Artesano Michoacano** I (daily 9am–8pm; free) has devoted separate rooms to handicrafts from different Michoacán villages, their dazzling craftsmanship rivalled only perhaps by that of Oaxaca. Farther east, beyond the beautiful **Templo de las Monjas** J, on Avenida Madero, is the 18th-century **Aqueduct**, with 253 arches. South of the aqueduct, in Morelia's largest park – the Bosque de Cuauhtémoc – is the **Museo de Arte Contemporáneo** (tel: 443-312 5404; Mon–Fri 10am–8pm, Sat–Sun 10am–6pm; free), which has very good exhibitions of contemporary art.

LAKE PÁTZCUARO AND JANITZIO

The very Spanish city of Morelia is uncharacteristic of the rest of Michoacán, which has remained strongly indigenous. Directly west of Morelia, surrounded by native villages, is **Lago de Pátzcuaro** ㉑, where the fishermen use distinctive butterfly-shaped fishing nets, and *pescado blanco*, a white fish unique to the lake, is a common menu item. There are boat trips to the island of **Janitzio**, in the middle of the lake, with its giant 40-meter (130ft) sculpture of Independence hero, José María Morelos. You can climb inside the statue, right up to the clenched fist, for a wonderful panoramic view.

Janitzio is especially known for its **Day of the Dead** celebrations (see page 90) on November 1–2, when local people cross the lake in a procession of candlelit canoes, bringing flowers, food, and other offerings to the cemetery in commemoration of their loved ones. In order to preserve the intimacy of the occasion, tourists are discouraged from attending the all-night vigil in Janitzio, but there are other cemeteries in the region where visitors are welcome to observe the celebrations.

PÁTZCUARO

The town of **Pátzcuaro** ㉒, on the south side of the lake, has whitewashed adobe houses with overhanging red-tiled roofs, colonial mansions with balconies and coats of arms, cobbled streets, and the smell of wood smoke in the air. This is the heart of Purépecha country; the Friday market is especially lively, although imported goods are taking over from indigenous wares.

All the main sights of Pátzcuaro, or Tarascan, are on or near the two central squares: first, the shady **Plaza Vasco de Quiroga**, which is named after the 16th-century bishop who dedicated his life to the welfare of the Purépecha, or Tarascan people; his statue stands in the center. On the east side of the square is the 17th-century **Casa del Gigante** (House of the Giant), former residence of the Counts of Menocal and still a private home. Other mansions have been converted into hotels, restaurants, and craft shops.

The **Plaza Gertrudis Bocanegra**, one block north, is named after an

Musician by the harbor, Pátzcuaro.

Janitzio Island.

Danza de los Viejitos (Dance of the Little Old Men), Plaza Vasco de Quiroga, Pátzcuaro.

Selling fresh corn tortillas on Plaza Vasco de Quiroga, Pátzcuaro.

Independence heroine. The busy town market is on the west side, while on the north side, the 16th-century *biblioteca* (library) occupies the former church of **San Agustín**. Inside, murals by the celebrated Juan O'Gorman illustrate the history of Michoacán. East of the plaza is the **Basílica de Nuestra Señora de la Salud**, a shrine for health-seekers from all over Mexico, who come to revere the statue of Our Lady of Health. Quiroga planned the basilica to be a majestic and enormous, five-nave cathedral, but unfortunately the majority of his plans were never completed.

The **Museo Regional de Artes Populares** (tel: 434-342 1029; Tue–Sun 9am–5pm), south of the basilica, on Alcantarillas, was founded in 1640 as the Colegio de San Nicolás by Don Vasco de Quiroga. The museum has a fine collection of regional handicrafts, including lacquerwork, pottery, textiles, and copperware from Santa Clara. The **Casa de los Once Patios** (House of Eleven Patios; daily 10am–6pm) southeast of the main square, is a craft center, with workshops and boutiques set around the courtyards of an 18th-century Dominican convent.

THE VILLAGES OF MICHOACÁN

On the eastern shore of Lake Pátzcuaro, the village of **Tzintzuntzán** (Place of Hummingbirds) is the ancient capital of the Purépecha, or *tarascos* as they were called by the Spanish. The Tarascans, unconquered until the Spanish arrived with their armor plate and cannons, have preserved their traditions, language, and way of life to this day, especially in the mountain redoubts. The ruins, also called **Tzintzuntzán** (daily 9am–5.30pm), and one of the chief ancient sites in Michoacán, consist mainly of a group of five *yácatas*, or round-based temples, on a reconstructed terrace that offers wonderful views of the lake and surrounding countryside. In the village, there is a large 16th-century Franciscan monastery in peaceful gardens; the olive trees are deemed the oldest in Mexico,

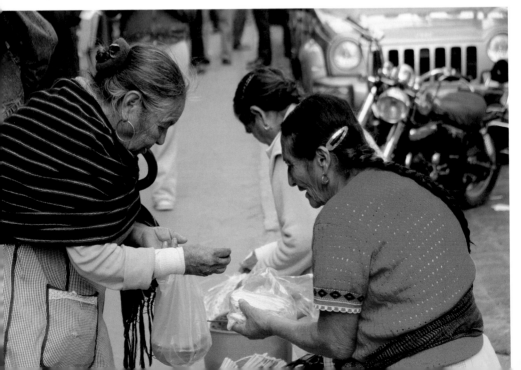

said to have been brought from Spain by Quiroga himself.

The area is dotted with indigenous villages, each known for its own special handicraft. Many of these are sold in the market town of **Quiroga**, which itself produces brightly painted wooden furniture and masks. South of Pátzcuaro, for instance, **Santa Clara del Cobre** (sometimes called Villa Escalante) is famous for its copperware, although no ore is now extracted from local mines. Guitars and all sorts of wooden handicrafts are made in the workshops of **Paracho**.

The town of **Uruapan** ㉓, 62km (39 miles) west of Pátzcuaro, marks the beginning of another Michoacán – the *tierra caliente*, or tropical lands. It is the center of a rich agricultural area known for its avocados. The town itself is famous for its lacquered trays and boxes, of which there is a good display in the **Museo Regional de Arte Popular** (tel: 452-524 3434; Tue–Sun 9.30am–3pm, 3.30–6pm; free), which is housed in one of the oldest buildings in Uruapan, the

16th-century **Huatapera** (built as one of the first hospitals). A few blocks west of the *Zócalo* (square), along Calle Independencia, is the entrance to the delightful **Parque Nacional Eduardo Ruiz** (daily 8am–6pm), a luxuriant tropical park that surrounds the source of the Río Cupatitzio. The country around Uruapan is remarkable. One very popular excursion, just 10km (6 miles) south, is to see the Río Cupatitzio cascading 25 meters (82ft) through lush tropical forests, over the **Tzararácua** waterfall.

Even more impressive is a trip to the still smouldering **Paricutín**, a volcano whose eruption in 1943 lasted until 1952, leaving whole villages buried, particularly San Juan Parangaricutiro, whose church tower still pokes up above the solidified lava. Miraculously, there were no fatalities. It is an extraordinary moon-like landscape, which is slowly sprouting with green life again. You can walk or rent a pony and guide in the Purépecha village of **Angahuan**, 30km (18 miles) northwest of Uruapan.

The church, San Juan Parangaricutiro, was trapped in the lava slide following Paricutín's eruption.

The Tzintzuntzán site contains many yacatas, a type of rounded temple platform.

📷 MEXICAN ICONS

Nostalgic, romantic, the charros with their sombreros, embroidered jackets, and daring horseback feats are an abiding symbol of Mexican tradition.

To describe a *charro* as just a Mexican cowboy is an injustice. He has become perhaps the country's most instantly recognizable symbol, an image of Mexican identity.

In the first decades of Spanish rule, only Spaniards were allowed to ride horses. However, when cattle ranches spread across central and western Mexico, they needed workers, and as well as Andalusians – prized by landowners for their riding skills – mestizos and indigenous horsemen were employed on the haciendas. The traditional Andalusian short riding jacket was adapted, with added Mexican ornament for special occasions; the Andalusian flat-brimmed hat evolved into the *charro*'s sombrero. Haciendas and the *charro* way of life extended over large areas, but are most associated with Jalisco state, also home to two other Mexican icons, tequila and *mariachis*; the latter, of course, also adopted *charro* dress.

Horsemanship displays had long been a feature of country fiestas, and the structure of such contests (*charrerías*) had become more formal. However, it was really only after the Revolution that the *charro* became an inescapable feature of Mexican popular entertainment, and *Lienzos Charros* (rings for *charrerías*) spread across the country. As Mexico urbanized, the *charro* became a nostalgic symbol of a simpler way of life. The great actor-singers of the golden age of Mexican cinema celebrated *charro* heroes: brave, passionate, loyal to friends and fierce with enemies, fun-loving, macho, endlessly flirtatious with women, but irresistibly charming. Nowadays, many Mexicans see this as a tired, kitsch stereotype, but the *charrería* still has a hold as Mexico's "national sport."

A charro demonstrating his impressive roping skills at the Lienzo Charro in Zacatecas.

Charro skills are based in country traditions and often passed from father to son; the earlier you start, the more you learn.

Ornate leather saddlery.

The coleadero, where a charro tries to throw a charging bull off balance, originated in Los Llanos de Apan, Hidalgo.

The charrería program

The biggest *Lienzos Charros* are in Mexico City and Guadalajara, where competitions are held on most Sundays, but there are rings in nearly every city. Full of music and color, *charrerías* are spectacular.

The show starts with a *desfile* or parade, as the competitors ride in to salute judges and public. The first *suerte* (event) is the *cala de caballo*, when each rider demonstrates his mastery over his horse by going full gallop across the ring, then coming to an abrupt stop inside a precisely marked rectangle and executing a series of movements before walking his horse out backward. Some of the most thrilling events are the *coleadero*, when a *charro* on horseback tries to throw a charging bull off balance and roll it over by pulling on its tail; and the *paso de la muerte* (pass of death), when a *charro* jumps from his saddle onto a bareback colt at full speed.

The last *suerte* is for women, who perform as a team, an *escaramuza charra*. They carry out intricate maneuvers that could be compared to dressage, except that they ride very fast, and no one could suggest it's an easy option. Plus, to remain feminine, *charras* must ride sidesaddle, and in long skirts.

Beautifully crafted boots of the finest leather are only one part of the charro costume.

A charro makes his entrance at full speed.

A charra and her steed.

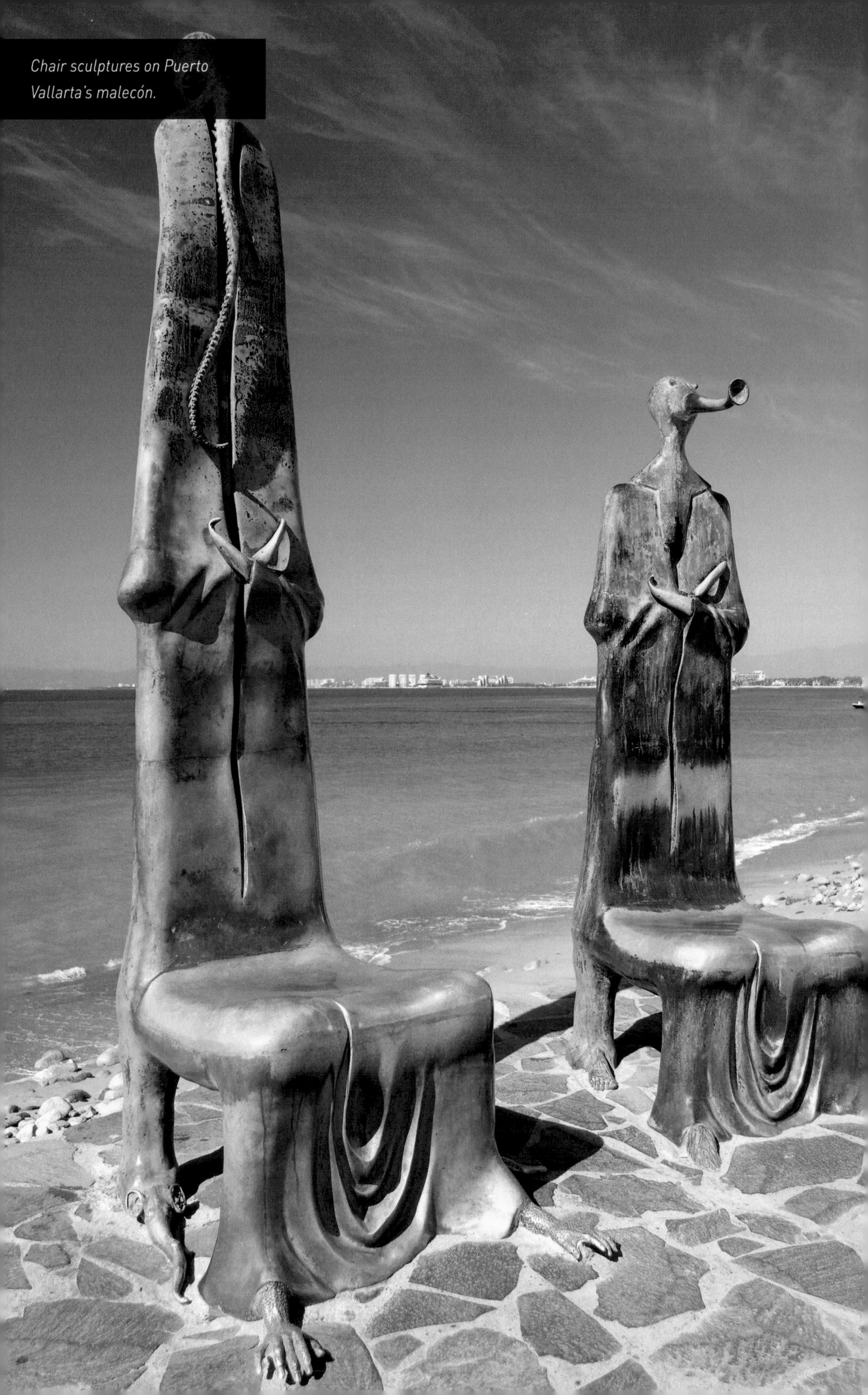

Chair sculptures on Puerto Vallarta's malecón.

ACAPULCO AND THE PACIFIC BEACHES

The Pacific coast has glamorous beach resorts with luxury hotels and all the facilities, but there are still secluded bays where you can just slip into a hammock and watch the tequila sunrise.

Acapulco, with its dramatic mountains sweeping down to the Pacific, was the first of the coastal resorts to achieve international fame as a hangout for the "beautiful people." Later, when the value of tourism as a major industry became apparent, Ixtapa was developed some 257km (160 miles) northwest. Puerto Vallarta comes next, and in between are just miles of beautiful coastline. Several major surf breaks, such as Sayulita and Pascuales, draw wave worshippers from around the globe.

ROMANTIC VALLARTA

Puerto Vallarta 24 owes its fame to Hollywood. It came to prominence with John Huston's 1964 filming of Tennessee Williams' *Night of the Iguana* on Mismaloya beach, just south of town. Richard Burton, who starred in the movie, subsequently bought a home nearby; his relationship with bride-to-be Elizabeth Taylor attracted much media attention, and it wasn't long before the tourists started arriving. Their house – at Zaragoza 445 – was formerly a museum but now the house has been gutted and the museum is closed. Many other movies have also been shot in the town since, including *Predator* with Arnold Schwarzenegger in 1987 and *Puerto Vallarta Squeeze* starring Harvey Keitel in 2002.

Our Lady of Guadalupe, Puerto Vallarta.

Vallarta lines the shore of **Bahía de Banderas**, one of the world's 10 largest bays, where migrating whales gather each spring; it is also a breeding ground for dolphins, and not surprisingly, there's good deep-sea fishing as well. Straddling the **Río Cuale**, the relatively unspoiled **Old Town** has white adobe houses with red-tiled roofs, donkey traffic, and cobblestones.

The **Templo de Guadalupe**, a central landmark, is topped by an imposing crown, a replica of that

Main attractions
Puerto Vallarta
Bahía de Banderas
Colima
Volcán de Fuego
Zihuatanejo
Acapulco
Isla de la Roqueta

Maps on pages 216, 252

worn by Maximilian's wife, María Carlota. Attractive bridges cross the river to an island, where there are art galleries, shops, restaurants, and a small **archeological museum** (Mon–Fri 10am–7pm; donation requested).

North of the old town, the **Zona Hotelera** is a long stretch of coast lined with luxury hotels that appears never-ending: almost as soon as construction of a hotel is finished, work begins on a new one close by. **Marina Vallarta**, a 178-hectare (440-acre) upscale resort area, has even more luxurious hotels, condos, and an 18-hole golf course. Parasailing, an easy and spectacular parachute ride behind a speedboat, is a popular pastime on several of Vallarta's beaches. Other water sports include snorkeling, scuba diving, jet-skiing, windsurfing, sailing, and deep-sea fishing for marlin, dorado, and tuna.

Playa Olas Altas and **Playa de los Muertos**, on the south side of Río Cuale, are the most crowded beaches, but there are several others farther south, beyond the city limits

at **Mismaloya** or **Boca de Tomatlán**. Boat or catamaran excursions can be arranged from Los Muertos pier to **Las Animas**, a tiny community with inexpensive hotels; **Quimixto**, where movie director John Huston built a house, and which is popular with divers; or **Yelapa**, farther on, which is a nice choice for those who want to escape the all-inclusive experience and try for something more low-key. You can choose between staying in a palm-thatched *palapa* or a small hotel, and (finally) there is internet at the cafés. It is also possible to rent a horse or *burro* (donkey) and venture into the jungle to the nearby waterfalls.

SOUTH OF VALLARTA

Those wanting a road trip will find that the route from Puerto Vallarta to Acapulco is worth the trip. It follows some of Mexico's finest stretches of coastline – with unspoiled beaches and some great surf spots – and passes through quaint villages. However, unless you plan on getting up

Parasailing on the Puerto Vallarta shore.

before dawn and driving until midnight, you'll want to stop overnight somewhere along the way. It is a long drive, but the effort will really be rewarded with seeing what Mexico once was, before the boom of development hit so much of the coastline. Towns still primarily depend on fishing and agriculture, and you will see numerous palm, mango, and pineapple farms. There is a plethora of *buteos* (buzzards), songbirds, and waterfowl so it's great for birders.

The road runs inland for a while and then passes **Playa Blanca**, a loud and busy Club Med facility, and **Pueblo Nuevo**, a budding US-style resort community. Then comes **Bahía Chamela**, upscale **Costa Careyes**, and the **Costa Alegre** ㉕, a 96km (60-mile) strip of relatively undeveloped coastline where the delightful bays have changed little since the Spanish galleons sailed these waters more than 400 years ago.

The next resort along the coast is **Barra de Navidad** ㉖, a sleepy town aimed mainly at vacationers from Guadalajara. It's worth stopping here

to enjoy the views or even surf if the waves are right. Deep-sea fishing is big, and for those wanting the beach but not quite ready for the boondocks, Barra de Navidad will fit the bill nicely. There's a nice tourist zone with hotels and restaurants, but very little of the push and brass of the big places – no touts, no hawkers. It's easy to sit and watch pelicans glide by as children beachcomb or play in the gentle waves. The same vacationers also head for **San Patricio Melaque**, just 2km (1 mile) along the beach. It was from this bay that Miguel López Legazpi sailed in 1564 to conquer the Philippines.

Manzanillo ㉗, just an hour away in the state of Colima, is a busy railhead and port, with narrow, traffic-choked streets, though sport fishermen may find rates are lower here (both for hotels and for fishing services) than in the more touristy destinations. There are a few good hotels in town, although the resort hotels and the best beaches are to the west of the bay around the **Santiago Peninsula**.

Boy on a Seahorse, Puerto Vallarta.

Las Hadas resort in Manzanillo.

☉ LGBTQ SCENE

Puerto Vallarta is Mexico's most out destination: LGBTQ tourism is particularly popular here, away from Mexico's usual ultra-machismo branding. **Playa de los Muertos** is the most renowned gay beach and here you will find the **Blue Chairs Beach Resort** (tel: 322-222 5040; www.bluechairs.com), easily the most lavish gay hotel in town and perhaps best for meeting people. More intimate accommodations are available courtesy of the stylish boutique **Rivera del Río** (tel: 322-150 6998; www.rivera delrio.com), where celebrities such as Raquel Welch have stayed. For nightlife, start with **La Noche** (Cardenas 257, until 3am) in the heart of the Zona Romántica, well known for its cocktails, then work your way up to a club like **Anthropology** on Plaza Río.

Selling colorful woven bags, made of ixtle fiber.

For the affluent, Las Hadas (The Fairies) complex, built by a Bolivian tin magnate, is a mixture of pseudo-Moorish, Mediterranean, and Disney styles. For those on a budget, look for the tiny ecotourism spots that have sprung up: a hammock and a parking spot right on an unblemished beach are hard to beat when you're paying only a fraction of the cost of an ordinary hotel. Surfers should make sure not to miss Pascuales, south of Manzanillo near the small town of Tecomán.

COLIMA

A short ride inland through lemon groves is the colonial city of **Colima** 28, the state capital and first Spanish city to be built in the west of Mexico. There are two worthwhile museums in Colima: the **Museo Regional de Historia** (tel: 312-312 9228; Tue–Sun 9am–6pm; free on Sun); and the even better **Museo de las Culturas de Occidente** (tel: 312-313 0608; Tue–Sat 10am–2pm, 5–8pm, Sun 10am–1pm), which exhibits a large and varied collection

A rococo Beetle.

of pre-Hispanic pottery from the cultures of western Mexico. Most notable are the pot-bellied Itzcuintli dogs for which Colima is renowned. Colima is a pleasant city of parks and gardens, and the surrounding countryside is dramatically dominated by two volcanoes: the still rumbling **Volcán de Fuego**, and its larger, extinct neighbor, the often snowcapped **Nevado de Colima**, which is popular with climbers.

IXTAPA AND ZIHUATANEJO

As they are served by the same airport and are only a few kilometers apart, Ixtapa and Zihuatanejo tend to be listed and lumped together as a unit, and indeed their boundaries have almost blended; but the characters of these two resort towns are wildly different. **Ixtapa** 29, like Cancún in the Yucatán and Huatulco, is the result of government-planned tourism. It came into existence in the 1970s, but now attracts almost half a million visitors each year, three-quarters of whom are Mexican, giving it slightly

more authenticity than its Yucatecan counterpart, which caters primarily to foreigners. Here you'll find a nice mix of guests from all over, and a much quieter vibe. There's also none of the March spring break madness that the "other" resort is famous for. Ixtapa's luxury high-rise resort hotels are strung out along the dramatic Playa del Palmar and around the Punta Ixtapa. The beach is beautiful and the sunsets sublime; however, there are numerous small pebbles that make barefoot walks less fun. As with any Pacific location, be cautious about undertow and errant waves.

Across a manicured roadway that runs past the hotels is a cleverly constructed mall that feels a little more like a village than just a strip shopping center. There are restaurants and juice shops interspersed with stores offering necessities and fripperies of all kinds. Shopping here is a major activity; there are more than 1,000 stores in these two resort towns, including trendy boutiques, silversmiths, goldsmiths, folk art, and handicraft markets.

In addition to its hotel zone, Ixtapa has luxury condominiums, several immaculate golf courses (one designed by Robert Trent Jones), a sheltered marina and all the most popular water sports. Boats leave from Playa Quieta (and less frequently from Zihuatanejo) for **Isla Ixtapa**, an island wildlife sanctuary lying a couple of kilometers offshore, with good swimming, excellent snorkeling, and a handful of beach restaurants.

Zihuatanejo ③ – or "Z" or even Ziwa, as it's known to anyone who has been there for any longer than a few hours – does more than merely cater to tourists: it is a real town with real people engaged in real activities. Getting around in either Zihuatanejo or Ixtapa, or from one to the other, is fairly easy; the hotels know what the prices for cabs are likely to be, and the drivers very rarely take advantage of unsuspecting tourists. The larger hotels often have shuttle services to and from the beaches or to their other satellite locations.

Pelicans in Ixtapa harbor.

Nevado de Colima.

A prime sunbathing spot in Acapulco Bay.

Unlike the sport fishing in the waters off Ixtapa, fishing is still a livelihood in Zihuatanejo as it provides food for both locals and visitors, although tourism is creeping in at a steady pace. Avid fishermen may want to try striking a deal with one of the local fishermen and tag along for the ride; most of the boats leave from the beach in the center of town, and a tasty lunch may be included in the price.

Facing the sea, on Paseo del Pescador in the center of town, is the small **Museo Arqueológico de la Costa Grande** (tel: 754-544 7552; Tue–Sun 10am–6pm), which offers an insight into the interesting culture and archeology of the coast of Guerrero. Ziwa is full of little restaurants of all kinds, and not surprisingly, those serving seafood are particularly popular.

Luxury condos overlooking the marina in Ixtapa.

Many of the hotels in Ziwa qualify as "budget" (Villas Miramar and Hotel Casa de la Palma are both good value), with a few notable exceptions such as La Casa Que Canta (tel: 755-555 7030; www.lacasaquecanta.com), a stunning building that cascades down the hill overlooking **La Ropa** beach; and the older, beautifully maintained and exquisitely landscaped Villa del Sol. For a change of pace, the tiny village and beach of **Playa Troncones** is a half hour's drive northwest of the resorts, and has recently garnered much attention among the surfing set. The beach runs for 5.5km (4.5 miles) with several unspoiled, secluded coves at the southeastern end. There are a few properties to rent, and surfers will want to head to Saladita, a prime reef break nearby which offers excellent surf; beginners should watch out for the sea urchins, or, better yet, leave this break to the more experienced.

ACAPULCO

Very recently, the press coverage here has not been good: drug wars and even beheadings have plagued this once-glittering tourist mecca, and even though the crime is almost never directed specifically toward tourists, the city is seeing fewer international visitors than it once did. It's unfortunate, but Acapulco is undeniably less popular these days. That said, it is not a place to be afraid of. Crimes likely to affect tourists are usually the petty kind, rarely violent, and even these are unlikely – though corrupt police officers have set up shop on rental cars heading toward the airport, threatening tourists with an expensive ticket and then offering to make a deal (see page 332).

While its golden years may be behind it, **Acapulco** ㉛ is still a fun spot to visit and is increasingly affordable, too. The economy here depends on tourism, so downturns are an excellent opportunity to take in what resorts have to offer at a bargain price. Stylish crowds of all ages and backgrounds come here to mix and mingle, hang out on the beaches during the day, and spend the nights dancing and drinking in the various bars and clubs. On or off the beach, the vibe is casual and relaxed.

Everyone here is looking for the same thing: fun.

BAHÍA DE ACAPULCO

At the west end of the large, sheltered Bahía de Acapulco is the traditional **Old Town**. Clustered around **Playa Caleta** , the original resort beach, some of the older hotels (reliable, but not luxurious) are still in operation. The rocky promontory of **La Quebrada** and the traditional Hotel El Mirador (tel: 744-483 1260; www.miradoracapulco. com) rises above the Old Town before the bay sweeps past the *malecón* (seafront promenade) and east toward the strip of modern resort hotels. The views are still stunning, and on a calm day you can look down from the mountains at the flat, silvery water, so still it has become a mirror. It's easy to find a spot to sit, order a beer, look out at the beach, or watch the activity on the white sand, and realize why this harbor became the mega-resort that it did. Acapulco continues to grow every year, and its rapid expansion eastward, in an area not far from the airport, has been influenced by the arrival of a toll road from Cuernavaca and Mexico City. In place of foreign tourists, Mexicans now flood the bars and discos, especially during Semana Santa (Easter), when nightclubs can be so packed you can stand for hours just trying to get in. Few Acapulco experiences are as authentic as dancing all night in the middle of a packed club, listening to the music and watching the smiles as favorite songs come on.

The **zócalo** (square), in the heart of town, is a reminder that this is Mexico and not just resortland. There are parks with benches and shade, a 1930s **cathedral** (tel: 744-482 1848; daily 10am–7pm, Thu until 9pm; free) with a mosque-type dome, open-air cafés, inexpensive restaurants, plenty of stores, and the town's largest **craft market**. There are also many small eateries, mostly catering to local people and Mexican tourists, that serve up wonderful fresh fish; be sure to ask for the catch of the day. Located across the boulevard is the **Malecón** and the docks where the deep-sea fishing vessels moor.

Acapulco cathedral.

Acapulco marina.

Fuerte de San Diego.

One event that sticks in the memory of all visitors to Acapulco is the emotion of watching the **high divers** at La Quebrada, an amazing spectacle that still hasn't lost its allure. For many tourists, cliff divers symbolize everything that makes Acapulco great: drama, danger, and flair. Every hour, beginning at 7.15am and ending just after midnight, young men execute dazzling swallow dives from a 40-meter (130ft) cliff into a narrow channel below; split-second timing is imperative for the divers to hit the water on the swell and not get dashed on the jagged rocks. Many divers train from boyhood, starting their jumps at the bottom of the cliff and working their way higher and higher as they gain experience and skill.

Acapulco's most historic landmark, the **Fuerte de San Diego** **D**, was built in 1616 to protect the port from mainly Dutch and English pirates. The fort was leveled by an earthquake in 1776, but was quickly rebuilt and has now been restored to house the small but interesting **Museo Histórico de Acapulco** (Tue–Sun 9.30am–6.30pm; free on Sun).

Leaving the warren of streets in old Acapulco, most tourists head along the 11km (7-mile) **Costera Miguel Alemán** **E**, a broad boulevard that stretches along the bay and is lined with high-rise hotels, restaurants, and little thatch-roofed bars advertising *la hora feliz* (happy hour) with drinks priced at three for the price of one. You can't miss the giant bungee jump tower or the Palladium disco, both landmarks that overlook the bay.

Hotel prices vary greatly with the time of year. The peak season with the best weather and highest prices is between mid-December and Easter and reservations should be made well ahead of time. The best fishing months are from November through May. Boats for big- and small-game fishing can be chartered for around $300 a day, either through the hotels or directly at the downtown Malecón (promenade). Sailboats, motorboats, pedal boats, and canoes can all be rented too.

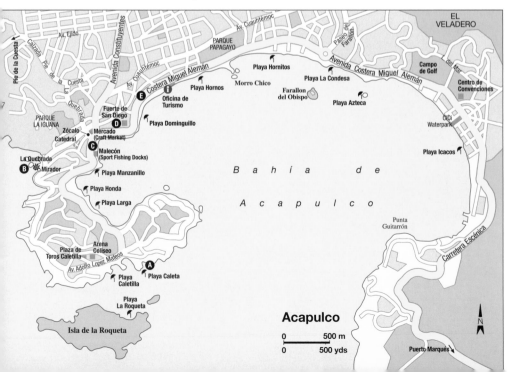

Some sections of the beaches in Acapulco can be polluted, although generally the sea is cleaner toward the east end of the bay; however, many tourists prefer to stick to the hotel swimming pools. All the usual water sports, from water- and jet-skiing to "bananas" and parasailing (easier than it looks), are readily available, while snorkeling is best in the shallow waters near **Isla de la Roqueta**. A glass-bottomed boat to the offshore island leaves from playas Caleta and Caletilla; en route you can see a huge diversity of aquatic plants and animals as well as the **Capilla Submarina** (Underwater Chapel), which is a wonderful submerged statue of the Virgen de Guadalupe (see page 22) placed here by local fishermen.

SUNSET AT PIE DE LA CUESTA

Some 8km (5 miles) north of town is the fishing village of **Pie de la Cuesta**. It is the best place to spend the day listening to the waves and watching the spectacular sunsets, but is not a good place to swim, as the undertow is vicious. A long sand bar peninsula sheltering the **Laguna de Coyuca** (abounding in catfish, snook, and mullet) is gradually filling up with modern villas and hotels catering to tourists. The fresh water lagoon is also very popular for water-skiing, sailing, and fishing trips.

LUXURY HOTELS

Taxis are reasonable and most hotels list the prices for the usual destinations. Make sure you agree on a price in advance, as taxis don't have meters. If you're on a budget, there are buses that run regularly along the Costera (see page 329).

On the way southeast to another popular beach at **Puerto Marqués**, in the next bay, you'll pass some of Acapulco's fanciest hotels, such as **Elcano**, **Las Brisas**, **Quinta Real**, and the **Camino Real** located at the bottom of a villa-studded hill. Each of these high-class resorts enjoys views of its own small bay, but people pay plenty for the privacy. Other high-end luxury hotels are spread out farther on, though they thin out eventually, leaving essentially unblemished coastline (often inaccessible) all the way to Puerto Escondido.

Bahía de Acapulco.

Cliff diver, Acapulco Bay.

⊘ THE CHANGING FACE OF ACAPULCO

In the 16th century, the large natural harbor of Acapulco was the only port authorized by Spain to receive the treasure-filled galleons arriving from China and the Philippines. The goods were transferred overland via Mexico City to the Gulf Coast port of Veracruz, from where they were shipped on to Spain. Over the next couple of centuries, something like 200 million pesos worth of silver was shipped out of Acapulco as payment for the silk, porcelain, spices, and ivory of the Orient. Naturally, the flourishing trade and rich shipments attracted pirates, freebooters, and the enemies of Spain. The Mexican War of Independence brought an end to the galleon trade and the town of Acapulco was forgotten until it was rediscovered as a resort during the 1930s. Over the next 70 years, Acapulco grew into one of the glitziest vacation spots in the world, rivaled (perhaps) only by Las Vegas or Rio.

Nowadays, everybody has heard of Acapulco, even if they have never been there, and despite the recent increase in drug crime, it remains a popular tourist destination both within Mexico and abroad. The beaches, nightlife, and the food keep people returning for more, and few sights are as iconic as its bronzed cliff divers plunging into the water from their bird-like perches on the rocks.

📷 SLICES OF PARADISE: MEXICO'S BEACHES

With all of 10,000km (6,200 miles) of coastline, Mexico offers an irresistible range of beach locations to escape to.

Surrounded by the warm waters of the Pacific, the Gulf of Mexico, and the Caribbean, Mexico has some of the most enticing tropical coastal scenery in the world: long, silky-soft beaches, soaring cliffs, and crystalline waters full of a dazzling array of marine life, from giant whales to kaleidoscopic shoals of tiny fish.

On both sides of Mexico there are big, multicolored resorts with every entertainment on hand, beginning with the two biggest, Cancún and – the favorite with Mexico City weekenders – Acapulco, followed by Cabo San Lucas, Mazatlán, Puerto Vallarta, Ixtapa-Zihuatanejo, and Huatulco on the Pacific, and Cozumel and Playa del Carmen on the Caribbean "Riviera Maya." Many of the surrounding beaches have been snapped up for giant all-inclusive resort complexes, with every activity on-site. If you prefer to evade the crowds, however, look farther – around Baja California and in northwest Mexico around Bahia Kino, south of Puerto Vallarta, along the coast of Oaxaca, on the southernmost part of the Riviera Maya – and you can find intimate, chic retreats with pampering spas and whole beaches all to themselves, or low-key, still scarcely developed hideaways.

Different places naturally have special attractions. The Pacific coast draws surfers from around the world, especially to Baja, Troncones, near Ixtapa and Puerto Escondido, in Oaxaca. On the Caribbean, the exquisite waters are more suited to swimming and relaxing, and a big draw is the seductive sand of the Yucatán's beaches itself, always soft, white, and cool. Offshore, though, magnificent coral reefs make this area the prime magnet for divers and snorkelers.

Catching a break at Puerto Escondido, the foremost surf center on the coast of Oaxaca.

Strolling across the sands of one of the many beautiful bays at Huatulco, a Pacific resort with both well-developed beachfronts and quiet hideaways.

Puerto Escondido is famous for its surfing, but is also home to quieter beaches like Playa Manzanillo which is safe for swimming.

The party gets going at Señor Frog's in Playa del Carmen.

Beach partying

Big and buzzing, Mexico's main resorts naturally all have plenty of places to continue the fun after dark – but with differences in style. Specialties of the giant resorts are huge mega-clubs – in Cancún, the biggest venues in Latin America – where once inside you have a whole assortment of bars, terraces, live shows, dance spaces, and music styles to choose from. Lines are long to get in and costs quite high – often upwards of US $45 – but all drinks and entertainments are included (although you still need to keep your waiter happy with frequent tips). For an older audience, in the same resorts there are also usually a few sunset or moonlight cruises available, often on "pirate ships," with dinner and show all-in.

Smaller, more hip resort towns, in contrast – such as Puerto Escondido, or Playa del Carmen – tend to have smaller, less expensive venues, with a less cheesy, more fashion-conscious style and music range, and all-night beach parties on the sand. In really small places, you'll usually have to be content with chatting in the local bar or stretching back in a hammock to gaze at the stars, although even the quietest beach village sometimes holds a fiesta on weekends.

Annual surfing competitions at Playa Zicatela, in Puerto Escondido, draw competitors from all over the world who come to surf the infamous "Mexican Pipeline".

Palms, turquoise sea and plenty of lounging-space at one of the Riviera Maya's many boutique resorts.

Playa la Entrega is popular with snorkelers on account of its crystal-clear waters and coral reefs.

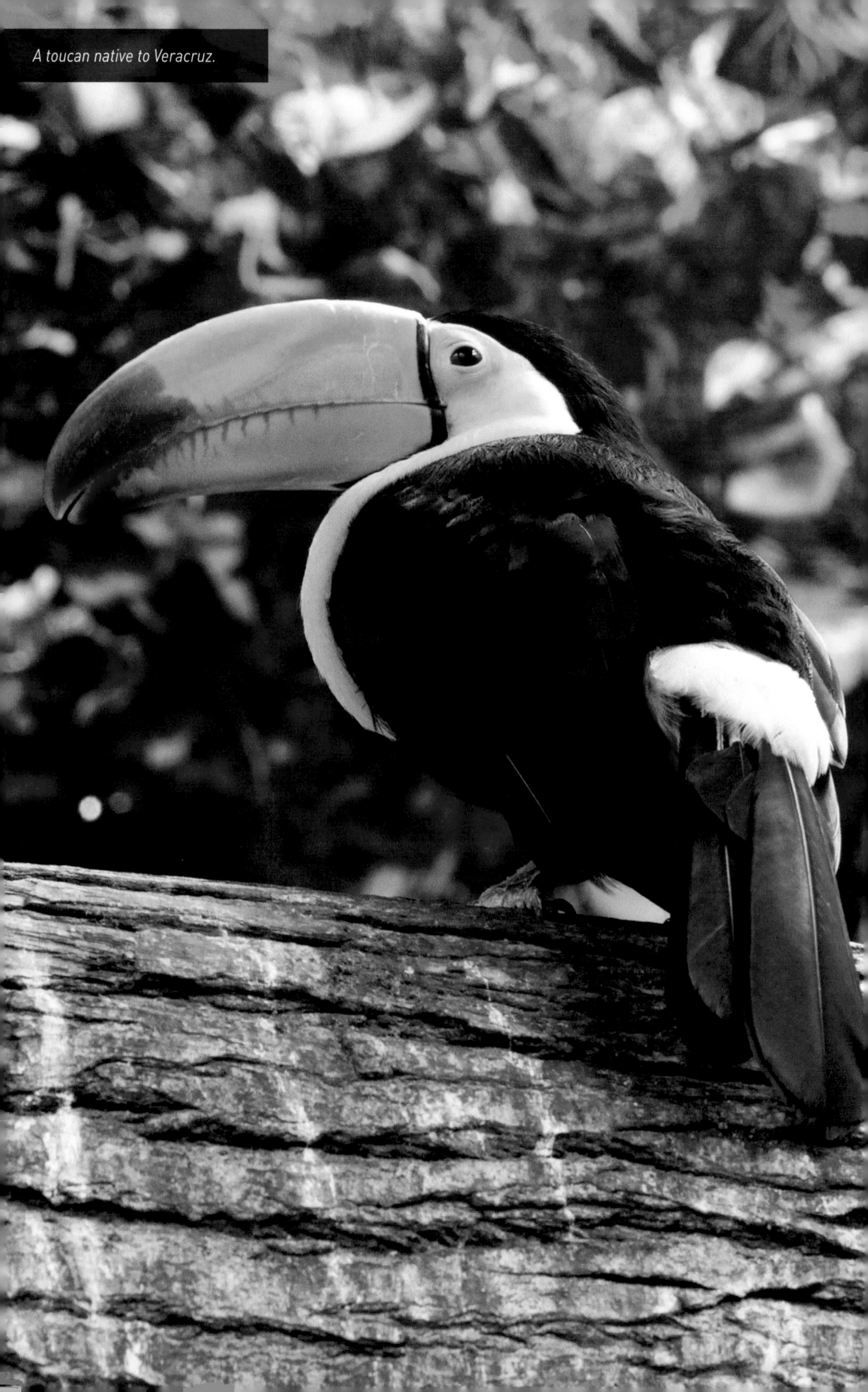

A toucan native to Veracruz.

THE GULF COAST AND THE SOUTH

With their beautiful beaches, lush forests, relaxed feel, and ancient cultures, Mexico's southern states have something for everyone.

Fishing boat moored at Playa Manzanillo, Puerto Escondido.

The east and south of Mexico offer perhaps more for the visitor in variety of landscape, cultural attractions and outdoor activities than any other part of the country. Hugging the Gulf Coast, Veracruz is one of Mexico's greenest states. Its beaches are not a scratch on those of the Caribbean or Pacific, but the state has much to offer, including the awe-inspiring ruins of El Tajín, the thrill of whitewater rafting, and the historical trail of Cortés. For music, dance, and fiestas, head for Veracruz itself, the most atmospherically appealing of Mexico's coastal cities.

The rugged landscapes of Oaxaca are very different, providing a home for more indigenous peoples than any other state in Mexico. Many live in severe poverty, but Oaxaca's peoples are highly resilient, and they and their handicrafts and traditions form a remarkable cultural tapestry. There is also the cosmopolitan colonial city of Oaxaca, dramatic ruins at Mitla and Monte Albán, and a beautiful Pacific coastline with surfers' hang-outs, such as Puerto Escondido and a mega-resort at Huatulco.

Humid, oil-rich Tabasco, home to the oldest Mesoamerican cultures, is the threshold of the Maya world. Chiapas is an extraordinarily varied state, changing in a few hours' drive from rain forest to pine-clad mountains. There are quaint colonial towns, traditional Highland Maya villages,

Textiles for sale.

the dramatic Sumidero Canyon, glittering lakes, and Palenque, Yaxchilán, and Bonampak, most sensational of all the Maya ruins.

After Chiapas, the flatness of the Yucatán comes as a shock. Visitors can easily alternate the azure colors of the Caribbean with visits to a spectacular variety of Maya ruins. Offshore, the Caribbean coast offers some of the finest diving and snorkeling in the world, while inland the Yucatán limestone is riddled with caverns, many of which form cenotes (water holes) exquisite for swimming. The Yucatán is also known for the special charm of its colonial towns – from Mérida and Campeche to sleepy Izamal – and for its mangrove and forest reserves, which protect a fantastic diversity of flora and fauna.

The voladores could show
bungee jumpers a trick or two.

THE GULF COAST

There's plenty to see in Mexico's greenest state: the highest mountain, the fastest rapids, the oldest civilization, the best museum outside the capital, and the liveliest plaza in the country.

México City

Veracruz is a long, narrow, tropical state that extends down the Gulf of Mexico. Its coast, including the historic port of Veracruz, is hot, humid and still relatively untouched by large-scale tourism.

In addition to being a center for three major pre-Hispanic cultures – Olmec, Totonac, and Huastec – Veracruz was Spain's gateway to the wealth of its Mexican empire. It was near the modern port of Veracruz that Hernán Cortés and his men first landed in 1519, and a short way to the north they founded the first permanent Spanish settlement in mainland America, the *Villa Rica de la Vera Cruz* or "Rich Town of the True Cross," before marching on to conquer the Aztecs in Tenochtitlán (see page 47).

Nowadays it is "black gold" that sails out of Veracruz; some of Mexico's biggest oil fields are in the north and south of the state, in Tampico, Minatitlán and Coatzacoalcos. However, with a population of more than 7 million, including some 650,000 indigenous people, Veracruz is also an important agricultural state, growing much of the country's sugar cane, vanilla, tropical fruits, and coffee.

THE OIL COUNTRY AND LA HUASTECA

The northern third of the state, between **Tampico** and Poza Rica

– both oil-refining towns – has little to detain most tourists. Tampico, with its huge modern harbor complex, has a sometimes-abrasive seaport atmosphere and excellent seafood. South of town is the **Laguna de Tamiahua,** where the islands and mangrove swamps can be explored in rented boats.

Far more enticing to most visitors is **La Huasteca ❶**, a fertile region west of Tampico that extends into the states of Tamaulipas, Hidalgo, and San Luis Potosí as well as

Main attractions

La Huatesca
Xilitla
El Tajín
Río Filobobos
Veracruz
Museo de Antropología de Xalapa
Pico de Orizaba
Laguna de Catemaco

Maps on pages 262, 265

All dressed up for Mardi Gras.

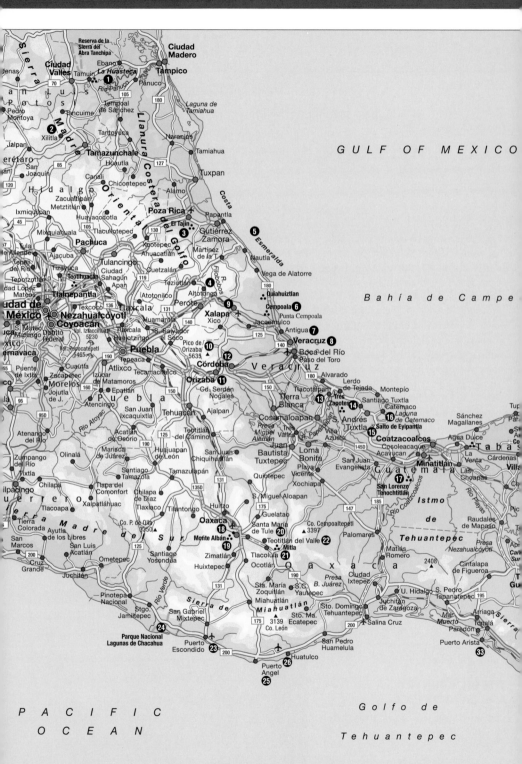

The Gulf Coast and the South

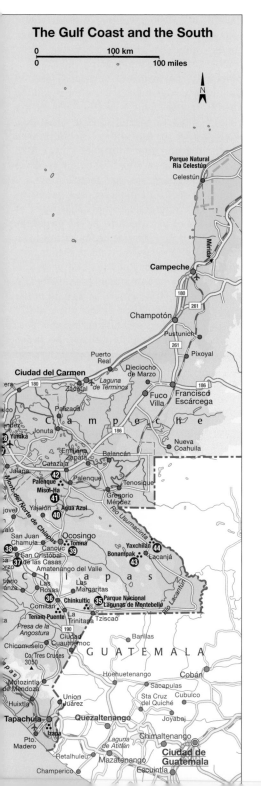

Veracruz. It is home to the Huastecs, one of the most intriguing Mesoamerican cultures. Their language is related to Mayan languages, and there are competing theories on when and why they migrated to La Huasteca from the far south of Chiapas or Guatemala, probably as long ago as 1000 BC. Huastec culture was at its strongest from about AD 1000 to 1500. In some ways they appeared very sophisticated, producing exceptional stone sculptures and ceramics, but their buildings were relatively simple, and Huastec men and women usually went naked, which led the Aztecs and the Spaniards to consider them primitive. The main Huastec archeological site is south of Ciudad Vallés in San Luis Potosí, at **El Consuelo**, also known as **Tamuín** or **Tamtoc** (daily 9am–5pm). The best places to see Huastec artwork are the anthropology museums of Xalapa (see page 268) and Mexico City.

The Huastecs were subjugated by the Aztecs around 1450 and later by the Spaniards, but many towns and villages maintain Huastec language and customs today (although the missionary friars eventually got them to wear clothes, including brilliantly embroidered smocks). One of the most characterful Huasteca towns is **Tamazunchale,** known for its Sunday market. Equally colorful are the local Day of the Dead celebrations (see page 90), when streets are carpeted with confetti and petals. Rainfall is heavy in La Huasteca, and the result is tropical vegetation of astonishing lushness and beauty. Many rare birds and butterflies are found here, attracting nature enthusiasts, and local shops sell mounted butterflies.

South of Ciudad Valles is one of the most extraordinary sights in all Mexico. A road leads through jungles of bamboo and banana plants to the remote village of **Xilitla ❷**, where English eccentric Edward James built his surrealist, Dalíesque retreat at **Las Pozas** (www.laspozasxil itla.org.mx; daily 9am–6pm; see page 264). The site has a series of concrete sculptures and seemingly half-finished, ethereal structures draped in lush forest.

FLYING MEN AND EL TAJÍN

The little Totonac town of **Papantla**, a favorite stopover for visitors to the ruins of El Tajín, has two claims to fame: it is Mexico's main vanilla-growing center, and the home of the **Voladores**

Statue of a Voladores de Papantla musician.

de Papantla. Their famous "dance" involves five "flying men," dressed in bird-like costumes. With ropes attached to one leg, four of the men, representing the cardinal points, launch themselves backwards in a kind of slow, serene bungee-jump from the top of a 32-meter (105ft) pole. The *voladores* revolve slowly around the pole and the rope unwinds until they gracefully reach the ground. Meanwhile, on a tiny platform at the top, the fifth man plays a reed flute and a little drum. Originally this spectacular performance was a solemn fertility ritual. These days it provides a means of economic survival, and *voladores* perform daily outside El Tajín ruins, and can be seen at many other touristic venues throughout Mexico.

El Tajín ❸ (daily 9am–5pm) was the most powerful center of the Classic-era Veracruz civilization, whose people may have been ancestors of the region's later Totonac inhabitants. Most of the city was built after about AD 600, and its period of splendor continued until around 1100–1200, when, possibly after attacks by primitive invaders, El Tajín declined quite rapidly.

The luxuriant surroundings and the way the site is almost hidden in the jungle make El Tajín all the more wonderful to visit. The lower part of the site – the first area beyond the entrance – seems to have been mainly used for ceremonial purposes, and feels almost like a forest of massive, awe-inspiring step-pyramids. The finest work of Tajín architecture is the oriental-looking **Pirámide de los Nichos**, with its 365 square insets or niches, one for each day of the solar year. The ancient ball game (see page 35) was extraordinarily important in the lives of El Tajín's people; there are 17 ball courts around the site, and relief panels along the walls of the **Juego de Pelota Sur** illustrate the ritual sacrifice of ball players.

To the northeast of the main area is the Plaza de Oriente, leading to the giant walls of the **Gran**

⌾ AN ENGLISHMAN'S CASTLE: LAS POZAS

Salvador Dalí described Edward James (1907–84) as "crazier than all the Surrealists put together." The son of a millionaire and a socialite, he was charming, refined, eccentric, and a prominent figure in British bohemia. He wrote poems himself, but was better known for using his wealth to sponsor the projects of his many friends – books, exhibitions, ballet companies – and collect art by Picasso, Magritte, Klee, and others. In the 1930s James discovered Surrealism, and was hooked. Dalí's famous sofa in the shape of Mae West's lips was first created for James' "dream house" at West Dean, near Brighton in England, a vast 300-room mansion. Besides Dali, he was also acquainted with Igor Stravinsky and Pablo Picasso.

In 1940 James moved to the USA, and then Mexico. In Cuernavaca he met a young man called Plutarco Gastelum, and hired him as his "manager." He first visited the remote Huasteca, a former coffee plantation, in 1945, drawn by its astonishing varieties of orchids and birdlife. James bought land in Xilitla and made it into a spectacular orchid garden and zoo, while Plutarco – who could be pretty eccentric

himself – built a large house, *El Castillo*, where he and his family all lived with the man the children called "Uncle Edward." In the 1960s, after a cold snap damaged many flowers, James decided to work in more solid form, imagining ever more bizarre – and larger – sculptures and fountains in concrete and metal. The structures, including bizarre concrete flowers, cost many millions of dollars to construct, even more than half a century ago. Between them he and Plutarco created a unique dream landscape, its surreal inventions intertwining unforgettably with the Huasteca forest. It became a hangout for many famous artists and writers interested in surrealism.

On his death James left Las Pozas to the Gastelum family, but with nothing for its upkeep, as his fortune had finally run out. It decayed for years, but in 2007 a foundation, Fondo Xilitla (www.xilitla.org), took over the estate to ensure its survival. The Castillo is now a very special guesthouse. The grounds, beside the sculptures, secrete a network of walkways, bridges, and temples, lacing an 8-hectare (20-acre) swathe of jungle beside some tumbling waterfalls.

Xicalcoliuhqui, which was probably a residential complex. The main residential area for El Tajín's elite was above the ceremonial center at **El Tajín Chico**, while higher up still, with a superb view over the entire city, was the palace of its rulers, the **Building of the Columns**. There is a site museum, and many other treasures can be seen in the Xalapa Museum (see page 268).

RAFTING AND BEACHES

Not far south of El Tajín is the foremost center for adventure tourism in Veracruz, along the **Río Filobobos ❹**. The river descends close to 1,000 meters (3,280ft) in around 65km (42 miles) to reach the sea at Nautla, passing through tree-shrouded canyons, whitewater rapids, placid pools suitable for swimming, and waterfalls like the 80-meter (262ft) -high *El Encanto*. **Tlapacoyán** is the main departure point for trips on the river. Some itineraries include visits to the remote archeological sites within the Filobobos Ecological Reserve, **El**

Cuajilote and **Vega de la Peña** (both daily 8am–5pm).

The beaches of Veracruz are less outstanding. The **Costa Esmeralda ❺** – in spite of its enticing name – is a stretch of very straight coastline between Tecolutla and Nautla, with palm-lined sands that fill up on local holidays. It can be an enjoyable base for visiting the area, but be prepared for modest beach towns with typical Mexican seafood restaurants along the sand, rather than upscale resorts.

There are dozens of small archeological sites along this coast, such as **Quiahuiztlán** (Tue–Sun 8.30am–5pm), overlooking the Gulf, which has a remarkable "Totonac Cemetery," with more than 100 tombs. Below it, the village of Villa Rica was the site where Cortés first founded Veracruz. Of particular historic significance is the fortified center at **Cempoala ❻** (daily 9am–5.30pm), which was the largest Totonac city when the Spaniards arrived in 1519, with around 30,000 people. Cortés and his men

> **⊙ Tip**
>
> The whole site of El Tajín covers around 10 sq km (4 sq miles), and is one of the hottest and sweatiest of Mexico's archeological sites. Take plenty of water and a hat, and if you intend to explore it fully allow plenty of time for rest stops.

Pirámide de los Nichos, El Tajín.

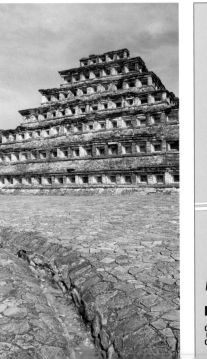

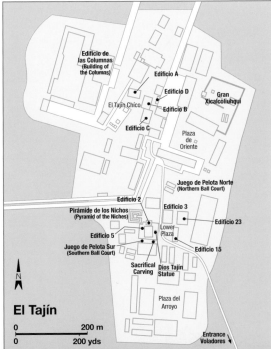

El Tajín

Edificio de las Columnas (Building of the Columns)
Edificio A
Edificio D
Gran Xicalcoliuhqui
El Tajín Chico
Edificio B
Edificio C
Plaza de Oriente
Juego de Pelota Norte (Northern Ball Court)
Edificio 2
Edificio 3
Pirámide de los Nichos (Pyramid of the Niches)
Edificio 23
Lower Plaza
Edificio 5
Edificio 15
Juego de Pelota Sur (Southern Ball Court)
Sacrificial Carving
Dios Tajín Statue
Plaza del Arroyo
N
0   200 m
0   200 yds
Entrance Voladores

Statue commemorating the city's development, on the Malecón in Veracruz.

were initially well received by the Totonacs of Cempoala (sometimes spelled Zempoala), and their chief struck an alliance with the Spaniards against the Aztecs, who had been exacting hefty tributes from the Cempoalans for years.

South of Cempoala, **La Antigua** ❼, founded in 1525, was the second location of Veracruz, and remains a little museum of early colonial architecture; the tiny **Ermita del Rosario** church dates from the 1520s, as does the ruined **Casa de Cortés** – although the conquistador never actually lived here.

EL PUERTO DE VERACRUZ: CITY OF SONG AND DANCE

When it comes to atmosphere, effervescence, and music, Mexico's largest port, **Veracruz** ❽ – often called *El Puerto de Veracruz* to tell it apart from the state – is the place to be. Its *zócalo*, the **Plaza de Armas,** is the liveliest in Mexico. By day, and for much of the night, it vibrates with *trios*, *marimbas*, *salsa*, and *danzón*. The palm-shaded square is lined with elegant white

Couples dance in the Plaza de Armas, Veracruz.

18th-century buildings, and *portales* filled with restaurants and cafés. There is organized music and dance several evenings a week, and itinerant musicians play at other times. Merrymaking reaches a crescendo in February during **Carnaval**, the week before Ash Wednesday. Veracruz has the biggest, loudest, most colorful Carnaval in Mexico, and people stream into the city to watch and take part.

In 1519 Cortés first landed on the Isla de Sacrificios, just off present-day Veracruz, but when he founded his new "town" shortly afterward he initially preferred a spot farther north at Villa Rica. Six years later he moved it south to Antigua, but it was not until the 1590s that Spanish governors transferred Veracruz to its definitive location, with the best harbor of all. The city, nevertheless, proudly traces its ancestry back to the first foundation in 1519.

MALECÓN AND MUSEUMS

A stroll along the waterfront promenade, the **Paseo del Malecón**, is an

essential pastime in Veracruz. Ships come and go, and you can take a boat trip round the harbor; stands and street vendors sell toys, cigars, amber jewelry, leather belts, and souvenirs. No trip to Veracruz is complete without a visit to the **Gran Café de La Parroquia**. An institution, this unpretentious café has been the city's prime location for socializing for two centuries. A much-discussed family feud meant that in 1994 the Parroquia had to move from its traditional location on the *zócalo* to its present site on the Malecón; fortunately, the waiters, regulars, and beautiful Italian coffee machines moved too. When you see the customers tapping, that's the sign to the waiters that their coffee needs topping up with hot milk – this constitutes *lechero*, and it's the way locals prefer to drink their coffee.

Traditional sightseeing in Veracruz is somewhat limited. The **Museo Histórico Naval** (tel: 229-931 4078; Tue–Sun 10am–5pm) on Calle Arista houses exhibits covering Mexico's naval history and the port itself. One block south, the **Baluarte de Santiago** (tel: 229-934 9981; Tue–Sat 9am–5pm, free on Sun) is the only remaining bastion of the Spanish fortified wall that surrounded the city until the 1880s. Its main exhibit is a collection of beautifully intricate pre-Hispanic gold jewelry, the *Joyas del Pescador* (Jewels of the Fisherman). Lost in a shipwreck centuries ago, they were discovered by a fisherman in 1976.

The small **Museo de la Ciudad** (tel: 229-200 2236; Tue–Sun 10am–5pm; free) has a thought-provoking section on slavery and the caste system in colonial Mexico. Two kilometers (1 mile) south along the *Malecón* above **Playa de Hornos** beach is the fine **Acuario de Veracruz** (tel: 229-931 1020; www.acuariodeveracruz.com; Mon–Thu 10am–7pm, Fri–Sun 10am–7.30pm), a state-of-the-art facility with spectacular tanks containing many kinds of marine life.

FORTRESS ISLAND

Across a causeway, on what was once an island, forbidding **San Juan**

Veracruz cathedral.

⊙ OLD WORLD TLACOTALPAN

Little Tlacotalpan is a gem of Veracruz. Set beside the vast Papaloapan River, it was an important port under Spanish rule and in the first decades of independence, when it acquired its special colonial architecture and well-shaded plazas. Then, when steamships and railroads came, Tlacotalpan was bypassed, and so the center of the town has scarcely changed since then. Although most of Tlacotalpan's old houses are modest in size, many have impressive facades of colonnades or arabesque portals; as a very Mexican touch, these European-looking neoclassical columns are painted in bright yellows, blues, and other tropical shades. Since 1998 the town, beautifully restored, has been a Unesco World Heritage site. Arriving in Tlacotalpan is like stepping into the past; though discovered by a fair number of visitors, it has retained its elegance and charm.

Tlacotalpan is exceptionally peaceful most of the time, but is by no means a museum. In addition to its buildings, it is known for its fiestas leading up to La Candelaria or Candlemas on February 2, one of the most colorful in Mexico. There are parades through the streets and on flower-decked boats on the river, plenty of food, drink, dancing, and the local *jarocho* folk music, and even Pamplona-style bull-running through the town. Local hotels get booked up well ahead.

Olmec heads, Museo de Antropología.

de Ulúa (tel: 229-938 5151; Tue–Sun 10am–5pm) guards the mouth of Veracruz harbor; the past 500 years of Mexican history can be told from the forbidding walls of this fortress, which has borne the brunt of many attacks – from the likes of Sir Francis Drake and 17th-century pirates to the navies of France, Britain, and the United States. During the dictatorship of Porfirio Díaz (see page 62) this was a notorious high-security prison, and its formidable, damp cells can be visited. A little farther south is the smaller island of **Isla de Sacrificios**, where Cortés first landed in 1519.

The beaches popular with *Veracruzanos* are south of the city at **Playa de Oro** and **Mocambo**. While the ocean water is warm, and the Gulf waves leisurely, they are really no match for the sands of the west coast or the Riviera Maya. For seafood, though, Veracruz is hard to equal. About 10km (6 miles) south of downtown Veracruz, **Boca del Río** is famed for its seafood restaurants (most open for lunch only, to about 7pm).

XALAPA AND ITS MUSEO DE ANTROPOLOGÍA

Although *El Puerto* is much larger, the state capital of Veracruz is actually the attractive university city of **Xalapa ⑨**, sometimes spelled Jalapa, in the hills 135km (84 miles) inland. Its climate is cool and damp, and the city is often shrouded in mist. Nevertheless, Xalapa enjoys a privileged setting: from the central **Parque Juárez** there are spectacular early-morning views of the **Cofre de Perote** volcano and, more distant, the **Pico de Orizaba** (see page 269). Just below the square, **El Agora** is a lively, multi-purpose arts center, and nearby is the **Pinacoteca Diego Rivera** (tel: 228-818 1819; Tue–Sun 10am–6pm; free), with some of Rivera's own work and contemporary art shows. Uphill from the park, the old neighborhoods have cobblestone streets of colorful houses, with sloping tiled roofs and wrought-iron balconies.

Xalapa's great highlight is in the northwestern suburbs, the outstanding **Museo de Antropología de Xalapa** (tel: 228-815 0920; www.xalapa.net/

antropologia; Tue–Sun 9am–5pm). The best anthropology museum outside Mexico City, it is spacious and light, with halls and sunny patios displaying priceless treasures of the pre-Hispanic cultures of the Gulf Coast.

The first rooms are dedicated to the Olmecs, the "mother culture" of Mesoamerica. The most striking pieces are naturally the celebrated colossal heads, dating from 1200–600 BC. The museum has seven of the 17 heads discovered so far, and the largest **El Rey** (The King), from San Lorenzo, dominates the first patio that you enter.

The next group of galleries is devoted to the Totonacs and other cultures from Central Veracruz. These include the haunting Cihuatéotl – terracotta figures of women deified after dying in childbirth – and the enchanting smiling figures, the most characteristic products of Classic-era Veracruz. The last rooms contain finely delineated **Huastec** sculptures and terracotta figurines.

The towns and countryside around Xalapa are also worth exploring. On the road toward Veracruz is the **Museo**

Ex-Hacienda El Lencero (www.xalapa.net/lencero; Tue–Sun 10am–5pm), the former estate of the dictator Santa Anna, which is now a delightful museum of colonial hacienda life. South of Xalapa is the colonial town of **Coatepec**, known for its fine coffee and orchid gardens, restaurants, and enticingly peaceful hotels, notably the Posada de Coatepec, a converted hacienda. The picturesque village of **Xico** is a short but beautiful drive away, through coffee plantations; an easy 2km (1.25-mile) walk leads to the spectacular **Cascada de Texolo** waterfall, featured in several movies.

Xalapa is also a base for rafting and adventure sports. In addition to the Río Filobobos to the north (see page 265), **Jalcomulco** on the **Río Pescados**, 30km (18 miles) south of Xalapa, is another popular center.

THE HIGHEST PEAK

Mexico's highest mountain, the **Pico de Orizaba** ⑩ (5,635 meters/18,490ft) is the third-highest peak in North America. Known to the Aztecs as Citlaltépetl,

Pico de Orizaba.

Papaya plantation.

or "Star Mountain," this extinct volcano last erupted in 1687. The main start-point for climbers is **Tlachichuca**, on the Puebla side. Only two of the 16 climbing routes are suitable for inexperienced climbers, and first-timers should always climb with a local guide.

Industrial **Orizaba** , on the Mexico City–Veracruz highway, has some fine colonial architecture, and the former **Palacio Municipal** is an extraordinary Art Nouveau construction in iron that was shipped over from Belgium in the 1890s. Also worth seeing are the 1926 mural by José Clemente Orozco (see page 114) in the current Palacio Municipal, and the paintings, colonial to contemporary, at the **Museo de Arte del Estado de Veracruz** (tel: 272-724 3200; Tue–Sun 10am–7pm).

A few kilometers farther east, busy **Córdoba** is one of the centers of Mexico's coffee industry. Its most interesting buildings are on or near the Plaza de Armas, the main square; best of all are the arcades of the **Portal de Zevallos**, along the north side, where several cafés serve the aromatic local coffee.

Making cigars in Salto de Eyipantla.

SOUTHERN VERACRUZ

Many of the rivers that divide up the hot, humid plains south of Veracruz city flow into the Río Papaloapan or "Butterfly River," which is 300 meters (985ft) wide by the time it reaches the Gulf. Beside it is the most atmospheric of the region's colonial towns, at **Tlacotalpan** (see page 267).

The small town of **Santiago Tuxtla** nestles in the foothills of the **Sierra de los Tuxtla**. It was in these hills more than 3,000 years ago that the Olmecs found the hard basalt stone they used for their extraordinary sculptures, even though the main Olmec centers were all many kilometers away to the east. At one end of Santiago's Zócalo, standing 3.5 meters (11ft 6ins) high and weighing almost 50 tonnes, is the largest of the Olmec colossal heads yet found. The **Museo Tuxteco** (tel: 229-934 9981; Tue–Sun 9am–5pm; free on Sun) has another head and fine pieces from nearby Olmec sites. A road leads 23km (14 miles) southwest to the largest of them at **Tres**

Zapotes (Tue–Sun 9am–5pm). There is little left at the ancient site itself, but the adjacent museum houses fascinating artifacts.

Not far from **San Andrés Tuxtla**, a sprawling cigar-making center is the turn-off for the **Salto de Eyipantla ⑮**. The road passes through fields of papaya, sugar cane, and tobacco before reaching this stunning waterfall, amid a perpetual cloud of mist.

The **Laguna de Catemaco ⑯** is a picturesque lake, 16km (10 miles) long, in the crater of an extinct volcano. Boat trips and other amenities can be found at the town of Catemaco, on the north bank. This is also a land of *brujos* (witch doctors), as you will soon see from the witch-related souvenirs for sale everywhere. The dividing line between authentic *brujos* and charlatans cashing in on tourists is very fine, but the tradition is real and goes back centuries. The annual gathering of *brujos* on the first Friday of March on Mono Blanco (White Monkey) hill outside Catemaco is now a tourist attraction itself.

Farther around the lake is **Nanciyaga** (tel: 294-943 0199; http://nanciyaga.com; daily 9am–5pm; charge depends on activities), a 40-hectare (100-acre) ecological reserve. Guided walks take you through pristine rainforest, and attractions include hanging bridges, traditional steam baths, pools of spring water for swimming, cabins, and a campground. Boat trips from Nanciyaga and Catemaco also go around the **Isla de los Monos**, which is inhabited by a colony of macaque monkeys brought here from Thailand for research purposes.

Some 37km (23 miles) beyond Acayucán are the remains of the oldest of all the pre-Hispanic "cities," at **San Lorenzo Tenochtitlán ⑰** (daily 8am–6pm; free). This was the first great Olmec center, which flourished from around 1300 to 900 BC. As at Tres Zapotes, the site mainly consists only of grassy mounds, and many sculptures found here have been taken to Xalapa and other museums, but there is still one colossal head and some remarkable carvings in the village museum.

Eyipantla waterfalls, near Catemaco.

Church of Santo Domingo,
Oaxaca city.

OAXACA

This southern state is rich in history, from the archeological magnificence of its pre-Hispanic cultures to its native-born leaders, Benito Juárez and Porfirio Díaz.

Oaxaca is indigenous country par excellence. Though the Zapotec and Mixtec indigenous peoples dominate the state, 16 other linguistically and culturally distinct groups live here too. No other Mexican state is as diverse. There's so much to see in the wild and wonderful state of Oaxaca: major archeological sites, tiny rural villages where people actually produce many of the country's best handicrafts, and the exquisite seashore that lies over the mountains from the high valley of the capital, which is also called Oaxaca. While recent increases in crime here have got lots of press, incidents are rarely directed toward tourists; as in most places in Mexico, tourists are welcomed and the vast majority will find they have few, if any, problems.

MOUNTAIN VISTAS

The city of Oaxaca is 548km (341 miles) from Mexico City and you can fly, go by train, or take the excellent and reasonably inexpensive toll road. The drive through the mountains is beautiful whichever road you take. If you don't want to take the toll road and go through Puebla you can stop at **Atlixco**, known for its bandstand and tiled benches and a dance festival held in September. The "tree of life," often thought to be from Metepec near Toluca, originated in **Izúcar de**

Atlixco's Huey Atlixcayotl festival.

Matamoros, which is a center for ceramics located a little farther south.

The state of Oaxaca was also the birthplace of two of Mexico's most prominent leaders: Benito Juárez, the country's first liberal president, was a Zapotec born in the hill village of San Pablo Guelatao, about 65km (40 miles) north of Oaxaca; and Porfirio Díaz, who seized the presidency in 1877 and stayed in power until the Revolution in 1910 was born here in 1830.

The Spanish city of Villa de Antequera de Guaxaca, now known simply

Main attractions
Oaxaca Centro
Teotitlán del Valle
Monte Albán
Mitla and the Tule tree
Puerto Escondido
Parque Nacional Lagunas de Chacahua
Puerto Angel and Huatulco

Maps on pages 262, 274

A cup of chocolate caliente, the Mexican version of hot chocolate, which mixes chocolate and cocoa beans.

A masked penitent in a Holy Week procession, Atlixco.

as **Oaxaca** (pronounced *wa-ha-ca*), was founded in 1529 near an indigenous settlement called Huaxyacac, which means "Place of Gourds." At an altitude of about 1,500 meters (4,920ft), its mountain climate is splendid – never too hot and never too cold. Oaxaca's center received Unesco World Heritage status in 1987 and still retains much of its old world charm, and ecotourism trips to remote ruins are growing in popularity.

The city has a population of a little more than 500,000 inhabitants and an unexpectedly cosmopolitan atmosphere. The indigenous influence is stronger here than in any other state capital, the Spanish colonial architecture is superb and well preserved, and there are some fine museums and a thriving artistic community.

Oaxaca is justly famous for its markets. The **Mercado de Abastos**, the Saturday market, is where the locals come to do their weekly shop. The buying frenzy takes place on a huge plot of ground next to the second-class bus station south of town, on the

Periférico (beltway). The fruit, vegetables, and pottery sections are particularly interesting. Otherwise, there's a hodgepodge of furniture, clothing, and kitchen equipment.

The **Benito Juárez market** and the adjacent **Mercado 20 de Noviembre** , both open daily, are more varied and attractive to visitors. Located on Calle 20 de Noviembre, just a few blocks south of the main square, they offer crafts (many of which are found in stands on the street outside the market), souvenirs of all sorts, flowers, and food (both raw and prepared). Photographers and cooks will find it particularly interesting for its huge mounds of dried peppers in a range of subtle colors and not-so-subtle flavors.

A shady bench in the beautifully planted **Zócalo** (plaza), the social hub of Oaxaca, is an excellent place to start a tour of the city. Alternatively, you can watch the world go by from the tables outside the many cafés and restaurants under the *portales* (arcades) around the square. The history of Oaxaca is illustrated in a mural that adorns

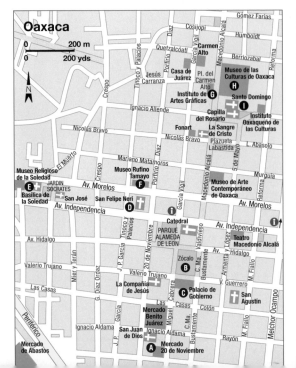

the staircase inside the imposing 19th-century **Palacio de Gobierno Ꞓ**, on the south side of the plaza.

To the north of the square, facing the adjacent **Alameda**, the vast **cathedral** has a fine Baroque facade; building started in 1554 but was only completed in the 18th century. In addition to its regular services, the cathedral is often used for concerts; dates and details are available from the **tourist office** on the corner of Independencia and García Vigil.

BAROQUE CHURCHES

Two blocks west of the cathedral, on Independencia, the church of **San Felipe Neri Ꞓ**, with its green stone Baroque facade, is where Benito Juárez got married. Farther along the same street, the 17th-century **Basílica de Nuestra Señora de la Soledad Ꞓ** (daily 9am–2pm, 4–6.30pm; free), also of green stone, has a lavish Baroque interior and houses a bejeweled statue of Oaxaca's much-revered patron saint, believed to possess miraculous healing powers. There is a small religious

museum behind the basilica (daily; donation), and delicious ice creams for sale on the plaza in front.

ANCIENT AND MODERN ART

Concentrating on esthetic rather than historical value, it took the 20th-century artist Rufino Tamayo (see page 115) more than 20 years to assemble his superb collection of pre-Hispanic artifacts. He then donated the pieces to his native city in the select **Museo Rufino Tamayo Ꞓ** (tel: 951-516 7617; daily 10am–2pm, 4–7pm; free), and they now make up one of the most important collections in the country.

More recently, Francisco Toledo – arguably Mexico's greatest living artist, who is also from Oaxaca – made a donation of his art collection to the city. Housed in his elegant former home, the **Instituto de Artes Gráficas de Oaxaca Ꞓ** (daily 9.30am–8pm; free, donations encouraged) displays a small but important collection of prints by internationally famous artists as well as the prominent Mexican muralists Rivera and Orozco (see page

The Baroque facade of Oaxaca's cathedral.

A quiet backstreet in Oaxaca.

112). The institute also has temporary exhibitions of graphic art.

Just north of the plaza, the **Museo de Arte Contemporáneo de Oaxaca** (MACO; tel: 951-514 2228; Wed–Mon 10.30am–7.45pm; free on Sun) is in a beautiful 18th-century building, with work mostly from the state of Oaxaca, along with some international exhibits.

The **Museo de las Culturas de Oaxaca**  (tel: 951-516 2991; Tue–Sun 10am–6.30pm; free on Sun), housed around the handsome cloisters of a Dominican monastery, is most noted for its spectacular collection of intricate Mixtec jewelry and other objects in gold, turquoise, obsidian, amber, conch shell, and glass. The pieces, dating from approximately AD 500, were found in Tomb 7 at nearby Monte Albán when it was uncovered in 1932. (They are often faithfully copied by local jewelers in gold or gold-washed silver, and sold in several of the city's better shops.) The museum also has interesting displays of textiles, clothing, household implements, and archeological relics.

The adjacent 16th-century former monastery of **Santo Domingo** , one of Oaxaca's noteworthy churches, has two handsome bell towers and a magnificent gilt and colored stucco interior. The exquisite giltwork reaches its crescendo in the dazzling 18th-century **Capilla del Rosario.**

SHOPPING OPPORTUNITIES

Oaxaca is a wonderful and exciting town for shopping. It is possible to buy handicrafts directly from the indigenous craftsmen and women, who come to town to sell their wares, chiefly handwoven rugs or *serapes.* A certain amount of bargaining is expected, although prices are often so low that it would seem insulting to beat them down any further.

From Santo Domingo, it is a short five-block walk back to the plaza along **Macedonio Alcalá**, a street lined with beautifully maintained colonial buildings and excellent shops selling crafts and jewelry, such as **La Mano Mágico**. On nearby García Vigil, **Artesanías Chimalli** has

Ball Court at Monte Albán.

authentic folk art and is reliable for shipping purchases.

It costs very little to join the **Biblioteca Circulante de Oaxaca** (tel: 951-518 7077; www.oaxlibrary.org; Mon–Fri 10am–7pm, Sat 10am–1pm), a private library with a fine selection of books in English and Spanish, many of them about Oaxaca and Mexico; the resident librarian, Ruth González, is an invaluable source of information and is also helpful if you just drop in to read a magazine.

Probably the most colorful of Oaxaca's legendary religious festivals is the **Guelaguetza**, which takes place in the Cerro del Fortín amphitheater on the first two Mondays after July 16. On December 23, the **Noche de los Rábanos** (Night of the Radishes), the plaza is filled with an extraordinary display of sculptures (often scenes of the birth of Jesus) which are made out of these intricately carved vegetables.

MONTE ALBÁN

What draws many people to Oaxaca is the proximity of its archeological wonders. The best time to see the ruins of **Monte Albán** ⑲ (daily 8am–5pm; free on Sun) is when it first opens in the morning. The grand Zapotec ceremonial center, about 10km (6 miles) west of the city, stands on an artificially leveled mountain top commanding a compelling 360-degree view. These majestic ruins were listed as a Unesco World Heritage site in 1987.

Monte Albán was established around 500 BC, although the city did not peak until 1,000 years later when the population reached 25,000. The entrance to the **Gran Plaza** is at the northeastern corner, between the **Ball Court** and the **Plataforma Norte**. In the center of the plaza, **Edificio** is known as the Observatory, while at the south end is the towering **Plataforma Sur**, Monte Albán's tallest building.

The **Palacio de los Danzantes** is on the west side of the square.

Archeologists have not yet agreed upon the meaning of the strange low-relief "dancers" carved on the walls of this building; the figures, which bear definite Olmec influence, have been interpreted variously as ball players, medical specimens, deformed persons, sacrificial victims, or slain enemies.

It is possible to go down into some of the tombs to see the ancient frescoes. In **Tomb 104**, in the northwest, there is a fine figure of Cocijo, the Rain God, whose forked tongue represents lightning; the treasures of **Tomb**, which belonged to a 14th-century Mixtec dignitary, can be seen in the **Museo de las Culturas de Oaxaca** (see page 276).

MITLA AND THE TULE TREE

About 10km (6 miles) from Oaxaca, on the road to Mitla, is the village of **Santa María de Tule** ⑳, which has a small craft market, a pretty church, and an enormous, 2,000-year-old *ahuehuete* tree (daily 9am–5pm) which, with a girth of 50 meters (164ft), is thought to be the widest in the Americas. Also

Stone relief, Mitla.

Geometric mosaics in Templo de las Columnas at Mitla.

⊙ Fact

There are so many archeological sites in Oaxaca that someone once suggested putting a roof over the whole state and calling it a museum.

known as the Montezuma Cypress, it is famous for the animal-shaped contours one can find in the gnarled bark.

Following the decline of Monte Albán, **Mitla** ㉑ (daily 9am–5pm; charge) became one of the most important Zapotec centers. The site's main structures, however, are Mixtec in style. The buildings, with their complex technique of inlaid stone, are reminiscent of the geometric friezes of the ancient Greeks.

The most intricate of the "mosaics" are in the **Patio de las Grecas**. In the **Patio de las Tumbas** there are two underground, cross-shaped tombs, one of which contains the **Columna de la Vida**; it is said that if you embrace this Column of Life, the gap left between your hands represents the years you have left to live. Unlike most ceremonial centers, Mitla was not abandoned after the Spanish Conquest, but remained inhabited well into the 16th century.

The church next to the site is built of stones taken from the ceremonial center. Outside the site entrance

Ancient cypress tree, Santa María de Tule.

there is an extensive craft market with some white, lacy handwoven shawls. Just off the plaza, the **Museo de Arte Zapoteca** (daily 10am–5pm), a research center for the University of the Americas, has an excellent collection of Zapotec artifacts on display and handicrafts for sale. The trip to Mitla can be combined with visits to other, less extensive, but nonetheless impressive ruins at **Dainzu, Lambityeco,** and **Yagul.**

Further southwest from Mitla, along country roads that pass agave plantations, is **Hierve el Agua**, a curious geological site of waterfall-like mineral deposits from overflowing thermal springs. On clear days the views over the rolling hills are pretty spectacular.

Several tour companies run minibuses with English-speaking guides from Oaxaca to the various archeological sites. The one to Monte Albán operates from the Mesón del Angel, and to Mitla from the Camino Real, Victoria, and Marqués del Valle hotels. People who prefer to explore on their

⊙ MAGICAL MEZCAL

Mezcal and tequila are often confused, but if there's a worm floating in the bottom, you've probably got a bottle of *mezcal*, though not necessarily a good bottle. The *gusano* worm makes little or no difference to the taste or strength, and some brands add one just for show. It is thought that in the past they were used to prove the veracity of the drink inside the bottle, as the high alcohol content helps to preserve the *gusano*. Hollywood and college students make much of the effects of eating the worm, but it does not have hallucinatory or other "magical" side effects. *Mezcal* differs from the more famous tequila in several ways, but primarily by taste. It is stronger, more complex, and more varied. By law, tequila must *not* have a worm in it. This doesn't mean *mezcal* is a superior drink: merely that there are fewer "golden rules" to its production, resulting in many types nationwide. The other main difference is that tequila is distilled from the sap of the blue agave, whereas *mezcal* is made from any type of maguey plant.

Drinkers of *mezcal* primarily opt to have it neat, most often as a shot, and sometimes with salt or a lime chaser. Unlike tequila, it is rarely an ingredient in cocktails. In Oaxaca, many people drink *mezcal* while nibbling at fried worms, the way other cultures might enjoy beer nuts. The city holds a *mezcal* festival each July. And finally, to dispel another myth: it does not contain mescaline, despite the phonetic similarity.

own can drive, negotiate an hourly rate with a taxi driver, or take a local bus that goes near but not directly to the sites. Many hotels and city bookstores sell specific guidebooks providing background and directions to the more established locations.

EXPLORING THE AREA

For an insight into life in this mountainous region, you could travel on one of the second-class buses to villages several jolting hours away, where many indigenous groups live in relative isolation. Oaxaca is one of the poorest states of Mexico; erosion is devastating and the farm laborers do not have enough land to support themselves. To supplement what they earn from farming, many Oaxacans have become artisans, and villages in the area surrounding Oaxaca offer opportunities to see them at work. Prices are much the same as they are in city markets, but much less than in Mexico City or other tourist towns.

In **Teotitlán del Valle** ㉒, a couple of kilometers off the main road to Mitla, it is sometimes possible to watch weavers creating designs from wool spun and dyed by the women of the household.

The fine Dominican church at nearby **Tlacolula** was built in the 16th century. Note the indigenous influence in the riotously decorated interior and the antique, tubular pipe organ. The town also has the best Sunday market in the region and is the place to get top-quality *mezcal*, sometimes flavored with herbs; bottles often include the coveted *gusano* worm that lives in the maguey plant.

South of Oaxaca, in the Mixtec town of **Cuilapan**, are the ruins of an early Dominican church and monastery. Independence hero Vicente Guerrero was executed here in 1831. Cuilapan was once a center for the production of cochineal, the scarlet dye made from female insects that feed on cacti. Used as a base for magenta hues in Europe, and even in the red coats of the British army, this dye was once so highly prized that its export was strictly controlled under Spanish rule.

⊘ Tip

B. Traven's short stories make excellent reading for anyone traveling in Oaxaca or southern Mexico.

Loom-weaver, Teotitlán del Valle.

Playa Zicatela is the main surfing beach in Puerto Escondido.

Playa La Entrega, Huatulco.

OAXACA'S COAST

Oaxaca has 480km (298 miles) of Pacific coastline with excellent beaches, quiet lagoons and good surfing. The highway from Acapulco (in neighboring Guerrero) to Salina Cruz (in Oaxaca) has been resurfaced, although it is still rough in many places. Puerto Escondido, Puerto Angel, and now Huatulco are the three best-known destinations. Although all have been badly hit by hurricanes, they were quickly repaired.

Of these three resorts, **Puerto Escondido** ㉓ has been in the business of tourism the longest, although it is by no means a sophisticated destination. Fishing is still an important source of revenue and the daily catch turns up fresh in the marketplace and on the table in local seafood restaurants.

The atmosphere in Puerto Escondido is low-key and relaxed with little to do but enjoy the sun, sea, and surf. The **old town** is on a hill above the bay. The main tourist area stretches from **Playa Principal**, where the fishing boats are berthed, to **Playa Marinero**, the swimming beach. Around the curve is the long, sandy beach at **Zicatela**, a magnet for surfers who come to ride the famous "Mexican Pipeline." Luckily for surfers, Playa Zicatela has a lethal undertow that keeps swimmers away.

Most tourist facilities are on or near the beach. The pedestrian walkway that parallels the bay through the tourist part of town is lined with shops selling silver, jewelry, and other trinkets.

There are simple but excellent seafood restaurants, such as Costa Hermosa and Junto al Mar, as well as bars that have live jazz and dance music starting at about 10pm and continuing far into the night. The most outstanding hotel in Puerto Escondido, the **Santa Fe**, stands at the point where the surf beach and the swimming beach converge. On the hill at the other end of town, **El Aldea del Bazar** is a handsomely designed hotel, although a taxi is needed to get to or from anywhere else.

SPECTACULAR WILDLIFE

Anyone with an interest in birds and other wildlife should consider a 60km

(37-mile) detour west of Puerto Escondido to the **Parque Nacional Lagunas de Chacahua** ㉔. *Lanchas* (small motor boats) can be rented in the village of El Zapotalito to tour the lagoons and their mangrove-edged islands.

It is best to come in the early morning or late afternoon to see the ibis, spoonbills, parrots, alligators, turtles, and many other creatures that inhabit the lagoons. There are also fine sandy beaches and sheltered coves; but bring insect repellent as the mosquitoes can be fierce.

PUERTO ANGEL AND HUATULCO

Even more than Puerto Escondido, **Puerto Angel** ㉕ is a sleepy resort with a tropical setting and superb sheltered beaches for people who want to relax, swim, and lie in the sun. The fishing village is on the east side of the bay, while swimming is better at **Playa del Panteón**, on the west side. Fresh seafood abounds and there are several comfortable, though not luxurious, hotels in the town. And if you want to get right back to basics, the long, sandy, palm-fringed beach of **Zipolite** is only 5km (3 miles) along the coast.

In contrast, **Huatulco** ㉖ has become a mega-resort, with marina, golf courses, scuba diving, and horseback-riding, somewhat overshadowing the emerald islands and sandy coast that made it famous. Beaches still sprawl along 35km (22 miles) of glorious coastline. Numerous resort hotels have been completed, including the Barceló, the Dreams Huatulco, the Camino Real Zaashila, the Quinta Real, and Las Brisas. The Punta Celeste archeological site just south of Tangolunda Bay is currently under excavation and access is limited.

There are boat trips from the harbor in the main Bahía de Santa Cruz to some wonderful beaches with excellent snorkeling. The purpose-built town of **La Crucecita**, 2km (1 mile) inland, is an integral part of the development, complete with a central plaza, restaurants, some inexpensive hotels, crafts markets, and a delightful marketplace.

Hand sculpture at Zicatela beach, Puerto Escondido.

⊘ PLAYA ZICATELA

Surfers have always drifted south from California to Baja's remote beaches, but the mainland has made a name for itself as well. With the resurgence in popularity of the sport, towns along the Pacific coast with good breaks have become more popular. Nowhere is that truer than at Puerto Escondido. Once a quiet fishing community known primarily for seafood and a few places to stay, this town is now synonymous with a break rivaled only by Oahu's North Shore: the Mexican Pipeline. While the town still retains a quiet, low-key tourist atmosphere, the surfing is anything but placid. Playa Zicatela is one of Mexico's greatest – and most dangerous – surfing breaks, in part because large waves break in shallow water. This is not a beach for swimmers, as strong currents run along the shore, making for undertows and rips that can pull even the strongest swimmer far from shore. Though famous, it is not for inexperienced surfers either: broken boards, separated shoulders, and other injuries are common. Use care and caution if you head out. On heavy surf you'll need a jet ski tow-in, but the rewards are adrenalin rushes and glassy glides down some of the most powerful, and perfect, wave faces Mexico can offer. Those who don't feel comfortable surfing can enjoy just hanging out and watching some of the world's greatest surfers strut their stuff on some of Mexico's best and biggest waves.

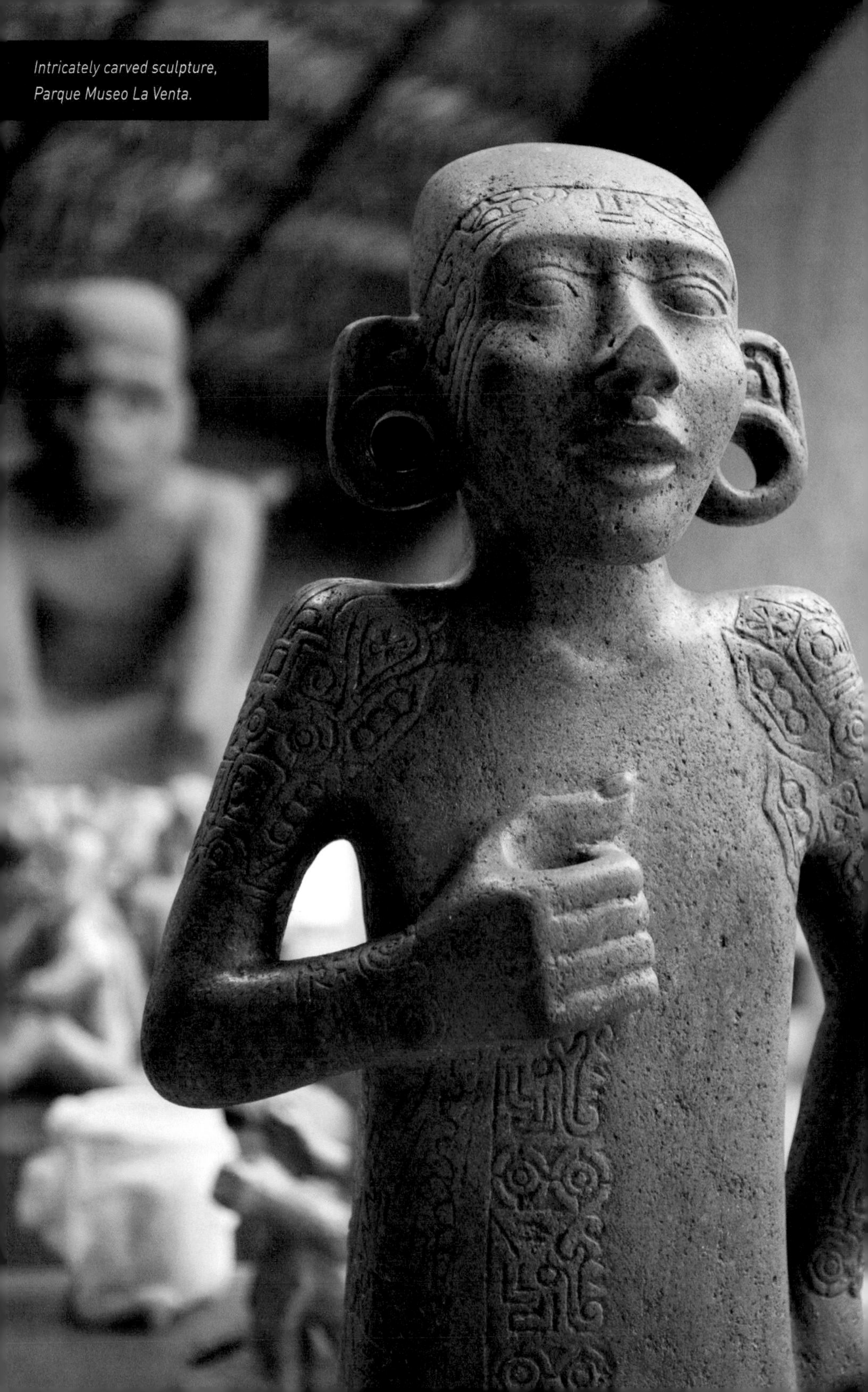

Intricately carved sculpture, Parque Museo La Venta.

TABASCO AND CHIAPAS

The two states of Mexico's southeast offer extraordinary contrasts, from the flat, humid, tropical delta of Tabasco to the mountainous subcontinent of Chiapas.

The two very different states of Tabasco and Chiapas span the country from the Gulf of Mexico to the Pacific, just east of the Isthmus of Tehuantepec, Mexico's narrow waist. They are the westernmost part of the region occupied, in pre-Hispanic times and today, by the Maya.

Green, tropical **Tabasco** is often wrongfully dismissed as an oil state to pass through on the way to Chiapas and the Yucatán. Much of this steamy, low-lying area is the delta of two giant rivers, the Grijalva and the Usumacinta, and the state is crisscrossed with meandering tributaries and palm-lined creeks that were used as trading highways by the oldest of Mexico's civilizations, the Olmecs, who inhabited this land 3,000 years ago. The ever-present water and green vegetation makes Tabasco a vivid contrast to the arid states to the west.

VILLAHERMOSA

In March 1519, after rounding the Yucatán peninsula, Hernán Cortés won his first victory in Mexico at Centla in northeast Tabasco – one of the spoils of which was his interpreter and later mistress, *La Malinche* – before sailing north to Veracruz. He left behind a small

outpost at the mouth of the Río Grijalva, which grew into a small town. By the 1590s, however, it was being raided by French and English pirates, and it was decided to move it upriver. Now called **Villahermosa** ㉗, it is the capital of Tabasco and, with close to 700,000 people, one of the busiest cities in southern Mexico.

A sleepy river town until the 1950s, Villahermosa has been transformed by the arrival of cars, air conditioning, and above all the oil boom of the 1970s, which led to it more than

◉ **Main attractions**
Comalcalco
Cañón del Sumidero
San Cristóbal de Las Casas
Chamula and Zinacantán
Agua Azul and Misol Ha
Palenque
Bonampak
Yaxchilán

Maps on pages 262, 294

Our Lady of Guadalupe church in Cupilco, near Villahermosa.

doubling in size and becoming a city of wide modern avenues (and sometimes horrendous traffic). The biggest expression of Villahermosa's oil wealth is the area around the **Tabasco 2000** complex, with a convention center, a shopping mall, lakeside parks and gardens, and upscale hotels.

The "old" center of the city – which is mostly 19th- or early 20th-century – is down below, beside the Grijalva, and known as the *Zona Luz* or "Zone of Light." It doesn't have the historic charm of Mexico's colonial cities, but does offer plenty of bustle and streetlife.

The city's greatest attraction, which largely escaped a major flood in 2007, is **Parque-Museo La Venta** (tel: 993-314 1652; daily 8am–4pm), in an exquisite jungle setting alongside a lake near Tabasco 2000. This unique open-air museum is a showcase for superb sculptures from the Olmec center of **La Venta**, 130km (80 miles) west of Villahermosa, which flourished from about 900–400 BC, after the still-unexplained decline of San Lorenzo in Veracruz (see page 271).

Initial excavations at La Venta were made in the 1920s and 1940s. Then, in the 1950s, the original site was threatened by oil drilling, and Tabascan poet and anthropologist Carlos Pellicer Cámara came up with the radical proposal to transport 32 of its massive monuments to Villahermosa for their protection. The result is spectacular: visitors "discover" the powerful sculptures amid lush forest plants, along paths around the park. Most celebrated are the colossal Olmec heads, more than 2 meters (6ft) tall, but equally dramatic are the altars, many showing priest-lords emerging from alcoves representing gateways to the underworld. Another feature of Parque La Venta is that it is intertwined with a zoo entirely of local wildlife (entry included in the ticket), so that as you walk around the monuments you can also see parrots, toucans, jaguars, and other exotic creatures.

The **Museo Regional de Antropología Carlos Pellicer** (tel: 993-312 6344;

Villahermosa's Government Palace.

Tue–Sun 9am–5pm), by the river, has a fine collection representing most of Mexico's ancient cultures.

COMALCALCO AND CACAO

Just east of Villahermosa is a popular natural attraction, the park of **Yumká** ㉘ (tel: 993-596 6704; http://yumka.org.mx; daily 9am–4pm), which contains a large area of native tropical forest and a safari park with exotic animals such as lions and hippos. More adventurous ecotourism trips can be made to forest waterfalls near Huimanguillo, off the Tuxtla Gutiérrez road, and to caves and sulfur springs in the **Sierra de Tabasco**, south of Villahermosa.

Comalcalco ㉙ (daily 8am–4pm), 62km (39 miles) from Villahermosa, is the westernmost ancient Maya city. It is also a remarkable demonstration of Maya adaptability. In most places, the Maya built in stone; in the soft, muddy delta this was impossible, so they built in stucco and brick. Most of its buildings date from AD 600–800. As you enter the site, you first come to the majestic **Plaza Norte**, surrounded by step-sided brick pyramids. Above it is the massive artificial mound of the **Gran Acrópolis**, with temples adorned with fine carvings; and the atmospheric **Palacio** that was home to Comalcalco's elite, with water-courses running through it to provide an early system of air conditioning.

In addition to being the oldest Mesoamerican culture, the Olmecs are also thought to have been the first people ever to cultivate cacao, or chocolate, in the Tabasco deltas in about 1000 BC. The area is still considered to produce some of the world's finest chocolate, and along the road south of Comalcalco town there is a modest *Ruta del Cacao*, with pleasant little cacao estates that are open to visitors, with tours, shops, and (of course) tastings.

INTO CHIAPAS

No state in Mexico offers such radical contrasts in landscape and climate as Chiapas. It has as many differences as whole countries: from dense, sultry rain forest around Palenque or on the Pacific coast, to spectacular mountain peaks, pine forest, crystalline waterfalls, and massive rock ridges in the Chiapas Highlands, another world where temperatures drop and the air feels completely different. The range of wildlife and vegetation is astonishing.

Like Oaxaca, Chiapas has a large indigenous population, making up about one third of the total. Long remote from the rest of Mexico, Chiapas has been known for chronic social problems, with many of its Maya communities, especially, living in severe poverty – the background to the Zapatista movement (see page 286). One effect of this conflict has been to draw more official attention to Chiapas than has been seen in decades, reflected in huge investment in new roads, which has made

The inscrutable features of a massive Olmec stone head in the open-air Parque Museo La Venta.

View of Tuxtla Gutiérrez.

THE ZAPATISTAS OF CHIAPAS

The newspapers may have moved on, but the Zapatista rebels remain spirited in their Chiapas village.

On 1 January, 1994 Mexico's political world was shaken to its foundations when armed Maya rebels, calling themselves the Ejército Zapatista de Liberación Nacional (EZLN, Zapatista National Liberation Army), emerged from the Lacandón forest and took over San Cristóbal de Las Casas and Ocosingo.

President Carlos Salinas and his government were stunned. The supposedly ignorant Indians seemed constantly able to wrong-foot them, represented by their balaclava-clad, multi-lingual non-Maya spokesman Subcomandante Marcos, whose sharp jibes at the established order made him one of the anti-globalization movement's first heroes.

In the background was a long-simmering conflict. From the 1940s, poor Maya in Chiapas were encouraged to move down to farm in the "empty" forest east of Ocosingo. However, with no formal title, they could be thrown off this land whenever it became more valuable, as happened with the expansion of commercial ranching from the 1970s.

After a few days the government agreed to a ceasefire, while the Zapatistas withdrew from the towns. The

EZLN leader Subcomandante Marcos.

resulting standoff has lasted ever since. The government declared its commitment to negotiate, but also poured troops into Chiapas. Local authorities often tacitly encouraged paramilitary groups to oppose Zapatista land claims. The conflict carried on at a half-hidden level, with flashes of violence usually far from media attention, as when 45 Zapatista sympathizers were murdered in Acteal in 1997.

In 1996 the government and Zapatistas signed a set of accords in San Andrés Larraínzar, which seemed to promise land rights and autonomy for indigenous communities, and since then have encapsulated the Zapatistas' core demands. However, nothing was done to put them into practice.

ZAPATISTAS TODAY

The Zapatistas began putting the San Andrés accords into practice themselves, linking the 2,000 villages they control across Chiapas to large "hub villages" or *caracoles* (snails), and developing their own system of participatory democracy.

Outposts of this network can be seen with Territorio Zapatista signs outside villages. In San Cristóbal, the Zapatistas seem part of the scenery. Economically the *caracoles* are weak, but supporters point to their achievements in building clinics and schools. The Zapatistas are generally happy to have foreigners around, since they believe this deters aggressive actions by others, as well as providing a much needed source of income.

Perhaps above all, though, the Zapatista movement struck a chord worldwide and has almost come to be seen as synonymous with justified, spirited resistance against the status quo. In 2016, the Zapatistas and the Congreso Nacional Indígena, a broad organization of different indigenous communities, put forward a female candidate known as Marichuy for the Mexican 2018 presidential elections. She was recognized by the election body but failed to collect the required number of signatures to be confirmed as a candidate; the signature process could only be completed online, or with smartphones, using clunky software that often took many hours to download in rural areas. Once again, indigenous communities felt that their needs had been sorely ignored.

many parts of the state a great deal easier to get to.

TUXTLA GUTIÉRREZ AND THE SUMIDERO

The state capital, **Tuxtla Gutiérrez** ㉚, is 290km (180 miles) south of Villahermosa. It is a modern city with a few specific attractions. The **Museo Regional de Chiapas** (tel: 961-613 4479; Tue–Sun 9am–6pm; free on Sun), in Parque Madero, has superb artifacts from the state's exceptional range of archeological sites. The fascination of the **Zoomat** or **Zoológico Miguel Alvarez del Toro** (tel: 961-639 2856; www.zoomat.chiapas.gob.mx; Tue–Sun 8.30am–4.30pm), on a hill south of the city, is that absolutely all of its more than 300 species are native to Chiapas, such as tapirs, jaguars, ocelots, and a dazzling array of birds. Many smaller animals are allowed to run freely around the park.

The most popular destination around Tuxtla is the **Cañón del Sumidero** ㉛, a giant gash over 1,000 meters (3,280ft) high and at times 2km (1.25 miles) wide, in the massive wall of rock north of the city. The Grijalva River used to become a whitewater torrent as it ran through it, but now, blocked by the dam at Chicoasén to the north, it is a broad, placid waterway. Boat trips run daily beneath the sheer cliff walls of the gorge, giving the opportunity to see a wide range of bird life and many bizarre rock formations. On one side of the gorge is the **Parque Amikúu** (daily 9am–5pm), an "ecopark" with jungle trails, kayaks for rent, a swimming pool, folkloric shows, and other attractions.

Boats to the Sumidero and the Parque Amikúu leave daily (8am–4.30pm) from **Cahauré** and the town of **Chiapa de Corzo** ㉜, 15 minutes east of Tuxtla, where there is a line of riverside restaurants by the *embarcadero*. The first Spanish settlement in Chiapas, founded in 1528, Chiapa has all the colonial charm that is missing in Tuxtla Gutiérrez. The huge octagonal well in the town plaza, dating from 1562 and called **La Pila**, is a remarkable

Great White Egret, Sumidero Canyon.

Sumidero Canyon.

Parachicos celebrate the day of San Sebastián, Chiapa de Corzo.

example of Spanish Mudéjar or Moorish-influenced architecture, the finest in the Americas. The beautifully airy cloisters of a former monastery are now the **Centro Cultural ex-Convento de Santo Domingo** (tel: 961-616 0055; Tue–Sun 8am–6pm; free), with exhibition spaces and the **Museo de la Laca**, dedicated to the lacquerware for which the town is famous.

Chiapa de Corzo is also famous for its wild, spectacular fiestas around the day of San Sebastián, January 20. Men dress up as *parachicos,* in bright ponchos, fur hats, and strange, pale-faced lacquered masks, which began as a way of satirizing the Spanish conquerors, while women wear elaborate, dazzlingly coloured skirts. They dance wildly around the town for days, and the fiesta culminates in a "battle of boats" on the river.

The Moorish-well, known as La Pila, in Chiapa de Corzo.

Another way to see the Sumidero is from the viewpoints *(miradores)* above the gorge, reached by a road from the west side of Tuxtla (signposted Chicoasén). *Combis* run there from central Tuxtla.

PACIFIC CHIAPAS

Southwest of Tuxtla are Arriaga and **Tonalá**, from where you can drive or get a *combi* to cover the 19km (12 miles) to **Puerto Arista 🕸**, so far the only "beach resort" in Chiapas. Crowds descend here from Tuxtla at Mexican holiday times, but the rest of the year the town, its huge beach, and its inexpensive seafood restaurants are very quiet.

The capital of the long coastal plain of the Soconusco is hot, busy **Tapachula 🕸**, Mexico's "gateway to Central America." Nearby, almost at the Guatemalan border, is the oldest Maya site in Mexico at **Izapa** (Wed–Sun 9am–5pm), dating back to 300 BC. Behind Tapachula the land rises extraordinarily steeply, to 2,000 meters (6,560ft) in just 60km (37 miles). Some of the coffee plantations on the high slopes, such as **Finca Hamburgo**, still owned by descendants of German and Swiss families who came here in the days of Porfirio Díaz, have been made into very special hotels. Far above the plain, they feel like a different world.

From **Huixtla**, 42km (26 miles) north of Tapachula, the highway north begins an incredible climb, before dropping down to meet Highway 190 near the Guatemalan border crossing at **Ciudad Cuauhtémoc**.

MONTEBELLO AND COMITÁN

From the border, the Pan-American Highway (Mexican Highway 190) climbs steadily into the central highlands, with superb views east toward Guatemala's mountains, looming hazily in the distance. At Trinitaria, an eastward turn leads onto the Carretera Fronteriza or Highway 307, which now follows the border for some 450km (280 miles) all the way to Palenque. After about 38km (23 miles) it passes through the **Parque Nacional Lagunas de Montebello** ㉟. Between precipitous, pine-clad slopes there are some 60 jewel-like lakes; also known as the **Lagunas de Colores**, they range spectacularly from turquoise and amethyst to dark emerald green and steely gray. Most people visit the lakes as a day trip, but there are rustic *cabaña* hotels in the largest village, **Tziscao**, right by a placid lake that extends into Guatemala.

Just west of the Montebello entrance, a road turns north to the Maya ruins of **Chinkultic**, astonishingly located on a near-vertical crag above a lake. However, access has become difficult owing to a dispute between local villagers and the state authorities, and before going there it's advisable to check on the situation at the Comitán museum. Back on Highway 190, a turning west leads 6km (4 miles) to the larger and more accessible site of **Tenam Puente** (daily 8am–5pm), with massive stone pyramids on an immense hill, giving sweeping views. These centers were on the southern borders of Classic Maya civilization, and are believed to have survived after the more famous cities farther north had collapsed.

Comitán ㊱ is known for its steep streets and broad plaza and as the home of Rosario Castellanos, Chiapas' greatest modern writer. As well as a

⊙ Tip

There are three main road crossings from Chiapas into Guatemala: at Ciudad Hidalgo and Talismán near Tapachula, and Ciudad Cuauhtémoc on Highway 190. Direct international buses run from Tapachula via Ciudad Hidalgo; on the other routes, you must get a Mexican bus to the border, then a Guatemalan bus on the other side. Most nationalities do not need a visa for tourist trips. It is not usually permissible to take a Mexican rental car into Guatemala.

Parque Nacional Lagunas de Montebello.

Hammocks for sale.

charming small-town atmosphere, good restaurants, and hotels, it has an attractive **Museo Arqueológico** (tel: 963-632 5760; Tue–Sun 9am–6pm; free), with many finds from Tenam Puente.

SAN CRISTÓBAL DE LAS CASAS

North of Comitán the highway continues climbing into the heart of Los Altos, the highlands of Chiapas. This is also the heartland of living Maya culture in the state, where many communities speak Mayan languages – Tzotzil in some, Tzeltal in others – wear traditional dress, and maintain beliefs that are a fascinating blend of ancient Maya tradition with Catholic elements brought by the Dominican friars. The women of **Amatenango del Valle**, on Highway 190, specialize in making beautiful earthenware pottery, using an open fire instead of a kiln, employing a technique dating back over a thousand years. Older women from Amatenango are instantly recognizable by their red and orange woollen smocks and long blue skirts.

Colorful street in San Cristóbal de las Casas.

At an altitude of 2,100 meters (6,890ft), **San Cristóbal de las Casas** ㉗, capital of Los Altos, is many visitors' favorite town in Mexico. It is a city of immense colonial charm, with mostly one-story houses with red-tiled roofs and walls in blue, green, and ochre around secluded patios, and the scent of wood smoke lingering in the air. The cool mountain air is sparkling, and plenty of likeable restaurants, surprisingly trendy cafés, and attractive hotels make this a very relaxing place just to spend some time and soak up the atmosphere.

San Cristóbal was founded in 1528 as the first capital of Spanish Chiapas. Formerly *Ciudad Real de Chiapa*, the "Royal City" of Chiapas, it was given its current name in honor of Bartolomé de las Casas, first bishop of Chiapas, who defended indigenous people against the excesses of the conquistadors. For centuries only Spanish-speaking people were allowed to live in the town, while the townspeople in turn rarely ever entered the Maya villages around them. This pattern has marked

Ø THE HIGHLAND WEAVERS

Among the Highland Maya, gender roles have traditionally been very set. Men's first role is to grow corn and keep livestock; the quintessential art of women is to weave. Ixchel, the most important Maya fertility goddess, was also goddess of weaving. In traditional communities, all women and girls weave from an early age. They do so using the Maya backstrap loom, examples of which can be seen on pots and figurines from the Classic era, before AD 800. It is made up essentially of two wooden rods, with the main threads stretched between them. One is attached, by a cord tied to both ends, to a post or tree, while the other is connected to a strap around the lower back of the woman, who works kneeling, moving backward and forward to stretch and relax the threads, and with a heavy wooden comb to pack down each row of colored cross-threads.

Each of the Highland communities has its own distinctive style of weaving, which soon become familiar. The bright flower-designs of Zinacantán are the most eye-catching and often the most popular, but in textile cooperatives you can also find the beautiful, extraordinarily intricate work of more remote villages such as San Andrés Larraínzar or Mitontic, the larger pieces of which are made with immense skill. And within each local style, each piece is also an individual creation of each weaver, using a great range of motifs, and no two pieces are ever the same.

society in the Highlands ever since, but the last few decades have seen a vast change, as the Maya have flocked down to the city not only for the daily market, but to live in its suburbs.

As in all Spanish colonial towns, there are fine churches. Alongside the zócalo (main square) is the cathedral, with a facade painted Highland-style in ochre and red. Calle Real de Guadalupe, running eastward from the square, has the highest concentration of restaurants and shops, many selling Highland weaving and jewelry of Chiapas amber. The finest of San Cristóbal's churches is the **Templo de Santo Domingo**, at the other end of Calle General Utrilla from the Zócalo, begun in 1547 but with a stunning 17th-century Baroque facade in yellow stone. The church is equally dazzling inside, with an overwhelming display of Baroque gilt.

Around Santo Domingo is the Mercado Indígena or **handicrafts market**, an irresistible place to browse through brilliantly colored clothing, mats, and other Highland products. Women from Maya villages come here every day to sell their own weaving and embroidery, as well as pottery, leather goods, and more modern things like toys and T-shirts. Some of the finest-quality weaving can be found in the cooperatives near the market, such as **J'pas Joloviletik** at Calle Utrilla 43.

One of the most distinctive products of Chiapas is fine amber, found especially in remote villages in the north of the state. San Cristóbal has a delightful **Museo del Ambar** (http://museodelambardechiapas.org.mx; Tue–Sun 10am–2pm, 4–8pm), in the former convent of La Merced, giving detailed information on how amber is formed, and with a delightful shop selling original jewelry. There are many more shops with attractive amber jewelry around the town, especially on Calle Real.

Chiapas is a key coffee producer in Mexico and, a block from Plaza 31 de Mayo, **Museo del Café** (Mon–Sat 8am–10pm) convivially marries information on the history of the coffee industry here with an atmospheric café. It's

⊙ Eat

San Cristóbal has some of Mexico's best vegetarian restaurants. La Casa del Pan, at Calle Real de Guadalupe 55, has delicious, imaginative variations on local dishes made with organic ingredients, and fabulous bread.

Ornate belltower, Comitán.

⊙ Tip

When visiting Chamula and Zinacantán for the first time, it is always better to go with a tour. In addition to explaining what you are seeing, tour guides have access to many places that are otherwise closed to outsiders. Some of the most satisfying, good-value tours are those of Alex y Raúl, who can be found with their bus every day in the Zócalo in San Cristóbal at 9.30am. On request they can also arrange trips to less-visited areas and Zapastista villages.

owned and run by a Chiapas coffee-growers cooperative.

A walk east from Santo Domingo leads to **Na Bolom** (tel: 967-678 1418; daily 9am–7pm), the former home of the Swiss writer and photographer Trudi Duby-Blom (1901–93) and her Danish husband, the archeologist and anthropologist Frans Blom (1893–1963). It is now a center that continues their work with the Lacandón Maya and other indigenous peoples of Chiapas, with a library and a guesthouse, but a great attraction is the house itself, with its patios, herb garden, and fascinating relics of the Bloms' life here.

To the north of town, the **Museo de la Medicina Maya** (tel: 967-678 5438; Mon–Fri 10am–6pm, Sat–Sun 10am–4pm, summer only) offers a great insight into traditional medicine in Chiapas.

THE HIGHLAND VILLAGES

No stay in San Cristóbal is complete without a visit to the Maya communities north of the city, at **San Juan Chamula** ⑱ and **Zinacantán**. They are very different. Chamulans keep sheep, and their traditional dress for men – nowadays worn over conventional clothes – is a coarse woollen smock in black or white; women wear long black woolen skirts and blue or white blouses bordered with embroidered strips. The people of Zinacantán, in contrast, are the great color-lovers of the highlands, and men and women wear beautiful multicolored smocks with intricate flower motifs. *Zinacanteca* weaving is, consequently, the most popular buy for visitors.

Tours from San Cristóbal include both villages, beginning at Chamula, 10km (6 miles) from the city, with a visit to the extraordinary church. As in all the highland villages, the religion of the Chamulans is a complex mix of Catholic and pre-Conquest Maya beliefs. Inside, there are no services or seats, but the floor is carpeted with pine needles and lit with hundreds of candles, and people come and go to consult traditional healers or *ilol*, sitting on the floor. At Zinacantán, typically, the church is more colorful, and the atmosphere less intense. As your guide will tell you, it is absolutely forbidden to take photographs in either of the churches.

Another easily accessible village is **Tenejapa**, 29km (18 miles) east. The road there passes through spectacular scenery, and there is a vibrant Thursday market.

TONINÁ AND THE WATERFALLS

Highway 199 runs down the 192km (119 miles) from San Cristóbal to Palenque and the steamy forests of northeast Chiapas. About halfway down is the market town of **Ocosingo**, where a turnoff leads 14km (9 miles) to one of the most extraordinary Maya creations at **Toniná** ⑲ (tel: 961-612 8360; daily 8am–5pm; museum Tue–Sun only). Instead of spreading over several pyramids like most Maya

⊙ THE PALENQUE ARCHIVES

Palenque has more Maya glyph inscriptions than any other city. The longest are the "king lists" around the walls of the temple at the top of the Temple of Inscriptions – now normally closed off, although some replicas are in the site museum. They give information about ten rulers of Palenque, from K'uk-Balam (Quetzal-Jaguar) who founded the dynasty in AD 431. They were made for the eleventh, Pakal "the Great," who became king aged 12 in 615 and died at 80 in 683, and who built the Inscriptions Temple as his monument and tomb.

Pakal had them carved for a reason. He had been born in a time of trial for Palenque: two kings had died without male heirs, and the city had twice been raided by Calakmul. He was only the nephew of the previous king, through his mother, who had ruled in his name while he was a child. Power in Maya cities normally passed only through the male line, therefore Pakal, despite his later victories, could still have been considered a usurper. The aim of his monument building was to restate emphatically his links to the dynasty and his right to rule. The point was made still more strongly by his son Kan-Balam II in the Cross Group carvings, which vividly portray the Maya concept of the shaman-king as an essential channel between his community and the heavens.

cities, Toniná is almost one giant structure, rising up a mountainside through seven levels and endless staircases, and looking more than any other Maya center like a work of science fiction. The excellent museum displays remarkable sculptures from the site. As a warrior state Toniná fought many battles with Palenque.

There are two more popular stops before Palenque. The 7km (4 miles) of breathtaking jungle waterfalls at **Agua Azul** 🐵, on Río Tulijá, are 4km (2.5 miles) off the main road. The most turbulent cataracts are – naturally – extremely dangerous, but if you walk up 1 km (0.5 miles) there are large, placid pools that are easy to swim in. A safer and often more enjoyable spot for swimming, which generally has a more relaxed atmosphere, is the pool beneath the 35-meter (115ft) waterfall at **Misol-Ha** 🐵, 22km (14 miles) from Palenque. Aside from the dangers of the waterfalls, Agua Azul is also a black spot for petty crime. Keep an eye on your possessions when swimming, and do not walk alone on the apparently empty paths farthest from the entrance.

PALENQUE

Looming out of the Chiapas jungle, the Maya ruins at **Palenque** 🐵 (museum tel: 961-612 8360; daily 8am–5pm, museum Tue–Sun 9am–4.30pm) are one of Mexico's great sights. They inspire awe and wonder, and yet the main area visited today represents barely 10 percent of all the temples, palaces, and other structures that graced Palenque in the 7th century AD, when it had a population of around 70,000. Palenque has been the site of many crucial discoveries in Maya archeology, including the deciphering of Maya glyph writing.

Rising up beyond the entrance is the massive pyramid of the **Templo de las Inscripciones** (Temple of the Inscriptions), a majestic symbol of Classic Maya architecture. At the top of its giant steps is a temple, where in 1952 archeologist Alberto Ruz Lhuillier discovered a sealed passageway that led to a burial chamber 25 meters (82ft)

Chamula woman dressed in traditional fabric.

Templo de las Inscripciones at Palenque.

> **Tip**

The main places to stay near Bonampak and Yaxchilán are the Lacandón-owned campamentos of often quite comfortable cabins at Lacanjá, and the Escudo Jaguar cabaña hotel at Frontera Corozal. Bonampak is on Lacandón land, so you must leave your car near the village and take a local taxi to the ruins. At Frontera Corozal, two boatmen's cooperatives offer trips to Yaxchilán: Pájaro Jaguar on the entry road and Escudo Jaguar (at the hotel).

A bas-relief at Palenque depicting Upakal K'inich, the son of K'inich Ahkal Mo' Naab III.

down, which contained a richly adorned tomb of a man, beneath a superbly carved sarcophagus lid. This was the tomb of the greatest of Palenque's kings, Pakal, the first Maya ruler identified by modern archeologists. Sadly, pyramid and tomb are now closed to visitors for their preservation, but there is a precise replica of the tomb in the Palenque museum. Another tomb in **Temple XIII** alongside, known as the **Tomb of the Red Queen** and believed to be that of Pakal's wife, is still open.

Opposite the pyramid is the **Palacio** of the kings of Palenque, a fascinating complex of rooms, courtyards, passages, and tunnels, crowned by a unique tower that may have been an observatory or a watchtower. Around its walls and columns are carved stucco panels, stone sculptures and inscriptions, showing events in the life of the city and celebrating its victories.

On the north side of the Palacio is a **Ball Court** and more small pyramids, forming the **Groupo del Norte** (North Group), while to the east a path leads across a stream to the three spectacular pyramids of the **Cross Group**, the **Temple of the Cross**, **Temple of the Sun** and **Temple of the Foliated Cross**. Built by Pakal's son Kan-Balam II, they have some of Palenque's finest carving, although again, nowadays they are often closed to visitors.

From beside the North Group a lovely path runs down through forest past waterfalls and the remains of residential areas to the museum (included in the site ticket), which as well as the replica of Pakal's Tomb has his jade death mask and other stunning treasures. The town of Palenque, 8km (5 miles) from the ruins, has a choice of hotels, restaurants, and services, but the most attractive places to stay are on the ruins road.

BONAMPAK, LACANJÁ, AND YAXCHILÁN

Two more spectacular Maya sites, Bonampak and Yaxchilán, are deep in the forest near the Usumacinta River, the frontier with Guatemala. They have become far easier to reach thanks to

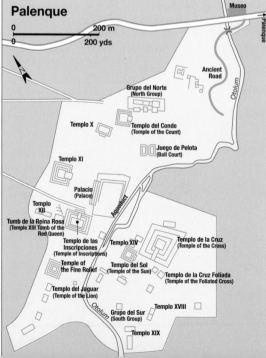

the Fronteriza highway around the Chiapas border to Comitán. One- or two-day tours are offered by many agencies in Palenque, but with a car it's easy to get there independently, with a stay at **Lacanjá** near Bonampak, one of the villages of the Lacandón, and the only Maya group never Christianized by the Spaniards. Nevertheless, discovering these remote sites still has a great feel of adventure.

Bonampak ㊸ (tel: 961-345 2824; daily 8am–5pm), shrouded in forest 148km (92 miles) southeast of Palenque, is quite small compared to the great Maya sites, but is of huge importance since it has, in one building, the one and only complete set of possibly hundreds of Maya mural paintings that has survived the ravages of the centuries. In vivid color and detail, the murals show the presentation of the son and heir of the lord of Bonampak, Chan-Muaan, in AD 790, followed by a bloody battle and further extravagant ceremonies that took place in the following two years, giving a matchless image of Classic-era Maya court life. All of Maya life is there – Chan-Muaan's queen and her maids, prisoners waiting to be sacrificed, bored-looking nobles chatting during a ceremony.

Yaxchilán ㊹ (daily 8am–5pm), was much larger than Bonampak, with a commanding position above the Usumacinta, and under Shield Jaguar II (reigned 681–742) and his son Bird Jaguar IV (752–68) was one of the most powerful cities along the river. There is still no access by road, and to get there you must take a boat from the little town of **Frontera Corozal**, 39km (24 miles) from Lacanjá, where there is also a boat crossing to Guatemala.

This all adds to the excitement of getting to Yaxchilán, first glimpsed through the trees on a crag above the river. Around its many temples there are superb relief carvings and stelae (standing stones), detailing momentous events in the lives of Yaxchilán's kings. Another feature of the site is the many howler monkeys, heard (and often seen) booming through the trees.

Woman aboard a boat on the Usamacinta river.

Maya mural paintings, Bonampak.

Beach at Tulum.

📷 YUCATAN'S NATURAL WONDERLAND

The Yucatán Peninsula and its Caribbean coast harbor magnificent natural treasures – hundreds of species of birds, animals, and colorful marine life, forming a diver's paradise.

Visitors to the Yucatán Peninsula often spend their time clambering over its awe-inspiring Maya ruins, sunning themselves on its gorgeous beaches, or exploring old colonial towns, but many birders, divers, and snorkelers flock here above all for its uniquely rich and diverse natural environment. The immense limestone slab that makes up the Yucatán is flanked for long kilometers by vast, virtually uninhabited fresh and salt-water coastal lagoons, which are home to a great many resident birds and provide winter quarters for millions of migrants from across North America. The Yucatán's *cenote* water holes, beautiful and mysterious (see page 315), and the huge subterranean rivers beneath them, filter minerals from the rock as they flow out to sea, providing rich nutrients for the Great Maya Reef, along the Caribbean coast. This is part of the second-longest coral reef system in the world, stretching for some 350km (218 miles) along the east coast of Yucatán and south past Belize to Honduras. Although narrower than the Australian Great Barrier Reef, this system reaches depths of more than 40 meters (130ft) around Cozumel, and at times the remarkable transparency of the water provides visibility up to 27 meters (90ft).

The Caribbean is one of the richest regions on earth in coral formations. Reefs, in turn, harbor an incredible variety and density of marine life. More than 50 species of coral, 400 of fish, and 30 gorgonians have been identified in the Yucatán reefs, along with hundreds of mollusks, crustaceans, sponges, and algae.

The loggerhead is one of the five species of sea turtle that come to the Yucatán to nest on the beaches from May to September.

Yucatán Jays, (Cyanocorax Yucatanicus) are relatively common. Juveniles are recognizable by their white-tipped tail features.

Pink flamingos breed in many of the shallow mangrove lagoons around the Yucatán coast, especially at Celestún and Río Largartos.

Divers in the upper caverns of the Dos Ojos cenote, near Tulum.

Diving destinations

There are many well-equipped locations from which to explore the Yucatán's underwater garden and coral mountains. Cozumel generally has the biggest variety of reefs, from shallow and ideal for beginners to giant wall dives, dropping sheer into the depths. Isla Mujeres, if sometimes crowded, also offers a good range of dives. On the mainland, friendly Puerto Morelos and busier Playa del Carmen are both excellent dive centers, while Akumal and Tulum have good open-water operators, and are now major locations for cave diving in nearby *cenotes*. The small dive operations on the Costa Maya, near Mahahual and Xcalak, offer a complete escape from any crowds (for slightly higher prices), and the chance to explore the vast, pristine Banco Chinchorro reef.

In general, the farther south, the better the condition of the reef. Hurricanes, notably Wilma in 2005, have done considerable damage to the coral, especially on Cozumel's inshore reefs. More long-term damage is being done by over-development, particularly the constant building of resort hotels down the Riviera Maya. These often obstruct the natural flow of nutrients out to sea from the mangroves and underground rivers, causing rapid coral deterioration. Only restrictions on building will halt this process.

Mexico's coastal mangrove forests are important ecosystems.

Spotted Eagle Rays can be seen among the reefs off Cozumel.

Cooling off in a jungle river.

Ruins overlooking the beach at Tulum.

THE YUCATÁN

Long separate from the rest of Mexico, the Yucatán Peninsula has special attractions: awe-inspiring Maya cities, a unique landscape, sultry colonial towns, sparkling Caribbean beaches, coral reefs, and a distinctive tranquility.

The Maya of the Yucatán were never subjugated by the Aztecs, nor by any of the cultures of central Mexico, and under Spain the peninsula, with its own governors, had little contact with the viceroys in distant Mexico City. There was not even a usable land link between the peninsula and central Mexico until the mid-20th century. In its isolation, the Yucatán got used to seeing itself as a world apart, with its own ways of doing things and its own particular synthesis of Maya and Spanish cultures. This blended with the uniqueness of the landscape – a giant, flat limestone slab, with no surface rivers but with mysterious rock pools called *cenotes* leading into vast underwater cave systems – to create a very special ambiance with a distinctive charm.

CONQUEST

The Maya of the Yucatán resisted the Spaniards longer than any other people in Mexico, despite being divided in traditional Maya style between some 19 small lordships. Cortés had sailed around the Yucatán without making any permanent landing, and it was not until 1526 that one of his former lieutenants, Francisco de Montejo, obtained from Emperor Carlos V the commission to be the *Adelantado* or "First Promoter" of the Yucatán. The following year he landed at Xel-Ha on

Quinta Avenida, Playa del Carmen.

the Caribbean coast – now one of the Riviera Maya's most popular snorkel parks – and tried to march inland, but after six months had to withdraw, having conquered nothing and lost more than half of his men to disease and Maya attacks. He tried again in 1531, landing near Campeche with his son, with the same name but known as Montejo *El Mozo* (The Boy), but this expedition also failed. Finally, in 1540 *El Mozo* tried again with his cousin, yet another Francisco de Montejo, known as *El Sobrino* (The Nephew). They took

Main attractions
Campeche
Uxmal and the Puuc Route
Mérida
Izamal
Chichén Itzá
Río Lagartos
Isla Mujeres
Cozumel
Tulum

Maps on pages
304, 308, 312, 314

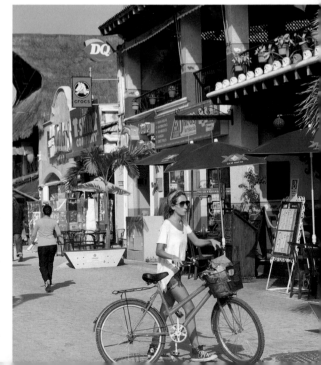

Good-quality handwoven Panama hats, made near Campeche, can be rolled up and will immediately resume their shape.

Spanish fortress Fuerte de San Miguel.

Campeche, then marched north to occupy the ruined Maya city of Ti'ho, where they resisted a bloody siege. They thought only divine intervention could explain their eventual victory, after a sudden collapse in Maya morale. In 1542, Mérida was founded at Ti'ho, as capital of the new colony.

The task of Christianizing the Yucatán was entrusted to Franciscan friars, led by Father Diego de Landa. The austere attitudes of the Franciscans can be seen in the plain, massive early colonial churches and monasteries across the Yucatán, with few architectural details. Another feature of colonial Yucatán was that, while in central Mexico the indigenous population fell disastrously after the Conquest, owing to European diseases, over-exploitation, and the complete disruption of the traditional economy, on the peninsula this decline was far less marked, and the Maya continued to make up half or more of the population.

Nationalist feeling in this sleepy colony was limited, and the ending of Spanish rule was extraordinarily peaceful: in 1821, when news reached Mérida that Spain had lost control of Mexico, the last Spanish governor called a meeting of prominent local citizens, told them that it was impossible for him to continue on his own, shook hands, and left. The Yucatán declared its sovereignty, together with a grudging, conditional adherence to Mexico. If the peninsula's criollo elite had had no great problems with Spanish rule, they were far more suspicious of "Mexicans." In 1839, in response to the authoritarian measures of Santa Anna, the Yucatán declared its independence, and in 1842 even succeeded in driving back an army sent to restore Mexican control.

CASTE WAR

This, though, was the prelude to the most extraordinary event in Yucatecan history, the "Caste War" of 1847–50. To fight their wars the Yucatecan elite did something the Spaniards had never done, recruiting the Maya as foot soldiers, offering in return land rights

⊘ HACIENDAS

Haciendas, aristocratic plantation houses, are emblematic of the Yucatán, with lofty ceilings and colonnaded terraces, ringed by exuberant tropical gardens. Built up from the 17th century to the *henequén* boom around 1900, most fell into atmospheric decline after the 1910 Revolution, but several have been reborn as very special hotels. A stay in a hacienda is one of the Yucatán's most seductive experiences. Several luxurious haciendas – at Temozón, Santa Rosa, and San José around Mérida, and Uayamón and Puerta Campeche in Campeche – are run by the same group (www.thehaciendas.com), all with gorgeous pools and restaurants. Hacienda Xcanatún, just north of Mérida, has some of the area's best dining. More modest alternatives include the laid-back Hacienda San Antonio Chalanté, near Izamal.

and lower taxes. These promises were never kept, and pent-up Maya rage reached boiling point. In 1847, the Maya rose up across eastern Yucatán and attacked the old colonial center of Valladolid. Panic spread through Spanish-speaking Yucatán, as town after town fell to the rebels, and whites and mestizos were massacred. At one point, the governor of the Yucatán, Santiago Méndez, sent letters to Britain, Spain, and the United States, offering the peninsula to whichever country would save its "civilized population" from certain death. The Maya came closer than any other native people in the Americas to regaining their land. Then, there was an equally astonishing turnaround. The Maya were village farmers, and would starve if they missed a planting season. In May 1848, as they prepared to assault Mérida, signs appeared that rains were going to come early that year; against protests from their chiefs, many went home, and lost their opportunity for ever.

While no foreign power wanted to get involved, Mexico sent troops, in return for the Yucatán rejoining the nation, and reprisals were as bloody as the earlier massacres. Nor did the war end simply. Some rebel Maya retreated into the empty southeast of the peninsula, where they established a "mini-state" around their new town of Chan Santa Cruz (now Felipe Carrillo Puerto) that remained outside Mexican control until 1901.

The war ended hopes of independence among white Yucatecans. The influence of the local elite was farther reduced when Campeche became a separate state in 1863, and in 1902 when the eastern Yucatán was made a Federal Territory, which in 1974 became the state of Quintana Roo.

Their frustrations were compensated for by new prosperity. Yucatán was finally found to produce something that was very valuable, as demand rose worldwide for sisal rope, made from henequén cactus, the "green gold" of the Yucatán. Under Porfirio Díaz, Yucatecan hacendados made vast fortunes, and Mérida became the most modern city in Mexico after the capital. After the Revolution, large areas of

⊘ Eat

Campeche has its own distinctive cuisine, cocina campechana, based on fish and seafood. Specialties include pan de cazón (hammerhead shark, chopped and baked in a tomato sauce between two tortillas), camarón al coco (shrimp in coconut), and arroz con pulpo (octopus and rice salad). The many enjoyable places to try it include the smart La Pigua, just outside the city walls at Avenida Miguel Alemán 179A, and the long-established traditional café La Parroquia, off the main square on Calle 55.

Campeche's twin-towered cathedral.

The Yucatán

0   50 km

0   50 miles

N

G U L F   O F

Reserva Ecológica
Estatal
Bocas de Dzilam

P
de Ba

Telchac
Puerto

Boca de Dzilam

Dzilam

⑩ Progreso

Chuburna

Chicxulub
Puerto

Xcambo

Chábihau de Bravo

Dzidzantún

Yatsino

Punta Baz

Sisal

Baca

Cansahcab

176

Xla

Reserva de laBiosfera
Ría Celestún

Dzibilchaltún

⑨

Motul

Temax

Tepakán

E

Punta Boxcohuo

Hunucmá

⑧ Celestún

261

Kinchil

Umán

Mérida
⑦

Aké

Seyé

Izamal **⑪**

Hóctun

Kantunil

Dzit

Bella Flor

Chocholá

261

Yaxcopoil

Acancéh

Tecoh

1800

Gruta
Bafankas

Libre
Unión

Piste

Y   u   c   a   t   á   n

180

Maxcanú

Mayapán

Telchaquillo

18

Sotuta

Chichén Itzá **⑫**

Xcala

Bahía de Campeche

Tankuché

Halachó
Becal

Oxkintoc

Muna

Mama

Mayapán

Tekit

Teabo

Lázaro
Cárdenas

Ticul

Mani

Calkiní

Uxmal
④

Teabo

Jaina
(Zac-Pol)

Pochoc

Kabáh
⑤

Oxkutzcab

Grutas de Loltún
⑥

Tekax de A.O.

Punta Nitún

Pomuch

Hecelchakán

Sáyil

Labná

Ticum

Peto

Tenabó

Xcalumkin

Xlapak

184

Tzucacab

Bolonchén

24

Boxol

261

Dzuiché

② Campeche

Chencoyi

Santa Rosa
Xtampak

Hunto Chac

José María
Morelos

Lerma

Cayal

Hopelchén

Polyuc

184

Tix

Seybaplaya

Tixmucuy

Nohyaxché

③

Iturbide

Dzibilnocac

Chunhubub

Balneario Acapulco

261

Edzná

Pich

Haltunchén

Chenko

Dzibalchén

Champotón
①

Moquel

Ruíz
Cortines

Hochob

San Enrique

Chencán

M   E   X   I

Q u i n t a n a

Huayahaca

180

Pustunich

212

Reserva de la

R o o

Pixoyal

250

M e s e t a

Tigrito

Isla del
Carmen

Puerto
Real

Chicbul

Biosfera de

d e   Z o h l a g u n a

Judas

Judas

Ciudad del
Carmen

Dieciocho
de Marzo

Ponte
Díaz Ordaz

Francisco
Escárcega

Lechugal

Calakmul

Dzibanché-
Kinichná

Bacal

Zacatal

Laguna
de Términos

261

Balamkú

Dzinapara

Conhuas

Becán

Xpuhil

Francisco
Villa

San
Ele

Coyoc

186

Lago
Sivituc

Chicanná

Xpuhil

Francisco
Villa

186

Buenavista

Río Bec

Tortuga

Escondido

Kohunlich

Candelaria

186

El Tigre

365

Reserva de la

Azul

Tomás
Garrido

Orange
Walk

Nueva
Coahuila

Biosfera de
㉝ Calakmul

Neustadt

Carmelita

Chablé

T a b a s c o

Calakmul

G U A T E M A L A

Sa

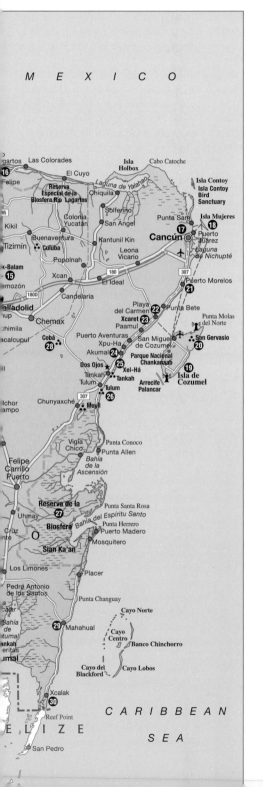

land were redistributed to villages, but *henequén* had already begun to lose its market to other fibers. The economy did not really revive until the tourist transformation began in the 1970s.

CAMPECHE STATE

One main road runs from central Mexico into the Yucatán: Highway 186 via Villahermosa and the shabby truck-stop town of **Francisco Escárcega**, from where 186 continues east to Chetumal and the Riviera Maya, while Highway 261 turns north for Campeche and Mérida. One other, much slower road, Highway 180, runs along the coast through the oil town of **Ciudad del Carmen**, once a pirate stronghold.

Highway 261 meets 180 just south of **Champotón ❶**, at the mouth of the northernmost river on this side of the peninsula, with the same name. The first two Spanish expeditions to Mexico led by Hernández de Córdoba and Grijalva both put in here in 1517 and 1518 looking for water, and both suffered in clashes with the Maya lord of Campeche, Moch-Cuouh. Champotón still has a Spanish fort, and a fishing harbor.

WALLED CAMPECHE

It is an easy 62km (40-mile) drive along the coast to **Campeche ❷**, the most complete Spanish fortified city in Mexico and one of the most romantic of its colonial cities. This was the first city founded in the Yucatán by the Montejos, and for centuries its only official port. Hence Campeche became an irresistible target for all the pirates who proliferated in the Caribbean from the 1580s. The city was attacked countless times, when its people had to take refuge in the monastery of San Francisco, north of the old town, while the buccaneers camped outside, demanding ransom to leave. Finally, the city's governors levied a special tax, and beginning in 1684 old Campeche was ringed with ramparts and *baluartes* or bastions, some of the most solid Spanish fortifications in the New World. In 1718, when the Spaniards expelled the last buccaneers from what is now Ciudad del Carmen, Campeche's pirate era came to an end.

After independence Campeche became a backwater, despite being given its own state in 1863. Its economy only revived with the discovery of oil offshore in the 1960s. As the oil boom gathered pace, modernity was seen as the way forward, and a plan was adopted called the *Resurgimiento* (Resurgence) of Campeche, which involved knocking down large parts of the old walls – some of which had already gone in the 19th century – and building an all-new modernistic square, **Plaza Moch-Cuouh**. In the 1990s, as tourism grew, this policy was completely reversed. Whole sections of wall were even rebuilt. Within the walls, gracious colonial houses with iron window-grilles were beautifully restored, and repainted in traditional colors – blues, greens, ochre. Old Campeche thus regained a huge amount of its historic charm, and in 1999 was declared a Unesco World Heritage site.

A walk around the circuit of bastions is an enjoyable way of getting a feel of the old city, beginning at the main plaza or **Parque Principal**. Overlooking it is the twin-towered **cathedral**, built over the course of three centuries and so with elements of several styles. Opposite, a typical Campeche house, the **Casa Seis** (daily 9am–9pm; free), restored in the style of a 19th-century merchant's residence, contains the tourist office. On the landward side of the plaza is the **Portales** building, with graceful two-story arcades hosting a restaurant overlooking the square.

An engraving of Chac, the Maya god of the rain, Uxmal.

There is an excellent sound and light show in the park every Sunday at 8pm.

Near the square are the **Puerta del Mar**, the "Sea Gate" that once led out to the port, and the **Baluarte de la Soledad**, which contains the **Museo de la Arquitectura Maya** (Tue–Sun 8am–5pm), with Maya stone stelae and carvings from around Campeche state. The next stop, heading clockwise, is the **Baluarte de Santiago**, inside which is a tropical garden, the **Jardín Botánico Xmuch'Haltún** (Mon–Fri 8am–9pm, Sat–Sun 9am–9pm). The longest surviving stretch of battlements is between the **Puerta de Tierra** or "Land Gate" and **Baluarte de San Juan**. You can walk along the top. Beside the gate there is also a fun museum about pirates, the **Museo de la Piratería** (daily 9am–5pm). The large **Baluarte de San Carlos** in the northwest corner has cannons, dungeons, and the **Museo de la Ciudad** (daily 8.30am–5.30pm), detailing the city's history.

Campeche's great museum treasures are not, however, in the bastions but some way outside the old city. The **Museo de la Cultura Maya** (Tue–Sun 8.30am–5pm) is in the **Fuerte de San Miguel**, a dramatic Spanish fortress on a hilltop to the south. Campeche state has a wealth of archeological sites, and the museum has many superb exhibits: most spectacular are the jade funeral masks from Calakmul, but other highlights include small clay figurines from Isla Jaina on the Gulf Coast, which show a very human aspect of Maya culture. Another fortress north of the city, **Fuerte de San José**, contains the **Museo de Barcos y Armas** (Museum of Ships and Weapons; tel: 981-811 6218; Tue–Sun 9.30am–6pm), detailing post-Conquest and maritime history. There are superb views from both fortresses.

Some 55km (34 miles) southeast of Campeche is the large Maya center of **Edzná** ❸ (daily 8am–5pm), which, like many, had its own building style, spectacularly represented by the Palace of

Five Stories, the largest multi-level structure in Maya architecture. The temples around it have especially intricate carvings. The region east of Edzná is known as the **Chenes**, from the Yucatecan Maya word for well (water can only be obtained here from deep wells). There are several remote archeological sites around the little town of **Hopelchén**, notably **Santa Rosa Xtampak**, and on the road north in Bolonchén is the **Xtacumbilxunaan** or Great Well, an awe-inspiring cave used as a water source for centuries. Tourist facilities in this area are very limited.

UXMAL AND THE PUUC

The landscape rises into Yucatán state and the Puuc Hills, which stand out in the flat Yucatán – *Puuc* is Maya for hill. Water here is even more scarce than in the rest of the peninsula, and in ancient times the supply was supplemented by collecting rainy-season water in *chultunes*, huge cisterns dug into the ground. Nevertheless, this was the setting for the emergence from around AD 650 to 950 of several Maya communities, around the great city of Uxmal, that developed the most refined of all Maya architecture, featuring an intricate interplay between natural and symbolic imagery and a dramatic rhythmic geometry. An unmissable part of the Maya world, the Puuc area can easily be visited from Mérida, 80km (50 miles) north.

The name **Uxmal ❹** (daily 8am– 5pm) means "thrice built," but it seems major building here only began late in the Classic period. Uxmal was at its peak under a king known as Lord Chac, who completed many of its finest structures in about 890–910. Only a few decades later, from about 920, Uxmal and the other Puuc communities declined rapidly, owing perhaps to a combination of overpopulation, soil exhaustion, drought, and defeat in war.

The first structure beyond the entrance is the partially oval **Pyramid of the Magician**, facing you, with steep steps leading up to a dramatic "monster-mouth" temple. Unfortunately, visitors are no longer allowed to climb them. Like most Maya pyramids, it was built up in many stages, but its name

Well-restored traditional houses near the church of San Franscisco, Campeche.

comes from a legend in which an *alux* or Maya spirit or leprechaun, the "Dwarf of Uxmal," built it in a single night in a test of strength with a local king.

Behind the pyramid are the extensively restored **Cuadrángulo de los Pájaros** (Birds Quadrangle) and the superb **Cuadrángulo de las Monjas** (Nunnery Quadrangle), a square plaza composed of four buildings that are each different, yet form a harmonious whole. For the full effect, walk around to the left and enter through the arch in the south building. The visual imagination of the Puuc builders is evident; carvings combine homey images – *Na* stick-and-palm huts that can be seen in Maya villages today – with intricate representations of vision serpents, channels to the gods. A recurring image is the Rain God Chac, recognizable by his long curved nose, who was especially important in the dry Puuc. Like many buildings at Uxmal, the "Nunnery" was given its name in 1658 by a Spanish Friar, Diego López de Cogolludo, on the basis of Spanish equivalents.

To the south is Uxmal's main **Ball Court**, beyond which is another huge artificial platform, created for the **Palacio del Gobernador** (Governor's Palace), which the archeologist Sylvanus Morley called "the most magnificent, the most spectacular single building in all pre-Columbian America." The name was apt for once, as this does seem to have been the residence of the lords of Uxmal. A figure of Lord Chac sits in the center of the 100-meter (328ft) frieze, the rest of which is a complex representation of the Maya calendar. As at the Nunnery, the frieze was made up by separately carving individual panels – more than 20,000 – on the palace, that were then fitted together in a giant jigsaw puzzle.

Sharing the same platform is the neat **Casa de las Tortugas** (House of Turtles), adorned with carved turtles, which the Maya associated with rain and creation. Beside the Palace platform are the older **Gran Pirámide** (Great Pyramid) and **Casa de las Palomas** (House of Pigeons), a large complex so-called because its roof comb, built as a base for long-lost sculptures,

Carved masks of the Rain God Chac at Codz-Poop at Kabah.

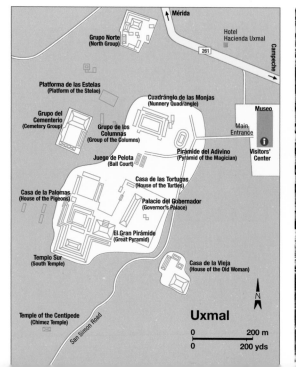

Grupo Norte
(North Group)

Hotel
Hacienda Uxmal

Mérida

261

Campeche

Platforma de las Estelas
(Platform of the Stelae)

Cuadrángulo de las Monjas
(Nunnery Quadrangle)

Museo

Grupo del
Cementerio
(Cemetery Group)

Grupo de los
Columnas
(Group of the Columns)

Main
Entrance

Pirámide del Adivino
(Pyramid of the Magician)

Visitors'
Center

Juego de Pelota
(Ball Court)

Casa de las Tortugas
(House of the Turtles)

Casa de la Palomas
(House of the Pigeons)

Palacio del Gobernador
(Governor's Palace)

El Gran Pirámide
(Great Pyramid)

Templo Sur
(South Temple)

Casa de la Vieja
(House of the Old Woman)

N

Uxmal

0   200 m
0   200 yds

Temple of the Centipede
(Chimez Temple)

San Simon Road

was thought to look like a dovecote. Down the path beyond it is a large arch, which stood at the end of a *sacbé* or Maya stone road to Kabah.

THE PUUC ROUTE

The smaller sites of the "Puuc Route" (all daily 8am–5pm) are spread along Highway 261 south of Uxmal and a road that turns east near Kabah. These sites are beautiful places to explore, both for their architecture and their surrounding woods full of birds. **Kabah 5** has a fine **Palacio**, but its highlight is the extraordinary **Codz-Poop** or Palace of Masks, with a facade of some 250 curled-nose masks of the Rain God Chac. An **arch** across the highway was the southern end of the *sacbé* from Uxmal.

A short way after the turn east, **Sayil** has one of the most elegant Maya palaces, with more than 90 rooms spanning three levels, and typical Puuc "drum column" facades. Farther along, **Xlapak** is a small site with one intricately carved temple, while **Labná** has the most beautiful of all Maya arches. Near the end of the route are the most

remarkable caves in Yucatán, the **Grutas de Loltún 6** (various guided tours daily 9am–4pm), which have the oldest evidence of human occupation in the peninsula – from 5000 BC – and have been used by the Maya in every era since then. The caverns are vast, with wonderful rock formations, bizarre changes in atmosphere, and underground gardens, as well as Maya relics.

The Puuc Route road ends by meeting Highway 184 at **Oxkutzcab**, one of several likeable towns along this road. **Ticul** is the largest, with good restaurants, and shops selling traditional ceramics. A detour east leads to **Maní**, with the massive, austere early Franciscan monastery where Father Diego de Landa lamentably burned hundreds of Maya manuscripts in 1562, thus eradicating one of the best recorded histories of any pre-Hispanic group.

MÉRIDA

Heart and hub of the Yucatán, **Mérida 7** is a city with a special blend of fine colonial architecture, tropical languor, and easy-going street life,

⊙ Shop

Mérida – especially the market area – is the best place to buy any kind of traditional local product: men's *guayabera* shirts, embroidered blouses, leather sandals. Handwoven Panama-style hats are mostly made in Campeche state, but the best ones still usually go on sale in Mérida. The best places to buy good-quality hammocks are the specialty shops on Calle 65, especially La Poblana, between calles 58 and 60.

Pyramid of the Magician, Uxmal.

Monumento a la Patria, Maya-inspired modern art, Mérida.

dubbed *La Ciudad Blanca*, "The White City," for its streets of colonial houses with whitewashed walls, behind which there are often secluded patios with gorgeous gardens of coconut palms and papaya plants. Many are now lovely small hotels, which helps make Mérida a great base for exploring the Yucatán.

Founded in the 1540s as capital of the whole peninsula, Mérida remains its biggest market. At the end of the 19th century, the city revived after the Caste War through the *henequén* boom, when its new millionaires spent their wealth on lavish homes along the all-new Paseo de Montejo, based on the Parisian Champs-Elysées. These ornate buildings combine with Franciscan austerity in Mérida's architectural mix.

PLAZA MAYOR AND THE MARKET

Central Mérida is compact, and easy to explore at a stroll. In line with Spanish colonial tradition, streets spread out in a grid from the main square; even-numbered streets run north–south, odd-numbered ones east–west.

Street leading to Catedral de San Ildefonso, Mérida.

With giant laurel trees giving shade, the broad **Plaza Mayor** Ⓐ (also known as the Plaza Grande, or the Zócalo) is a natural place to begin a walking tour. On the east side is the massive, rather stark **Catedral de San Ildefonso** Ⓑ, the oldest cathedral in mainland America, completed in 1598 (Santo Domingo, in the Dominican Republic, is the only older one in the Americas).

The spacious building beside the cathedral contains the **Museo de Arte Contemporáneo de Yucatán** or **MACAY** (tel: 999-928 3258; www.macay. org; Wed–Mon 10am–6pm; free), with modern Yucatecan art and interesting temporary exhibits.

The first large Spanish building completed in Mérida, well before the cathedral, was the **Casa de Montejo** Ⓒ on the south side of the plaza, built as the home of the Yucatán's conquerors, the Montejos. In the 1980s most of it was rebuilt and is now a Citibanamex bank, but it retains its extraordinary plateresque portico, with the Montejo coat of arms, and flanked by two giant figures of Spanish conquistadors, their feet on screaming

heads, presumably representing the Maya. On the west side is the **Ayuntamiento** or city hall, with an 18th-century loggia. Presiding over the north side are the colonnades of the 19th-century **Palacio de Gobierno** ◐ (daily 9am–4pm; free), with the city's tourist information office and powerful murals around its patios by Fernando Castro Pacheco, evoking the history of the Yucatán.

From the plaza a walk south down Calle 60 and east on Calle 65 leads to the **market**, Mérida's giant bazaar, which spreads over several blocks. In front of the main market, at the crossing of calles 65 and 56, is the **Museo de la Ciudad** ◒ (Tue–Fri 9am–6pm, Sat–Sun 9am–2pm; free), with informative displays on the history of the city, and temporary art exhibitions. A few blocks away on Calle 50 are two surviving gates from the Spanish city wall built around Mérida in the 18th century.

CALLE 60 AND PASEO DE MONTEJO

After the Plaza Mayor, the other great hub of Mérida is the north stretch of Calle 60, which runs up from beside the cathedral. On the corner of calles 60 and 61 you can get a horse-drawn carriage or *calesa* ride up to Paseo Montejo. One block up from Plaza Mayor is **Parque Hidalgo**, one of the best squares for people-watching, beside which is the **Iglesia de la Tercera Orden** ◒ (also called Iglesia de Jesús), originally built for the Jesuit Order in 1618, and more ornate than the Franciscan churches.

A five-block walk east along Calle 59 leads to another, more typically austere church, **La Mejorada**, on a quiet plaza. Nearby are two delightfully individual museums: the **Museo de la Canción Yucateca** (Calle 57; Tue–Fri 9am–5pm, Sat–Sun 9am–3pm) relating to the Yucatán's traditional music; and the **Museo de Arte Popular de Yucatán** (Tue–Sat 9.30am–6.30pm, Sun 9am–2pm; free on Sun), with beautiful handicrafts from around Mexico.

Back on Calle 60, at the corner of Calle 55 is **Parque Santa Lucía**, one of the prettiest of Mérida's old squares and the venue for the *Serenatas*

◔ Eat

Lunch in Progreso (see page 313) is a great way of sampling local food and getting a feel of local life. Seafront restaurants such as Los Pelícanos and Flamingos all have delicious fresh fish and ceviches of conch, shrimp, and octopus, and are packed with family groups every weekend.

Colonial-style ironwork, Mérida.

◔ THE TWO SIDES OF FATHER LANDA

Father Diego de Landa (1524–79) is a very ambiguous figure in Yucatán and Maya history. Founder of the monastery at Izamal and first head of the Franciscans in Yucatán, Landa admired the virtues of courage and willpower that the Maya shared with Christianity and was awed by their accomplishments. In 1566 he wrote a report titled *Relación de las Cosas de Yucatán* (Relation of the Affairs of Yucatán), which is the most complete account we have of Maya life on the verge of the Conquest. Rediscovered in a Spanish library in the 19th century, the *Relación* also contained information that was indispensable for the deciphering of the Maya calendar and, later, Maya glyph writing.

However, this can now be viewed as a classic example of conquerors rewriting the history of the defeated. In 1562, after he discovered that many Maya were still holding their old rituals in secret, Landa furiously ordered that a mass *auto-da-fe*, or religious trial for heresy, be held at Maní, where suspected pagan backsliders were beaten and tortured, and every Maya artifact the friars could find was destroyed – including a great number of books written in Maya script. With that in mind, it's hard to imagine Landa's book providing a source of information even close to equal in historic value with those original Maya works. Today, sadly, only four Maya manuscripts survive.

Pink flamingos, Celestún.

Part of the Nunnery at Chichén Itzá.

Yucatecas every Thursday at 9pm, performances of local music and dance. Mérida provides a delightful range of free entertainment. Every Saturday night, Calle 60 is closed to traffic and taken over by salsa bands and food stands, the prelude to the all-day *Mérida en Domingo* every Sunday, which also features displays of the main Yucatecan folk dance, the jarana. Every night there are events, presented more for locals than tourists. The free English-language magazine *Yucatán Today* has the full program (see page 342).

A few blocks farther up from **Parque Santa Lucía**, a turning right leads to the very different **Paseo de Montejo**, with broad, tree-lined sidewalks. Opulent French- or Italian-style mansions can be seen between more modern buildings. One of the grandest, the 1909 Palacio Cantón, is now the **Museo de Antropología e Historia G** (Tue–Sun 8am–5pm), which provides an excellent background to visits to the peninsula's Maya sites. There is also an excellent collection of Aztec artifacts here.

DAY TRIPS FROM MÉRIDA

The mangrove lagoons at **Celestún 8**, 90km (56 miles) west of Mérida, provide breeding grounds for flocks of pink flamingos and other water birds. Boats to see them depart daily (6am–5pm) from the **Embarcadero** at the entrance to Celestún village; tours are also offered by many Mérida agencies. Carry on through the village and you will find a long, white beach.

North of Mérida, Maya **Dzibil-chaltún 9** (daily 8am–5pm) was one of the oldest continuously occupied sites in the Americas, dating back to 500 BC and still occupied when the Spanish arrived. One of the most striking structures is the **Templo de las Siete Muñe-cas** (Temple of the Seven Dolls), through the doors of which the sun pours on the morning of the Spring equinox, March 21. There is also a stunning *cenote* (water hole), **Xlacah** (open for swimming) and an excellent site museum.

Campeche was long the Yucatán's only port because the peninsula's northwest coast is a long sandbar, with very shallow sea beyond it; to

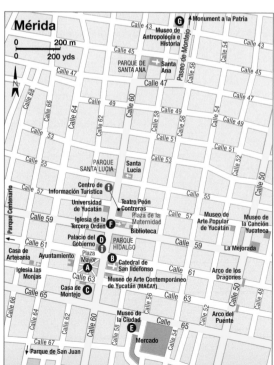

compensate, the harbor at **Progreso** ⑩ is at the end of a giant quay built out to sea, now 6km (4 miles) long. Behind it, Progreso's beaches make it a favorite weekending spot for *Meridanos*, with terrace restaurants along the seafront.

IZAMAL

A short detour east from Mérida leads to **Izamal** ⑪, known as *La Ciudad Dorada*, "The Golden City," because its old buildings are painted yellow-ochre: horse-drawn carriages clop through cobbled streets, and little disturbs the tranquil pace. Nowhere else in Yucatán are the Maya and Spanish traditions so closely intertwined. Izamal was a Maya pilgrimage center, and the remains of pyramids are scattered around the town, notably the immense **Kinich Kak Mo** (daily 8am–6pm). Izamal is dominated, though, by the **Monasterio de San Antonio de Padua**, largest of the Franciscan monasteries, founded by Diego de Landa in 1549. Huge and simple, in yellow and white, the monastery occupies an old Maya pyramid-platform, and has an equally huge atrium or courtyard, built to contain open-air services for the newly converted Maya.

Opposite the monastery an imaginatively renovated old house is now the **Museo de Artesanías** (www.centroculturalizamal.org.mx; Mon–Sat 10am–8pm, Sun 10am–5pm; free), with beautiful exhibits of traditional craftwork, and a shop. It also provides information on artisans currently working in Izamal.

CHICHÉN ITZÁ

Chichén Itzá ⑫ (daily 8am–4.30pm), voted one of the "New Seven Wonders of the World," is the most famous and most visited of all the Maya sites. It is often crowded, and visitors can no longer climb up most of its giant structures. Nevertheless, the extraordinary scale and ambition of Chichén Itzá cannot fail to be awe-inspiring.

It is paradoxical that Chichén should be the best-known Maya city, for its "Mayan-ness" has long been debated. The severe, flat-walled style of its Castillo pyramid and other major structures is very unlike other Maya cities, more reminiscent of central Mexico, and

⊘ Tip

At both Chichén Itzá and Uxmal there are sound-and-light shows at the ruins, every night at 7pm (Nov–Mar) or 8pm (Apr–Oct), which are included in the admission ticket, although there is an extra charge for headphone commentary in languages other than Spanish. To attend you must go back to each site after visiting during the day. The presentations are spectacular, and at Chichén Itzá the show recreates the "Descent of Kukulcán" effect on the stairway of the Castillo.

Castillo de Kukulcán, Chichén Itzá.

The Observatory, Chichén Itzá.

Cenote Yokdzonot, near Chichén Itzá.

different from other more traditionally "Maya" buildings at Chichén. It used to be widely believed that around the year 1000 the Yucatán was invaded by Toltecs from Tula in the Central Highlands, who took over an older Maya city of Chichén and added their own "Toltec-Maya" city.

This theory has been largely discredited, above all because it has been shown that the "Maya" and "Toltec" buildings at Chichén were built in roughly the same period, mostly from about AD 800 to 950. The argument is still open, but it seems fairly clear that Chichén Itzá was always an unusually mixed community, where Yucatán Maya and "Mexicans" (groups of migrants, not an "invasion") lived alongside each other. Chichén rose to splendor from about 700 and dominated northern Yucatán after defeating Cobá around 860. It also survived the "Maya Collapse" longer than other major cities, but was finally abandoned around 1200.

THE MONUMENTS OF CHICHÉN

Dominating the view as you enter the site is Chichén Itzá's "sacred mountain,"

the **Castillo de Kukulcán**. It is a giant representation in stone of two of the three Maya calendars, the *haab* and the *tzolkin*: its four staircases have 91 steps each, which, including the platform at the top, total 365, the number of days in a year; each side has 52 panels, representing the 52-year cosmic cycle.

It is also aligned, with extraordinary precision, with the movements of the sun. Every year, on the Spring equinox (March 21), thousands come to Chichén Itzá to witness the "Descent of Kukulcán," the astonishing play of sunlight on the northern staircase. As the afternoon progresses, the sun picks out the great feathered serpent carved beside the staircase, beginning at its tail and moving down to its head, "bringing it alive." On the Fall equinox (September 21), the "snake" appears to ascend the pyramid.

On the northwest side of the central plaza is the great **Ball Court**, the largest in Mesoamerica, and vastly bigger than the older courts in most Maya cities. Games must also have been played in a different style, with teams of around

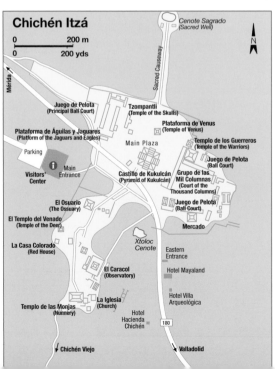

Chichén Itzá

0 — 200 m
0 — 200 yds

Mérida

Cenote Sagrado (Sacred Well)

Sacred Causeway

N

Juego de Pelota (Principal Ball Court)

Tzompantli (Temple of the Skulls)

Plataforma de Venus (Temple of Venus)

Plataforma de Águilas y Jaguares (Platform of the Jaguars and Eagles)

Templo de los Guerreros (Temple of the Warriors)

Parking

Main Plaza

Main Entrance

Visitors' Center

Castillo de Kukulcán (Pyramid of Kukulcán)

Juego de Pelota (Ball Court)

Grupo de las Mil Columnas (Court of the Thousand Columns)

El Osuario (The Ossuary)

Juego de Pelota (Ball Court)

El Templo del Venado (Temple of the Deer)

Mercado

La Casa Colorada (Red House)

Xtoloc Cenote

Eastern Entrance

El Caracol (Observatory)

Hotel Mayaland

La Iglesia (Church)

Hotel Villa Arqueológica

Templo de las Monjas (Nunnery)

Hotel Hacienda Chichén

180

Chichén Viejo

Valladolid

seven, who had to get the ball through the stone rings on each side. The superbly carved panels along the bottom of the walls show headless figures with writhing snakes symbolizing blood coming out of their necks, suggesting that losing players were decapitated.

Beside the Ball Court a path leads to the **Cenote Sagrado** (Sacred Well), 60 meters (197ft) in diameter. It appears to have been used only for rituals (another *cenote*, the **Xtoloc**, was Chichén's main water source). Many rich offerings have been retrieved from it, but there is no solid evidence that people were thrown into it as human sacrifices.

Back at the plaza, on the east side is the squat **Temple of the Warriors**, with, at the top, the celebrated statue of the reclining **Chacmool**, holding a receptacle for the hearts of sacrificial victims – although visitors are no longer allowed up to see it. The temple takes its name from the columns in front, carved with portraits of more than 200 warriors, priests, and other figures. They lead to the **Court of the Thousand Columns**, once the main market area. The forest of columns once supported wood and palm roofs.

South of the plaza are the more "Maya" buildings of Chichén. The most prominent is the fascinating **Observatory**, known as the **Caracol** (Snail) because of its spiral-like drum tower, with slots for tracking the movements of the stars. Beyond it, the buildings the Spaniards called the **Nunnery** (Templo de Las Monjas) have Puuc-style carvings.

Some 5km (3 miles) east are the **Grutas de Balankanché ⑬** (daily 9am–5pm), another of the Yucatán's great cave systems. Like the Loltún caves, this labyrinth of chambers, leading down to a magical underground pool, was used by the Maya for centuries, and many relics have been found here.

VALLADOLID AND RÍO LAGARTOS

Valladolid ⑭ gives an enjoyable taste of Yucatecan small-town life to anyone heading west from Cancún. As in all old colonial towns the hub of local life is the broad plaza, with the tall, white **cathedral**. A short walk west leads to the

Banco Chinchorro is covered with beautiful corals.

☉ UNDERGROUND WORLD

From the surface the Yucatán can appear to be a great, flat expanse of forest, with no rivers, hills, or other natural landmarks. These are below ground. Rainwater runs straight through the limestone, forming an immense labyrinth of caves and subterranean rivers. Seven of the 10 longest underground rivers in the world have been discovered here, including the longest of all, the Ox-Bel-Ha system around Tulum, which so far has been explored to a distance of 180km (112 miles).

Any hole in the rock that allows access to underground water is a *cenote* (a Spanish version of Maya *dzonot*). They can be huge pools open to the sky (where a cave roof has fallen in, centuries ago) or dark tunnels leading down to subterranean cathedrals. Spellbinding to explore, they are magical places in which to swim and snorkel.

Among the most popular swimming *cenotes* is the magnificent Dzitnup near Valladolid. However, every village in the Yucatán once needed to have a *cenote* nearby, and many village *cenotes* are now open to visitors. Guides in Mérida offer *cenote* snorkel tours. Several famous *cenotes* are around Tulum, now the world's foremost center for cave diving. For beginners, a good place to get a taste of cavern diving, snorkelling, or even cenote ziplining is Hidden Worlds Rainforest Adventures (www.rainforestadventure.com), north of Tulum, at one of the entrances to the Ox-Bel-Ha caves.

Brightly colored houses on Isla Mujeres.

The dock at Isla Mujeres.

semi-fortified church and monastery of **San Bernardino Sisal**, begun in 1552.

In the middle of Valladolid is the town's original water source, **Cenote Zací**, but its water is now dirty. Around 5km (3 miles) west of the town, however, is the unmissable **Cenote Dzitnup** (daily 8am–5pm), a subterranean cathedral, with a vast, arching cavern above a perfect pool of clear turquoise water that is irresistible for swimming. A short walk away is the almost equally spectacular **Cenote Samula**, though it gets fewer visitors.

North of Valladolid, Highway 295 leads to the coast. After 18km (11 miles) a side road leads to a remarkable Maya site at **Ek-Balam** ⑮ (daily 8am–4pm), extensively excavated only since the 1990s. Its greatest feature is the extraordinary mouth-shaped tomb entrance of **El Trono**, with some of the finest Maya carving. The road ends at the laid-back fishing town of **Río Lagartos** ⑯, on a long lagoon populated by flamingos and countless other water birds. Local boatmen offer trips, and there is also excellent fishing. Seeing birds at Río Lagartos is a more relaxed experience than it is at Celestún.

CANCÚN

Virtually every kind of modern architectural fantasy can be found in the Hotel Zone at **Cancún** ⑰; neo-Parisian mansions rub lawns with Las Vegas-Baroque and neo-Maya pyramids. Cancún provides luxuries on tap and on a big scale: glittering restaurants, eye-popping nightclubs, stunning pools with swim-up bars.

Now the biggest resort in Mexico – and the Caribbean – Cancún's legendary attractions are, naturally, its warm, turquoise sea and long, long beaches of wonderfully soft, powdery white sand that never gets hot underfoot. To take advantage of them, all sorts of water activities are on offer (although scuba diving and snorkeling are better farther south or on the offshore islands).

No one really noticed these beaches until 1969, when the Mexican government looked around for a location for a new resort on its then empty Caribbean coast to match Acapulco on the

Pacific, and the narrow sandstrip of Cancún was chosen. The first hotel opened in 1971, and building has gone on ever since. Cancún has had its setbacks, such as Hurricane Wilma in 2005, which stripped away sections of the beach, subsequently "rebuilt" with sand dredged up from the sea bed. Nevertheless, Cancún has a natural tendency to bounce back, and after every stumble – hurricanes, financial downturns – construction picks up again on a bigger scale.

HOTEL ZONE AND DOWNTOWN

There are two parts to Cancún. The main beach hotels and biggest malls and nightclubs are all along the strip of Cancún island, often known just as the **Hotel Zone**, shaped like a "7" on the map, and with one road, the **Boulevard Kukulcán**, along its 23km (15-mile) length (places along it are identified by kilometer markers, Km 14, Km 16 and so on). The island encloses a mangrove lagoon, the **Laguna Nichupté**. The biggest hub of activity is around the bend in the "7," near Km 9, with the **Convention Center** and the loudest nightclubs, such as **Dady'O** and **Coco Bongo**.

The biggest shopping zone is farther south around Km 11–13, with the **Flamingo Plaza** and **Kukulcán Plaza** malls and the upscale **La Isla** "shopping village." At Km 17 is the Maya site of **El Rey** (daily 8am–4.30pm), a Postclassic-era trading settlement. Though small it gives a clear sense of having been a small town, with a main street and central plaza. Opposite is the best of Cancún's public-access beaches at **Playa Delfines**, with crashing surf. Beaches around the north side of the "7" have more tranquil waters for swimming, but tend to be more crowded.

The other part is **Ciudad Cancún** (or **Downtown**), the town at the north end of Boulevard Kukulcán first built as a dormitory area for Hotel Zone workers. After 40 years and with a population of more than 600,000, this is now a city in its own right. Its main streets of **Avenida Tulum** and **Avenida Yaxchilán** have attractive, reasonably priced restaurants, with plenty of Mexican atmosphere, and there's a busy market, Mercado 28. The bus station, banks, other services, and more economical hotels are also here. As the Hotel Zone has filled up, resort development is spreading up the coast to the north, especially around a marina, **Puerto Cancún**.

With typical **Cancún ostentation, the Museo Subacuatico del Arte** (http://musamexico.org) is, quite literally, a museum under the sea. In the water between Cancún and Isla Mujeres, hundreds of sculptures are submerged at various depths, making this a must-see for divers. Most tour agencies will offer packages.

ISLA MUJERES

Puerto Juárez, just north of Cancún, is the passenger ferry port for **Isla Mujeres** ⓲, site of the first Spanish landing in Mexico in 1517, when Hernández de Córdoba and his men saw figures of the Maya goddess Ixchel, and so gave

⊙ Tip

Cancún is not designed for strolling, but local buses (routes R1 and R2) run from Avenida Tulum in Ciudad Cancún all the way down Boulevard Kukulcán and back again, more or less 24 hours daily, with very frequent services during the day. The fare is around $2, no matter how far you travel. Taxis are abundant: fares are officially higher in the Hotel Zone than Downtown, but the rule is: get an idea of the current fares (published in free magazines) and always agree the fare *before* you get in the cab.

Cancún beach resort.

Swimming with performing dolphins at Xcaret.

it the name "Island of Women." No longer the remote backpacker paradise it once was, the little island is still a less glitzy alternative to Cancún. A narrow strip 8km (5 miles) long, Isla is easy to explore by rented bicycles, scooters or the local favorite, golf carts.

Isla town has preserved its tiny, sandy streets, full of souvenir stores and dive shops, and some of its old wooden houses in candy-box colors. The best beach is **Playa Norte**, across the top of the town, and Isla is an excellent snorkeling, diving, and fishing center, with the **Manchones** reef nearby. Boat trips to the bird sanctuary at **Isla Contoy** are also available. On the island's west coast is a family attraction at **El Garrafón** (www.garrafon.com; daily 10am–5pm), a natural lagoon with a dolphin pool and easy snorkeling (although the coral is now in poor condition), and the **Tortugranja** (daily 9am–5pm), a turtle conservation center.

COZUMEL

Playa del Carmen.

Mexico's largest island, **Cozumel** ⑲, the "Island of Swallows," was a place of pilgrimage for the Postclassic Maya, with a shrine to the goddess of fertility, Ixchel. In the 1960s French oceanographer Jacques Cousteau made it known that as well as fine, sheltered beaches it had some of the world's richest offshore reefs, and Cozumel became a popular choice for divers and snorkelers on Mexico's Caribbean coast.

Tourism thus began on Cozumel before Cancún existed, and the island and its little capital **San Miguel de Cozumel** retain a less hectic, cozy, family feel. San Miguel is now also a major cruise ship port, with two large terminals, and the waterfront **Malecón** (Avenida Rafael Melgar) is lined with handicraft and jewelry stores, where cruise passengers can buy tax-free goods. Large resort hotels are mostly along the beaches north and south of the town.

From San Miguel a straight road runs to the east coast, passing the turn-off to the ruins of **San Gervasio** ⑳ (daily 8am–3.45pm), the main town of Maya Cozumel, with large structures and plenty of lizards in quiet woods. Cozumel's east coast is empty and windswept, with a few sheltered coves. The road turns south to follow the shore down to **Faro Celarain Eco Park** (daily 8am–5pm) at **Punta Sur**, with a lighthouse and lagoons with crocodiles, flamingos, and other birds. Some of Cozumel's most popular beaches are along the southwest coast, such as **Playa San Francisco**. Only 8km (5 miles) before San Miguel is Cozumel's most popular (and often crowded) location at **Parque Chankanaab** (daily 7am–5pm), a snorkel park around a lagoon in a botanical garden.

Cozumel's greatest jewels are in the seas around it. Although Hurricane Wilma damaged the coral of inshore reefs near San Miguel, such as **Paraíso** and **Chankanaab**, they are slowly recovering and still full of fish. Other renowned reefs such as **Palancar** off the southwest coast offer a spectacular range of diving. Snorkeling is not an

inferior option here, as you can still see a stunning range of marine life. There are around 60 dive operators on the island, which also offer snorkel trips.

THE RIVIERA MAYA

For many years, Cancún and Cozumel were the only tourist centers on the Mexican Caribbean. Since the 1990s, opulent retreat hotels and all-inclusive resorts have spread all the way along the 131km (81 miles) to Tulum, down the coastline now labeled the Riviera Maya. One consequence of this boom is that access to some of the finest bays is now difficult for non-hotel guests.

The first major stop south of Cancún, after 36km (22 miles), is **Puerto Morelos** ㉑, which, before Cancún, was actually the largest village on this coast. Mellow and relaxing, it has a fine long beach, excellent restaurants, and a protected inshore reef for great diving and snorkeling. Another 25km (15 miles) south are some of the most exquisite palm-lined bays on the whole coast. Some, notably at **Punta Bete**, are still open to all, while others now contain the

Riviera's most opulent resorts, especially **Hacienda Tres Ríos** and **Mayakobá**, with its PGA-standard golf course.

From there it's not far to the phenomenon that is **Playa del Carmen** ㉒, the passenger ferry port for Cozumel and second-largest center on the coast after Cancún. A tiny village in the 1980s, its population is now more than 200,000. So fast is its growth that it changes identity every few years: a backpacker hangout in the mid-1990s, it is now exploding with luxury condominiums. Playa still has a different style to Cancún: its main artery is a long pedestrian street, the **Quinta Avenida** (Fifth Avenue), giving much more of a sense of streetlife. Nightlife in Playa is also much more hip than in the mega-clubs of Cancún. Playa is another excellent diving center, with high-quality operators.

Just south of Playa is one of the Riviera's most popular attractions, the family friendly "eco-archeological theme park" of **Xcaret** ㉓ (tel: 1-800-292 2738; www.xcaret.com; daily Apr–Oct 8.30am–10pm, Nov–Mar 8.30am–9pm). Created around a lagoon that was once the Maya port of

The Maya trading town of Tulum.

Tropical fish on a coral reef, Cozumel.

> **Tip**

To make the most of a Calakmul visit, it's best to stay in one of the hotels at Xpuhil or Chicanná (112km/70 miles from the ruins) and get up very early to get to the Biosphere Reserve – wildlife, of all kinds, is most active in the mornings. Guides can be contacted through the tourist information hut in Xpuhil, or Río Bec Dreams hotel. There is no bank or ATM in Xpuhil, the area's only town, so take enough cash, in pesos, and plenty of insect repellent.

Polé, it has a semi-underground snorkeling river, dolphins, a beach, a zoo, a live show, and a dazzling butterfly garden.

Puerto Aventuras is a purpose-built marina surrounded by condos and large hotels, while at **Xpu-Ha** many of the fabulous bays are now occupied by large resorts. On the landward side of the highway are some *cenotes*, for a cooling swim. At 40km (25 miles) from Playa del Carmen, **Akumal ㉔**, famous for snorkeling and diving with turtles, has condos and medium-sized hotels well-spaced out around beautiful arching beaches, especially the enchanting **Media Luna** (Half Moon) bay. Akumal means "place of the turtles," and, carefully protected, they still breed here in the summer months. Shortly beyond Akumal, "snorkel heaven" signs lead to the very popular snorkel park at **Xel-Ha ㉕** (www.xelha.com; daily 8.30am–6pm), around a gorgeous, if often crowded, coastal lagoon.

TULUM AND SIAN KA'AN

The Riviera ends at the ruins of **Tulum ㉖** (daily 8am–5pm), one of the most prominent Maya coastal trading towns in the Postclassic era, from around 1200–1530. One of few enclosed Maya settlements, architecturally it is relatively crude, but few sites have a more spectacular setting, on cliffs above a beach. It stunned the Spaniards of Grijalva's expedition when they first saw it, with a fiery beacon on top of the **Castillo** pyramid, as they sailed down this coast in 1518.

Tulum gets many visitors, so most of its buildings are now roped off. The wall around the site on three sides – the fourth being the sea – probably only marked off the inner core of the city, the reserve of lords and priests, while a larger population lived outside. In addition to the Castillo, other striking buildings at Tulum include the two-level **Temple of the Frescoes** and small **Temple of the Diving God**. Both have images of a god-figure diving into the sea, possibly related to fishing.

Tulum's other treasure is its fabulous beach, which runs for 11km (7 miles) all the way to the Sian Ka'an reserve. This is the foremost home of the palm-roofed beachside *cabaña* on the Riviera, a wonderful place for relaxation, with a wide

Nohoch Mul pyramid, Cobá.

choice of cabins, from luxurious to basic wood-and-palm huts. The rapidly growing village of Tulum Pueblo, 2km (1 mile) inland, has ATMs and other services.

Any extension to the Riviera is blocked off by the **Sian Ka'an Biosphere Reserve** ㉗, a vast swath of virtually uninhabited forest, savanna, mangroves, freshwater lagoons, and reefs that is home to a huge variety of flora and fauna including monkeys, tapirs, crocodiles, and more than 400 species of birds. Tours – among the Riviera's best experiences – are available from Tulum and Muyil. A very bumpy dirt road also runs down to the lonely fishing village of **Punta Allen**, where modest guesthouses offer total tranquility. The coastal lagoons of Ascension Bay are considered among the best fly-fishing grounds in the world.

COBÁ

From Tulum a road leads inland 45km (28 miles) to **Cobá** ㉘ (daily 8am–5pm). This was one of the greatest Maya cities and the largest in northeast Yucatán from around AD 500–850. Its power was challenged by the rise of Chichén Itzá, and Cobá's defeat appears to have led to its decline from about 860. It was an unusually dispersed Maya city, with centers spread between lakes and linked by *sacbeob* (*sacbé*, in singular) stone roads. Around 800 the longest of these roads ever found, nearly 100km (62 miles) long, was built from Cobá westward to Yaxuná, a strongpoint in the wars with Chichén.

Because the site is so spread out, a visit to Cobá involves a real forest walk and a sense of intrepidity, with the chance to see plenty of birds (it is recommended to rent one of the bicycles available at the entrance). The largest area is the **Cobá** group, between two lakes, with a Ball Court and large pyramid. If you arrive early to avoid the crowds, head straight for the **Nohoch Mul** pyramid, which at 42 meters (138ft) high is the tallest in the Yucatán. Elsewhere in the woods there are finely carved stelae.

COSTA MAYA TO CHETUMAL

South of Tulum, Highway 307 bends inland around Sian Ka'an. Another 76km (47 miles) south a road turns off east for the **Costa Maya**, the latest stretch of Yucatán coast opened up for tourism. The road meets the sea after 56km (35 miles) at **Mahahual** ㉙. Hurricane Dean set back development here in 2007, but reconstruction has been fast, and a dock for cruise ships reopened a year later. Along the beach south of the town, there are Tulum-style beach *cabañas* and stylish small hotels.

The paved road continues south just inland for 59km (37 miles) to end at **Xcalak** ㉚. Lacking Mahahual's cruise traffic, this sand-street village has a still more laid-back feel, and along the beach north of Xcalak are some of the Yucatán's most utterly tranquil small hotels. Some 20km (12 miles) offshore is a paradise for divers and snorkelers at **Banco Chinchorro**, a huge atoll with pristine coral. Operators in Xcalak and Mahahual have equipment for trips to the reefs.

Inland, Highway 307 continues past the lovely **Laguna de Bacalar** ㉛, a

Pyramid el Castillo, Tulum.

giant *cenote*, fed by underground rivers, that's wonderful for swimming. **Bacalar** town has lakeside hotels and restaurants, and the **Fuerte de San Felipe Bacalar** (Tue–Sun 9am–7pm), a squat Spanish fortress built for protection against pirates in the 18th century, which is now a museum with great views.

Farther south again, **Chetumal** ㉜, the state capital of Quintana Roo, is a small, very tropical, modern city, with great waterfront restaurants. Often dismissed by tourists, it nevertheless has a couple of interesting attractions if you are passing through. At the city's entrance is the intriguing **Monumento Cuna del Meztizaje**, with elaborate depictions of Gonzalo Guerrero and his daughter Malinche (see page 48), an important figure in Mexican history as the mistress of Hernán Cortés. The town's **Museo de la Cultura Maya** (Tue–Sun 9am–7pm; free on Sun) is generally considered to be the most comprehensive museum on Maya culture. Nearby is the road crossing into Belize.

THE RÍO BEC AND CALAKMUL

Highway 186 heads west from Chetumal across the peninsula to Escárcega, completing the "Yucatán Loop." Along or not far off the road is a remarkable wealth of archeological sites. Around 60km (37 miles) west is the side road to one of the most beautiful Maya sites at **Kohunlich** (daily 8am–5pm). Surrounded by giant fan palms, its greatest treasure is the **Palace of the Masks**, with a staircase lined by six serene *mascarones*, giant heads believed to represent the city's rulers.

As the road crosses into Campeche it enters the **Río Bec** region, which contains an extraordinary concentration of archeological sites with a distinctive style, often featuring monster-mouth temples combined with peculiarly steep, theatrical pyramids. Several are near the highway: **Chicanná** (daily 8am–5pm) has some of the most spectacular temples, but the highlight is **Becán** (daily 8am–5pm), a walled city containing a maze-like complex of palaces and intimate plazas.

A separate but unmissable site is reached from a turn-off 45km (28 miles) west of Becán, from where it's another 60km (37 miles) to the ruins. **Calakmul** ㉝ (daily 8am–5pm), extensively excavated only since the 1990s, is the most important recent discovery in American archeology. This was possibly the largest Maya city, and its wars with Tikal had a huge effect on Maya history. Looming up out of the forest, the site centers on the largest of all Maya pyramids, **Structure II**. It is within the **Calakmul Biosphere Reserve**, Mexico's largest rain forest reserve, so you may also see monkeys, coatis, an array of birds, and even jaguars. Back on Highway 186, 5km (3 miles) west of the Calakmul turn is another small site, **Balamkú** (daily 8am–5pm), which has one of the largest surviving Maya stucco friezes, an astonishing mass of strange imagery.

Ceramics shop, Costa Maya.

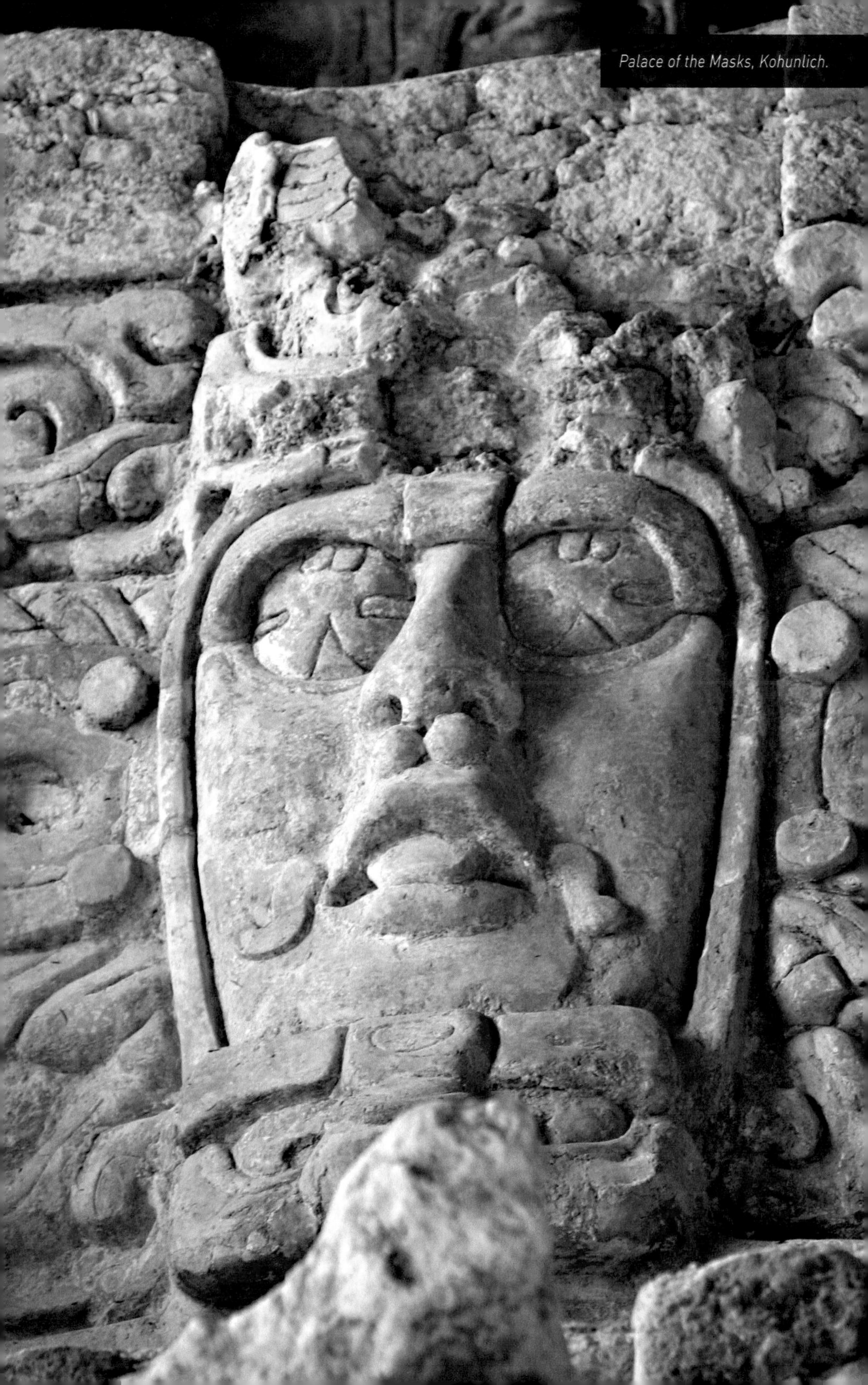

Palace of the Masks, Kohunlich.

Casa de los Azulejos,
Mexico City.

MEXICO

TRAVEL TIPS

TRANSPORTATION

TRANSPORTATION

GETTING THERE

By air

Mexico's main gateway airports are Mexico City and Cancún, which can be reached by direct flights from many US and Canadian cities, as well as several cities in Europe and Central and South America.

From the US and Canada: There are frequent scheduled flights from most large US and Canadian cities to Mexico City and Cancún; airlines include Aeroméxico, Air Canada, Alaska Airlines, American, Continental, Delta, North West, and United. Flights are most numerous from Los Angeles, Houston, Miami, Chicago, New York, and Toronto, but there are also many from other cities. Some airlines, especially Aeroméxico and Continental, also fly to other Mexican cities, such as Los Cabos, Monterrey, Puerto Vallarta, Guadalajara, Villahermosa, and Mérida.

From Europe: There are direct scheduled flights to Mexico City from Amsterdam, Frankfurt, London, Madrid, and Paris, and to Cancún from London, Manchester, Madrid and Brussels. The main carriers are Aeroméxico, Air Europa, Air France, British Airways, TUI, Iberia, KLM, and Lufthansa.

From Asia: All Nippon Airways flies to Mexico City from Tokyo.

If you cannot fly directly to your destination in Mexico, connections can be made on domestic flights via Mexico City with Aeromar, Aeroméxico, VivaAerobus or Interjet, which between them provide flights all around the country.

There is a proliferation of **discount air fares** at different times of the year. Check out travel and airline websites for the best prices for both international and domestic flights. In addition to scheduled services, there are often low-cost direct **charter flights** available, especially to Cancún, from the US, Canada, and many parts of Europe.

When you arrive at Mexico City, Cancún or any other airport, there are special taxis for getting to your final destination (see page 327 To and from the airport). If you do not have any Mexican pesos when you arrive, change at a bureau de change desk or withdraw from an ATM only the amount you need for a taxi, and then get more cash near your hotel. Do not make it evident that you have any large amount of cash when passing through Mexico City airport.

By sea

Cruise ships frequently include a Mexican port in their voyages, and from the US, a selection of one- to three-week cruises is available. Caribbean cruises departing from New Orleans, Tampa, Miami, Fort Lauderdale, and some other ports regularly stop at Cozumel, and less frequently at Progreso and Mahahual. Numerous cruises along the west coast of Mexico start from Los Angeles or San Francisco, and some can also be boarded in San Diego, Portland, Seattle, or Vancouver: they may stop at Ensenada or Los Cabos in Baja, Mazatlán, Puerto Vallarta, Manzanillo, Ixtapa-Zihuatanejo, and Acapulco. Cruises are a leisurely, comfortable way of getting to Mexico, but usually give you only one day in each port of call.

To travel to Mexico in your own boat you must have full documentation for the boat, including **registration** and **proof of ownership**, full insurance, and full passports for everyone on board. Fishing and radio **licenses** should also be obtained in advance; Mexican consulates and marine insurance brokers can advise about **current requirements.**

If, as many people do, you plan to sail down Baja to Mexico's west coast, and are doing so for the first time, it's naturally essential to get

⦿ Airline numbers

Air Canada
Tel: 1-888-247 2262 (US and Canada); 0871-220 1111 (UK)
www.aircanada.com

American Airlines
Tel: 1-800-433 7300 (US and Canada); 020-7365 0777 (UK)
www.aa.com

British Airways
Tel: 0844-493 0787 (UK)
www.britishairways.com

Delta
Tel: 1-800-221 1212 (US and Canada); 0871-221 1222 (UK)
www.delta.com

United
Tel: 1-800-864 8331 (US and Canada); 0845-607 6760 (UK)
www.united.com

US Airways
Tel: 1-800-428 4322 (US and Canada); 0845-600 3300 (UK)
www.usairways.com

Mexican Airlines

Aeromar
Tel: 01800-237 6627 (Mexico)
www.aeromar.com.mx

Aeroméxico
Tel: 1-800-237 6639 (US and Canada); 01800-021 4000 (Mexico)
www.aeromexico.com

Interjet
Tel: 1-866-285 9525 (Mexico)
www.interjet.com.mx

Volaris
Tel: 01800-122 8000 (Mexico)
www.volaris.com

as much information as possible on charts, weather conditions, etc., and if possible to take a crew member who has sailed these waters before.

By bus

Bus travel is an essential means of getting around in Mexico (see page 329), and there are some direct long-distance bus services into Mexico from the US (notably from Brownsville, Texas), and many more from Mexican cities just south of the border. However, unless you live near the border or have more time than money, flying to the area you want to visit and then using buses is a better bet.

By car

To drive a US or Canadian vehicle into most of Mexico you must get a **Temporary Import Permit**, which can be done at all main border crossings, at the *Módulo de Control Vehicular* desk in the Customs Post *(Aduana)*. To obtain one you must present the originals and at least two photocopies of the following documents: your passport; current driver's license; and the car registration papers, which must be in the name of the passport holder. You must also have a Mexican Tourist Card, which you should therefore get at Immigration before visiting the *Aduana*. It is also best to have a credit card, to pay for the permit (around $44) and as a guarantee against over-staying your permit. There are higher charges for RVs and anything towed behind the main vehicle. You can pay for the permit in cash, but if so you must leave a large cash bond as the guarantee. The permit is valid for 6 months, during which you can enter and leave Mexico as you wish, but when you finally leave be sure to visit a **Mexican Customs Post** again at the border to have the permit cancelled; if you do not, you will be considered to have overstayed the permit and a fine will be charged against your credit card, or you will forfeit the cash bond.

Temporary Import Permits can also now be obtained from many Mexican Consulates in the US, for a slightly higher fee, and procedures can also now be initiated online, saving time, but the website (www.banjercito.com.mx) is mainly in Spanish, and the cost is again higher. AAA (American Automobile Association) offices near the border also help with paperwork and advice.

Note that special conditions apply in Baja California, where Temporary Import Permits are not required for US and Canadian vehicles. Sonora state has an **"Only Sonora"** program, under which drivers are provided with permits for free (which also takes very little time) so long as they do not go beyond the state. Elsewhere along the border, Import Permits are often not strictly required in the **"Frontier Zone"** (roughly 20km/12 miles into Mexico), but since security and other procedures have been tightened up, in practice it's best to have one.

Details of these procedures can change, so check before you travel. You must also obtain **Mexican car insurance**, as US and Canadian coverage is not valid in Mexico. There are several auto insurance offices at nearly every border crossing, and the AAA also provides advice for members. Better deals, though, can often be had by getting your insurance in advance, through services such as www.sanbornsinsurance.com or www.mexbound.com. Details of cover can vary widely, so shop around online, and always check the small print.

It is also worth noting that, due to on-going violence between drug cartels along the whole of the northern Mexican border and in nearby cities such as Monterrey, driving from the US into Mexico does come with a level of risk. For more on driving in Mexico, see page 331.

GETTING AROUND

Almost 250,000km (150,000 miles) of free and toll roads make Mexico's cities, towns, and most villages accessible by car. If you don't drive yourself, buses provide a comfortable and economical way to see every part of the country, and for fast journeys there is an extensive domestic airline network. The only passenger trains left in Mexico are on tourist routes such as the spectacular Copper Canyon line from Chihuahua, but Mexico's long coastline and some frequent ferry services make going by boat an easy way to travel in some areas.

To and from the airport

At most Mexican airports only special authorized airport taxis are allowed to take arriving passengers into town. Except at Cancún, there are not many airport buses. Airport taxis are more expensive than standard cabs but are well regulated and safe. At Mexico City airport, *Taxi Autorizado* stands are easy to find just beyond the arrivals area. It's good to have an idea in mind of the whereabouts of your hotel or final destination in the vast city; Mexico City is divided into various zones for airport taxis, and the fares for each of them are posted at each stand. You buy a ticket at the stand, and then present it to a driver of the relevant company outside the building. There is usually a choice between standard cars, or vans for larger groups. A cab from the airport to the Zona Rosa, for example, location of many hotels, should cost around US$16–20. It is also usual to tip the driver. If you are not going to Mexico City itself, there are buses from the airport to some nearby cities such as Cuernavaca, Puebla, and Toluca, which leave from near Area D.

When leaving Mexico City, any cab can take you to the airport, but as usual in the city (see page 330), it is best to get a hotel to call a cab for you, and to be clear on the price first.

At Cancún, the main authorized transportation are the large **colectivo vans**, which wait outside Terminals 2 (used by Mexican airlines and many charters) and 3 (used by most US and European airlines). Fares are around US$15 per person; from the airport they drive all the way along the Hotel Zone to Ciudad Cancún, dropping passengers at their hotel, but if, for example, you are staying in Ciudad Cancún, this will take more than an hour; also, they are not obliged to leave without a minimum of eight passengers, so at slack times you may have to wait. *Colectivos* also leave more or less hourly for Playa del Carmen, via Puerto Morelos. There are also airport buses, which run from outside Terminal 2 (there's a free shuttle bus to here from Terminal 3), usually several times an hour to the bus station in Ciudad Cancún (not the Hotel Zone), and once or twice an hour to Puerto Morelos and Playa del Carmen. Fares are much lower than colectivos (around $3). Individual standard cabs are not available, but to go direct to any specific location on the Riviera it can be both quick and economical, especially for a family or a group, to book a **private van** transfer through services such as www.cancunvalet.com or www.cancuntransfers.net.

When leaving, again, any cab from Cancún or any of the Riviera towns will take you to the airport, but agree the price first. Regular buses run from the bus stations in Ciudad Cancún and Playa del Carmen.

Smaller airports all have their own local airport taxis, fares for which are generally reasonable, and there's rarely any need to wait. Again, any **local cab** can take you to the airport. Some airports have bus services from nearby cities, but they are often at very inconvenient times.

By air

Getting between different parts of Mexico by land often involves long drives, but as a fast alternative there are plenty of **domestic airline services**. Deregulation has led to the big traditional carriers Aeroméxico and Mexicana being joined by several low-cost operators. Every state capital has at least a few flights daily to Mexico City, and there are also airports near all the main tourist areas, such Los Cabos, Ixtapa-Zihuatanejo, and the main airport of southern Mexico: Cancún. One disadvantage of the network has been that since deregulation there have been relatively few direct inter-regional flights, so getting to many destinations has required changing flights in Mexico City's huge **Benito Juárez airport**. However, more options are becoming available.

Toluca, only 60km (38 miles) west of the capital, is being developed as an "alternative" airport for overloaded Mexico City, used particularly by the low-cost airlines

Cruise ships dock in Cozumel, one of the Caribbean's busiest ports.

VivaAerobus, Interjet, and Volaris; and other regional hub airports are Guadalajara, Monterrey, and Cancún. Mexico's largest airline has a lower-cost arm flying smaller aircraft that are intended to open up more regional routes – Aeroméxico Connect – so it's always worth looking around to see what routes are available, to save travel time. Flying via Toluca in particular can be much cheaper than going through Mexico City.

There is a good deal of fare competition on popular routes (such as Mexico City–Cancún), and airlines frequently announce **special offers**, including flight and hotel combinations, but prices are more static on routes with fewer operators. All Mexican airlines now take online bookings, but for complicated flight combinations you may find good deals in local travel agents.

In some parts of Mexico small airlines operate local **"bus flights"** with small turboprop aircraft. Aerotucán (www.aerotucan.com.mx) flies between Oaxaca and Puerto Escondido and Huatulco; Mayair (www.mayair.com.mx) runs a frequent shuttle between Cancún and Cozumel. En route, you naturally see much more than from a standard jet.

By boat

Ferries run between Baja California and the mainland, and cover the short distances between the Yucatán mainland and the Caribbean islands of Cozumel and Isla Mujeres. The Baja ferries make long journeys across the deep Gulf of California, which gives the traveler the chance to appreciate both the peninsula and the mainland without making the extremely long and hot drive around the Gulf.

Baja California ferries

Make sure you have the latest timetable, as boats don't leave every day (visit www.bajaferries.com), or ask at your hotel for ferry information. If you are coming from the US, ask a travel agent or insurance agent at the border for an up-to-date timetable.

The northernmost route, operated by **Ferry Santa Rosalía** (www.ferrysantarosalia.com), connects the port of Santa Rosalía with Guaymas, leaving Santa Rosalía on Tuesday, Wednesday, Friday, and Sunday, and returning from Guaymas on Monday, Tuesday, Thursday, and Saturday. A similar schedule applies between Mazatlán

and La Paz. There are cabins on the ferries running from Topolobampo to La Paz and from Guaymas to Santa Rosalía, as well as a public (not very comfortable) salon area. Food and drink are available on the ferries. Double-check schedule information as boats are sometimes delayed.

Yucatán ferries

Reservations and schedules are not a problem for the frequent, short ferry trips from Cancún and the Riviera Maya to the offshore islands of Cozumel and Isla Mujeres. Passenger ferries to Isla Mujeres run from Puerto Juárez, just north of Cancún. Two companies – **Magaña** and the newer **Ultramar** – run the service, but their docks (the Estación Marítima and the Gran Puerto Cancún respectively) are very near each other, and fares (around US$3 per adult) and schedules are also similar. Both companies have ferries to Isla every half-hour from around 6am–11.30pm; from Isla, Magaña generally has a last boat around 8.30pm, but Ultramar runs until 11pm–midnight. The crossing time is around 25–30 minutes. The car ferry to Isla Mujeres runs from Punta Sam, at the end of the road north of Puerto Juárez. There are usually five sailings daily in each direction, and fares are around US$25 for a car and two people.

Passenger ferries to Cozumel leave from Playa del Carmen, and journey time is around 30 minutes. Again there are two companies, Mexico and Ultramar, which both have sailings usually every hour on the hour (with less frequent services in the middle of the day) from Playa 6am–11pm, and from Cozumel 5am–10pm. Fares are around US$10, but special offers can often be had. Car ferries to Cozumel run from Puerto Calica, 10km (6 miles) south of Playa del Carmen, with from four to seven sailings daily in each direction. Fares are around US$30, for a car and two people.

By train

Aside from a handful of upscale operations on limited lines, there is only one passenger train still operating in Mexico. This is the spectacular Chihuahua–Pacífico railroad, through the amazing Copper Canyon to Los Mochis on the Pacific coast, officially the Ferrocarril Chihuahua–Pacífico but known as El Chepe (www.chepe.com.mx).

By bus

One can go virtually anywhere in Mexico by bus. Hundreds of bus companies crisscross the country, with vehicles ranging from big, modern, fast, air-conditioned models to small *combis* and vans for village routes. In virtually every part of Mexico, the bus system is the most economical way to get around.

There are two basic categories of Mexican buses. First-class buses are air-conditioned, have comfortable reclining seats, videos showing movies, toilets at the back, and often free coffee and soft drinks. Seats are assigned, and all baggage is carefully checked in and out. First-class buses run between cities and main towns, with only a few set stops on each route, have a pretty precise schedule, and are generally very punctual. There are also some more expensive "extra-luxurious" or "Executive Class" buses on busy routes, which generally means they have more leg room and almost bed-like seats. Ordinary first-class fares are still very reasonable, and unless you take flights this will be the best way to make any longer journeys in Mexico.

Second-class buses run on local routes and also often follow the same ones as first-class, but stop whenever anyone asks them to, and so take much longer. They are a good deal cheaper, tickets cannot be bought much in advance, seats are not assigned, and baggage is just put into overhead racks or the bus's side compartments rather than checked in (so you need to keep more of an eye on it). Second-class buses have also generally been more basic, but nowadays many – such as the buses that go up and down the Riviera Maya, which are described as *Intermedios* (between the two classes) – have comforts close to first class, including air conditioning. Using second-class buses is essential for getting to many places that do not have a first-class bus route, but using them for long journeys is usually not worth the saving, given how long they take.

The third element in the system is the mass of *colectivos* or *combis*, small vans of different sizes that ply the same routes as second-class buses (but are even cheaper) or serve places too small to justify even a second-class bus route. This is a very personal way of traveling: to find a *colectivo* to a particular place

you often have to ask, and they leave when they have enough passengers, and stop when asked. Nevertheless, they are licensed, and have set fares for each route, and drivers are generally very punctilious about returning change. Even the remotest village in Mexico has some kind of *colectivo* service, so nowhere is inaccessible.

Buying tickets

You can reserve and buy first-class, luxury-class, and some second-class bus tickets in advance at bus stations, by phone, or, increasingly, online through the websites of the individual companies. Online bookings, however, are sometimes difficult with a non-Mexican credit card. In addition, **Mi Escape** (tel: 55-5784 4652, www.miescape.mx) sells tickets for many bus companies in central and southern Mexico, and has handy "Ticket Shops" in many areas of Mexico City and other cities, which, if you cannot book online, help you avoid an extra trip to the bus station. There is no extra charge for buying through Mi Escape. For busy times of the year, especially Mexican holiday seasons such as Christmas and Easter, make reservations well ahead. If you make several stops, buy your seat for the next stage of your trip as soon as you arrive – otherwise you may have to stay longer than you intended.

In second-class bus stations, you generally line up on the day to buy a ticket at the relevant window. At the point of origin of the bus you must usually have your ticket before you get on the bus, rather than buy it on board. This does not apply if you join the bus later in the route.

Bus stations

In most cities, there are separate first- (*estación de autobuses de primera*) and second-class (*de segunda*) bus stations, while *combis* run from squares or individual garages. Exceptions include Cancún, which has one station for all services. In some cities, notably in Oaxaca and Chiapas, individual second-class companies have kept their own, separate depots, which can be confusing.

Mexico City, as often, is an exception because of its huge size. There are four big stations for first- and most second-class buses to different parts of the country. Some buses stop at more than one station, but to save time it's best to know which one you need:

Terminal de Autobuses del Norte
Eje Central Lázaro Cárdenas 4907
Colonia Magdelena de las Salinas
www.centraldelnorte.com
Metro: Autobuses del Norte, Line 5.
Buses for the north of the country – roughly beyond Manzanillo on the Pacific side, including Baja California, or beyond Poza Rica on the Gulf side.
Terminal Central de Autobuses del Sur
Avenida Tasqueña 1320
Colonia Campestre Churubusco
Metro: Tasqueña, Line 2
Buses bound for points south and southwest of Mexico City, such as Cuernavaca and Morelos, Taxco, Acapulco, Oaxaca, and Chiapas.
Terminal de Autobuses del Poniente (Terminal del Observatorio)
Avenida Sur 122, Colonia Real del Monte
Metro: Observatorio, Line 1
For Toluca and Mexico state, Michoacán, Jalisco, Nayarit, Sinaloa, and other points west.
Terminal de Oriente (tapo)
Zaragoza 200
Metro: San Lázaro, Lines 1 and B
Buses to the east and southeast, including southern Veracruz, Tabasco, northern Chiapas, and the Yucatán Peninsula.

All these bus stations are well away from Downtown to avoid traffic problems. As at the airport (see page 327), there are authorized taxi stands at each terminal for getting cabs into the city, and these are the most reliable option to use. The stations are well policed, but be careful with your bags while walking around the Mexico City stations.

Baggage

Officially, the amount of baggage each passenger can take with them is limited to 25kg (55lbs) on first-class buses, but this is not usually enforced. On second-class buses there is virtually no limit, although you will often have to load it yourself.

Bus companies

There are many bus companies around Mexico, but the following are the major first-class companies, serving different parts of the country:
ADO, tel: 55-5133 2424, 01800-280 8887, www.ado.com.mx
The largest company in southeast Mexico, particularly Veracruz, Tabasco, Chiapas, and the Yucatán

A VW Beetle taxi deftly navigates Mexico City.

Peninsula, which also has services from Mexico City.

Enlaces Terrestres Nacionales (ETN), tel: 01800-800 0386, www.etn.com.mx
Mexico City and Mexico state, Aguascalientes, Michoacán, Jalisco, and other areas of west-central Mexico.

Estrella Blanca, tel: 01800-507 5500, www.estrellablanca.com.mx
Large company with services in every part of Mexico except Tabasco, Chiapas and the Yucatán Peninsula.

Estrella de Oro, tel: 01800-900 0105, www.estrelladeoro.com.mx
Mexico City to Morelos, Guerrero, Ixtapa-Zihuatanejo, and Veracruz.

Estrella Roja, tel: 01800-712 2284, www.estrellaroja.com.mx
Mexico City to Puebla and Cholula, and some other destinations.

Omnibus de México, tel: 01800-765 6636, www.odm.com.mx
Mexico City, Jalisco, Zacatecas, and many destinations in northeast Mexico.

Primera Plus, tel: 01800-375 7587, www.primeraplus.com.mx
Mexico City to Jalisco, Guanajuato, León, and the Pacific coast.

City buses

City buses are a very economical (under US$0.50) way of getting around, and in Mexico City can be an enjoyable means of getting to places not well served by the metro, seeing the city and getting close to local life. That is so long as you are prepared to be adaptable and try some Spanish, and so long as you only try to use them outside of peak times – after 10am in the morning, and before about 4–5pm in the afternoon. During the long peak hours, buses are incredibly crowded, slow, and often impossible to board.

Local buses in Mexico City come in different sizes, from rather more comfortable full-size buses to the hundreds of *peseros*, medium-sized minibuses, or small *combis*, known in the capital as *micros*. The easiest to handle is the *Metrobus* which runs up and down dedicated lanes on the Avenida Insurgentes, with big modern buses and set stops almost like metro stations; special tickets are required (not the same as metro tickets) which can be bought at the stops. Using any of the other city buses (especially *peseros* and *micros*) requires a little practice, and it helps a lot if you can ask for explanations (such as where a bus is going) in Spanish. One complication is that they do not usually have clear route numbers; instead, destinations are written on the windshield, so to get the right bus you need to know not only where you're going but also the names of some places close to it. You should be aware of the potential for pickpocketing and other petty crime on Mexico City buses (especially when they are crowded). Notice when people are close to you, and do not attract attention by showing that you have large amounts of money, or wear easily stealable jewelry. Always have change when you use buses, and do not try to change large bills.

Guadalajara is served by air and bus services, and there are several *cuota* (toll) highways that connect it to cities nearby. Streets are wide, though crowded, and much of the driving action is on Juárez or Vallarta. Guadalajara is a "walking" city, with generally safe, easy to follow streets. Local buses are the most economical way to get around – a 10- or 15-minute ride only costs a few pesos.

Other cities all have their own local buses. Similarly they do not generally have route numbers, but using them is usually a much calmer business than in the capital, and in tranquil cities such as Mérida they provide an easy way to get around. In most cities there are also local *combis*, but, again, it is difficult for newcomers to identify where they are going. Many tourist cities such as Puerto Vallarta and especially Cancún have bus services that are much easier for foreigners to use, and even have easy-to-identify route numbers.

By metro

Mexico City has an excellent subway (metro) system, officially the STC (Sistema de Transporte Colectivo, tel: 55-5709 1133; www.metro.df.gob.mx), which for much of the day is a very quick as well as convenient way to get around the city. Stations are well lit and the trains are very quiet, and a small free map of the network is available at most stations. All lines are open Mon–Fri 5am–midnight, Sat 6am–midnight, Sun 7am–midnight; tickets cost only around US25¢, and it's best to buy them in strips of five or 10, to avoid lining up each time you use the system. In the south of the city, the system is extended by the *Tren Ligero*, an overground light rail line that runs from Taxqueña metro to the gardens of Xochimilco.

There is a possibility of petty crime on the metro – as in any giant city – but so long as you are reasonably careful traveling on the system is pretty trouble-free in the middle of the day. However, stay away from it during rush hours (usually 7.30–10am, and 5.30–8pm), when, like all Mexico City public transportation, it gets atrociously crowded, and the risk of pickpocketing is much greater (note, though, that at peak times there are also special **women-only carriages**, usually at the front or back of each train). It is not advisable to use the metro in the center and east of the city late at night. Don't plan, either, on using the metro to get to the airport or bus station with your luggage; no large bags are permitted, especially at peak traveling times.

By taxi

Mexico City

As has been well-publicized, there have been particular problems with crime in Mexico City taxis, so special care is advisable; follow a few basic precautions, and you can travel without any difficulties. The city has a bewildering variety of taxis, and the local authorities occasionally relicense all the thousands of taxi drivers in a bid to root out **"pirate cabs"** and increase passenger safety. All cabs, except some hotel and airport taxis, which have set fares by zones, now have meters *(taximetros)*.

If you are a newcomer to the city, and especially if you do not speak good Spanish, it will always be best to get a hotel to call a cab for you (larger hotels all have ranks outside) or to find an official taxi rank (called a *sitio*, and signposted in the street) and get a cab there. **Sitios** all have phone numbers, so it's a good idea to note down the number of a local rank and use it when necessary; there are also 24-hour phone cab services, such as **Taxi Mexico** (tel: 55-1495 3545) or **Servitaxis** (tel: 55-5516 6020, www.servitaxis.com. mx). Hotel and phone taxis are more expensive than street cabs, but still cheap by international standards, and you have a guarantee of security.

If you cannot find a *sitio* and need to get a cab in the street, only hail one of the larger, more modern cabs, in white with a red stripe along the side or in burgundy and white or gold. A properly licensed cab should have a white license plate with a capital letter followed by five numbers. The old green and white cabs are the cheapest, but also have the most risk of crime, so it's best to avoid them.

Always look for the driver's photo ID, which should be displayed on the dashboard of the cab. Also check that the driver has turned on the meter.

Other towns and cities

In other parts of Mexico traveling by taxi is far less problematic and this level of caution is not generally necessary, so there is rarely a problem in hailing cabs in the street. However, note that in most cities and towns taxis do not have meters. Instead, there is a set fare for the whole town, or a system of fares by zones. It is a good idea to be aware of the current local rates: hotels can advise, and in most tourist areas they are listed in free English-language magazines. As a general rule it is advisable to agree on the fare before you get in the cab – and reject anything exaggerated. Except in tourist areas drivers will usually only speak Spanish, so try, at least, to know your numbers.

In some cities (such as **Villahermosa** and **Tabasco**) it is customary for taxi drivers to cruise up and down popular routes, especially at peak times, and pick up several passengers on a *colectivo* basis, who each pay part of the fare. When you want a taxi to yourself to go to a specific location, you may have to phone for one (again, best done through hotels), or pay a bit more. *Colectivo* taxis naturally blend into *colectivo* minibuses, and in small towns and country districts the only difference between them is the size of vehicle. Small town and rural taxis will take passengers long distances, so long as you agree a price first. Similarly, Toluca airport taxis run to Mexico City, those in Villahermosa will happily take you to Palenque (a 2hr drive) and those from Tuxtla Gutiérrez will go up San Cristóbal de las Casas, for around US$40.

In **Mérida**, Yucatán, the city has introduced metered taxis, but there are also still taxis (generally white with a red stripe along the side) that are meter-less and use the old set fare-zone system. Metered taxis are nearly always cheaper, especially for short journeys, so it's best to use them when possible. Local phone taxi services, such as **EconoTaxi** (tel: 999-945 0000) or **Taxiseguro** (tel: 999-922 64 64) all use metered cabs.

Cancún and the **Riviera Maya** have thousands of taxis, mostly licensed from Cancún, Puerto Morelos, Playa del Carmen, or Tulum. They do not have meters, but instead there are complicated scales of official rates for each area. Current rates are often posted outside bus stations, and listed in free magazines such as *Cancún Tips* and on several local websites; hotels should also have them. One peculiarity of the taxi rates in Cancún is that they are based on the idea that tourists should pay more than locals, so fares are higher for any journey to or from the Hotel Zone than in Ciudad Cancún. Taxis from any of the major centers will usually take you anywhere on the Riviera, for the right price. However, Riviera cab drivers – especially in Cancún – have a bad reputation for exploiting the confusion this system produces among recent arrivals, with exaggerated prices and other scams. Again, try to get an idea of current rates soon after you arrive, and *always* agree a price before you get into a cab.

Isla Mujeres and **Cozumel** each have unmetered local taxis with a fare scale for the whole of each island, not just the main towns. Current rates are posted at the ferry landings.

By car

While buses, *colectivos,* and local taxis can get you to just about every part of Mexico, if you want to explore with more freedom – and with more

☉ Day without a car

In an effort to combat pollution, Mexico City and Mexico state operate a "Day Without a Car" *(Hoy No Circula)* program based on the last number of your license plate. The program restricts circulation between 5am and 10pm to cars with plates ending in 5 and 6 on Mondays; 7 and 8 on Tuesdays; 3 and 4 on Wednesdays; 1 and 2 on Thursdays; and 9 and 0 on Fridays. In addition, vehicles may not be used on one Saturday each month, depending on the last digit of the license number. Some vehicles that meet special low emissions standards are exempt. These regulations are quite strictly enforced. Also at times when pollution levels are becoming particularly high, an extra level of restriction comes into operation, which allows vehicles with plates ending in odd or even numbers only to be used on alternate days. On certain public holidays, restrictions are lifted and all cars are allowed to circulate. This program has not met all the hopes that were placed in it – in part because locals have invented many ways to get around it – but is kept in force since it is thought that without it, pollution would return to its 1990s levels.

Hoy No Circula is also applicable to foreign-plated vehicles, and most rental cars and vehicles from other Mexican states, based in the same way on their license numbers. However, owners of foreign vehicles can obtain a *Pase Turístico*, giving exemption from the scheme, so long as their car is less than eight years old and passes a brief emissions test. Details are available from tourist offices.

control over your time – it will be much better to have your own car. Major roads are mostly of a high standard, and a growing number of fast toll highways cut journey times between major regions of the country. Their tolls (cuotas) are relatively high, and many local drivers do not use them, but this means that they are often empty, and so very fast. Among the most important cuota **highways** are those from Mexico City to Guadalajara, Acapulco, and Veracruz (via Puebla), and that from Mérida to Cancún.

Local and village roads are often slow, particularly in mountain regions, but in most parts of the country they are now paved, with bumps and potholes the farther you go from main routes. Some remote places can only be reached by dirt track, notably in protected natural areas.

For the requirements needed to bring your own vehicle into Mexico from the US or Canada, see page 327.

Car rental

It is straightforward to rent a car in Mexico. All the major international car rental agencies are represented here, and there are also many local agencies. Resort hotels often have recommended agencies, but you will often find better deals if you shop around. There is a big choice of agencies in resort areas and some larger cities; in smaller cities there may be only one or two, with a limited choice of vehicles, so if you expect to be driving any distance it is generally advisable to rent in one of the **regional car-rental centers** – such as Puerto Vallarta, or Mérida and Cancún in the Yucatán – rather than arrive in a small city such as Tuxtla Gutiérrez and expect to find a car available there.

Renting a car is especially popular in the Yucatán Peninsula since, because it is so flat, it is easy to drive around; in more rugged areas, driving is less attractive, so there may also be fewer agencies. Mérida agencies often have the Peninsula's best rental deals.

To rent a car you need to be **over 21** and have your **passport, driver's license,** and a **credit card**. Small agencies in particular often give discounts for payments in cash, but you still need a credit card for a deposit. Most car rental deals now include **unlimited** mileage (kilometraje ilimitado), and lower basic rates that are generally a false economy. During peak vacation times, it's advisable to book a car in advance. Nowadays, naturally, some of the best rental rates can be obtained by booking online, directly with an agency or through one of the international car-rental websites. It is usually costly to drop off a car in any place other than where it was rented.

When you collect your car, the agency should show you that the tires and spare wheel are in good condition, and that the car has the necessary jack. It should also have a fold-up red warning triangle, which you should place 50 meters (165ft) behind the car if you ever have to stop on a highway.

Insurance

Your car rental agreement will usually include **Collision Damage Waiver** (CDW) insurance. However, be aware that in Mexico this normally covers you only for the total loss of the car – in which case, you will still generally be liable for 10 percent of the value of the vehicle – and does not cover daños parciales or "partial damage," minor knocks, and collisions such as a broken fender or windshield. Additional, comprehensive cover is often available, but it can be expensive. When Mexican drivers have minor collisions with other vehicles, they usually settle the matter with an exchange of cash, without recourse to insurance. This is an added incentive to drive carefully.

If you bring a US or Canadian vehicle to Mexico, you must get a Mexican insurance policy (see page 327). It is advisable to get the most comprehensive one you can afford.

Fuel

All gasoline in Mexico is sold by the state oil company, **Pemex**. Some gas stations are now independently operated, but prices are generally the same throughout the country – more expensive than in the US, but still low by world standards. All **Pemex** gasolineras have diesel and unleaded (magna) fuel, and many also have a higher-grade unleaded gas called Premium. Gas stations rarely accept credit cards. When arriving at a gasolinera, check that the attendant sets the pump at zero before filling the car, to avoid being overcharged. Attendants will usually offer to clean your windshield, check tires, check your oil, and so on, for a tip.

Pemex gasolineras are easy to find in cities and resorts, but in rural areas there may only be one in a district's main town, and on some highways they are spread out over long distances. When making long trips, fill up before starting out, and again every chance you get.

Safety tips and rules of the road

In Mexico City, and some other cities such as Monterrey, traffic is hectic enough to deter any visitor from driving, and this is rarely the most convenient way to get around. Elsewhere, though, there are no special problems with driving in Mexico. The chief things to look out for, especially in small towns and villages, are topes or **speed bumps**. Children, old people, and animals have priority on Mexican country roads, not vehicles, and topes are intended to slow traffic down as quickly as possible. They come in different styles and sizes, from large humps that can really batter a car if you hit them at speed to rows of ridges called vibradores. Many are signposted, with signs such as "Topes a 100m," but others are not, so you always need to look out for them. It is best to avoid driving outside towns at night, because roads are rarely lit and topes, potholes, and other dips in the road are much harder to spot. Except when overtaking always keep an extra distance from vehicles in front of you, as they may have to brake suddenly for a tope.

Other things to bear in mind are that Mexican drivers rarely use blinkers (indicators) to indicate that they are about to turn left or right, but may put on hazard warning lights as an indication they're about to make a maneuver in either direction (buses and combis especially do this when they are about to stop). Also, drivers of slow trucks often put on their left blinkers as a helpful sign to drivers behind them that it is safe to pass.

Those renting a vehicle should beware of unscrupulous police officers who target rentals (or foreigners) heading out of town. This has been reported particularly in Acapulco on the way to the airport,

Open highway, Puuc region.

but is of concern in many places, particularly in isolated areas near major tourist destinations. Cars are stopped and bribes are asked for. This is annoying, but be polite at all times. If you do not wish to pay the bribe, insist on paying the ticket at the station. They may remove your license plates and insist you pay... or they may just decide it's easier to let you go. Do not threaten or insult them at any time.

Breakdown services

The **Green Angels** *(ángeles verdes)* is a free government-run drivers' assistance service that patrols Mexico's major highways in green-and-white radio-equipped vehicles. They can offer first aid, minor repairs to your vehicle, or an emergency supply of gas and oil. You pay only for the parts used and for gas and oil. The Green Angels (emergency number: 078) operate daily 8am–8pm. Most speak some English. If you have more than a minor problem in a rented car, call your rental agency as soon as possible, and follow their advice.

Always carry water for the radiator, a jack, and spare tire (or two, in rugged, remote areas of the country), fuses, and any other spare parts that might need replacing – even if you're not prepared to do the repair yourself. You can count on the Green Angels for mechanical know-how but not for parts specific to your make and model (and away from the main roads you may well be on your own).

Nearly every village will have at least one mechanics' workshop

(mecánico) – who, you may be surprised to find, can often handle repairs to any kind of vehicle – and a tire repair shop (a *llantera* or *vulcanizadora*). Due to country roads in bad condition and dirt tracks, flat tires can be quite common. If you have a flat and can then get to the nearest *llantera* on the spare, they will make an immediate repair to the burst tire for very little money, and, if necessary, you can then get a new tire in the nearest town.

Road signs

Many road signs are international, others assume a knowledge of Spanish. If you don't understand a road sign, slow down and be prepared to stop.

Parking

Parking is restricted in most city centers. Where parking is prohibited the curb is painted yellow or red. If you park illegally the police may tow the car away (or, in Mexico City, clamp the wheels) with surprising speed, and to get it released you must pay a fine. Where on-street parking is permitted, the stretch of street will often be "administered" by an *aparcacoches*, a man with a red rag who points out spaces to arriving drivers, stops traffic to allow them to park, and watches over the car while it is there, for a few pesos.

In all city centers there are plenty of paid parking lots (*estacionamientos*, marked with a large "E" sign) and, as charges are not huge, it will generally be better to find one rather than waste time

driving around looking for a space on the street. For a tip, attendants will usually wash the car too. In central Mexico City, Monterrey, and the modern areas of some other cities there are often giant multistory parking garages. If you are driving into any city, try to get a hotel with its own parking lot, and leave the car there while in the city.

In small towns finding parking space is rarely difficult, but you still need to avoid parking next to any painted curbs.

Distances and driving times

Driving times in Mexico will vary a lot depending on the kinds of roads you use. On *cuota* highways you can travel very fast; on country roads, because of the need to slow down for towns, villages, and *tope* speed bumps, average speeds are much lower. The relationship of distance to driving time is also very variable. In the flat Yucatán or the Gulf Coast you can expect to get around fairly quickly at an average of around 90kph (56mph) between towns, but in the mountains of Oaxaca or Chiapas journeys will take far longer.

The following are only rough averages. All driving times are without any allowances for stops.
US Border (Brownsville, TX)–Mexico City: 964km (600 miles), 12hrs
US Border (Brownsville, TX)–Cancún: 2,333km (1,450 miles), 30hrs
US Border (San Diego)–Cabo San Lucás: 1,711km (1,063 miles), 24hrs
Mexico City–Puerto Vallarta: 906km (563 miles), 11hrs
Mexico City–Acapulco: 382km (237 miles), 4–5hrs
Mexico City–Veracruz: 406km (253 miles), 4–5hrs
Mexico City–Palenque: 930km (578 miles), 14hrs
Mexico City–Oaxaca: 452km (280 miles), 6–7hrs
Mexico City–Cancún: 1,630km (1,012 miles), 22hrs
Oaxaca–Puerto Escondido: 290km (180 miles), 5–6hrs
Oaxaca–Palenque: 815km (506 miles), 15hrs
Palenque–San Cristóbal de Las Casas: 191km (118 miles), 5hrs
Palenque–Mérida: 555km (345 miles), 7–8hrs
Mérida–Cancún: 320km (199 miles), 3–4hrs by *cuota* highway, 4–5hrs by ordinary road.

A

Accommodations

Choosing accommodations

Hotels in Mexico cover every option – from luxury grand hotels and chic design venues in cities, through opulent beach resorts and spas, down to palm-roofed forest cabins and simple *posadas* and hostels with rooms for under 200 pesos per night. A growing network of traveller's hostels, often with an international vibe, rival budget to mid-range hotels for comfort, usually with communal facilities. Around the main resort areas – Puerto Vallarta, the Riviera Maya – there are ever more all-inclusive resorts, with every amenity on-site.

Virtually every kind of hotel in Mexico can now be booked online. If you are staying in a large resort hotel, or one of the bigger city hotels, you will generally get better rates by booking them as part of a package through a travel website or tour operator, with flight included, than if you simply book a room direct from the hotel. Hotel costs naturally vary a great deal across the country – in the most popular resort areas and major cities they can be as high as US or European levels, but in other areas – Chiapas, Michoacán, cities not fully on the tourist track – even luxurious old colonial haciendas can be remarkably economical, with beautiful rooms for around US$60 or less.

Several kinds of Mexican hotel have distinctive attractions. Dotted along both the Pacific and Caribbean coasts, set apart from the bigger resorts, are exquisite, ultra-stylish beach retreats with everything you need for serious pampering, including acres of beach and pristine forest to themselves. Increasingly, across the country – and especially in colonial towns such as Oaxaca or Mérida – the trend is very much to revamp characteristic old Spanish colonial houses or *haciendas* (colonial-era estate houses with a landholding), and convert them into hotels. These are almost always built around inviting patios, with fabulous grounds and gardens, and have an irresistible charm. Haciendas are particularly prevalent in the traditional farming areas – Jalisco, Morelos, and the Yucatán – and present great opportunities to get out into an otherwise hard-to-access isolated rural heartland. As haciendas were usually built on plantations or small farms, they often come with optional hands-on eco-activities, ranging from horseback-riding to observing traditional handicrafts.

RVs and camping

Amenities for camping and, particularly, traveling with an RV in Mexico have expanded a good deal since the 1990s, and there are RV parks with good hook-ups, laundries, showers, and other amenities in many parts of the country. They are most numerous along the peninsula of Baja California and along the Pacific coast around Puerto Vallarta, but there are also well-equipped parks in many other areas, such as around Lake Pátzcuaro in Michoacán, or at Paamul near Playa del Carmen on the Riviera Maya, where many RVers spend the winter.

If you want to camp, many RV sites also offer camping space. Other popular camping locations include Palenque, near the ruins, and many backpacker hostels around Mexico offer camping space in their yards and gardens. It is not usually a good idea to try "wild camping" in open country, above all if you do not speak good Spanish. You may find that even remote parcels of land belong to an individual or a community, who will resent you camping without permission. For safety's sake, stick to campsites or beaches where others are already camping.

For more information on both RV travel and camping in Mexico, the most comprehensive one-stop guide is the *Traveler's Guide to Mexican Camping*, published by Rolling Homes Press (www.rolling homes.com). Other handy sources include *On the Road in Mexico* (www. ontheroadin.com), *The People's Guide to Mexico* (www.peoplesguide.com) and www.rversonline.org.

Addresses

Most Mexican cities have a grid street system, bequeathed by the Spaniards, with straight streets spreading out from a Zócalo or main square. In Mexico City and many other cities streets have names, which makes finding addresses fairly simple, although since streets are long it is very useful to have the name of the nearest cross-street and the building number. In the vastness of Mexico City and some other cities the name of the official district or *colonia*, attached to addresses, is also important in finding one's way around. Note that some popular area names do not have official status; the Zona Rosa, for example, is divided between colonias Cuauhtémoc and Juárez.

Puebla and many cities in southern Mexico have a much more confusing system that identifies streets by numbers. Streets running east–west are often (but not always) called *Avenidas*, those going north–south are *Calles* (Streets). The two big streets that form the axis of the grid, running through the Zócalo, are generally the Avenida Central and Calle Central; Avenidas north of Central may be numbered evenly Avenida 2 Norte (North), 4, 6, etc., while to the south they will be Avenida 1 Sur (South), 3, 5, etc. Streets west of Calle Central may be Calles 2 Poniente (West), 4, 6, etc.; to the east they will be Calle 1 Oriente (East), 3, 5, etc. There are also other number variations, without splitting odd and even numbers. This system produces combinations like "Avenida 5 Sur Oriente," (5 South, East), which will be in the southeast corner of the grid. This takes some time to get used to.

In the Yucatán most towns use a simpler street-numbering system: even numbers generally run north–south, odd ones east–west. Since streets are, again, very long, cross-streets are customarily given with addresses in the following style, Calle 55 No. 533, x 64 y 66 (Calle 55 No. 533, between calles 64 and 66).

Admission charges

All archeological sites and most museums in Mexico are administered by the *Instituto Nacional de Antropología e Historia* (INAH). The INAH has set scales of admission charges for its sites: smaller sites cost around US$2.80 per person; medium-sized sites and museums around $3–4.50; the largest and most famous sites (Teotihuacán, Chichén Itzá, Uxmal, and some others) are around $8.50, plus about $1 per vehicle to park. The charges at privately owned museums and attractions are generally around $3 or less. Admission is free on Sundays to INAH sites only for Mexican citizens and residents. Everyone else must pay at all times.

Budgeting for your trip

As in any country, there are variations in average price levels across Mexico, which can very roughly be divided into four – although within each area there can also be big price differences. The major resort areas are generally the most expensive, especially if you stay in the most "touristed" areas; Mexico City is a zone by itself, with the biggest range, from very high to very economical; most other cities are, overall, a bit less expensive; and in many small towns, rural areas, and some states such as Chiapas, prices are much lower. Taking this into account, an attractive mid-range hotel in the third of these areas – most cities other than Mexico City, including the colonial cities like Oaxaca – can cost around $80–90 for a double room, sometimes with breakfast; below $40, rooms in the capital and resort areas will tend to be pretty basic, although elsewhere you can find great bargains. A decent full meal will cost around $15–18 or less (although there is always plenty of much cheaper food available), a beer about $1.50–2. Added to this are transportation costs: a first-class bus ticket for a long trip (for example, Mexico City–Oaxaca) will be around $30, a taxi ride in most cities will be about $2–3.50 (more in Mexico City and resort towns). Renting a car will cost around $50 a day.

Overall, therefore, in most parts of Mexico you can travel around very comfortably spending around $60–70 a day per person, but it's also possible to travel for much less by taking advantage of budget options.

Children

Mexico is a very family-oriented society, and there are few places that do not admit children. Mexicans often travel in family groups, and most hotels have some big family rooms *(habitaciones familiares)* with several beds, which are very economical. Children are seen in most restaurants, including the very plush ones in Mexico City (although there they will be expected to sit at table and behave), and even many *cantinas*, where kids are not admitted during the week, have "family days" on weekends. Restaurants do not usually have special children's menus but will often try hard to meet special requests, and many menus are so varied that there is nearly always something children will like. If children are picky about food, in all resort areas and most towns there are pizzerias and outlets of international fast-food chains. Familiar drinks brands are always available, but for more natural treats the local *juguerías* and *paletería-nevería* stands with fresh juices and own-made ice creams are ideal.

Entertainments for kids are naturally easiest to find in the big resort areas where, along with hotel pools and beaches, there are plenty of rides and water parks. Especially popular attractions are the "eco-parks" such as Xcaret on the Riviera Maya, which give a family-friendly introduction to the tropical environment, and the chance to snorkel in complete safety. Elsewhere, rides and other kids' entertainments often appear in city centers and plazas at weekends. Mexican fiestas, big and small, are often magnetic for kids – so long as they can cope with the crowds – and always include more rides and children's activities.

Climate and clothing

Central Mexico

Mexico City, Guadalajara, and many other cities lie in the Central Highlands where the climate is pretty temperate year-round. Most of this area is also south of the Tropic of Cancer, which runs across Mexico just north of Mazatlán and Zacatecas and creates particularly distinctive weather patterns, including excessive rainfall during the wet season.

Dry season (October to June)

The weather is hot, although cities at higher altitudes rarely get excessively hot; in an average year, Mexico City's highest temperature will be around 31°C (88°F) and Guadalajara's around 35°C (95°F). In Mexico City, the hottest months are April and May, toward the end of the dry season, but even then average temperatures are only in the upper 20s°C (low 80s°F). This is the most popular time to visit Mexico, but at those high altitudes temperatures drop noticeably at night, falling to around 0°C (32°F) in January and February. Altitude and mountainous terrain also create impressive local climate variations, and some areas are known for especially cold winters, notably

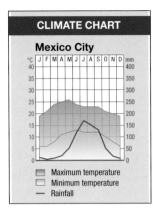

CLIMATE CHART

Mexico City

Legend:
- Maximum temperature
- Minimum temperature
- Rainfall

Toluca, Mexico's highest state capital.

Wet season (June to October)
The wet weather at this time, especially in July and August, can be almost constant. Mexico City has rain nearly every day, usually for a couple of hours in the afternoon.

What to wear
In cities and in provincial towns, casual clothes are all you need at most times, but it would not usually be acceptable, even in hot cities, to walk around public places in beach wear or (for men) very short shorts, and most especially not when visiting churches. In cities like Mexico City and Guadalajara, even casual wear is smart, particularly for going to most good restaurants (long pants and a pale-colored shirt for men, modest dress for women). A sunhat is essential in hot and shade-free places; equally, bring a long-sleeved top/jacket for travel in the cooler mountainous areas.

Baja California
Baja is mostly north of the Tropic and has very low annual rainfall. Temperatures are more comfortable where the land is cooled by sea breezes on the southern tip of the peninsula and along the Pacific coast. Desert areas are cold at night.

Fall (September to November)
The weather is at its wettest, particularly in the late fall.

Summer (June to August)
Summer temperatures can vary significantly, although 30°C (86°F) can be expected. On average, Ensenada's temperature will not rise above 35°C (95°F); but San Felipe, on the Gulf of California, may soar to 48°C (118°F).

What to wear
Remember to pack your swimsuit, sunhat, and beach gear: in coastal towns here beachwear is even acceptable in most restaurants in the evening, except the formal ones.

Northern Mexico
Northern Mexico is largely desert. As you head east toward Monterrey, the climate becomes wetter and more moderate, but remains very hot in summer. However, even on the tropical Gulf Coast, temperatures can fall quite low in winter as cold air plunges south from the US.

Summer (June to August)
The days are exceptionally hot in summer – well above 38°C (100°F). Mountainous areas are cooler.

Winter (December to March)
In winter, days are often dry and cool, although temperatures may drop below freezing at night.

What to wear
Pack a sweater or jacket: this area can get very cold at night despite generally warm daytime temperatures in summer. Hiking boots are necessary for visiting the Copper Canyon area. Bring casual-smart clothes if going out in the evening (shirt and long trousers for men, long dress or other modest clothing for women).

The Pacific coast
Along the Pacific coast, temperatures are cooler at night than in the south, but otherwise similar. In an average year, the maximum temperature in Mazatlán or Puerto Vallarta is in the mid-30s°C (mid-90s°F). Acapulco has daily highs of 27–32°C (80–90°F) year-round, seldom falling much below 21°C (70°F) at night, and Pacific breezes keep temperatures bearable.

Summer (June to August)
North of Mazatlan, the coast becomes desert, and summertime temperatures are extreme, with temperatures frequently above 38°C (100°F). The coast south of Puerto Vallarta conforms much more to the tropical wet and dry season, meaning summer can also be very wet.

Winter (December to March)
Winter varies depending on which part of the coast you are on, but in general is dry, with pleasantly warm daytime temperatures.

What to wear
Remember beach gear, but bring hiking shoes for exploring the coastal national parks. If you are traveling anywhere in the June to October rainy season, you'll want some kind of waterproof coat.

Southern Mexico and the Yucatán peninsula
The southern area has some of the most variable weather in Mexico – some regions are dry while others have nearly 500cm (187in) of rainfall a year. Terrain has a huge effect on climate, and so, for example, the cool mountain climate of San Cristóbal de las Casas is completely different from the steamy rain forest weather of Palenque, 190km (118 miles) to the north. On the Yucatán Peninsula, weather is entirely tropical. Daytime temperatures are generally in the upper 20s°C (low 80s°F) year-round, and night-time temperatures seldom go below 16°C (60°F).

Wet season (June to October)
This part of the country, particularly the Yucatán, is prone to hurricanes during the wet season (see below). One consequence of climate change is that around the Gulf of Mexico the distinction between dry and rainy seasons has become less clear, and the rain storms that once came almost exclusively during the wet season now come during the earlier part of the year too, while months such as August can be rain-free for days at a time.

Dry season (October to June)
In the main winter tourist season in the Yucatán (December–March) temperatures are ideal, rising to a peak of around 38°C (100°F) toward the end of the seca (dry season) in May–June. In Oaxaca, more than 1,500 meters (5,000ft) above sea level, the night-time temperature in January can fall below freezing, but at the end of the dry season in May or June, at midday it can rise to nearly 38°C (100°F). On the Riviera Maya temperatures are generally a little more moderate than in the interior. Around the Gulf of Mexico, climatic variations of recent years have meant that rain storms are now far more common during the first few months of the year.

Hurricanes
Both the Gulf and Pacific coasts are vulnerable to hurricanes, with the Yucatán region most at risk. The official hurricane season runs from June through November, but

whether any major storms will develop during that time is unpredictable beyond a few days. Mexico, especially the Yucatán and Riviera Maya, has some of the best hurricane precautions in the Caribbean, and visitors are warned well in advance of any dangers. The best source of information on hurricanes, including current conditions, is the US **National Hurricane Center**, www.nhc.noaa.gov.

What to wear

If you are traveling anywhere in the June to October rainy season, you will want to take some kind of waterproof coat. Pack a sweater, fleece, or jacket for going to the Chiapas highlands. Even though this area is hot, it's good to have some long pants and at least one long-sleeved shirt or top, to protect against sunburn, insect bites, and scratches from bushes whenever you explore archeological sites and forest paths. Beachwear is de facto in the Riviera Maya area and even acceptable in most restaurants; in other areas something a little more formal will be required for going out in the evening.

Crime and safety

As has been well publicized, there has been a serious upsurge in violent clashes between the Mexican authorities and drug cartels in parts of Mexico, especially since President Calderón launched his offensive against the cartels in 2007 (see page 73). The solution remains elusive. President Pena Nieto's policy in this regard proved ineffective. Despite arrests of high-profile cartel leaders, the drug war's death rate spiked to an all-time high in 2017, then was beaten once more in 2018. President López Obrador has promised to tackle the issue from a new angle, which may see a less confrontational approach and therefore a decline in bloodshed. In any case, this violent crime mainly affects certain areas – border cities such as Tijuana, Ciudad Juárez and Nuevo Laredo, Culiacán in Sinaloa, although Monterrey has also been badly hit by drug crime. The truth is it has very rarely had any direct effect on tourists. There is a certain greater risk in Acapulco, but other resort areas have been pretty peaceful. Throughout the Yucatán the crime rates in general

are noticeably lower, although caution is always recommended. Overall, foreign visitors – unless they actually go looking for danger – are far less likely to be affected by this sort of violence than the more "traditional" problems of petty crime, bag-snatching, and so on. And the risks of these can be greatly reduced by following a few sensible precautions.

The risk of petty crime is, in general, highest in parts of Mexico City, but even there it's easy to have a trouble-free trip by following a few ground rules. Special care is needed when using taxis (see page 330) and you should avoid using the metro during peak times. Be especially aware of people around you in the Centro Histórico, and in any markets. Elsewhere and in most other cities it's much easier to drop your guard, but it's always best to keep to these rules:

Don't walk around dark, empty streets at night.

In any crowd, always keep your bag in front of you with your hand on it, and be aware of anyone standing especially close.

When you sit in a restaurant or café, always keep your bag in view and close to hand, preferably on your lap, on an empty chair, or on the table in front of you. Never leave bags on the floor or hanging from a chair back.

Use ATMs at banks only during business hours. Try to use them only where there are plenty of people around.

In bars, never leave your drink unattended.

The long arm of the law.

Don't carry all your credit cards or large amounts of cash.

Try to split your important possessions between different bag compartments, rather than storing them all together.

Lock your bags whenever you leave your hotel room, and do not leave valuables lying around in the room.

If you have a car, try to park in hotel or other attended parking lots or garages.

If you use second-class buses, try to put your bags in the overhead racks nearest to you, and keep an eye on them.

Police forces and military checks

If you are the victim of any kind of crime, report it as soon as possible to the nearest police post. If you have been robbed it is unlikely the items can be recovered, but you will need a police statement for an insurance claim. In many resorts there are special tourist police (*Policía Turística*) units, with English-speaking officers.

On many roads drivers may be stopped by military checkpoints. They are checking for shipments of drugs or weapons, and are rarely ever interested in tourists, who are usually waved on their way. If, however, you are discovered in possession of any illegal drugs you can expect severe penalties.

Customs regulations

All visitors arriving in Mexico must fill out a customs form (usually given out on incoming flights). When you hand it in at the airport,

after clearing immigration, you will be asked to press a button by a kind of traffic light. If it comes up green, you go straight through; if red, your bag will be searched. The purpose of this system is to ensure that customs checks are random. In addition to their personal effects visitors entering Mexico are allowed certain amounts of some goods (see below); other items may be subject to duty and require an import permit. For specific requirements for taking US or Canadian vehicles into Mexico, see page 327. When leaving Mexico, it is expressly forbidden to take out any pre-Columbian artifacts without authorization, and there are severe penalties for doing so, with very little chance of appeal.

Customs allowances

These include the following; for a full list, visit http://omawww.sat.gob.mx, which has the relevant pages in English.

Cigars and cigarettes: For each visitor aged over 18, up to 400 cigarettes, or 50 cigars, or 1kg (2.2lbs) of tobacco.

Currency: Up to US$10,000 or the equivalent in cash. Amounts above this level are not liable for duty but must be declared.

Alcohol: Visitors aged over 18 can bring in up to 3 liters (100 fl. oz) of wine or liquor.

Electrical equipment: One laptop computer and one CD or other audio player, and two still or video cameras, per person, as long as they are for personal use and not re-sale.

Disabled travelers

Traveling around Mexico has its problems for people with restricted mobility, but things have been improving, albeit from a very low level. Many streets in Mexico City and other cities now have wheelchair ramps cut in sidewalks, and many state museums now have access ramps. In many situations, it's necessary to rely on the great helpfulness of Mexican people – ask for assistance on buses, ferries, or in public buildings, and great efforts will usually be made to find an elevator, fit in a chair

or otherwise accommodate you. Archeological sites tend to have stony paths that are difficult to negotiate, but the larger ones now often have smoother walkways.

To make the most of a trip to Mexico it's best to plan carefully, and be aware that costs will unavoidably be higher than for other travelers. The best places to stay will be the big beach resorts, where some hotels have fully adapted rooms, and even those that do not are easier to get around. In the colonial cities, some hotels have attractive ground-level rooms. A rented car or taxis will be the best way to get around.

Cancún Accessible (tel: 998-884 2156; www.cancunaccesible.com), Mexico's first specialized travel company for disabled visitors, can provide tours, accessible transportation, accommodations, and other services around the Riviera Maya and Yucatán.

Eating out

Street food and market cocinas

One of the great attractions of eating in Mexico is the sheer range and quality of "street food" available. Mexicans are enthusiastic snackers, and every town, even every village, has a selection of small hole-in-the-wall shops and stands selling *antojitos* like *tacos*, *tortas* (filled bread rolls), treats for kids like *marquesitas* (waffle-like cones filled with *cajeta* sweet toffee or cheese) and other specialties, and at weekends and during fiestas there are even more. Hence, you're never short of alternatives if you don't feel like a full meal. Some visitors shy away from all street food for hygiene reasons, but if you take reasonable care to avoid the most basic or badly tended stands you can try some of Mexico's most distinctive (and economical) dishes without any great risk. One other peculiarity of Mexico is that the food at some simple **street-stands** can be as good or better than that of many restaurants, and good taco-stands have a high local reputation, so look out for ones that draw a crowd.

Some of the biggest and most varied clusters of street-food outlets are those in and around markets, which open early in the morning and often close in mid-afternoon. Inside town markets there are usually rows of simple restaurants called *cocinas económicas* (cheap kitchens) that, again, are great places to get a very economical full meal of local specialties, with plenty of atmosphere included.

Restaurants and loncherías

In cities and most towns there will be a choice of restaurants, which, since many people eat out for breakfast, generally open early and stay open all day. In villages there may only be one or two simpler, cheap **loncherías** (from the English lunch), which often blend into **taquerías**. They close quite early (around 7–8pm) and generally do not serve any alcohol. Also, one feature of some of the best traditional Mexican restaurants is that they are not open in the evenings, closing around 6pm, as after breakfast the second main meal of the day has traditionally been a big, leisurely *comida fuerte* or "strong meal" from about 2pm through the afternoon, followed only by a snackish meal at night. Hence, a late lunch is often the best time to sample some of the most interesting Mexican cuisine. In all cities and tourist areas there are also plenty of restaurants with a more flexible, international timetable. Mexican restaurants of all kinds – even *cantinas*, at weekends – admit children, and make them welcome.

Bars and cantinas

In addition to the usual international-style drinking places found in cities, resorts, and hotels, there are some with a distinctively Mexican flavor, notably the *cantina*. The cheapest *cantinas* are very basic, male places for heavy drinking, but there are also many more refined, less rough-edged *cantinas* often with beautiful traditional decor – especially in Mexico City – where women can feel comfortable, particularly on weekends. *Cantinas* serve a special kind of food, small snacks similar to Spanish tapas called *botanas*, of which there is a vast variety. One is served with each drink, and traditionally they get bigger with each successive drink, but by tradition you also pay only for the drink, not the *botana*, so this is an amazingly cheap as well as convivial way to eat.

Ice-cream stands

Another feature of the Mexican street is the number of ice-cream stands, often called a *Paletería-Nevería*. The best offer a big range of made-on-the-spot fresh fruit *paletas* (ice lollipops) or *nieves* (ices in a tub). Most also have a selection of juices, and so double as a *juguería* (see above).

Electricity

Mexico uses the same 110 volt, 60 Hz, electrical system as the US and Canada, with the same flat two-pronged plugs. Anyone from areas with other systems should bring plug adaptors, as they are very difficult to find in Mexico.

Embassies and consulates

Mexican embassies abroad

Australia
14 Perth Avenue, Yarralumla, act 2600, Canberra; tel: 02-6273 3963; http://embamex.sre.gob.mx/australia
Canada
45 O'Connor Street, Suite 1000, Ottawa, Ontario K1P 1A4; tel: 613-233 8988; https://embamex.sre.gob.mx/canada
Ireland
19 Raglan Road, Dublin 4; tel: 3531-667 3105; https://embamex.sre.gob.mx/irlanda
New Zealand
Amp Chambers, Level 2/187 Featherston Street, Lambton, Wellington 6011; tel: 644-472 0555; https://embamex.sre.gob.mx/nuevazelandia
UK
16 St George Street, London W1S 1FD; tel: 020-7499 8586; www.sre.gob.mx/reinounido
US
1911 Pennsylvania Avenue NW, Washington DC 20006; tel: 202-728 1600; http://embamex.sre.gob.mx/eua

In Mexico City

Canada, the UK, and especially the US also have consulates in various other parts of Mexico, details of which will be on the embassy websites.

Australia
Rubén Darío 55, Col. Polanco; tel: 55-1101 2200; www.mexico.embassy.gov.au
Canada
Schiller 529, Col. Polanco; tel: 55-5724 7900; www.canadainternational.gc.ca/mexico-mexique
Ireland
Boulevard Ávila Camacho 76, 3rd Floor, Col. Lomas de Chapulpetec; tel: 55-5520 5803; www.dfa.ie/irish-embassy/mexico
New Zealand
Jaime Balmes 8, 4th Floor, Los Morales, Col. Polanco; tel: 55-5283 9460; www.nzembassy.com/mexico
UK
Río Lerma 71, Col. Cuauhtémoc; tel: 55-1670 3200; http://ukinmexico.fco.gov.uk
USA
Paseo de la Reforma 305, Col. Cuauhtémoc; tel: 55-5080 2000; https://mx.usembassy.gov

Emergency numbers

General Emergencies: 060 is the shared number most commonly used for the police and all emergency services, but in some parts of Mexico the number used is **066**.
Health Emergencies: 080 (in Mexico City; in other areas, just try **060 or 066**).

However, rather than use the common emergency number it can be more efficient to call the service you need direct, particularly the local Red Cross (Cruz Roja) if you have a medical emergency: numbers of local police departments and ambulance services are in the phone book, and hotels should have them.

Etiquette

Mexicans, traditionally, lay great emphasis on courtesy. This has nothing to do with social class, and in country areas poorer people actually tend to be more polite than the wealthier members of the community. Indigenous people, especially, value traditional courtesies highly, and can appear positively ceremonious in the way they deal with strangers; if you respond in a casual manner this will appear contemptuous and aggressive rather than informally friendly.

An essential aspect of courtesy is to make at least some effort

with Spanish, even if it is only with a simple greeting like *buenos días* (good day) or a *por favor* (please). When entering a shop, a restaurant or any other business it is usual to say *buenos días* (or *buenas tardes*, good afternoon, after around 1pm) first before saying what you want. Among country and especially indigenous people, it will also be appreciated if you follow this with an introductory question – *¿Le puedo hacer una pregunta?* or "Can I ask you a question?" – before, for example, asking directions in the street. When you have finished, always say *gracias* and *adios* clearly and with emphasis. Getting brusquely to the point and going about one's business is not highly valued. When introduced to someone by name, Mexicans shake hands, and do so again whenever they meet again, and when they take leave of one another. Women (but not many Indigenous women) nearly always greet anyone they are on friendly terms with, men or women, with a kiss on the cheek.

Mexicans believe it is less rude to accept an unwanted invitation, and fail to appear, than to refuse it. Equally, notions of punctuality are pretty vague, and any appointments are kept to only roughly.

Around Tulum and Playa del Carmen on the Riviera Maya, and Puerto Escondido and some other locations on the Pacific, topless and sometimes nude bathing are now effectively permitted, but in general Mexicans are not very tolerant of nudity or too much exposed flesh. In towns and above all in churches you should avoid any public exposure that might offend – for example, men walking around shirtless, and anyone wearing very short shorts.

Festivals

Listed here is just a small selection of Mexico's hundreds of fiestas and fairs, month by month, but every town has at least one special event during the year, and cities have several. Information on upcoming fiestas can be found at local tourist offices and in the local press. Check dates before you go, too, as many vary slightly from year to year. (See pages 9 and 87.)

January

6: Día de Reyes, Feast of Epiphany or "Three Kings": the traditional day for children to receive Christmas gifts. There are parades led by "The Kings" in most cities across Mexico.

February

late January or February: Carnaval, during the week before Lent: among Mexico's biggest carnival fiestas are those in Huejotzingo, Puebla; Tepoztlán, Morelos; Acapulco, Guerrero; Mazatlán, Sinaloa; Veracruz; Campeche city; and Mérida, Yucatán, all with several days of parades, floats, eating, and dancing. A very special *Carnaval* takes place in San Juan Chamula, Chiapas, an extraordinary mix of Maya and Catholic traditions.

March

March or April: Semana Santa (Holy Week) sees a wide variety of celebrations and processions all over Mexico.
March: Festival del Centro Histórico, Mexico City: a three-week cultural extravaganza in the historic center, with opera, rock, movie screenings, and other events, often in open-air venues and including an international range of artists.

April

April–May: Feria Nacional de San Marcos, Aguascalientes: the largest of Mexico's *ferias* or fairs, given "national" status: for nearly four weeks Aguascalientes hosts stock sales, food displays, parades, *charro* shows, bullfights and cockfights, a beauty pageant, many other shows, and daily parties.

May

5: Cinco de Mayo, Puebla: holiday commemorating the Mexican victory over the French army at Puebla in 1862; in Mexico (in contrast to parts of the US with large Mexican populations) this is a relatively minor holiday.

June

24: San Juan Bautista (John the Baptist): especially colorful fiestas are held in San Juan Cosalá, on Lake Chapala, Jalisco; Coatetelco, Morelos; San Juan Chamula, Chiapas; and on Cozumel.
29: Día de San Pedro y San Pablo. As with most saints' fiestas, celebrations go on for several days around the actual date; among the most attractive are the big street fiesta in Tlaquepaque, near Guadalajara, Jalisco, and the processions in Pochutla, Oaxaca.

July

16: Nuestra Señora del Carmen. Festivals in the San Ángel district of Mexico City, Catemaco, Veracruz, and Ciudad del Carmen, Campeche. At Catemaco, the procession of the Virgen del Carmen traverses the streets accompanied by traditional marimba music and then takes to the water, passing the place where she originally appeared to a fisherman in the 17th century.
Last two Mondays in July: La Guelaguetza, or *Lunes del Cerro* (Mondays on the Hill), Oaxaca: A stunning display of the dances, music, crafts, and other traditions of all the many cultures of Oaxaca state, held on a hill outside Oaxaca city.

August

Usually 5–20: Feria de Huamantla, Huamantla, Tlaxcala. The most spectacular of many celebrations across Mexico around the Feast of the Assumption (August 15), culminating in "the night no-one sleeps"
10: San Lorenzo, Zinacantán, Chiapas: San Lorenzo is the patron saint of many Chiapas towns and at Zinacantán they mark the occasion with some of the most intriguing Highland Maya ceremonies, accompanied by the community's own, almost unearthly music.

September

14: Día del Charro. A special day to celebrate Mexico's horseback-riding traditions: the biggest events are in Guadalajara, but there are also *charro* parades in Mexico City and many other cities.
15–16: Independence Day. Major celebrations begin on the night of the 15th, commemorating Hidalgo's *Grito* or call for Mexican independence, and are followed by other events and a national holiday on the 16th.

October

Mid-October–November: Festival Internacional Cervantino, Guanajuato: Mexico's première arts festival, with a prestigious range of international participants.

November

October 31– November 1–2: All Saints' Day and Día de los Muertos (Day of the Dead). The dead are commemorated in slightly different ways all over Mexico. Some of the most impressive events are at Pátzcuaro and Isla Janitzio, Michoacán, at San Andrés Mixquic, near Xochimilco in Mexico City, and in Oaxaca.

December

12: Nuestra Señora de Guadalupe, Mexico City: The most important religious festival of the year: vast crowds visit the shrine of Our Lady of Guadalupe, and all over the country groups of *guadalupano* pilgrims can be seen in the days up to December 12 running along roads to the capital or to their local shrine to the Virgin.
24–25: Navidad (Christmas): the night of Christmas Eve (La Noche Buena) is the heart of Christmas celebrations, with Midnight Masses followed by very late family dinners, and Christmas Day itself is a very quiet holiday.

☉ Medical treatment

If you need medical assistance, the best place to call on will be one of the modern private clinics that are found in Mexican cities and resort areas, and then claim on your insurance. Such clinics have high-quality facilities, and near-invariably have some English-speaking staff. Hotels should be able to recommend one, and/or provide a list of local English-speaking doctors (or dentists). If you call the embassy or consulate of your home country (see page 339) they will also have a list of multilingual doctors. In small towns and country areas the only facilities will usually be a local public health center (*Centro de Salud*), which can handle basic emergencies perfectly well, but anyone with a more serious problem will need to be moved to the nearest private hospital.

Health and medical care

No one should travel in Mexico without a comprehensive travel insurance policy, covering loss or theft of their belongings, cancellations, and all medical eventualities, including emergency repatriation by air if necessary. Mexico's public health system is fairly limited, and for foreigners it is essential to have private health insurance. Many credit card companies provide some coverage for medical and/or legal emergencies for trips paid for with their card, but check whether this is sufficient for your needs. If you intend to try out any adventure sports activities – such as scuba diving – you may need additional cover or a specialized sports insurance policy, so check carefully how far your policy extends, and shop around to find the best options.

Health precautions

At most times – that is, except during exceptional crises such as the 2009 swine flu outbreak – there are no inoculations that are obligatory for travelers to Mexico. However, it is advisable to be inoculated against polio, tetanus, and hepatitis A, and, if necessary, to have a typhoid booster shot. Cholera is also present in some areas, so you may wish to be immunized against that too. There is a risk of malaria in forest areas of the Gulf Coast, Campeche, and Chiapas, so some travelers take a course of antimalaria tablets, but discuss the risks with your doctor before taking any such pills, as they can have strong side effects. Dengue fever, another fly-born infection, affects local people in some areas, but the best way to avoid it is to steer clear of any pools of stagnant water.

If you fly into Mexico City, the combination of altitude and air pollution can leave some new arrivals weak and listless, with headaches and other symptoms. Take it easy during the first days you are there, to get acclimatized.

It's a good idea to bring a basic medical kit, including medication for diarrhea and stomach cramps, insect repellent, aspirin or an equivalent, antiseptic wipes and cream, Band Aids, sunscreen, and any prescription drugs you may need.

Drinking water and hygiene

The risks of ingesting any tap water in Mexico are often exaggerated, but in general, the essential rule is still to drink only bottled, purified water (agua purificada). This is guaranteed clean water, not mineral water (agua mineral), which is a lot more expensive. Purified water is sold in all grocery stores, supermarkets, and pharmacies, and in all restaurants, and all hotels of mid-range level and up provide it free for their guests. Travelers in Mexico have commonly been advised to refuse to have ice in their drinks or to buy anything at street juice stands, but nowadays virtually every restaurant and stand also uses agua purificada to make ice and fruit-juice mixes, so there is very little risk in this either. At the same time, the standard of mains water in most parts of Mexico has also been improving, so you are unlikely to catch anything by swallowing a little water while in the shower.

Overall, the best ways to reduce the likelihood of getting any stomach complaints while in Mexico are simply to avoid the most basic lonchería restaurants and any street-food stands with obviously poor hygiene standards, and to be reasonably sensible about eating any high-risk foods such as seafood that is not clearly fresh. If you buy any fruits or vegetables yourself, rinse them with purified water, or peel them. If you are camping out or traveling in any remote areas, where you may run out of purified water, be prepared to purify water yourself: either boil it for 20 minutes or more (depending on altitude), or use purification tablets.

Hospitals

Private hospitals will be listed in the local phone book under Centros Médicos or Hospitales, and will normally have large ads making clear the services they offer and whether they have English-speaking staff. The following are some reliable options around the country:

Mexico City: Centro Médico ABC, Avenida Observatorio, Colonia Américas; tel: 55-5230 8000, emergencies 55-5230 8161; www.abchospital.com.

Guadalajara: Hospital México-Americano, Colomos 2110, Guadalajara, Jalisco; tel: 33-3642 3333; www.hma.com.mx.
Acapulco: Hospital Magallanes, Wilfrido Massieu 2, Acapulco, Guerrero; tel: 744-469 0270; http://minisitios.seccionamarilla.com.mx/hospitalmagallanes.
Mérida: Clínica de Mérida, Avenida Itzáes 242, Mérida, Yucatán; tel: 999-942 1800; www.clinicademerida.com.mx.
Cancún: American Hospital, Plaza Las Américas, Avenida Tulum Sur 260, Cancún, Quintana Roo; tel: 998-881 3400; www.amerimedcancun.com. This same US-owned group also has hospitals in Puerto Vallarta and Cabo San Lucas.

Pharmacies

Well-stocked pharmacies (farmacias) are plentiful in Mexican cities, and there is usually one in every small town. In cities, there is nearly always at least one that is open 24 hours daily, often on or near the main square. Pharmacies stock not only prescription drugs, but also a wide range of products such as cosmetics, condoms, purified water, and telephone cards (see page 345).

Internet

Internet access is very widely available across Mexico, and has made up for the inadequacies of the mail system. Internet cafés are abundant in cities and there is usually at least one in small towns, so checking email is never a problem. Charges are usually around $1–2 an hour, or more in resort areas. In addition, many hotels, even mid-range or budget ones, now offer Wi-fi connections, often for free (in remoter areas connections may be very slow, but they usually work). Email is now the most reliable way of keeping in touch while in Mexico, and of making hotel reservations.

Left luggage

There are left-luggage lockers in each of the main terminals at

Mexico City airport and at most other airports, usually near the Departures area. In Mexico City, they are often in great demand. First-class bus stations (including all the Mexico City terminals) often have staffed left-luggage counters, and if you have a bus ticket for the next few days you can often check bags into the bus company's own luggage storage (guarda equipajes) room.

LGBTQ travelers

Mexican attitudes to sexuality and gender are, like those to many things, often contradictory. There is a strong strain of homophobia in parts of Mexican culture, but also a good deal of tolerance and increasing broad-mindedness. And with an assertive gay rights movement that enjoys some protection from the political left, and with that spectrum in power, things are looking up. A series of laws against anti-LGBTQ discrimination have been passed, and roughly half of the country's states have legalized same sex marriage, with more to come.

Mexico City has an energetic LGBTQ scene, centered in the Zona Rosa, and elsewhere there are sizeable communities in Monterrey, Mérida and, especially, Guadalajara. Of the beach towns, the hub is Puerto Vallarta, close to Guadalajara, followed by Cancún. In some cities and small towns, particularly further north, LGBTQ life may remain more underground. On the other hand, among Mexico's many, many surprises are the Zapotec communities such as Juchitán and Tehuantepec in eastern Oaxaca, where society is essentially matriarchal and women prize having gay sons, as being more help to them in their old age.

An extensive listings site for LGBTQ-friendly venues can be found here www.gaymexicomap.com.

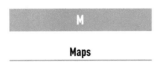

Maps

Completely accurate maps are oddly hard to obtain in Mexico. Many states have ongoing road-building schemes, and many

Embracing wireless internet in Querétaro.

maps are not updated frequently enough to catch them all, so you can find new roads not marked on any map. Tourist offices and free local English-language magazines commonly provide free maps, which are useful, although often a little sketchy. The most thorough maps are those of each state produced by the official *Secretaría de Comunicaciones y Transportes* (SCT), but some are now seriously out of date. The maps and road atlases of Mexico's main commercial map publishers, Guía Rojí and Editorial Independencia, are good for the capital, most cities, and areas around them, but sometimes less so for rural areas. If you intend to tour around, and haven't brought enough maps with you, stock up in Mexico City or in any shop that has a good map stock.

Media

Newspapers and magazines

Mexico has a great many daily newspapers. Mexico City papers that are also distributed around the country include the prestigious *Reforma*, *Excelsior*, *El Universal*, the more popular-style *uno más uno*, the erudite left-wing *La Jornada*, and business-oriented *El Financiero*, and every state has two or more papers of its own. In Mexico City there are also several good entertainment guides. In English, *The News* (www.thenews.mx) is a fairly limited daily published in

Mexico City, and the *Miami Herald* has a Cancún edition that is distributed around the Yucatán.

Major international magazines such as *Time* and *Newsweek* are readily available on newsstands in the capital, major cities, and the big resort areas, but are scarce elsewhere. Sanborn's restaurant branches generally have a newsstand with a selection of the foreign press.

In many tourist areas, inland and especially around the coasts, there is at least one local free magazine published in English, such as *Baja Times* in Baja, *Tourister* in Ixtapa-Zihuatanejo, *Yucatán Today* in Mérida and *Cancún Tips* and several others on the Riviera Maya. They are distributed in hotels, tourist offices, restaurants, and other venues, and while they are advertising-led they are handy to pick up, since as well as basic maps they also contain other useful information (such as current taxi rates).

For websites with news and information on Mexico, see page 346.

Television and radio

Except for those in really remote areas, or boutique retreats that deliberately avoid it, nearly every Mexican hotel has TV, and a great many, even in lower price ranges, now have cable or satellite systems offering a variety of channels. These will include a great many Mexican ones with their favorite mix of soap operas (telenove-las), entertainment spectaculars, chat shows, sensationalist news, classic Mexican movies, and soccer, and a choice of channels in English. In addition, US and British TV shows and movies are often shown even on Mexican channels in English with Spanish subtitles. Anyone with some knowledge of Spanish can also get insights into local life by flicking around the many small-scale local channels.

There is an even bigger number of radio stations, most of them broadcasting Mexico's own music, of different kinds.

Money

Mexico's currency, the *peso*, comes in denominations of 20, 50, 100, 200, 500, and 1,000 peso bills, and there are coins for 1, 2, 5, 10, and 20 pesos, as well as flimsy coins of 10, 20, and 50 *centavos* of a peso. Since the global financial crisis of 2007–8 the peso has generally stood at around 12–14 pesos to the US dollar.

Along the US border and in big resort areas like Cancún, many shops and businesses accept US dollars, and prices may be labeled in both currencies. However, if you pay in dollars you will usually end up paying slightly more than if you had changed your money into pesos.

When getting spending money in Mexico it is best to be able to use a variety of methods – some US dollars in cash, and through ATMs (it is best to bring a couple of different cards, in case one doesn't work). If you are traveling from Britain or most other countries, always take a little cash in US dollars. Mexican banks generally give very bad exchange rates for non-dollar currencies (Euros and Canadian dollars may be less of a problem). Credit cards are widely used in Mexico, especially in hotels, big stores, and dive shops, and are effectively essential for renting a car. It is much less common to use them in restaurants, and in markets and street stores you must have some cash (in pesos). ATMs are also plentiful in cities, and there is usually at least one in the main town of each district. Given the time it can take to change money in Mexican banks,

and the fact that withdrawing money through an ATM can cost less than bank commissions, this is often the most convenient way to get money, but it is not advisable to rely on ATMs completely. There may be none in remote areas, so check on the local situation – hotels will be able to advise you. For this reason it is good to have some dollars in cash (which many hotels will exchange).

Note that owing to security concerns you should always notify your credit card company before traveling to Mexico, as otherwise you can find that your card is blocked without warning.

Changing travelers' checks or cash can involve standing in long lines and they are increasingly difficult to change. Furthermore, some bank branches do not change money at certain times (such as during the afternoon). This is a big reason why it's often much easier just to use an ATM. Before joining a line at a bank, always check if there is a special currency exchange (cambio) counter. It will always be quicker to change money in bigger branches than smaller ones. All banks are closed on Sundays and public holidays.

Outside of banking hours, in any tourist area there will be several small *casas de cambio* (money exchanges), where rates are sometimes quite reasonable. Avoid changing money in hotels, which habitually give very poor rates. There are also exchange desks at all airports, which nearly always give bad rates. If you have no pesos, change only as much as you need for a taxi to your hotel, and then get cash from an ATM.

Whenever you change money, avoid being left with only big-denomination notes (especially 500 or 1,000 pesos), which will be hard to break in most shops and restaurants.

Taxes

Airline passengers leaving Mexico must pay a departure tax, generally of around 1,200 pesos ($60). This is now nearly always included in the ticket price, but with a few, usually budget, flights you may have to pay (in cash, not by card) at check-in. Mexico has a sales or value added tax (IVA) of 15 percent (10 percent in some border states) which is charged on most transactions, and

most states charge a 2 percent accommodations tax, which is added to hotel bills.

Tipping

Many Mexicans depend on tips to make up for low wages, so it is a good principle to follow to tip generously and often. In restaurants and bars in most parts of the country, the usual rate is around 10 percent of the check; in resort areas this rises to around 15 percent. Some restaurants add around 10 percent to the check, but if the service has been good it will be appreciated if you also leave some cash.

Hotel porters and bellboys are usually tipped around 5–10 pesos, for chambermaids about 10 pesos per night. Tour guides are tipped according to the tour price and the quality of their performance. It is not, however, usual to tip taxi drivers, unless they have been especially helpful, for example with luggage.

There are also many people who are customarily given small tips for a range of small services. At gas stations there will often be a boy who will clean your windshield for a few pesos, and it's usual to tip the main gas attendant if they provide any extra services such as checking your tires or oil. Boys or old men who guard areas on a street, guide you into one of "their" parking places and then watch over your car till you come back are given 2–5 pesos. More formal parking attendants are tipped 5 pesos or more.

Opening hours

Opening hours vary a little around the country, with a greater tendency to get everything done in the morning, and then take a long *siesta* break through the afternoon, the farther south you go. Office hours are widely variable, but in most areas they open 9am–2pm, then close for lunch, reopening from 4–6pm. In cities, many stores may also observe a long lunch break, opening from around 8.30–1 or 2pm and again from 4–8pm, but there are also plenty that stay open all day, 9am–9pm. In small towns and especially villages shops are often just open through the day, for whenever there's any business. Markets generally begin business early, around 7am or earlier, and may be shutting down by about 2 or 3pm. Most city shops are closed on Sundays, but in small towns and villages this can be a busy market and shopping day.

Banks are traditionally open Monday–Friday 8.30am–1pm and Saturdays 9am–1pm, but many now stay open much later, often through the afternoon to 5–6pm or later.

Cathedrals and major city churches have their own timetables, and are often open all day, but village churches commonly open their doors early, at sunrise, but are nearly always closed in the afternoons, roughly from around 1pm to 4 or 5pm. They are then left open until after dark.

Except in beach resorts, business throughout Mexico slows to a near-standstill during Easter week, between Christmas and New Year, and around the major fiestas.

Photography

All the major types of camera equipment, memory cards, and so on are available in Mexico, in resort areas and the main cities, where there are often specialist stores that should be able to provide any more technical equipment. However, they are relatively expensive, so bring everything you need with you if you can.

There are a few restrictions on photography at archeological sites and museums administered by the Instituto Nacional de Antropología e Historia (INAH). Tripods cannot be used without a permit, and an extra fee must be paid to use a video camera, but there are no limitations on the use of hand-held still cameras. At the larger archeological sites these controls are keenly enforced.

Indigenous peoples often resent being used arbitrarily as photographic subjects by wandering tourists. This is not because, as is often said, they think cameras "steal their souls," but because they greatly value courtesy (see

Etiquette) and find it insultingly impersonal for a complete stranger to take their picture without asking. If you wish to take any pictures in indigenous communities, always greet people and ask first (¿Le puedo hacer una foto?); where there are plenty of tourists around, you may also be asked for money. There is a complete ban on picture-taking in many indigenous churches and other buildings in villages in highland Chiapas and many other areas. If you take any tours into indigenous areas your guide should make clear when it is acceptable to take photos.

Postal services

Main post offices (oficinas de correos) are found in all main towns and are usually open Monday–Friday 9am–6pm, and often Saturday 9am–1pm. Offices in small towns and villages commonly open for shorter hours, and close for lunch. Stamps (estampillas) are sold in post offices and any shop with the sign Expendio de Estampillas. Mail boxes are generally small metal boxes attached to walls in two shades of blue and marked Servicio Postal Mexicano. In towns and outside some main post offices there are often large red boxes marked Buzón Expresso, but mail posted in them goes only marginally faster.

The Mexican mail service is inexpensive but erratic, and often very, very slow. Hence email is now a much better means of maintaining any kind of communication – postcards and letters will generally arrive, but it's hard to say when. If you have anything important you need to send, a good alternative to standard mail is to use Mexpost, a courier service that is run by the post office but is quite efficient: packages sent within Mexico usually arrive the next day, to the US within two days, and to Europe in about a week. Available at most main post offices (but not small ones), it still costs less than most commercial courier companies. However, all the main international courier services (FedEx, UPS, etc.) are available in most Mexican cities.

You can also receive mail at Mexican post offices, although, if possible, it would be better to have the item sent to a hotel. Letters sent

Public holidays

The following are Mexico's official holidays, when all businesses throughout the country are closed for the day.
January 1 New Year's Day
February 5 Constitution Day
March 21 Birthday of Benito Juárez
March/April Maundy Thursday, Good Friday, Easter Monday
May 1 Labor Day
May (Last Monday) Spring Bank Holiday
September 16 Independence Day
November 20 Revolution Day
December 12 Virgin of Guadalupe
December 25 Christmas Day

for general delivery/poste restante should be clearly addressed to your name (in capitals, underlined) and then Lista de Correos followed by the zip code and the name of the relevant town and state, as in CP 77510 Cancún, Quintana Roo, México. When you go to the post office where you are expecting mail, ask for the Lista de Correos, and take your passport.

Religious services

Mexico remains a predominantly Catholic country, but a wide variety of evangelical Protestant groups are also active, especially among indigenous people. In many cities and resort areas there is at least one Catholic church that holds services in English some time each week, and there are also expatriate Protestant churches and church groups. Local free magazines (see Media) will have details of services in English in each area. There is also a large Jewish community in Mexico City, particularly in Roma, Condesa, and Polanco.

Shopping

The sheer range of Mexican traditional handicrafts is stunning: every part of Mexico has its own distinctive traditions, and some areas are especially rich in the quality of their work – such as Puebla, Taxco in Guerrero, Oaxaca, or Chiapas (see page 106). Few visitors can resist shopping in Mexico, and for some, hunting for original craftwork and similarly distinctive items can be the primary purpose of their visit. The price range is nearly as wide as the range of items available, so take your time and choose wisely. Serious craftwork enthusiasts should plan to travel extensively in the countryside – the best work will often be found closer to where it is made. You may also be lucky enough to watch craftsmen and women (*artesanos* or *artesanas*) at work. If you're particularly interested in any type of craftwork, it's best to do some advance research on the best towns and villages to head for, and the kind of work they do; otherwise, check around in the nearest city to get an idea of the most distinctive local products.

Some large stores, and sometimes even market traders, will pack and ship large purchases to your home for a reasonable charge.

Smoking

Officially, smoking is only permitted in outside spaces, such as patios or terraces.

Student travelers

At some museums and other public buildings there are small discounts on admission for students. In most

Public phone on Isla Mujeres, in the Yucatán.

cases they are intended for Mexican students only, but since the situation is not clear, if you have an international student card you may be able to get the corresponding discount.

T

Telephones

White *Lada* public phones of Telmex, Mexico's main phone company, can be found easily in all but the remotest spots in the country. They work with phone cards (*tarjetas lada*), which are available for 30, 50, or 100 pesos from Telmex shops and any store with a blue-and-yellow *Ladatel* sign (pharmacies nearly always sell them). Instructions are posted up in different languages in each phone booth, and when you insert the card the display on the phone will tell you how much credit you have left on the card. By pressing a button you can also change the display from Spanish to English.

In villages that do not have Lada phones there is always a local *Caseta* or phone office, identified by a blue-and-white Telmex *Teléfono Público* sign. At these you write down the number you want to call and it is dialed for you, and you then take the call from a booth. In cities there are also many private phone centers (*locutorios*) that use the same system.

Telmex charges are quite low for local calls but can go up sharply for anywhere outside your immediate area, and are high for international calls. If you need to make an international call, rather than watch a phone card running out very quickly, it will be better to make the call from a *caseta* or phone center, and then pay in one go when you have finished. This will also work out a little less expensive. Making any phone call from a hotel is generally particularly expensive.

The number of cell phones has been growing prodigiously in Mexico, as it has everywhere else in the world. Signal coverage is now good around cities and most towns, although the more remote rural areas remain "holes" in the network. Mexican cell phones operate on the same 1900 frequency band as in the US, so phones from Europe or elsewhere must have a quad- or triband facility. The cost of using a

foreign cell phone in Mexico is steep, so if you expect to use a phone much it can be more economical to get a low-cost model pay-as-you-go Mexican phone. In all cities there are plenty of phone shops of Telcel, Movistar, and other companies that have frequent competitive offers.

Usually the best, and cheapest, way to make a call from Mexico is to find an establishment with free Wi-Fi in exchange for your custom and send a message or use a calling app that way.

Phone codes

To make any call within Mexico but outside your immediate area, you must first dial an access code (**01**), followed by an area code (often called *el Lada*). In some big cities the area code has two digits (Mexico City 55, Monterrey 81, Guadalajara 33), followed by an eight-figure number; everywhere else the area code has three digits (Cuernavaca 777, Puerto Vallarta 322, Acapulco 744, Mérida 755, Cancún 998) and individual numbers have seven figures. *Lada* codes are given with all phone numbers listed in this guide.

Mexican cell phone numbers have the same area codes, but to call them you may need to use another access code instead of 01, usually **044** or **045**. Numbers beginning **01 800** are toll-free.

International dialling codes

To call Mexico from abroad: +52 followed by Lada area code and the number.
To call abroad from Mexico: Australia 00 61; Irish Republic 00 353; New Zealand 00 64; South Africa 00 27; UK 00 44; US and Canada 001.

Telephone enquiries

Operators for internal services speak Spanish only, but international operators are English-speaking:
For directory enquiries within Mexico, dial 040.
For international enquiries and operator-assisted long-distance calls, dial 090.

Time zones

Most of Mexico is usually in the same time zone as US Central Standard Time (GMT minus 6 hours). Exceptions are the states of Chihuahua, Sonora, Sinaloa, and

Baja California Sur, which usually follow Mountain Standard Time (GMT minus 7 hours) and Baja California Norte, which is usually in the same zone as US Pacific Time (GMT minus 8 hours). However, Mexico moves onto Daylight Saving Time later than the US, on the first Sunday in April, and ends it earlier, on the last Sunday in October, so for a few days each year the time zones of the two countries are not synchronized. In addition, Sonora state does not observe Daylight Saving at all, so during the summer months it is effectively on Pacific Time, the same as Baja California Norte.

Toilets

Public toilets are quite scarce in Mexico, except in airports, bus stations, museums, malls, and archeological sites. Those that do exist usually charge a couple of pesos for entry. In an emergency, restaurants or cafés are often the best bet; ask for *el servicio* or *el lavabo*. If you're concerned about hygiene, chain restaurants will always be pretty clean.

Tourist information

Mexican Government Tourist Offices (MGTO)

The umbrella website for Mexico's tourism authorities worldwide is: www.visitmexico.com

Canada
2 Bloor Street West, Suite 1502, Toronto, Ontario M4W 3E2; tel: 416-925 0704
1 Place Ville Marie, Suite 1931, Montreal, Quebec H3B 2C3; tel: 514-871 1052
999 West Hastings Street, Suite 1110, Vancouver, British Columbia V6C 2W2; tel: 604-669 2845

UK
Wakefield House, 41 Trinity Square, London EC3N 4DJ; tel: 020-7488 9392

US
152 Madison Avenue, No. 1800, New York, NY 10016; tel: 212-308 2110 ext. 103
2829 16th Street North West, 4th Floor, Washington DC 20009; tel: 202-265 9021
1880 Century Park East, Suite 511, Los Angeles, CA 90067; tel: 310-282 9112
225 North Michigan Avenue, Suite 1850, Chicago, IL 60601; tel: 312-228 0194

5975 Sunset Drive, Suite 305, South Miami, FL 33143; tel: 786-621 2909 ext. 13
4507 San Jacinto, Suite 308, Houston, TX 77004; tel: 713-772 2581

Local tourist offices

Every state in Mexico has its own tourist office, based in the state capital, and many cities also have their own municipal information offices. The quality of local tourist offices varies a great deal. In some the staff is well-informed, up to date on local developments, and very helpful; others may employ students who have no specific knowledge and are there only to give out leaflets. Websites, local independent tour companies, and, where they exist, local English-language free magazines (see Media) are in general much more useful sources of information than official tourist offices. Tourist offices can be particularly unreliable regarding travel information, so always check bus timings, for example, with the relevant company rather than rely on anything told to you by tourist offices. The following are some of the more useful tourist information services around Mexico, but as said there is at least one in each state, and more in coastal resorts.

Acapulco
Avenida Costera Miguel Alemán 187; tel: 744-484 4159 or 744-484 7264; https://visitacapulco.travel

Baja California Norte
Juan Ruíz de Alarcón 1572, Zona Río, Tijuana; tel: 01800-028 0888 or 664-682 3367; www.bajanorte.com/en

Cabo San Lucas
Calle Flor de Pitaya, Lote 30, Mza 7, Fracc. Jacarandas, Cabo San Lucas; tel: 624-143 1346, from US and Canada tel: 11-52-624-143-1346; www.loscabosguide.com

Campeche
Main public information office: Casa Seis, Calle 57 (on Parque Principal), Campeche; tel: 019-816 1782; www.campeche.travel

Guadalajara (Jalisco State Tourist Office)
Avenida Morelos 102, Plaza Tapatía; tel: 33-3668 1600; http://visita.jalisco.gob.mx

Puerto Vallarta
Zona Comercial Continental Plaza; tel: 322-224 1175; www.visitpuertovallarta.com

Mérida and Yucatán
Main city information offices: Teatro Peón Contreras, Calle 60, by Calle

57, Palacio Municipal, on the Plaza Mayor, and Ayuntamiento de Mérida Calle 59 between calles 52 and 50; tel: 999-928 1966; www.merida.gob.mx/turismo

Mexico City (Distrito Federal)
Nuevo León 56, Colonia Hipódromo; tel: 01800-008 9090; https://turismo.cdmx.gob.mx

Oaxaca
Avenida Juárez 703, Centro Histórico; tel: 951-502 1200; www.oaxaca.travel

Puebla
Boulevard Héroes del 5 de Mayo, No. 402 Paseo de San Francisco, Puebla; tel: 01800-326 8656 or 222-246 2490; http://puebla.travel/en

San Cristóbal de las Casas
Palacio Municipal, Avenida Miguel Hidalgo 1 (on the Zócalo); tel: 967-678 0665 or 01800-280 3500; www.turismochiapas.gob.mx

Veracruz
Palacio Municipal, corner Zaragoza and Lerdo de Tejada, on the Zócalo, Veracruz; tel: 229-200 2200; www.veracruz.gob.mx

Websites

See also the state tourist sites listed under Tourist Information Offices
www.mexperience.com. Very clear information, interesting background articles, and a booking service.
www.mexconnect.com. More of a magazine-style site, Mexico Connect has an inspiring range of features on many aspects of Mexico.
www.inside-mexico.com. Inside Mexico, a guide to living in Mexico produced by expat residents.
www.thetruthaboutmexico.com. Informative antidote, written by Mexican residents, to "Mexico=chaos" media reporting.
www.planeta.com/mexico.html. Eco Travels in Mexico, a useful source for discovering small-scale and eco-tourism travel possibilities.
http://mexicomike.com. A huge amount of useful information for travelers, and particularly good for drivers.
http://thepeoplesguidetomexico.com. Seemingly never-ending essays and information about Mexico are given from regional, culinary, living/working, and numerous other perspectives.
www.zihuatanejo.net. Local guide to Ixtapa-Zihuatanejo and Troncones.
www.yucatanliving.com. Imaginative site produced by Mérida-based expats.

www.yucatanwildlife.com. Covers every aspect of the peninsula's astonishing wildlife, and tour options.

TOUR OPERATORS AND TRAVEL AGENTS

The companies below provide a range of travel services and tours, from the US, the UK, and within Mexico.

Adventures Mexico, www.adventures-mexico.com. Based in the Yucatán, this boutique tour company offers day trips and long tours of the region and Central Mexico.

Andale... Mexico, www.andalemexico.com. Based in Mexico City and Queretaro, this Internet tour agency with international offices offers a much broader than average range of trips and other services around Mexico.

Authentic Copper Canyon, tel (US): 217-369 9897, http://authenticcop percanyon.com. Tailor-made trips to Copper Canyon and locations across Northern Mexico, including visits to the indigenous Tarahumara people.

Go... with Jo, tel (US and Canada): 1-800 999 1446, www.gowithjo.com. Texas-based company with range of trips around Mexico, run with a personal touch.

Journey Latin America, tel (UK): 020-3432 1523, www.journeylatiname rica.co.uk. One of the best sources in the UK for flight-only deals and other itineraries in Mexico and around Latin America.

Journey Mexico, tel (US/Canada): 1-800 513 1587, www.journeymexico. com. Mexico-based tour company with an emphasis on bespoke, luxury trips around the country, with some good sample itineraries.

Mexico City Explorer, tel (Mexico): 55-5564 8807 or 01800-505 5807 www.mexicocityexplorer.com.mx. Tours of every part of the capital, and an exciting range of trips to other parts of the country.

STS Travel, tel (US and Canada): 1-800-648 4849, www.ststravel.com. US student travel service, with spring break deals a specialty.

Turibus, tel (Mexico): 01800-280 8887 or 55-5141 1360, www.turibus.

⊙ Weights and measures

The metric system is used throughout Mexico.

com.mx. Open-topped double-decker buses that provide daily tours of Mexico City, Puebla, Veracruz, and Mérida. Passengers can get on and off as many times as they wish during the day.

V

Visas and passports

US, Canadian, Australian, New Zealand, British, and other EU citizens do not need a visa to enter Mexico as tourists for up to six months, but visas are required by nationals of South Africa and certain other countries (for details in English, visit the Mexican Immigration Department website, https://consulmex.sre.gob.mx or consult local Mexican consulates). US citizens need a full passport to travel to and from Mexico by air, and a passport or other WHTI (Western Hemisphere Travel Initiative) compliant document, such as a US Passport Card, to cross the border by land or enter by sea (for details of the WHTI, visit the State Department site, http://travel.state. gov). Canadian citizens can officially still enter Mexico with only ID and a birth certificate, but if they transit through the US they must have a WHTI-compliant document, and in practice it's much simpler just to have a full passport. All other travelers must have full passports valid for at least six months from the date of entry. These rules are subject to change. Please double check before you travel.

All air travelers must also fill in a Mexican Tourist Card (FM1), which is handed out on incoming flights, and then stamped at immigration with the length of your permitted stay. Keep it with your passport and then give it up when you leave. Do not lose it, as if you do not have a Tourist Card when you leave you can be fined and delayed.

If you enter Mexico by land from the US, you do not need a Tourist Card for visits to the *Zona Fronteriza* or "Border Zone" (roughly 20–30km/12–18 miles from the border) of up to 72 hours, but if you intend to go farther or stay longer you should get one at a border crossing. When traveling by air the charge for a tourist card is absorbed into the

ticket, but if you enter Mexico by land from the US, Guatemala, or Belize you must pay a fee of around $20. This has to be paid at a government bank office at the border, which can be a little time consuming. There is a special arrangement for travelers visiting Mexico on cruise ships, so that they do not need a tourist card.

At most airports and US crossing points immigration officers give most visitors stays of 90 or 180 days, but travelers entering from Guatemala or Belize may be given only 30 days or less. If you wish to get an extension, the best thing to do is go to the Immigration Department office in Cancún (*Instituto Nacional de Migración*, Avenida Uxmal by Avenida Nader; tel: 998-881 3560), which is open Mon–Fri 9am–1pm, and generally grants tourist extensions very promptly. There are also INM offices in all main cities.

W

Women travelers

Women traveling alone or with another woman in Mexico are likely to attract some attention from Mexican men. To minimize unwanted attention, it's best to dress in a relatively restrained manner, and, if such a situation arises, to avoid making eye contact; make it clear that you have better things to do and walk purposefully on. In public places and by day this attention is unlikely to be aggressive or persistent, and is often pretty frivolous. However, it is important to avoid empty, dark streets and obviously dubious areas at night, and if you want to take a long walk, try to recruit fellow visitors to come along. Groups of three or more women and women with men are very unlikely to be bothered. In general, men in country areas are often shy and very courteous with all foreigners, including women; you are more likely to find a more aggressive, insistent atmosphere in the biggest cities and biggest resorts.

The most basic traditional *cantinas* still do not admit women, except at certain times. This is scarcely any loss, as most truly justify the tag "drinking dens." More comfortable *cantinas* that do admit women are generally very easy to identify.

PRONUNCIATION TIPS

Although many Mexicans speak some English, it is always good to have some basic Spanish phrases at your disposal, and outside the main tourist areas it will be essential to get around and to deal with restaurants and hotels. In general, Mexicans are delighted with foreigners who try to speak the language, and they'll be patient – if sometimes amused. Pronunciation is not difficult. The following is a simplified mini-lesson:

Vowels
a as in *bad*
e as in *bed*
i as in *police*
o as in *holly*
u as in *rude*
Consonants are approximately like those in English, the main exceptions being:
c is hard before **a**, **o**, or **u** (as in English), and is soft before **e** or **i**, when it sounds like **s**. Thus, *censo* (census) sounds like *senso*.
g is hard before **a**, **o**, or **u** (as in English), but before **e** or **i** Spanish **g** sounds like a guttural **h**. In country areas **g** before **ua** is often slightly suppressed, so that *agua* sounds more like *awa*.
h is silent.
j sounds like a guttural h.
ll sounds like y.
ñ sounds like ny, as in *señor*.
q is followed by **u** as in English, but the combination always sounds like **k**, not **kw**. ¿Qué quiere Usted? is pronounced: Keh kee-er-eh oosted?
r at the beginning of a word and **rr** within them are heavily rolled.
x between vowels sounds like a guttural **h**, eg in Mexico or Oaxaca.
y alone, as the word meaning "and", is pronounced **ee**.
Note that **ch** and **ll** are separate letters of the Spanish alphabet; if looking in a phone book or dictionary for a word beginning with **ch**, you will find it after the final **c** entry. A name or word beginning with **ll** will be listed after the final **l** entry (**ñ** and **rr** are also counted as separate letters.)

USEFUL WORDS AND PHRASES

Note that everyone in Mexico understands OK, which has become part of everyday Mexican language.
please *por favor*
thank you *gracias*
you're welcome *de nada* (literally, for nothing)
I'm sorry *lo siento*
excuse me *con permiso, disculpe* (if, for example, you would like to pass) *perdón* (if, for example, you have stepped on someone's foot)
yes *sí*
no *no*
Can you speak English? ¿Habla (usted) inglés?
Do you understand me? ¿Me comprende?/¿Me entiende?
I don't understand *No entiendo*
this is good *(esto) está bueno*
this is bad *(esto) está malo*
hello *hola*
good morning *buenos días*
good afternoon *buenas tardes*
good night/evening *buenas noches*
goodbye *adiós*
Where is...? ¿Dónde está?
exit *la salida*
entrance *la entrada*
money *dinero*
credit card *tarjeta de crédito*
tax *impuesto*

AT THE HOTEL

Where is there an inexpensive hotel? ¿Dónde hay un hotel económico?
Do you have a double/single room? ¿Tiene una habitación doble/sencilla?
With a double bed *con una cama matrimonial*
With twin beds *con dos camas*
For one night/two nights *para una noche/dos noches*
Does it have air conditioning? ¿Tiene aire acondicionado **or** clima?
Does it have a bath or a shower? ¿Tiene baño o ducha?
Can I see the room? ¿Puedo ver la habitación?
Is there a room with more light? ¿Hay alguna habitación con más luz?
dining room *el comedor*
key *la llave*
swimming pool *alberca, piscina*
Can you cash a travelers' check? ¿Puede cambiar un cheque de viajero?

EATING OUT

In Spanish, *el menú* is not the main menu, but a fixed menu offered each day (usually for lunch) at a lower price. The main menu is *la carta*.
restaurant *restaurante*
budget restaurant *lonchería, cocina económica*
café, coffee shop *un café*
A coffee please *Un café, por favor*
Please bring me... *Tráigame por favor...*
beer *una cerveza*
cold water *agua fría*
hot water *agua caliente*
soft drink, soda *un refresco*
cheap set menu *la comida corrida*
breakfast *desayuno*
lunch *almuerzo/comida*
dinner *cena*
first course *primer plato*
main course *plato principal*
Another beer, please *Más cerveza, por favor*
The bill/check, please *La cuenta, por favor*
To get the attention of a waiter (waitress) ¡Señor! (¡Señorita! ¡Señora!)
Can I pay by credit card? ¿Puedo pagar con tarjeta de crédito?

cambio *change*
tip *propina*

SHOPPING

market, market place *el mercado*
I want/I would like *Quiero...*
How much is it (this)? *¿Cuánto es (esto)?*
It's very expensive *Es muy caro*
Can you give me a discount? *¿Me puede dar un descuento?*
Do you have...? *¿Tiene usted...?*
I will buy this *Voy a comprar esto*
Please show me another *Muéstreme otro (otra) por favor*
Just a moment, please *Un momento, por favor*

COMMUNICATIONS

post office *los correos; la oficina de correos*
public telephone *un teléfono público*
cell/mobile phone *teléfono móvil, celular*
letter *la carta*
postcard *la tarjeta postal*
stamp *una estampilla*
Is there a Net café near here? *¿Hay un centro de internet por aquí?*

PLACES

police station *la delegación de policía*
embassy *la embajada*
consulate *el consulado*
bank *el banco*
hotel *un hotel*
apartment *un apartamento*
restroom *el sanitario/el lavabo/el baño de hombres/mujeres*
ticket office *la oficina de boletos, taquilla*

TRANSPORTATION

airplane *el avión*
airport *el aeropuerto*
ferry boat *el ferry, el transbordador*
small boat *lancha*
subway *el metro*
train *el tren*
first class *primera clase*
second class *segunda clase*
deluxe *de lujo/ejecutivo*
How much is a ticket to...? *¿Cuánto es un boleto a...?*
I want a ticket to... *Quiero un boleto a...*
return ticket *boleto redondo* or *boleto de ida y vuelta*

Please stop here *Pare aquí, por favor*
Straight ahead please *Derecho, por favor*
How many kilometers is it from here to...? *¿Cuántos kilómetros hay de aquí a...?*
How long does it take to go there? *¿Cuánto se tarda en llegar?*
left *a la izquierda*
right *a la derecha*
What is this place called? *¿Cómo se llama este lugar?*
I'm going to... *Voy a...*

On buses

bus *autobús/camión de pasajeros*
express bus *el camión directo*
bus station *estación de autobuses, central camionera*
first/second class *primera/segunda clase*
bus stop *parada*
reserved seat *asiento reservado*
Where does this bus go? *¿A dónde va este autobus?*
When does the next bus leave for...? *¿Cuándo sale el próximo autobus para...?*
Where does it leave from? *¿De dónde sale?*
I am getting off here! (to call out to a local bus or colectivo driver when you want to get off) *¡Bajan por favor!*

On the road

car *un carro, un automóvil, un coche*
Where is a gas station? *¿Dónde hay una gasolinera?*
a repair garage *un taller mecánico*
tire repair shop *una llantera, una vulcanizadora*
auto parts store *una refaccionaria para coches*
fill it up, please *lleno, por favor*
Please check the oil *Cheque el aceite, por favor*
radiator *el radiador*
battery *la batería*
jack *un gato*
towtruck *una grúa*
mechanic *un mecánico*
tire *una llanta*
spare wheel *la llanta de repuesto*

Taxis

taxi *el taxi*
taxi meter *taximetro*
taxi stand *el sitio de taxis*
Please call me a taxi *Pídame un taxi, por favor*
What will be the fare to...? *¿Cuánto sera para llevarme a...?*

DAYS AND MONTHS

Monday *lunes*
Tuesday *martes*
Wednesday *miércoles*
Thursday *jueves*
Friday *viernes*
Saturday *sábado*
Sunday *domingo*
January *enero*
February *febrero*
March *marzo*
April *abril*
May *mayo*
June *junio*
July *julio*
August *agosto*
September *septiembre*
October *octubre*
November *noviembre*
December *diciembre*

⊘ Numbers

Numbers
1 *uno*
2 *dos*
3 *tres*
4 *cuatro*
5 *cinco*
6 *seis*
7 *siete*
8 *ocho*
9 *nueve*
10 *diez*
11 *once*
12 *doce*
13 *trece*
14 *catorce*
15 *quince*
16 *dieciséis*
17 *diecisiete*
18 *dieciocho*
19 *diecinueve*
20 *veinte*
21 *veintiuno*
25 *veinticinco*
30 *treinta*
40 *cuarenta*
50 *cincuenta*
60 *sesenta*
70 *setenta*
80 *ochenta*
90 *noventa*
100 *cien*
101 *ciento uno*
200 *doscientos*
300 *trescientos*
400 *cuatrocientos*
500 *quinientos*
1,000 *mil*
2,000 *dos mil*
10,000 *diez mil*
1,000,000 *un millón*

FURTHER READING

NON-FICTION

The Conquest of New Spain Bernal Díaz del Castillo. A simple soldier's tale, delightful to read, that is one of the world's greatest eyewitness accounts.

Chronicle of the Maya Kings and Queens Simon Martin and Nikolai Grube. Remarkable overview of the huge amount that has been learned about Classic Maya history in the last 30 years.

The Fall of the Ancient Maya David L. Webster. Explores the great question of what happened to the Maya via a fascinating analysis of the nature of ancient Maya culture.

First Stop in the New World: Mexico City, the Capital of the 21st Century David Lida. Up to the minute, very sharp account of the contemporary megalopolis: one to challenge plenty of stereotypes.

Five Families Oscar Lewis. Lewis spent many years studying Mexico's "culture of poverty" and interviewing its victims.

Incidents of Travel in Central America, Chiapas, and Yucatán and **Incidents of Travel in Yucatán** John L. Stephens. First published in 1841 and 1843, these books remain among the greatest of all travel books, and have never been out of print. Stephens and illustrator Frederick Catherwood had many adventures, made remarkable discoveries, and were instrumental in revealing the lost Maya civilization to the world.

Insurgent Mexico John Reed. Exciting account of the 1910 Revolution by the reporter famous for his coverage of the Russian Revolution.

The Labyrinth of Solitude Octavio Paz. Nobel-Prize winner Paz was the best known (outside Mexico) of all Mexico's intellectuals, and this book is a must for going beyond a superficial understanding of the psychology and culture of contemporary Mexicans.

The Log from the Sea of Cortés John Steinbeck. Steinbeck tells of an expedition to gather biological specimens from the Sea of Cortés off Baja California, and beautifully evokes its natural riches.

The Lost Chronicles of the Maya Kings David Drew. A very readable overview of Maya history and culture.

Maya Cosmos Linda Schele, David Freidel, and Joy Parker. A richly suggestive examination of Maya beliefs in the past and present. The late Linda Schele played a huge part in expanding knowledge of the Maya and her other books with co-authors (*Blood of Kings*, *Forest of Kings*, *The Code of Kings*) are equally fascinating.

☉ Send us your thoughts

We do our best to ensure the information in our books is as accurate and up-to-date as possible. The books are updated on a regular basis using local contacts, who painstakingly add, amend and correct as required. However, some details (such as telephone numbers and opening times) are liable to change, and we are ultimately reliant on our readers to put us in the picture.

We welcome your feedback, especially your experience of using the book "on the road". Maybe you came across a great bar or new attraction we missed.

We will acknowledge all contributions, and we'll offer an Insight Guide to the best letters received.

Please write to us at:
Insight Guides
PO Box 7910
London SE1 1WE

Or email us at:
hello@insightguides.com

Mayan Tales from Zinacantán Robert M. Laughlin. A fascinating collection of folktales and dream-stories.

Mexican Postcards Carlos Monsiváis. Acute mini-portraits of many aspects of Mexican life, from one of the country's leading contemporary writers.

Mexico: A Biography of Power Enrique Krauze. Krauze is one of Mexico's most respected contemporary historians and political analysts, and his book presents an iconoclastic view of the country's modern history.

Mexico: From the Olmecs to the Aztecs Michael D. Coe and Rex Koontz. An excellent survey of all the ancient Mexican cultures, by one of the most eminent authorities in the field.

Oaxaca Journal Oliver Sacks. Charming book in which the eminent neurologist follows up another of this passions – the search for Oaxaca's rare ferns.

Our Word is our Weapon Subcomandante Marcos. The Zapatista spokesman presents his radical view of the state of modern Mexico.

The Oxford History of Mexico M.C. Meyer and William Beezley. Scholarly yet engaging one-volume history.

Sliced Iguana: Travels in Unknown Mexico Isabella Tree. Entertaining reports on the chaos of the capital, the matriarchal communities of Oaxaca, and more of the many quirky surprises of modern Mexico.

The Teachings of Don Juan: A Yaqui Way of Knowledge Carlos Castañeda. This and other books by Castañeda provide an imaginative insight into spiritual experience – but don't believe every word. Also *A Separate Reality*; *Journey to Ixtlán*; *Tales of Power*; *The Second Ring of Power*; and *The Eagle's Gift*.

Viva México; a traveller's account of life in Mexico Charles Macomb Flandrau. The charming, unhurried account of a British traveler of 1908; some of Flandrau's insights into Mexican character are absolute gems.

Zapata and the Mexican Revolution John Womack Jr. A vivid account of the life of Mexico's most legendary revolutionary.

FICTION

The Burning Plain/El Llano en Llamas Juan Rulfo. Some of the most powerful Mexican literature: a collection of short stories in which Rulfo's spare, suggestive prose gives the reader a deep understanding of the mestizo culture formed during the colonial era. Rulfo's great masterpiece was the novel **Pedro Páramo**, an intense, allegorical evocation of the memory of violence and its place in rural Mexico in the years after the Revolution. It is said to be an important precursor to magical realism.

Like Water for Chocolate/Como Agua para Chocolate Laura Esquivel. The 1990 bestseller novel about family life, food, and the Revolution. Wit, humor, irony, and more blend into a very readable book. Also by the same author is **Swift as Desire**, a sad and funny tale about the importance of love.

Mexico James A. Michener. This book follows the story of a journalist sent to report on the meeting in a small town between two of the world's greatest matadors. It endures as the most important literary work about bullfighting in Mexico.

Mexico City Noir Paco Ignacio Taibo. Taibo is Mexico's most popular modern crime writer, and his thrillers featuring the down-at-heel detective Hector Belascoarán Shayne are vividly entertaining portrayals of the modern country and its often apparently chaotic nature.

The Border Trilogy Cormac McCarthy. McCarthy's evocatively written trilogy – *All the Pretty Horses*, *The Crossing*, and *Cities of the Plain* – takes place on the US–Mexican border in the 1940s and 1950s and is a stirring insight to the differences and similarities either side of what has long been one of the world's most poignant frontiers.

The Night of the Iguana Tennessee Williams. Powerful drama made famous by the movie starring Richard Burton.

The Plumed Serpent D.H. Lawrence. Lawrence takes on profound problems – the meaning of life and death, the relations of man to man and woman to man – and argues for a profound change in Mexico.

The Power and the Glory Graham Greene. Mexico was really only a conveniently dramatic backdrop to Greene's meditations on religion, desperation, and commitment, since he knew and understood little about the country, but this novel about a lost priest during the 1930s anti-Catholic campaigns remains powerful.

The Treasure of the Sierra Madre B. Traven. No other foreign author has written so much and so well about Mexico as the mysterious B. Traven (his identity is still a matter of controversy). Most of his books are set in

southern Mexico, and his knowledge of that area is astounding. Others to look out for are: *The General from the Jungle*; *The Rebellion of the Hanged*; *March to Caobaland*; *The Bridge in the Jungle*; and *The Carreta*.

Under the Volcano Malcolm Lowry. Lowry's astonishing masterpiece about an alcoholic British consul drinking himself to death in Cuernavaca centers around despair, but in the process it reveals an intense engagement with the Mexican environment.

Where the Air Is Clear Carlos Fuentes. The first, and often considered the best, work by Mexico's most esteemed modern writer. As in all Fuentes' major works, Mexico City, with all its infinite contradictions, is as much a character as any individual: the narrator is a rather mysterious man who spends his life listening to and watching fellow inhabitants of the capital, of every social stratum, as they attempt to cope with the conditions of their lives. See also **The Death of Artemio Cruz** in which he writes from the perspective of a man on his deathbed; of life, love and regret. **The Old Gringo** about an American caught up in the Revolution.

ARTS, CRAFTS, AND TRADITIONS

Arts and Crafts of Mexico Chloe Sayer. Excellent photographs, and includes step-by-step instructions for making traditional Mexican craft items.

Art and Time in Mexico photographs by Judith Hancock Sandoval, text by Elizabeth Wilder Weismann. Well-illustrated overview of colonial art and architecture.

Days of Death, Days of Life: Ritual in the Popular Culture of Oaxaca Kristin Norget. In-depth study of the popular culture of one of Mexico's most distinctive cities.

Great Masters of Mexican Folk Art Cándida Fernández de Calderón. Superb examples of traditional crafts, beautifully illustrated, with an illuminating text on the lives of the makers.

The Maya Textile Tradition Linda Asturias de Barrios and others, with photographs by Jeffrey Foxx. Magnificently illustrated examination of the intricate complexity of textile-making in traditional Maya communities.

Mexican Churches Eliot Porter and Ellen Auerbach. A lavish collection of photographs from around the country.

Mexicolor: The Spirit of Mexican Design Melba Levick, Tony Cohan, and Masako Takahashi. Fittingly, one of the most colorful books ever published, which beautifully explores Mexico's culture and love of color.

BIRDS AND WILDLIFE

A Field Guide to the Mammals of Central America and Southeast Mexico Fiona A. Reid. The essential aid for anyone wildlife-spotting in Oaxaca, Chiapas, or the Yucatán.

A Guide to the Birds of Mexico and Northern Central America Steve N.G. Howell and Sophie Webb. A well-illustrated handbook, and an excellent starter for anyone visiting Mexico who is interested in birds.

Marine Mammals: Baja California-Sea of Cortés-Pacific Coast Uko Gorter. A very thorough, illustrated guide in Rainforest Publications' Mexico Field Guides series.

Southern Mexico Traveller's Wildlife Guide Les Beletsky. Handy one-volume guide covering birds and land and undersea life.

FOOD AND DRINK

The Cuisines of Mexico Diana Kennedy. Resident in Mexico for more than 50 years, British writer Diana Kennedy is *the* authority on Mexican food and cooking, in English, and her books are both readable and practical.

The Food and Life of Oaxaca Zarela Martínez. Perceptive, intimate account of the role of food in the life of Oaxaca, also with usable recipes.

Tequila! A Natural and Cultural History Ana Valenzuela-Zapata and Gary Paul Nabhan. The lowdown on the culture surrounding Mexico's most famous lubricant.

OTHER INSIGHT GUIDES

Insight Guide: *Guatemala, Belize and Yucatán* provides in-depth coverage of this beautiful area, with revealing features and stunning photography.

Explore: *Cancún & the Yucatán* offers intrepid travelers a series of carefully curated self-guided tour routes around the peninsula.

CREDITS

INSIGHT GUIDE CREDITS

Distribution
UK, Ireland and Europe
Apa Publications (UK) Ltd;
sales@insightguides.com
United States and Canada
Ingram Publisher Services;
ips@ingramcontent.com
Australia and New Zealand
Woodslane; info@woodslane.com.au
Southeast Asia
Apa Publications (SN) Pte;
singaporeoffice@insightguides.com
Worldwide
Apa Publications (UK) Ltd;
sales@insightguides.com
Special Sales, Content Licensing and CoPublishing
Insight Guides can be purchased in bulk quantities at discounted prices. We can create special editions, personalised jackets and corporate imprints tailored to your needs.
sales@insightguides.com
www.insightguides.biz

Printed in China by CTPS

All Rights Reserved
© 2019 Apa Digital (CH) AG and
Apa Publications (UK) Ltd

First Edition 1983
Tenth Edition 2019

www.insightguides.com

Editor: Helen Fanthorpe
Updater: Paul Stafford
Author: Luke Waterson
Head of DTP and Pre-Press: Rebeka Davies
Update Production: Apa Digital
Managing Editor: Carine Tracanelli
Picture Editor: Tom Smyth
Cartography: original cartography Berndtson & Berndtson, updated by Carte

CONTRIBUTORS

This new edition was commissioned and edited by Helen Fanthorpe. It was thoroughly updated by Paul Stafford, a writer who has lived in Mexico and travelled the country extensively on and off.

This version builds on earlier work by Luke Waterson, Ray Bartlett, Donna Dailey, Patricia Díaz, Andrea Dubrowski, Guillermo García-Oropeza, Mike Gerrard, José-Antonio Guzmán, Margaret King, Felicity Laughton, Wendy Luft, Ron Mader, Barbara McKinnon, Kal Müller, Mike Nelson, Nick Rider, Barbara Ann Rosenberg, Chloe Sayers, and John Wilcock.

ABOUT INSIGHT GUIDES

Insight Guides have more than 45 years' experience of publishing high-quality, visual travel guides. We produce 400 full-colour titles, in both print and digital form, covering more than 200 destinations across the globe, in a variety of formats to meet your different needs.

Insight Guides are written by local authors, whose expertise is evident in the extensive historical and cultural background features. Each destination is carefully researched by regional experts to ensure our guides provide the very latest information. All the reviews in Insight Guides are independent; we strive to maintain an impartial view. Our reviews are carefully selected to guide you to the best places to eat, go out and shop, so you can be confident that when we say a place is special, we really mean it.

Legend

City maps

- Freeway/Highway/Motorway
- Divided Highway
- Main Roads
- Minor Roads
- Pedestrian Roads
- Steps
- Footpath
- Railway
- Funicular Railway
- Cable Car
- Tunnel
- City Wall
- Important Building
- Built Up Area
- Other Land
- Transport Hub
- Park
- Pedestrian Area
- Bus Station
- Tourist Information
- Main Post Office
- Cathedral/Church
- Mosque
- Synagogue
- Statue/Monument
- Beach
- Airport

Regional maps

- Freeway/Highway/Motorway (with junction)
- Freeway/Highway/Motorway (under construction)
- Divided Highway
- Main Road
- Secondary Road
- Minor Road
- Track
- Footpath
- International Boundary
- State/Province Boundary
- National Park/Reserve
- Marine Park
- Ferry Route
- Marshland/Swamp
- Glacier   Salt Lake
- Airport/Airfield
- Ancient Site
- Border Control
- Cable Car
- Castle/Castle Ruins
- Cave
- Chateau/Stately Home
- Church/Church Ruins
- Crater
- Lighthouse
- Mountain Peak
- Place of Interest
- Viewpoint

INDEX

MAIN REFERENCES ARE IN BOLD TYPE

INSIGHT ⊙ GUIDES

OFF THE SHELF

Since 1970, INSIGHT GUIDES has provided a unique perspective on the world's best travel destinations by using specially commissioned photography and illuminating text written by local authors.

Whether you're planning a city break, a walking tour or the journey of a lifetime, our superb range of guidebooks and phrasebooks will inspire you to discover more about your chosen destination.

INSIGHT GUIDES

offer a unique combination of stunning photos, absorbing narrative and detailed maps, providing all the inspiration and information you need.

PHRASEBOOKS & DICTIONARIES

help users to feel at home, when away. Pocket-sized with a free app to download, they go where you do.

CITY GUIDES

pack hundreds of great photos into a smaller format with detailed practical information, so you can navigate the world's top cities with confidence.

EXPLORE GUIDES

feature easy-to-follow walks and itineraries in the world's most exciting destinations, with our choice of the best places to eat and drink along the way.

POCKET GUIDES

combine concise information on where to go and what to do in a handy compact format, ideal on the ground. Includes a full-colour, fold-out map.

EXPERIENCE GUIDES

feature offbeat perspectives and secret gems for experienced travellers, with a collection of over 100 ideas for a memorable stay in a city.

www.insightguides.com

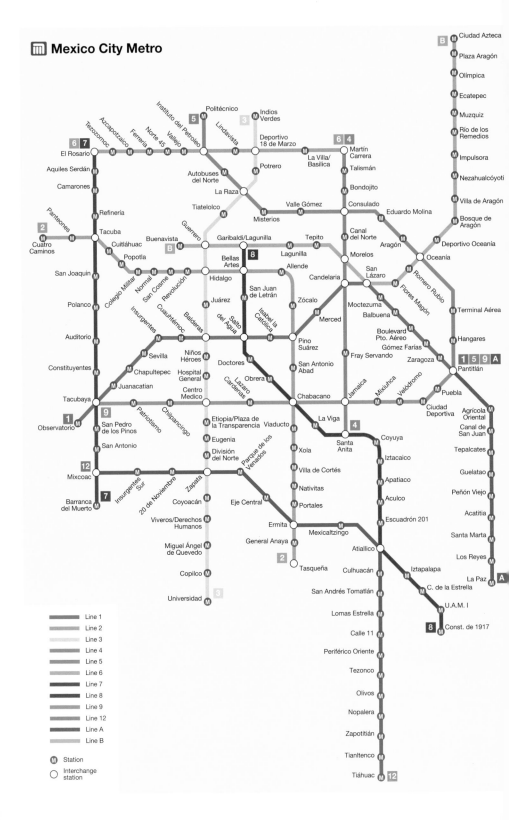

Mexico City Metro

B Ciudad Azteca
Plaza Aragón
Olímpica
Ecatepec
Muzquiz
Río de los Remedios
Impulsora
Nezahualcóyoti
Villa de Aragón
Bosque de Aragón
Deportivo Oceanía
Oceanía
Terminal Aérea
Hangares

1 5 9 A Pantitlán

El Rosario
Aquiles Serdán
Camarones
Refinería
Tacuba
Cuitláhuac
Popotla
San Joaquin
Polanco
Auditorio
Constituyentes
Tacubaya
Observatorio
San Pedro de los Pinos
San Antonio
Mixcoac
Barranca del Muerto

Politécnico
Indios Verdes
Deportivo 18 de Marzo
Potrero
La Villa/Basílica
Martín Carrera
Talismán
Bondojito
Consulado
Eduardo Molina
Valle Gómez
Misterios
Canal del Norte
Aragón
Tepito
Morelos
San Lázaro
Candelaria
Zócalo
Merced
Moctezuma
Balbuena
Boulevard Pto. Aéreo
Gómez Farías
Zaragoza
Puebla

Autobuses del Norte
La Raza
Tiatelolco
Garibaldi/Lagunilla
Bellas Artes
Hidalgo
Juárez
San Juan de Letrán
Isabel la Católica
Pino Suárez
Fray Servando
Niños Héroes
Sevilla
Chapultepec
Hospital General
Doctores
Obrera
San Antonio Abad
Juanacatian
Centro Medico
Chabacano
Jamaica
Mixiuhca
Velódromo

Romero Rubio
Flores Magón

Ciudad Deportiva
Agrícola Oriental
Canal de San Juan
Tepalcates
Guelatao
Peñón Viejo
Acatitla
Santa Marta
Los Reyes
La Paz **A**

Etiopia/Plaza de la Transparencia
Viaducto
La Viga
Santa Anita
Coyuya
Iztacaico
Apatiaco
Aculco
Escuadrón 201
Iztapalapa
C. de la Estrella
U.A.M. I
8 Const. de 1917

Eugenia
Eugenia
División del Norte
Zapata
Coyoacán
Eje Central
Viveros/Derechos Humanos
Miguel Ángel de Quevedo
Copilco
Universidad

Xola
Villa de Cortés
Nativitas
Portales
Ermita
General Anaya
Mexicaltzingo
Atiallico
Tasqueña
Culhuacán
San Andrés Tomatlán
Lomas Estrella
Calle 11
Periférico Oriente
Tezonco
Olivos
Nopalera
Zapotitlán
Tianltenco
Tiáhuac **12**

Line 1
Line 2
Line 3
Line 4
Line 5
Line 6
Line 7
Line 8
Line 9
Line 12
Line A
Line B

M Station
O Interchange station

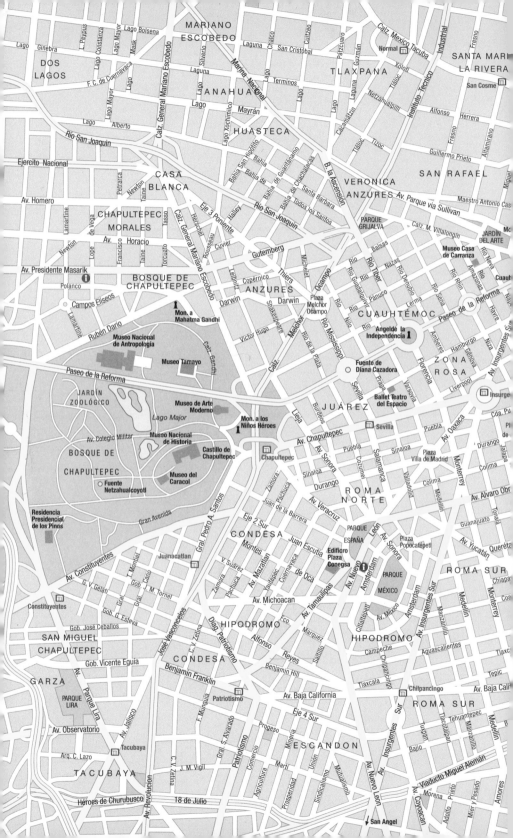